D0085644

SOCIAL WELFARE

Policy and Analysis

THIRD EDITION

ANDREW DOBELSTEIN
University of North Carolina

THOMSON

BROOKS/COLE

AUSTRALIA • CANADA • MEXICO • SINGAPORE • SPAIN • UNITED KINGDOM • UNITED STATES

THOMSON

BROOKS/COLE

Executive Editor: *Lisa Gebo*
Assistant Editor: *Shelly Gesicki*
Editorial Assistant: *Sheila Walsh*
Marketing Manager: *Caroline Concilla*
Marketing Assistant: *Mary Ho*
Production Coordinator: *Mary Vezilich*
Print Buyer: *Vena Dyer*

Permissions Editor: *Karyn Morrison*
Production Service: *G & S Typesetters, Inc.*
Copy Editor: *John Mulvihill*
Cover Designer: *Roger Knox*
Cover Photos: *Getty Images*
Compositor: *G & S Typesetters, Inc.*
Printer: *Transcontinental Printing–Louiseville*

HV
95
.D62
2003

COPYRIGHT © 2003 Brooks/Cole, a division of
Thomson Learning, Inc. Thomson Learning™ is a
trademark used herein under license.

ALL RIGHTS RESERVED. No part of this work covered
by the copyright hereon may be reproduced or used in
any form or by any mean—graphic, electronic, or
mechanical, including but not limited to photocopying,
recording, taping, Web distribution, information
networks, or information storage and retrieval systems—
without the written permission of the publisher.

Printed in Canada
2 3 4 5 6 7 06 05 04 03

For more information about our products, contact us at:
Thomson Learning Academic Resource Center
1-800-423-0563

For permission to use material from this text,
contact us by: **Phone: 1-800-730-2214**
Fax: 1-800-730-2215
Web: http://www.thomsonrights.com

Library of Congress Control Number: 2002102019

ISBN 0-534-50986-X

Brooks/Cole–Thomson Learning
511 Forest Lodge Road
Pacific Grove, CA 93950
USA

Asia
Thomson Learning
5 Shenton Way #01-01
UIC Building
Singapore 068808

Australia
Nelson Thomson Learning
102 Dodds Street
South Melbourne, Victoria 3205
Australia

Canada
Nelson Thomson Learning
1120 Birchmount Road
Toronto, Ontario M1K 5G4
Canada

Europe/Middle East/Africa
Thomson Learning
High Holborn House
50/51 Bedford Row
London WC1R 4LR
United Kingdom

Latin America
Thomson Learning
Seneca, 53
Colonia Polanco
11560 Mexico D.F.
Mexico

Spain
Paraninfo Thomson Learning
Calle/Magallanes, 25
28015 Madrid, Spain

50681950

CONTENTS

PREFACE

The much-heralded welfare reform of 1996 has settled in as a major departure from traditional and established welfare policy. Proclaimed to "replace welfare as we know it," according to former President Clinton, Temporary Assistance to Needy Families (TANF) as this latest welfare reform is called, was crafted to change the system of welfare through a number of initiatives designed to remove any idea of welfare entitlement. TANF's welfare changes confirm a number of shifts in the direction of welfare policymaking that, historically, have played an important part in shaping present American social welfare policy. Perhaps most significantly, the 1996 welfare reform confirms a long-held American dissatisfaction with welfare. That a Democratic president initiated, supported, and advocated a welfare reform that restricted access to welfare by economically needy families, in the face of long-standing liberal Democratic efforts to establish a right to welfare and to expand welfare programs, speaks clearly to this dissatisfaction. (See, for example, my *Moral Authority, Ideology, and the Future of American Social Welfare*, Chapter 4.) With the confirmation of the long-held fact that no one likes welfare, even though many need it, the dreams of many leading welfare reform advocates have been dashed.

But the changes in welfare signaled by TANF go much deeper than confirming a dislike for welfare. TANF also takes the federal government out of its traditional role as custodian of American income-maintenance policies. The creation of the TANF block grant turns welfare custodianship over to the states. To understand the significance of this change one must recall the decade of the 1960s and the period of President Nixon's administration when the federal government proposed taking full and complete responsibility for all income-maintenance activities. Or one must revisit President Johnson's effort to create the "Great Society" by expanding the social welfare role of the federal government. The devolution of welfare responsibility to the states has shifted the policy agenda of the federal welfare administration, the Department of Health and Human Services (DHHS), toward matters that traditionally were state policy issues: children's issues such as child abuse and family preservation. Even medical care as reflected in the recent State Child Health Insurance Program (SCHIP) put the states in charge of a Medicaid-derived health program.

Amid recent court decisions that restrict the authority of the federal government over that of the states in matters of public policy, efforts to privatize portions of Social Security, and a national political climate that continues to rebel against increased amounts of government regulation, the social welfare architecture laid down almost 70 years ago shows signs of aging in the new American political economy of the twenty-first century. Thus while the programs discussed in this text remain mainstays of American social welfare policy, our nation seems to be entering a new phase that will shape the social welfare policy agenda of the future.

While we have grown content with the present social welfare arrangements, we are now forced to move on to new forms of social welfare. But whether these new forms will better serve those in need remains a serious question. The political support for these traditional welfare programs seems, more and more, to depend on shifting their focus to others than the very poor. For example, the states' use of TANF funds has not focused on low-income populations exclusively, but instead has made these public funds available to expand programs to individuals and families above the poverty line. Thus, on the one hand we may be becoming a nation very dependent on public programs, such as publicly supported child care and programs for older people. On the other hand, all too often the neediest are denied the use of these public programs because funds are not adequate to stretch upward to serve more middle-income families.

Universalizing these programs and services, as discussed in Chapter 8, not only makes them more expensive but also detracts from the specific purposes they were created to address. The term "welfare for the rich" continues to be heard more and more, while the resources that would fund welfare for the poor seem to be drying up.

In addition to this text, the student will have access to a valuable online appendix at the publisher's resource center website: http://socialwork.wadsworth .com/socialwelfarepolicy/.

At this site, the student will be able to find information on about 40 programs, such as Social Security, Medicaid, and homeless shelters. An *Instructor's Manual* (ISBN 0-534-50987-8) is available to adopters of the text.

Developing the third edition of this book was, as usual, aided by many people. First, my students are constant critics, and their criticisms helped me refocus several sections of this book, as did comments from outside reviewers: Freddie Avant, Stephen F. Austin State University; Sheying Chen, CSI/CUNY; Sandra Cross, Western Washington University; Richard Hoefer, University of

Texas at Arlington; Golam Mathbor, Monmouth University; Marciana L. Popescu, Andrews University; and Karen Staller, University of Michigan. I have many other people to thank for their contributions to this new edition, but I especially want to mention Harrold Jones for his willingness to work on some of the tables and to my wife, Susan, who continues to give encouragement both to my work and to the social work profession.

Foremost, perhaps, this edition is dedicated to the students who will soon become professionals in the service to others. Yours is a great challenge in a world that seems to be moving away from our traditional values and beliefs. I hope you remember the special honor conferred on you by serving the needs of others.

—Andrew Dobelstein

SOCIAL WELFARE

Policy and Analysis

THIRD EDITION

THEORIES AND METHODS OF POLICY ANALYSIS

The December sun sets suddenly in the North Carolina mountains, drawing the precious heat of the day with it. John, a social worker from the local Community Action Agency, and I bump up the country road to Mr. Riggsbee's house, thrown side to side as his 1980 Chevy four-wheel negotiates the rocks, ruts, and sharp turns.

"Lived up here all his life," John explains. "Been by hisself since his wife died 'bout a year ago. Don't drive no more. Daughter in Yadkinville comes on weekends to visit. Takes his laundry home with her. Brings it back the next week. Wants him to move to one of those assisted living places in Yadkinville, but he won't go. Says he lived all his life here. Says he might as well die here. It's his home."

"How old is he?" I ask.

"'Bout 90. Not sure. We try to come up here every week. See how he's doing."

"How does he get by?"

"If tweren't for the Elderly Nutrition Program run by the Senior Center, he'd be lost. Daughter brings food when she comes. They come up with food three days a week. He makes it last. He's a mountain man. He knows how to make do."

The Chevy's lights push the growing darkness to the sides of the road. The cold begins to seep into the truck. My feet are warm. My fingers are getting cold. Up ahead a small yellow light stutters through the swaying trees.

"There it is," John announces.

We pull up closer to the light and stomp up onto the porch.

"Hey, Mr. Riggsbee!" John calls out. "Anybody home? Brought that feller from the university with me like I said. OK to come in?" No answer.

John opens the door latch, pushes the door in, and pulls me in after him.

"Cold out there. This here's the university feller. Name's Frank."

"Glad to meet you, Mr. Rigssbee. Thanks for letting me come."

Mr. Rigssbee sits in a rocking chair by the woodstove. His eyes are bright. He nods his head in my direction. An acknowledgment, I wonder?

The woodstove sends out a different kind of heat. It seems to reach out and get right into my body. I can feel the cold behind me, but the stove warms me through.

Mr. Rigssbee is clean and dressed in a wool plaid shirt. His ruddy face shows the lines of age. The dim light from a small lamp covers the room in an orange glow. Beyond this main room to the right is what seems to be a kitchen. To the left is another room, maybe the bedroom. John is talking with Mr. Rigssbee, asking whether the seniors brought him his food today, if he has enough wood cut, if his daughter visited, if he's taking his medicine, if he remembers he has to go to the doctor next week, and so forth. Mr. Rigssbee sits there silently, rocking slowly in his chair, nodding occasionally as John talks.

I try talking with him. He rocks and nods, and the corner of his mouth turns up, occasionally, as if in a smile. But "Yp" and "Nope" are all I can get out of him. As my eyes grow accustomed to the light I notice that there are cracks in the wooden walls of the house, and that is why my back is cold.

After about an hour, filled intermittently with John's questions and long periods of silence, we get up to go.

"Be seein' you, Mr. Rigssbee," John announces. "You call now if you need to, you hear?"

Mr. Rigssbee nods.

"I liked meeting you, Mr. Rigssbee. You take care, now," I say as I stand to go.

"Thanks for comin," he responds.

As we step out into the biting cold, John says, "He enjoyed his conversation with you, I could tell."

What conversation? I wondered.

As we bounce back down the mountain, John answers my many questions. One reason Mr. Rigssbee won't move is that he receives Supplemental Security Income (SSI), about $179 per month, and this is not enough to pay the monthly costs for assisted living. Doesn't want his daughter to pay. He does not get Social Security because he always worked on the farm and never had to pay Social Security taxes. He would have to sell his place to have enough to afford assisted living. Then again, his 50 acres wouldn't bring much money even if he did sell it. Like all mountain people, his life is attached to the land. It provided him with a livelihood all his life. It's part of him. He wants his daughter to have it, even though she doesn't want it.

Because he gets SSI he is also eligible for Medicaid; so his doctor visits and his medicine are paid for. The county has a transportation service for people like Mr. Rigssbee who are financially and physically dependent. This is how he gets to the doctor and occasionally to the grocery store. The Elderly Nutrition Program delivers him a hot noon meal three days a week. The Community Action Agency that John works for administers an Energy Assistance Program, so Mr. Rigssbee has enough wood for his stove, most of the time, along with the wood he gathers himself during the summer. The Community Action Agency also administers a Weatherization Program, and sometime this winter yet, workers will be coming out and insulating his house. His church, Primitive Baptist Church, has a "telephone line," whereby each day he gets a check-in call from a volunteer. If there is a problem or an emergency, either Mr. Rigssbee or someone else calls John at the Community Action Agency and they go out and check on him. He has a little garden that he works in the summer, and "puts up" some beans and tomatoes he uses during the winter. He is lonely since his wife died, and one day, John reasons, he'll get a call that Mr. Rigssbee has gone to join her. But until then he is doing about as well as can be expected, all things considered.

One thousand or so miles away in Chicago, Yesheeta scrunches down closer to her older sister, pretending not to hear her mother calling. Despite the threadbare blankets, Yesheeta tries to squeeze the last bit of warmth from the bed before getting dressed. Her mother calls again, sharply. "Yesheeta, get up. You have to get dressed. You'll miss your bus."

Yesheeta does not want to miss her bus.

Yesheeta is four years old. She goes to a Head Start program for low-income children, whose aim is to put them on an even footing with children from more affluent households when they start school. Yesheeta goes to an inner-city school, where most of the children come from poor or nearly poor households. Some children Yesheeta's age will be going to private preschool programs where they start their learning. Yesheeta's Head Start program does the same thing, but it also includes minor medical care for the children, lunches, and breakfast, and it is the thought of breakfast that stirs Yesheeta into action. Toast, eggs, warm grits with butter, sometimes hot chocolate. Yesheeta is by the door when the bus pulls up outside, and with a quick goodbye to her mother she is out the door.

Tiquela, Yesheeta's older sister, is in second grade. Her bus will be coming shortly, so she pulls on her clothes, brushes her hair, and makes herself a cup of hot tea. She puts a white clip-on bow in her hair because today she has to make a report to the class and she wants to look her best. She is trying to make good grades, but social studies is her hardest subject. Her school serves breakfast and lunch too, but Tiquela is often too busy talking with her friends to be bothered about breakfast.

Yesheeta and Tiquela's 19-year-old mother, Ms. Smith, is on welfare, Temporary Assistance to Needy Families (TANF). She was living with her mother and her mother's boyfriend, but when her mother's boyfriend kept trying to have sex with her she decided to move out and get an apartment on her own. Her mother's boyfriend is probably Yesheeta's father, but Ms. Smith is not sure. She is sure she does not want to get pregnant again, and she wants to try to make something out of her life. So she found an apartment on Okenwald Avenue, and the welfare department is helping her get ready for employment. Today she does not have to report to work training, so her social worker is coming to visit her.

Joan is a first-year social work student. Her field placement is with the Cook County Department of Social Services. Ms. Smith is her first client. She has met Ms. Smith in the office, and today she has scheduled a home visit. Joan takes the El to 42nd Street and transfers to the bus. As the bus slowly winds its way east, Joan notices that more and more African Americans are on the bus. The bus stops. Whites get off. African Americans take their place. By the time it gets to Okenwald Avenue, Joan is the only white person on the bus, and she feels very uncomfortable. People seem to be staring at her. A young African American male sits in the empty seat next to her, and in spite of her liberal attitudes Joan's skin begins to itch with anxiety.

Joan gets off the bus and walks to Ms. Smith's apartment.

"Scary! Just scary," Joan reports to her supervisor when she gets back to the office.

The stairs to the apartment were littered with trash. The walls that were not broken out were covered with layers of graffiti. Ms. Smith had three dead-bolts on the door, and she used all three after she let Joan into the apartment. There was a kerosene heater in the main room and a broken-down sofa that Joan was invited to sit on, which she did with great reluctance. The bathroom was filthy. The tub had a crack in it that made it unusable. A bare light bulb hung above the empty medicine cabinet. Each bedroom had a mattress on the floor, each piled with rumpled coverings of assorted types. But the kitchen was clean. Immaculate, compared with the rest of the apartment. Still, Joan declined a generous offer of a cup of coffee.

All in all, though, Joan reported, Ms. Smith seemed to be doing OK. She was upbeat about the possibility of getting a job and eventually getting a better place to live. She was learning to use the computer and had just learned how to get on the Web. Maybe in her job, she hoped, she would be able to "surf the Web," and then she could help Tiquela with her homework. She told Joan that everybody uses computers now, and she was sure that once she mastered it she could get a good job.

At first Ms. Smith resented the fact that the welfare office made her either get a job or get into some sort of job training. She thought it was nobody's business what she did with her life, and she told her previous social worker so. But the social worker told her that if she did not get a job she could not get welfare, and the thought of moving back with her mother was chilling. Now she is glad that she is expected to get training and get a job.

"Welfare was the way of life for my mother," she told Joan. "I want my kids to have a better life than I had."

"My girls are doin' real good," she explained to Joan. "Yesheeta loves her school, and I go and help out every week. I'm going there as soon as you leave." She told Joan, "I'm learning how to read to Yesheeta, and they have books I can bring home and read to her. Look at this one with all the pictures!"

Ms. Smith is also pleased that both schools give the children breakfast and lunch.

"Sometimes we don't have much food in the house toward the end of the month, but I know they can always get something to eat at school," she confided to Joan.

Finally, more than two thousand five hundred miles to the west, 16-year-old Angeline DeMarcos sits in the West Los Angeles Public Health Clinic, waiting nervously for her appointment with Sally Alonzo. Angeline is four months pregnant and is waiting for her second prenatal checkup. Angeline met Nurse Alonzo the last time she came to the clinic when she was sent by the nurse at her school. Nurse Alonzo told Angeline it was all right to call her Sally.

Sally called Angeline back to the examining room, took her blood pressure, and listened to the fetus with her stethoscope. In a few minutes Dr. Johnson came in. She listened with her stethoscope, too, measured Angeline's growing stomach, felt around her stomach a bit, and announced. "You have a healthy little baby growing inside you, Angeline. Keep up the good work." And she left.

Angeline straightened her clothing as Sally explained things to her about what to eat, what she could and could not buy with her special food stamps, how to take care of herself during the next few months. Suddenly, without warning, Angeline began to cry, and then to sob hysterically. Sally tried to soothe her, but Sally's kind words only made Angeline sob harder.

Sally left the room, and in a few minutes an older woman came in.

"Tell me what's wrong, my sweet girl" the woman coaxed. "What is it that is making you cry? Do you feel all alone, and having a baby frightens you?"

"Sí!" Angeline sobbed. Then she began to talk.

The baby's father, José, had a good job in construction. He was 19 and lived in Angeline's neighborhood. She started to go with him even though she was still in school. They were going to get married as soon as Angeline finished. She was in love with José. They had made all kinds of plans. She knew right away she was pregnant, but she did not say anything to Jose or her family. Finally she went to the school nurse, who sent her to the Health Department in order to get into the Women, Infants, and Children (WIC) program. Then José got picked up by the INS.

"He said he had his Green Card," Angeline sobbed. "Before they sent him back to Mexico he told me they had made a mistake, and he would be back in a couple of weeks, but I haven't heard from him. I'm all alone, all alone." She stopped crying.

The woman listened carefully. She talked about some options that Angeline had, and Angeline was firm that she wanted to deliver the baby and keep it. The woman explained how it would be possible for Angeline to finish school, and that they could contact Legal Aid and see what could be done about locating José. If he was illegal, at least there might be some correspondence, and maybe something could be done to enable his return, although Angeline should not get her hopes up about this. The woman also said she would meet with Angeline's parents and try to help them understand the situation Angeline found herself in, and discuss with them some of the resources that might be made available to Angeline and the family as she got closer to the time of giving birth.

"We have some time to work on these things," the woman said softly. "When you go out, tell the receptionist you want to see me next week, and we will begin to work on these things."

Riding the bus home Angeline felt much better about everything. She made up her mind that this evening when her mother got home from work she would tell her everything.

SOCIAL PROGRAMS ARE CREATED BY SOCIAL POLICIES

Elderly Nutrition. Energy Assistance. Supplemental Security Income. Social Security. Medicaid. Community Action Agency. Weatherization. Head Start. School Lunches. WIC. Public Health. Legal Aid. These and many other social programs and agencies are the resources human service professionals employ as they attempt to help people through difficult life experiences. But where do these social programs come from? How are they created? What are they supposed to accomplish? What are the rules that determine who can get what kinds of help? The answers to these and other questions are found in the policies that create the social programs. Just as the carpenter reports to work with a box full of tools to frame a house, so too the human service worker brings social programs as the tools for helping people. But how are these tools used?

When we go to the grocery store we might pick up a quart of milk and a dozen eggs without giving any thought to how these products got on the shelf. If we were studying to be agricultural scientists, however, we would study a great deal about how those products got on the shelf. We would need to know how eggs and milk were produced, the rules that governed their transport and storage, and how they were introduced to the people who bought them. In the same manner, the human service worker must know how social programs are produced, what was intended by creating them, what rules must be followed in using them, and what persons can use which programs. In other words, in order to use social programs to help persons in need, we must study the social policies that created them.

Some human service workers need to understand the policies that create social programs in order to help their clients, just as John helped Mr. Rigssbee, as Joan helped Ms. Smith, and as Sally and her coworker helped Angeline. Other human service workers, supervisors, for example, need to understand some welfare policies so that they can weave social programs into the service fabric of their agencies. They need to know what social programs fit best with what their social agency is trying to accomplish. Still other human service workers will be in positions to modify existing social policies and create new ones so as to make social programs more useful for those who need them. Understanding social welfare policy, therefore, is a foundation for the entire human service enterprise.

The development of social welfare policy and its transformation into social products is often seen as dull and boring. Yet one cannot pick up a newspaper

6

or watch the evening news without confronting social welfare policy. President George W. Bush announces a "faith-based" social initiative. Congress considers "privatizing" Social Security. Congress creates a program to house the homeless. Falling state revenues force reductions in Medicaid spending. To many people, these policy developments have little meaning beyond their face value. But human service professionals who understand the policy contexts of these initiatives are able to grasp their full meaning and understand the larger ramifications of such social policy developments.

The purpose of this text is to help human service professionals, at whatever level of practice, understand the context of social welfare policy, as well as understand the specific social programs the policies create. Thus the text is divided into two parts. The first part of the text deals mostly with developing an understanding of how social welfare policy comes about. The second part deals with the major social welfare policies and their programs. The division of this text into parts is somewhat arbitrary. Policies create programs, and the need to modify programs requires the re-creation of policies. Yet dividing this text into parts allows students and teachers to divide their attention between theories and methods of policy analysis and development and America's major social welfare policy subjects. In many ways this is a division between theory and practice. Part I contains information that will provide a theoretical foundation for understanding how policy analysis fits into America's policymaking system and some methods by which policy analysis tasks are accomplished. Part II applies these theories and methods to familiar social welfare policy areas, or sectors, that are continually examined as Americans search for new answers to long-standing domestic problems.

Part I of this text seeks to help the student understand the place of policy analysis and development in the vast complex of public decision-making in America. Public decisions are a product of political processes that depend on a variety of information. Sometimes we think of information about constituency preferences, interest group programs, and the influence of the powerful—"political information"—as less important in policymaking than the facts and figures of a particular issue under consideration—"scientific information."

Policy analysis provides a good deal of the information necessary for political decisions. Policy analysis must take into account both "political" and "scientific" information; as it does so, policy analysis often provides a bridge between the two kinds of information, giving decision makers a firmer foundation on which to make decisions. Chapter 1 provides some ways of understanding policy analysis and development that show the different purposes that policy analysis may serve and how these different purposes influence policy development processes. In so doing, Chapter 1 provides a working definition of social welfare policy, and discusses how social welfare policy generally fits into the scheme of things in our contemporary American society.

Chapters 2 and 3 provide a framework for understanding how policy decisions are made in the American system. Knowing where decisions are likely to be made is very important to knowing what kind of information policy analysis must supply. Some decisions are made in different branches of government.

Others are made at the state or local levels of governance. Still others may depend on an interplay between public and private sector activity. Each decision center has somewhat unique information requirements in the policy development process.

Chapter 4 examines different approaches to policy analysis and development. It provides three models of policy analysis that can be adapted to the specific information requirements of the various policy decision centers, and describes a number of techniques of data collection, analysis, and presentation.

Part I therefore provides a theoretical orientation to social welfare policy analysis and development that shows the wide variability in its application. Variability, however, can be managed when it is clear what kind of information is required in specific policymaking settings. Once the theory of policy analysis is understood, the actual tasks of policy analysis within the context of specific policy problems, the substance of Part II, can be better understood.

UNDERSTANDING SOCIAL WELFARE AS A PART OF PUBLIC POLICY

CHAPTER I

INTRODUCTION: THE LABYRINTH OF SOCIAL WELFARE POLICY DEVELOPMENT

In 1994, an outspoken Republican congressman, Newt Gingrich, sought to win Republican control of the U.S. House of Representatives in that year's elections by proposing a "Contract with America." The "contract" proposed items Republican representatives agreed to promote if they were elected to office. One such item was welfare reform. Curiously enough, this Republican pledge was not unlike the pledge Bill Clinton made during his presidential campaign when he pledged to "end welfare as we know it."

Essentially, the welfare reform legislation under consideration in 1995 (H.R. 4) proposed to deny cash assistance to teenage mothers and to reward states for reducing out-of-wedlock births. But almost immediately these welfare policy proposals raised several policy problems. According to some anti-abortion groups, such as the National Right to Life Committee and the U.S. Catholic Conference, this legislation could prompt unmarried mothers, and particularly teenagers, to have more abortions. These groups sought to amend pending welfare reform legislation to have these provisions removed. However, other anti-abortion groups, such as the Family Research Council and the Christian Coalition, supported these provisions of the bill as providing the means to take a strong, traditional, conservative stand against out-of-wedlock births and teen pregnancy.

With strong Republican support, welfare reform (H.R. 4) passed the House of Representatives by a vote of 234 to 199 on March 24, 1995. But when it could not win support from the Senate, H.R. 4 was attached to the 1995 budget bill. Wrangling over the 1995 budget bill went well beyond the beginning of the new fiscal year in October. When Congress finally sent President Clinton a budget bill in December 1995, he vetoed it, largely because of the welfare reform package included in the bill. The president's veto resulted in a federal government shutdown lasting almost three weeks. After further political wrangling, Congress separated welfare reform from the budget bill. President Clinton signed the budget bill, but he vetoed the now free-standing welfare reform bill. Congress had adjourned and welfare reform looked dead.[1]

Then, in January 1996, Representative E. Clay Shaw (R-FL), chairman of the Subcommittee on Welfare Reform of the House Ways and Means Committee, revived the legislation as H.R. 3734, and led it through modifications sufficient to win the president's approval. These modifications provided state incentives to, rather than statutory requirements for, reducing out-of-wedlock births, thereby reducing the tension that developed over this contentious issue. The president announced on July 31, 1996, that he would sign the compromise legislation. The House of Representatives approved the Conference Committee report on July 31, 328 to 101, and the Senate approved it August 1, 78 to 21. On August 22, 1996, the president signed the Personal Responsibility and Work Opportunity Act (PL 104-193), making welfare reform a reality.

Exactly what President Clinton meant by his campaign promise "to end welfare as we know it" was not clear, although he talked frequently about his experiences as governor of Arkansas, and of putting people to work instead of giving them welfare. It seemed to matter very little that the country was still digesting welfare reforms created by Congress in 1988, the Job Opportunity and Basic Skills (JOBS) program, and that the JOBS program had fallen far short of its political objectives. The dismal history of work-mandated welfare programs going all the way back to the 1967 Work Incentive (WIN) program was being repeated in yet another form. Nor did it seem to matter much that Congress had amended welfare programs in significant ways in every session of Congress since the Social Security Act was passed in 1935. Would we ever get it right?

At about the same time as the 1992 presidential campaign, a group of Republican staff members in the House of Representatives began to get together informally to think about and study welfare in the United States. The staffers were encouraged, if not led, by welfare counsel of the House Ways and Means Committee, Dr. Ron Haskins. Haskins had developed considerable academic experience in social welfare policy analysis before going to work for Congress. And, as a former Marine, he knew how to lead, as well as how to follow, and when it was right to do one or the other.

The interesting feature of this informal group was that the staffers who met and talked came from different congressional committees or subcommittees, all of which had some authority over one or another welfare-type program. Perhaps the group was emboldened by the fact that Republicans were not in control of either Congress or the White House, or perhaps by the information that they began to collect with the help of the Congressional Research Service on the range, complexity, and cost of welfare spending.[2] Maybe they were driven by partisan politics, as some later suggested. But one fact emerged from these meetings: if welfare was ever to get workable "reforms," committees had to give up jurisdiction over some of their programs, just as the federal government would have to give up its direction of social welfare programs, which it had guarded so jealously for the previous sixty years.

There are many reasons why congressional committees want to maintain jurisdiction over specific programs (see Chapter 3). The most important is political: constituencies develop around specific programs, and these constituencies help to reelect the representatives who refund and expand the programs they control. Block grants would lessen jurisdiction as well as erode political support for committee chairs and members. Looking on themselves as members of the "loyal opposition," this group of staffers had little hope of achieving the kind of welfare reform they envisioned, and so they could be expansive in their proposals. For example, they even discussed wresting the Food Stamp Program away from the Agriculture Committee and making it part of the income-maintenance block grant, a proposal that finally sank the welfare reform proposed by President Carter some years earlier.

Then the unexpected happened. The 1994 congressional elections put the Senate and the House of Representatives in Republican control, placed more Republicans in governorships, and a large number of state legislatures changed from Democratic to Republican control. The 1994 elections were the most stunning in thirty years, and many conceded that the outcome was due to the Contract with America, which Newt Gingrich introduced into the campaign itself. From state houses to the White House, Republicans boasted the contract was what turned the political tide, while Democrats grumbled that the contract was a political ploy that could not be carried out.

One element in the Contract with America involved reforming welfare by denying welfare benefits to unmarried teenagers, denying welfare to children born out of wedlock while their mother was receiving welfare, and putting people to work. The Clinton staff was in a difficult position inasmuch as it was proposing welfare reform that was remarkably similar to that in the Contract with America. But the real surprise came to the staffers in the House of Representatives who had been working on their block-grant proposals.

"All of a sudden we were ahead of the power curve," one staffer commented. "We had a well-thought-out welfare reform proposal and tentative agreements from the committees about program jurisdiction. I couldn't believe it. We were in the driver's seat and far out in front."

Another staffer commented: "Here we were, in control of the House, and leadership pushing to implement the Contract while it still had currency among House Republicans. We turned to Ways and Means, and they said, 'I think we have something you might like.' And like it we did."

But there was still much work to do. Staff crunched numbers and showed how the proposal would reduce spending. Governors, many of them newly elected, grabbed at the opportunity presented by the block grants. State flexibility had been the cry of most governors since the small social service block grants were created in 1984.

Not everything ran smoothly. Agriculture balked at putting food stamps into the block grant, even though the new chairman was somewhat favorably disposed to the idea.

"Agriculture needs an urban base," one staffer commented. "Farming makes up such a small portion of agriculture spending today, and of our constituency, that without urban spending, agriculture would be lost. And you need to remember," the staffer continued, "welfare is big business, not so much in the amount we spend for benefits, but who carries out the programs. In agriculture, grocery stores are big beneficiaries of food stamps, as are those in the computer industry who are developing 'debit card'–type spending mechanisms, and those who are constantly investigating fraud. Food stamps is big business, and agriculture had to hang on to it."

The 1996 welfare reform represented a great change in the direction of social welfare policy and programs. Throughout the following chapters some of these changes will be discussed from the perspective of how the income-maintenance provisions of this reform affect existing policy debates and program activities. But before we explore the specific elements of these most recent welfare changes in Chapter 5, we must understand the larger picture of policy development in the United States. For as important as this most recent welfare reform is in its own right, it also provides an example of the basic purposes served by all social welfare policy in the American system. The development of this most recent welfare reform not only offers important lessons in how social welfare policy is made in America, but provides important insights into what exactly social welfare policy is, and the purposes social policy serves in the American political system.

SOCIAL POLICY AS A SOCIAL CONSTRUCT

Social policy is often thought about in terms of programs, but it also serves a more general and important set of social functions. When Congress created its 1996 welfare reform, it created public policy. The preceding pages illustrate many of the themes that make up public policy as it is experienced at a single point in time. Welfare as we know it today has existed as part of the Social Security Act since 1935, and its programs have been changed almost every year since then. The 1996 changes are more and less important program changes than earlier welfare changes. All program changes were created by changes in public policies, but these recent policy changes were built upon previous changes. All these policy changes give meaning and substance to the basic purposes of creating social welfare policy in the first place.

Any single public policy serves a number of specific and general purposes. The 1996 welfare reform made changes in who gets benefits and how benefits are provided. Additionally, the vast network of agencies that provide these services has changed as the 1996 welfare reforms have been put into place. For example, many congressional representatives support block grants for welfare precisely because they believe these welfare changes will reduce the influence of federal and state administrative bureaucracies in providing welfare benefits. Such combinations of specific and general purposes of public policy vary from policy to policy, and the 1996 welfare reforms are no exception. While specific purposes of public policy satisfy specific constituencies, like families that need welfare support, the general purposes of social policy satisfy expectations of the larger community. In general, social policy satisfies one or another of five purposes, all of which can be found in the 1996 welfare reform. The 1996 welfare reform (1) solved a social problem; (2) located the public interest; (3) identified and legitimized special social goals; (4) provided a context for resolving conflicting values; and (5) established the direction for future social activity. The following sections look more closely at each of these five general purposes.

Solving a Social Problem

The words "social problems" conjure up vivid images of street violence, abused and neglected children, prostitution, and homelessness. To say that public policy solves these problems overstates the case. Rather, we can say that public policy "addresses" social problems, or that social policy tries to solve social problems. In reality, America's social problems, particularly the big social problems like crime and homelessness, are seldom "solved" in the sense that once policies are created, these problems cease to exist. Yet it is still important to think of public policy as actions that try to solve social problems.

There are several reasons why public policy does not "solve" social problems, as problem solving is usually understood. In the first place, not everyone sees problems in the same way. Often what one person thinks is a problem may seem completely normal to another person. Problems emerge when values are applied to existing life conditions. Take the example of abortion, mentioned above as part of the debate over the 1996 welfare reforms. Some people value life so highly that they see taking life at any stage as wrong. Thus because of their values they believe abortion is wrong. For other people, it is not that they do not value life, but to them choices over life and death often have to be made. These persons argue that life-and-death choices should be made by the person responsible for carrying out the choice. Because of these beliefs, this group values individual choice. In many ways, of the three most cherished American values, life, liberty, and the pursuit of happiness, two values, life and liberty, are in conflict in abortion debates.

Thus different people place higher or lower values on life circumstances. For some, abortion is legally and morally wrong; for others, abortion is about giving women (and men) the freedom to choose what is right and wrong. Solving a problem for one person may create a problem for someone else with different values. In this sense, a problem may not be solved. Values drive problem identification, just as values drive the solutions we seek in the form of public policy. From identifying the problem (the beginning), to selecting a policy to deal with the problem (the ending), the whole of public policy development is driven by values.

Social problems come in various forms and sizes and do not necessarily mean that a society is in serious trouble. American society is a highly complex, diverse mix of people. The economic system that energizes the United States and the political institutions that order it are founded on the belief in individual choice and maximum participation, which foster increased diversity. American society operates pretty well most of the time. Public activities are undertaken to enhance private interests. But this picture of success emerges from a context of constant change, adjustment, readjustment, and accommodation. Some of these changes create problems, such as the need for a constant supply of decent housing, that involve large social and geographic sectors. Some problems, such as relocation of displaced textile workers, involve smaller, discrete sectors. All are important. The idea of a dynamic society constantly dealing with problems through public policies is important to an understanding of the purposes of public policy, and explains, in part, the constant efforts to reform welfare.

This complexity of American society is yet another reason why public policy does not solve a problem in the usual way one understands problem solving. For example, social relationships among racial and ethnic groups in American society constitute a serious, continuous problem. In the 1960s, the Civil Rights Act and the Voting Rights Act were public policies developed to ease social tension and improve social relationships. But despite the importance of these policies, African American and white populations have not reconciled their differences. Though some progress has been made, African Americans remain largely segregated socially, economically, and geographically, a source of serious conflict as the African American population continues to receive so little of the total public resources. This is a serious problem that continues as an agenda item for public policy.

Across the nation, large numbers of Spanish-speaking people are migrating to the United States from Mexico and South American countries. Latin Americans are the fastest growing population in the United States today, making most of the Southwest a bilingual culture. The influx of immigrants, both legal and illegal, caused such a strain on California's public resources that Californians approved a 1994 referendum that prohibited spending public resources on illegal immigrants, with the threat of denying public services to thousands of people. California's courts ordered a delay in implementing that particular policy, and eventually the policy was abandoned. Thus a public policy designed to resolve a problem brought about by American diversity appears to make the problem worse by withholding resources from those who may need them.

Solutions to problems may range from conservative to liberal policy choices, depending on how the problems are perceived. In reviewing health-care delivery, Alan Shostack, a sociologist, has demonstrated how the problem of inadequate care might be resolved by different approaches depending on how the problem is understood. If, for example, inadequate care is viewed as a result of too many people asking for too many services because public and private insurance companies will pay for these services, a policy to restrict access to health care by raising fees might seem to resolve the problem appropriately. On the other hand, if the problem is seen as the inability of the health-care industry to provide basic care to the average person, one might conclude that the health-care industry has too many interests competing for high profits—drug companies, large hospitals, equipment manufacturers, nursing homes—and thus suggest that the government regulate the costs and profits of health-care providers.[3]

Solutions to problems may also take the form of policy choices aimed at specific groups in the population, for instance, women, minorities, and children; or they may prompt policies that enhance the well-being of everyone, including special groups. The first of these types of policies has been called *residual*. Residual policies are created on the assumption that although political, economic, and social systems operate effectively most of the time for most people, residual problems remain that have to be accommodated by public policies.

The second kind of policy is called *institutional*. These policies assume that solutions to problems have to be applied universally and usually are accomplished through some change in existing institutions.[4] The differences between institutional and residual policies can be illustrated by comparing the Social Security retirement program (Old Age Survivor and Disability Insurance, OASDI) with financial assistance to the aged (Supplementary Security Income, SSI). OASDI is based on the assumption that protection of income in retirement requires a universal restructuring of our economic system; in this case the government taxes everyone and reserves these funds for everyone's use in retirement. SSI, on the other hand, provides limited financial resources to older people when their equity in OASDI is so marginal that they need additional financial resources.

In summary, public policy resolves problems, but the way each problem is understood becomes important for how that problem is resolved. In many cases, the particular view taken toward a problem is a *normative orientation:* one in which a standard for viewing the problem has already been established. This standard is often one based on values or ideology, and policy analysis usually accepts these values as facts, leading to a decision. However, for any problem a number of conflicting normative orientations may exist. Poverty, for example, is a social problem for which many policies have been established; in fact, many of the policies discussed in this book were designed to deal with the problem of poverty. Some people take the position that poverty is the fault of the individual; others see poverty as a problem of the social system (as when African Americans or women are discriminated against in employment); still others may see poverty as the result of an inequitable distribution of money and power. And although these views reflect personal ideologies and beliefs about poverty, they are advanced as basic facts in debates over policy. They constitute normative orientations on poverty.

Policy analysis and policy choice must come to grips with normative orientations, because the prevailing or public views on a subject often reflect values held by the larger society. Sometimes these prevailing views reflect deeply held religious convictions, as with the abortion issue. Sometimes they reflect the particular values of a policy analyst or the values of the method of analysis itself. Sometimes they reflect the values of the decision maker. Thus normative orientations are evident not only in the ways problems are identified, but also in the ways policy alternatives are examined. Chapter 4 presents three models of policy analysis; each model also includes recognition of normative issues. In subsequent chapters that examine specific policy subjects, the normative orientations to each problem are stated as clearly as possible so that they can be considered in the analysis itself.

Locating the Public Interest

The public interest is an elusive but extremely important concept in policy development. The whole purpose of democratic government is service to the public. The acts of such a government are presumed to reflect the preferences of the governed. When they do not, the governed attempt to bring the government into line with public preferences, through a range of available political activities such as voting, decrease in public support for government, and, unfortunately on occasion, civil unrest.

Charting the public interest is extremely difficult in a complex society. Different people and different groups of people usually want different things, another example of the influence of normative orientations. People also want change, which reinforces the idea that the public is "fickle." In the 1960s, for example, the American public seemed to be asking for greater freedom of choice over the termination of pregnancy. By the 1980s, the American public seemed to be asking government to restrict the choice. By 1996 abortion had again opened old debates, and compromised policy development, as seen in the welfare reform debates. Presently, the same normative concerns that shaped earlier debates over abortion are emerging in debates on stem cell research. (See Chapter 10.)

Public opinion is very hard to measure. Public opinion polls provide some gauge, as do statements from major public actors, but these may be superficial or fleeting reflections of the public interest. For example, after winning election to a second term of office, President Reagan talked about his victory as proof of positive public support for his policies, yet his percentage of the popular vote was less than one point greater than that of his opponent, Walter Mondale, and opinion polls showed that a majority of the electorate disagreed with his policies, even though they liked him. In the 2000 election, George W. Bush won the Electoral College vote even though he lost the popular vote to Albert Gore. Yet President Bush claimed to have a public mandate to implement his tax reduction policies.

Public opinion translates only crudely into public policy. Public opinion is an expression of the masses, but policy is shaped by elites. Thus public opinion may not always be converted into results that reflect broad public interests. For example, public opinion may favor an equitable tax system, but tax policies leave tax systems inequitable.

Nevertheless, public policy does provide an important locus of public interest. A number of publics will be involved in the creation of any public policy. A president or a governor may initiate a policy proposal after a number of individuals and groups associated with an issue have come to some conclusion about the dimension of the problem, its normative orientation, and proposed solutions. A legislator may undertake to develop policy. Many publics, many individuals, and many groups interact in the policymaking process. All policymakers have to be sensitive to a variety of public orientations. Thus in the process of developing policy, a considerable amount of public consensus is achieved, so that by the time a public policy is developed, it offers a pretty good indication of how the American public is oriented toward the issues at stake.

By locating the public interest, public policy freezes public thinking and public action on an issue at a particular point in time. Because the processes of policy development are complex and time consuming, public policy is not likely to be on the cutting edge of new issues. In any dynamic society the circumstances that give rise to an identifiable problem are changing constantly, as are the political institutions that reformulate public interests into public products. As a result, it often seems that no sooner has a public policy emerged than there are pressures to change it. In this dynamic environment, the public is frequently apt to question whether government and public representatives in government are responding to public wishes. Whether or not publics should be involved in policy development is not in question: publics are involved, often in complex ways. Thus when a public policy process has been completed, public interest is reflected in the policy; the public interest in the issue emerges from the process and becomes clear.

Identifying and Legitimating Social Goals

Because it is closely associated with locating the public interest, public policy identifies and legitimates social goals. Although we visualize policy development as a progression from problems to goals, such may not always be the case. Goals may preclude problems or may exist independent of them, and social goals frequently determine the framework of discourse that surrounds most policy debate. Goals are most frequently thought of as desired states of affairs. A goal is an image of the future, which provides a guiding framework for many actions that follow. Goals also provide a measure of social progress, which can be gauged by how much has been achieved with respect to the vision set forth by the policy. Public policy serves to identify goals and confer legitimacy on them. Thus through the development of public policy a particular set of ideas become formalized goals, and movement toward or away from these goals can be charted, as the 1996 welfare reform illustrates. President Clinton's goal "to end welfare as we know it" conferred legitimacy on work as a precondition for welfare, a preference in welfare policy dating all the way back to passage of the Social Security Act itself. (See Chapter 5 in particular.)

The development of the "War on Poverty" is another example of the goal-setting purpose of social policy. On January 8, 1964, President Lyndon Johnson went before Congress with his state of the union message. Reporting on the state of the union is required of new presidents, and these messages frequently outline the policy objectives (social goals) of the new administration. In this particular address, Johnson introduced a bold new goal: the elimination of poverty in America. "This administration today, here and now, declares unconditional war on poverty in America," he proclaimed. "Our aim is not only to relieve the symptoms of poverty, but to cure it, and above all, prevent it."[5] This statement inaugurated an effort later called the "War on Poverty," a centerpiece of the Johnson administration's Great Society. This announcement and the activities that followed formed the framework of the Johnson administration's social policy. They were goals, and they were also public policy.

President Johnson's declaration of war on poverty provided a context for a number of specific policy proposals. He asked Congress to develop and expand 11 major programs: (1) Appalachian development, (2) youth employment, (3) expanded food stamp distribution, (4) a national service corps (VISTA, Volunteers in Service to America), (5) more stable unemployment insurance, (6) extension of minimum wage coverage, (7) federal aid to education in impoverished communities, (8) construction of more hospitals and libraries, (9) hospital insurance for the aged, (10) expanded public housing, and (11) federal aid for mass transit.

This cornucopia of policy initiatives was an astute summary of the direction of the nation under the Kennedy administration. The general mood of the nation had suggested to President Kennedy that poverty was unacceptable. In 1959, Michael Harrington had exposed the ravages of poverty in the United States, and public opinion seemed to support efforts to deal with it. For example, President Kennedy had managed to initiate a limited food stamp program, but many of his social initiatives could not find their way through an entrenched Congress.[6] President Johnson's message to Congress set forth policy objectives that reflected a buildup of broad interests in dealing systematically with poverty. On August 20, 1964, Johnson signed legislation that further clarified the social goal of the policy initiatives presented in his state of the union message: America's objective would be to afford the poor some security and to enable them to "move with the majority along the high road of hope and prosperity."[7] This legislation was the Economic Opportunity Act, which created a range of programs that were used for the next twenty years to reduce poverty in the nation. Thus a diffuse goal, reducing poverty, was legitimated through the social policies of the Great Society and its programs.

Creating a Context for Resolving Conflicting Values

Public policy is designed to solve public problems, and the resolution of a problem often depends on the normative orientation of the problem solver. The solution of a problem for one group of persons may raise problems for another group. Johnson's proposals to eliminate poverty provided opportunities and support for many people with low incomes, but they also burdened state and local governments with complex federal programs, causing political backlashes that have endured ever since. In 1981, for example, President Reagan proposed reducing the burden of federal programs on states by creating block-grant programs that would allow states flexibility in dealing with social problems. In exchange, he solicited agreements from governors that they would accept reduced amounts of federal funding in exchange for relief from federal regulations. The resulting reductions in funding, combined with a significant economic recession, brought thousands of people back into poverty and ill health, and the percentage of citizens living in poverty reached the level that had existed before Johnson's policies were instituted.

Again in 1996 governors sought more freedom from cumbersome federal programs, and Congress answered with more block-grant programs. Similar complaints about welfare programs in the 1990s brought about the TANF block grants to states. Sometimes these adverse or conflicting elements of policy are identified as "unintended consequences" or "unanticipated events" of policy choices. Unintended consequences represent efforts to even out competing value positions among different groups. Most commonly the competition is between those who have and those who do not. The long-held idea that the United States is a "community of publics," and the concomitant notion that this community will express itself in a democratic policy that at least satisfies the greatest number, if not the greatest good, is increasingly under fire. Years ago, C. Wright Mills, who had focused his attention on the divisions among groups, claimed that American society has never been a community of publics, but is instead severely stratified. "At the top, members emerge as elites of power. The middle does not link the bottom with the top. The bottom is politically fragmented and increasingly powerless." [8] Mills's claims continue to ring true today.

Understanding public policy thus requires understanding power. Power, and "power elites," as Mills terms them, are extremely important to the analysis, development, and realization of public policy. Power has been defined as "the capacity to overcome part or all of the resistance to induce changes in the face of opposition." [9] In this view, power itself has no value exclusive of its expression; the purposes to which power is put give it value. In the policymaking process, once questions of value are decided, few conflicts arise over using power to implement policy. Power struggles are more apt to transpire over agreements about the values themselves. In other words, power struggles concern values and the choice of normative positions. Mills and others who describe American society as elitist argue that power in the hands of a few gives those few a great advantage in determining the normative orientation toward an issue; consequently this elite exercises great influence in the direction of public policy.

Amitai Etzioni distinguishes between power *assets* and the *exercise* of power. [10] Possession of the potential to act confers power assets, which may be converted into *expressions of power,* but are not necessarily used in this way. Groups or individuals who hold power assets tend to calculate whether to exercise power or not. Consequently, expressions of power are often made even when power is not exercised outright. For example, an individual or a group, perhaps a small labor union, may choose not to act (that is, not to exercise power) because it calculates that the power that could be exercised by another group, for example, management, would be greater; hence by exercising its power in a strike the union would lose the struggle. However, the threat of exercising that power (a power asset) might force management to some concession. This distinction between the assets and the exercise of power is extremely important in policy analysis, since power influences normative orientations, or the "policy agenda," as many analysts call it.

Because American society is composed of many groups, representing a variety of values, promoted by a variety of elites, a constant ferment stirs the policy agenda. In fact the number of goals on the agenda is so great that there are insufficient resources to realize all of them. Consequently, groups moving toward realizing particular goals will tend to resist any perceived competitors. Cooperation under these circumstances is difficult to achieve, and conflict is more likely to be the dominant mode of interaction. When cooperation is achieved, as it often must be when dealing with complex public problems, it is frequently imposed by another party. For example, cooperation between labor unions and management may be achieved because the Department of Labor also has power assets that can be brought to bear to compel cooperation on policy matters. This type of cooperation is often engineered by mediators who bring the parties to the bargaining table. In Etzioni's words, "Power and cooperation are, thus, not a mutually exclusive pair of concepts; cooperation often has a power base, and power is exercised through cooperation."[11]

In this view, public policy development provides an environment in which power exchanges can take place either cooperatively or through conflict. Since power assets are not equally distributed, and since changes in power relationships take place through the application of power, public policy development provides the framework in which power can become restructured.

An example of the restructuring of power through policymaking can be seen in Edward Banfield's and Martin Myerson's study of the development of public housing policy in Chicago in the 1950s. The city had decided to expand considerably its public housing. Once that decision had been made, the struggle for control of land and money began in earnest. A variety of conflicting claims over site selection, the occupants of the proposed housing, and construction had to be resolved. The ensuing scramble was a competition for shares of city resources and, eventually, for the authority to give the city itself control of the process by which resources would be distributed: "The 'Big Boys' could get and keep power enough to run the city only by giving favors for the maintenance of [their power] base. The people of Chicago probably did not fully realize the price that was being paid to assemble enough power [to build the housing]."[12]

Setting the Direction for Future
Social Action: Policy and Planning

Policy builds on policy, and in this incremental form, public policy sets the course for further social development. In the United States at least, public policy appears as a process of changes leading to a better society. Some may want to protect the environment; others may want to improve housing or health care;

still others may want to redistribute income and wealth. Yet these different actions only seem separate. In fact they constitute a single process. Human urgings for a better society are deeply imbedded in the American ideology, and Americans believe that a systematic, orderly process of policy development will lead to good for society. This belief stems from a positivist ideology that originated in the writings of Auguste Comte, the founder of sociology, and in the literature of utopias. The influence of positivist thought in policy analysis is examined in detail in Chapter 4, but it is important here to understand the essential support that positivism gives to public policy. The very idea of policy, a committed direction, in contrast to uncoordinated activities, attests to the positivist belief that society can be improved, and positivism gives compelling vitality to the idea that social policy leads, eventually, to social reform. Again, the 1996 welfare reform policy serves as an example. Advocates for this reform accepted the idea that it would decrease the need for welfare in the future.

The close connection between public policy and future change, and the underlying belief that changes will produce a better society, explain in part the close historical relationship between the activities of social planning and social policy. The application of scientific knowledge to practical problems marked the beginning of the systematic study of why social change takes place, or how social change can be managed and directed. This planning tradition emerged from the American city planning movement and the social and municipal reform efforts of the early 1900s.

This spirit of reform was consistent with the ideological orientation toward positivism, the belief that science could and would create a better society, and was so far-reaching in its influence on American social institutions that any consideration of policy analysis must acknowledge this early history. Largely because of increased pressure for change from settlement house workers and other social reformers, state legislatures and municipal governments began to set aside portions of land for parks and other public purposes. As far as the cities were concerned, developing parks and other public facilities was consistent with efforts, already under way for several decades, to ensure safe water supplies, adequate waste disposal, and public safety and fire protection. In Chicago, the philanthropist William Kent gave land for Jane Addams's Hull House. The great landscape architect Frederick Law Olmsted conceived New York's Central Park as a place in which city dwellers could experience "a day in the country," based on the ideal of humanizing the urban experience.

To achieve the objectives proposed by the reformers, municipalities had to develop plans not only for new parks but also for the many other community resources believed to be essential to a decent life in urban America. This planning required not only information about what might be possible, but also reform in the structure and character of local government, for municipalities needed additional staff to execute these new projects. Moreover, reformers sought to protect these public accomplishments by insisting that the increasing number of public officials be chosen by popular elections rather than through patronage, thus giving further authority to the rational, as opposed to political, nature of this form of policy development.

As the twentieth century progressed, this blending of scientific information with social reform and city planning led to the emergence of social planning as a defined discipline and specific sector of activity. Herbert Hoover created the President's Research Committee on Social Trends in December 1929.[13] Among its members were the political scientist Charles E. Merriam of the University of Chicago and Howard W. Odum, a sociologist at the University of North Carolina who had helped to establish its school of social work. Although the committee was commissioned to develop plans to guide the country through the economic calamity of the Great Depression, Hoover gave only nominal support to this work, perhaps because he underestimated the impact of the worsening economic circumstances. The depression, however, did reveal serious flaws in the American economic and social structure, and Hoover's Research Committee provided intellectual energy for President Roosevelt's "brain trust," which eventually did help create the social plans that lifted the nation out of the depression and led the way to establishment of the federal role in policy development under the Social Security Act.

The close association between social sciences and social policy development is much too broad to be examined here, but briefly it may be said that the emerging base of social knowledge fused with ideas that a better social order could be planned and realized. "It was in this context that applied social science, first in the form of statistics and demography, and later in the form of established disciplines of sociology, economics, political science, and public administration, rose as a challenge to the practical problems of understanding and controlling the complexities of society."[14]

The relationship between policy analysis, policymaking, and various forms of social and physical planning has continued to the present day. Policy documents are often called "master plans." Nearly every local community in the United States—cities, counties, and even multijurisdictional organizations—has its planning boards or planning councils. The purpose of these planning groups is to develop policy, usually about necessary land use. These policies eventually become incorporated into something called a "comprehensive plan." For example, the small town of Carrboro, North Carolina adopted a policy that stated, in part, that for purposes of land use, mobile homes would be treated in exactly the same way as homes permanently constructed on a site. This policy became part of Carrboro's land-use plan. Now when an individual or a corporate group contemplates using land in Carrboro, the treatment of mobile homes must be considered along with many other planning factors. The mobile home policy sets the agenda for further policy development and therefore remains in close association with an ongoing process of planning.

Similarly, the Social Security Act, along with the many amendments to it over the years, is both a policy document and a planning document. For example, as public policy, Title II of the act provides federal support for a public retirement program. As a planning document, Title II requires the anticipation and implementation of sophisticated financial provisions for retirees, including the projection of national economic performance as far as fifty years into the future as well as a series of population projections so that economic guarantees can be supported over this period of time.

CLASSIFYING SOCIAL POLICY

The diversity of social policy prohibits general statements about how public policy is analyzed and developed. Policy is categorized most frequently according to who makes it and what purposes it serves. Such classification schemes are useful insofar as they provide common points of departure for thinking about social policy proposals, but social policy as a concept must be defined before classification can be discussed reasonably. Throughout this text, public policy is understood in the following way: *A public policy is an action (or in some cases, an inaction) usually undertaken by government, directed at a particular goal, and legitimated by the commitment of public resources.* A detailed discussion of this definition introduces the next chapter, but for the purposes here of classifying public policy this definition restricts our consideration of public policy to *activity of government.* On the basis of this definition, public policy can be categorized and its different purposes can be explained by identifying those who make it.

Administrative Policy

Administrators most frequently make public policy. In general, administrators are persons who work in government agencies or well-defined corporate organizations that have responsibility for carrying out programs. Thus they make policy within the context of a particular program, or policy, or problem. For example, Donna Shalala, secretary of Health and Human Services in the Clinton administration, and former governor Tommy Thompson, President George W. Bush's secretary for the same department, and their respective administrative staffs, never made policy about airports or interstate highways because these policies are made by the Department of Transportation. Administrative policymaking may be restricted further by the function of administrators. Because their primary responsibility is to implement programs (and policies), administrators cannot make policies that would create new programs or change the policies that established the existing programs. As a result of this narrow frame of reference, administrators are required to develop policy that is carefully measured against established program mandates.

The "Baby Doe" regulations of 1985 demonstrate the limited scope of administrative policymaking and the consequent need to apply scientific knowledge to the policymaking process.[15] Congress included a provision in the Child Abuse Prevention Act of 1984 that failure to provide treatment to disabled newborns would constitute abuse and neglect; doctors could be held legally accountable for failing to provide needed medical treatment. The Department of Health and Human Services (DHHS) was required to implement this program within the framework of a format unique to administrative policymaking: regulations. These regulations required the DHHS not only to stay within the bounds of the Child Abuse Prevention Act but to avail itself of highly technical information in developing its policy. Answers to questions such as, "What constitutes imminent danger?" and "What is medically indicated treatment?" had to be extracted from detailed expert knowledge.

Legislative Policy

The legislative process of policymaking or, in more common terms, the development of statute law, is a human labyrinth. Figure 1.1 shows how an idea is translated into statute law in Congress. The process is similar in the states, although some of the elements, like the number of times a bill may have to be read, will be different. The character and substance of a proposal may be obvious enough when the legislative process begins, but those may change or be lost altogether during the twists and turns of the process. The intrigue of the legislative process not reflected in Figure 1.1 is legendary. A more complete explanation of the significance of policy analysts for the legislative process is provided in Chapter 2.

Legislators are a diverse lot. They are elected from geographically defined districts: 535 of them to the U.S. Congress, and often more than one hundred to each state legislature. These districts—urban or rural, rich or poor, with Anglo, Hispanic, African American, or Asian American constituencies—are as diverse as the country itself. Legislators are thus to bring to legislative forums widely divergent views about problems and what should be done about them. Most legislators are educated as lawyers, but many are "professional politicians"; they see lawmaking as their vocation, and they want to keep their jobs. All, except 100 senators in the U.S. Senate, stand for election every two years. Legislators have no job tenure. For this reason, and others related to their working environment, legislators are very sensitive to the concerns of their constituents.

Legislators create statute law. Because of the authority behind it and the general deference given to it, statute law establishes our most formidable public policy. And because of the wide diversity of the viewpoints of the participants and the complicated legislative process, it is also the most difficult to create. Yet precisely because it is so formidable, legislation is sought most frequently in the development of public policy. Legislation is a good example of policy that fixes future courses of action. When a law is made, all the other policymakers— administrators, executives, and judges—are brought into action.

In contrast to administrators, legislators have almost no limitation on the scope of their policymaking. The only limit on legislators as they make policy is that they must not make unconstitutional laws. However, often the constitutionality of a legislative action is not decided until after the law has been implemented. Much legislative activity takes place within committees; these are intended to address different subject areas but are not strictly limited forums of discussion. Just about anything is open to legislative policymaking, and creating new policies is as much a part of legislation as modifying old ones. Social

FIGURE 1.1 | A MODEL OF HOW CONGRESS MAKES A LAW

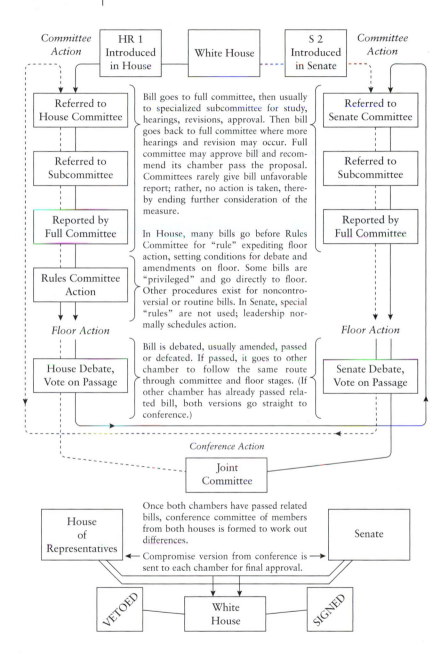

science knowledge, an administrative asset, is not very useful to legislators, because the legislative process is so complex and because the legislators' actions are so closely connected to the desires of their constituents (or interest groups). In other words, legislative policymaking is highly politicized.

Executive Policy

Political executives do make policy, but their policymaking is limited by their primary responsibility of carrying out policy made by others. In most cases political executives are elected officials, such as the president, governors, and mayors. Others, such as heads of administrative agencies, may be appointed. The secretary of the Department of Health and Human Services, for example, is not elected to the post, but chosen by an elected official (the president) and confirmed by other elected officials (members of Congress). The superintendent of a local school system may be elected by the citizens of the school district or may be appointed by the school board that is elected by the citizens. Private corporations, including nonprofit welfare organizations, often designate a chief executive officer (a CEO) as the person responsible for proposing and carrying out policy. Thus administrators and executives share some limitations in their activities as policymakers. Both operate within a limited scope, and both are forced to rely heavily on technical information, because their primary policymaking responsibility is in relationship to carrying out or implementing programs.

The overlap between executives and administrators is best exemplified by the Reagan administration's expanded use, in its second term, of the Office of Management and Budget (OMB) to direct the policymaking of administrative agencies. Because the president has considerably more executive control over the OMB than over administrative agencies, the OMB has increasingly been asked to review proposed policies to determine if they conform to guidelines set down by the president. Before Reagan was elected president, reviews were made of issues in a very general way. This informal review approach was exemplified most clearly by President Ford in 1974, when he required only that policy with inflationary implications be reviewed by the OMB. Reagan expanded this authority in 1981 when he created the Task Force for Regulatory Relief to review the propriety and necessity of policymaking (regulations) in the other administrative agencies. In 1981 he also issued an order giving the director of the OMB authority to "designate any proposal and rule as a major one" (and thus subject it to OMB review) and to "waive sections [of proposed regulations] involving [Regulatory Impact Analysis]." [16] As one commentator put it, "There is no doubt that the February 17th order [EO 12291] developed a centralized review mechanism in the White House with power to 'crack the whip' to bring agencies in line with Reagan's objectives . . . a power play that shifts power from the regulatory agencies to the OMB." [17] This illustrates that a wide range of actions by administrators may receive careful scrutiny from executives and may even require their approval. The implications of this trend in policy development are discussed in Chapter 2. At the very least, this trend has increased the need for social science information among executives and administrators.

Judicial Policy

The policymaking activities of judges differ from those of administrators, executives, and legislators. Traditionally, judges are expected to restrain their personal values in deference to precedent and tradition. In other words, judges read existing law (statute and case law) and make policy based on their interpretation of whatever policy already exists. It might be said that judges do not make policy so much as they affirm and clarify policy on the basis of what other policymakers have already done.

This traditional view of judicial policymaking has received considerable examination since Theodore Becker's pioneering analysis of the judiciary. Many have viewed the actions of judges as political (an "objective application of a political law" in Becker's words), but Becker himself attempts to locate the judicial system within the larger political framework of American government. In his view the political actions of judges are not aberrant forms of judicial behavior, but an integral part of the system of checks and balances in the American system. Specifically, he argues that in "a bargaining type of policy formation which is highly sensitive to pressure, courts allow for unimproved solutions as conflicts reach high levels." [18] This view of judicial policymaking corresponds to the view that the function of public policy is to resolve conflicts over allocation of resources.

There are many outstanding instances where judicial policymaking has broken with the traditional view of judicial behavior. *Baker v. Carr* (1964) forced reapportionment in the states. *King v. Smith* (1963) forbade the states to deny aid to children by questioning the moral fitness of their homes. The greatest example of judicial policymaking will probably remain *Brown v. Board of Education* (1954), which overthrew racial segregation in this country by deciding that separate schools did not constitute equal schools.

Despite its wide-ranging authority in terms of subject area, judicial policymaking is circumscribed by the limits placed on judicial authority: issues must be brought before the court, and they must be issues about constitutionality. Because judges must rely more on legal information than on social science, the courts are perhaps not as much partners with social scientists in the policymaking process as are legislatures.

The Media

Television, newspapers, and radio may not make policy, but they profoundly influence it. The reporting on the events of September 11, 2001, revealed the powerful role of the media in policy development. Not only their presentation of vivid images of the attacks on America, but their selective emphasis on specific aspects of these events helped to mold public opinion and thus direct support for America's policy response to these attacks. The media derive power from constitutional guarantees of free speech, and while media executives are careful not to overstep free speech boundaries, the dramatic ability to present one or another side of a controversial issue gives the media an often overlooked role in the development of social policy. The media as a shaper of social policy needs further study and articulation.

CONCLUSION

Although public policy seems to be an elusive concept, it becomes clearer as the purposes it serves are examined. Public policy represents a social benchmark, showing where American society stands on specific matters. Thus, Americans are concerned about abortions: *Roe v. Wade* and the Hyde Amendment summarize where the nation stands on this matter. Americans are concerned about the welfare of children: the Social Security Act and resulting regulations identify how Americans respond to these issues. Americans are worried about clean air and water: the EPA's Superfund states the nation's position on the environment. For housing concerns there is the Housing Act and tax credits for home mortgages. The list goes on and on; for every issue there is some policy that identifies the position of America's citizens.

Within this litany of social policy, policies often overlap one another both in time and in substance. Social policy is like an elaborate mosaic of American society. Change one part, and the entire mosaic changes. For this reason it is difficult to discuss the major social policies, how they are developed, and how they are analyzed, without giving some consideration to the general picture of public policy as a social construct.

The 1996 welfare reforms, as important as they are, represent only another piece in America's constantly changing social fabric. Denying welfare benefits to children born out of wedlock may seem more like a social policy a foreign country might produce. Such a policy only makes sense when seen in the context of the whole of American social welfare policy directed toward children and their needs. In this context a small policy change, a new piece added to the mosaic, makes the whole look different when in fact the "new look" is very much a product of all that has gone on before.

As one comes to understand the purposes of public policy, it becomes more evident that public policy is an expression of the whole citizenry. Public policy represents a collective choice (not always evident as an overt choice) made through the instruments of governance. If these instruments do not work well, the policy will not adequately address the issue put before it. People within the institutions of government, and to a lesser extent persons in large public and private corporations, make policy, and consequently there is a public process by which policy is made. Policymakers need information and a method for making policy. An understanding of policy analysis, therefore, becomes important.

These subjects are discussed in subsequent chapters. Chapters 2 and 3 examine in greater detail the processes of policymaking and the interaction in that process of those who make policy. Chapter 4 discusses methods of policy analysis and identifies the kinds of information that are important for the type of analysis undertaken, and discusses how this information is examined, what analytic procedure is most used with which kind of information. Once this framework for social policy analysis is developed, Part II of this book, consisting of analyses of some of the most evident public problems of the day, can be seen as an applied social policy study.

QUESTIONS FOR DISCUSSION

1. What are the purposes for the development of public policy?
2. How can inaction be the origin of public policy development?
3. What positive roles might interest groups play in the development of public policy?
4. The 1996 welfare reform, and its recent reauthorization, has set a new course for the development of welfare policy in the United States. How does this new direction reflect the general purposes for public policy outlined in this chapter?

2

C H A P T E R

SOCIAL WELFARE
POLICYMAKING

INTRODUCTION

This text explores social welfare policy from the way it is made to the products it produces. But in order to understand the social welfare policy story, one must recognize that social welfare policy is a special form of public policy. The processes by which social welfare is made correspond to policymaking in general. This chapter, then, examines general policymaking processes, illustrating how those processes come together to form policy from the perspective of the social welfare observer. In this way the uniqueness of social welfare policy can be distilled from the more general policy process.

The process of policymaking may seem as difficult to understand as the idea of policy itself. Policymaking usually begins when a problem is identified and suggestions are made about what to do about it. However, the rest of the process may be hard to follow. Contrary to many policymaking myths, there is no center of policymaking activity, nor are there routine, established policymaking activities. Instead, policymaking involves diverse actions, spanning many different policy decision centers. Those who actually make policy, "the policymakers," differ widely as well. The individual policymakers and policymaking activities involved in passing a law, for example, are quite different from the persons and activities that produce administrative regulations to implement the law. Yet both legislators and administrators make policy. The information needed for policymaking, too, is as varied as the policy process. All policy decisions need information, but the kind of information depends on the point in the policy process at which analysis is conducted and a policy is expected. Understanding policymaking thus entails a clear understanding of who is making the policy, when information is likely to be needed, and what kind of information is likely to be required. Although a detailed examination of the policymaking process cannot be undertaken in this book, some discussion of the process is necessary to clarify why we have the many kinds of social welfare policy and programs discussed later in this book. Knowing who actually makes the policy and what kind of information is used to make the policy helps brings clarity to a very complex policy development process.

THE SOCIAL POLICY DEVELOPMENT SPECTRUM

Chapter 1 offers a basic definition of public policy: *A public policy is an action (or in some cases, an inaction) usually undertaken by government, directed at a particular goal, and legitimated by the commitment of public resources. More narrowly: Social welfare policy is a subset of public policy concerned with allocating social resources in order to improve individual and community well-being.* Yet these statements, and others like it, belie the complexity of public policy and its development. The action may be taken in the public sector by any unit of government, or by several units of government acting together. Statutes enacted by legislatures and decisions made by courts are public policies, as are administrative rules and regulations and the actions of chief executives and their staffs. Usually governmental units must act together to produce a public policy, as when the legislature passes a law that an executive must approve. Sometimes governmental units act alone, as when administrative agencies change regulations. Such complexities in public policymaking are repeated at the federal, state, and local levels of government, all of which have sufficient authority to develop public policy, independently or cooperatively with one another.

Policymaking might also take place in private, nongovernmental sectors. When an automobile manufacturer decides to close a factory, or when the Chase Manhattan Bank raises its prime interest rate, or when the AFL-CIO decides to call a strike, public policy has been made. Similarly, for-profit firms and nonprofit corporations at the state and local levels make public policy. For example, a metropolitan hospital may decide not to take Medicaid assignments, or a local Salvation Army center may set policy that would exclude homeless people with children from one of its shelters because of lack of space. Knitting together the strands of public- and private-sector decisions and actions adds another level of complexity to the policymaking process. Recently, the Boy Scouts of America decided to exclude gay males as scoutmasters, a private organization policy that has had a ripple effect on both private and public organizations. Deeming the policy offensive to gay and lesbian individuals and groups, many public agencies took steps to deny the Boy Scouts use of their facilities. National parks refused to let the Boy Scouts use their facilities free of charge. Many public schools revoked their charter agreements with the Boy Scout councils. United Way agencies were asked to deny funding to Boy Scouts as long as the Boy Scout policy was in place. *Private-sector policymaking therefore becomes public policy when it engages public problems.*

Public policy development is further complicated by interlocking goals. As appealing as it may be to think that public policies address single goals, it is virtually impossible to identify a policy goal that does not interlock with others in one way or another. Improving secondary education, for example, involves raising teacher salaries, using schools as a community resource, and promoting stable families with adequate incomes. Achieving each goal contributes to realizing the others. Deciding which goals to address requires a decision process that may precede systematic analysis of the problem itself. Because even individual goals are understood differently, concentrating on a single goal may compromise policy analysis and policy decision-making. For example, in 1996, policy analysis of welfare reform concentrated on the single goal of putting people to work. But different policymakers understood the goal differently. Thus the most recent welfare reform (TANF—see Chapter 5) included provisions to reduce out-of-wedlock births, promote stable two-parent families, reduce welfare rolls, and reduce child poverty. Should all have to work, or could some be excused? Should only two-parent families be eligible for welfare? Welfare reform falters over disagreements on implementing these diverse goals. The multiple welfare reform goals continue to be sorted out as welfare reform policy is fine-tuned, old programs eliminated, and new programs established.

Committed resources legitimate public policy. Resources can be committed in a variety of ways, including both present and future commitments, and resources are committed from varied governmental and private-sector units. Categorical grant-in-aid programs, for example, commit resources of the federal government, but only if state governments adopt federal policies and commit their own resources as well (see Chapter 3). Through the commitment of resources, public policies attain power over the distribution of resources that, for policy analysis purposes, must be examined in terms of those who gain from the distribution and those who lose. Even though the resources may be directed at an agreed-on goal, the implications of distribution often spread well beyond specific policy goals. Consequently, a public policy undertaken to achieve one objective may in fact achieve the opposite because of the way resources are provided. Few would have guessed, for example, that a federal policy granting accelerated depreciation for business investments during 1981–85 would actually inhibit capital investment because corporations "sold" tax credits to each other. In the same way, the 1996 welfare reform set a five-year "cap" on receiving welfare benefits, but in 2001 this "welfare cap" had negative consequences for many families as the once robust American economy began to falter.

The wide scope of policy development suggests the complexity of attempts to analyze it. The type of policy analysis called for in most cases is determined by the point(s) in the policy development process where a particular policy decision is likely to be made. Figure 2.1 is a simplified model of the stages in policy development, with an example drawn from the Social Security retirement program. Notice how the character of policy development might differ between stages 1 and 4. At stage 1, a variety of possible social goals might be examined, with prospective policies accompanying each. Stage 4 might include policy considerations of program implementation, as, for example, when con-

FIGURE 2.1 | PARADIGM OF THE POLICY DEVELOPMENT PROCESS

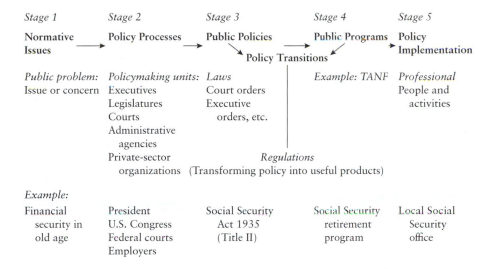

Stage 1	Stage 2	Stage 3	Stage 4	Stage 5
Normative Issues	Policy Processes	Public Policies	Public Programs	Policy Implementation
		Policy Transitions		
Public problem: Issue or concern	Policymaking units: Executives Legislatures Courts Administrative agencies Private-sector organizations	Laws Court orders Executive orders, etc.	Example: TANF	Professional People and activities
		Regulations (Transforming policy into useful products)		

Example:

Financial security in old age	President U.S. Congress Federal courts Employers	Social Security Act 1935 (Title II)	Social Security retirement program	Local Social Security office

sidering the impact of regulations on different populations. At stage 4, analysis might be confined to a single goal, although the distributional impact of alternative implementation strategies could receive considerable attention. The model and example of policy development in Figure 2.1 suggest that there is no clear center point in the policymaking process, and likewise that there is no single strategy or technique that can be applied in policy analysis (an issue that receives detailed attention in Chapter 4).

Figure 2.1 also shows that a policy process begins when a problem or issue takes on a public character and policy actors are excited into action. The process of policymaking does not end, however, with a specific policy event. Congress created welfare reform, and the president signed it into law in 1996, but this policy document had to be translated into program forms that people could use. To do so required additional policymaking by administrative agencies. Policymaking also takes place in the implementation process, usually by administrators who have considerable knowledge of existing programs. Finally, professional people implement programs, usually in face-to-face contact with the citizenry in the environment where the issue or concern was first raised.

Figure 2.1 is a linear model, but in reality policy development may be initiated at any of the five stages and may end at any of them. Sometimes a policy action will create a policy that is not implemented. In 1962, for example, Congress and the president created the Mental Health Services Act, designed to develop community-based care for persons with psychiatric problems. But no public programs were developed until 1964, mostly because financial commitments to the policy were limited and the states were slow in developing their own resources to implement the policy.

The 1988 welfare reform, like many other social policy changes, illustrates the incremental nature of social welfare policy development. It is not unusual for social policies to take several years to develop. The 1988 social welfare legislation that created the Job Opportunity and Basic Skills (JOBS) program was first proposed by the 97th Congress, and was finally turned into public policy two and a half years later by the 100th Congress.[1] The pace at which Congress created the 1996 welfare reform, a period spanning two sessions of Congress, is characteristic of the way Congress proceeds with social welfare issues. However, the 1996 welfare reform legislation was also preceded by over five years of granting waivers in the Aid to Families with Dependent Children (AFDC) program that gave the states considerable flexibility to do many of the things in welfare administration that found their way into the 1996 reform legislation. The discussions that appear later in this book of specific policies present a good picture of the length of time it takes social welfare issues to mature into social welfare policies.

Public Problems—Stage 1

Public problems are discussed in some detail in Chapter 1. The policy development paradigm suggested by Figure 2.1 is designed to take into account those values that shape the contours of the problem subject to policy deliberation, while acknowledging that values shape the policy solutions (see Chapter 4). Thus issues subject to policy deliberation may change as they are worked through the policy process, depending on how values shift as the problem may be redefined.

Policymaking Units—Stage 2

Two important assumptions about policy analysis underlie the following discussion: first, policy is made at all the five stages represented in Figure 2.1; second, the kind of policy analysis required depends on the needs of the policymaker. Because all policy units in the American system (executive, legislative, etc.) do indeed make policy, both independently and in concert with other policymaking units, it is important to understand the operating context of each unit in order to determine its policy analysis needs and tailor the analysis to the policy-deciding tasks. Thus some grasp of the various constraints on policy analysis that affect these units is necessary. Table 2.1 summarizes the decision-making environment of and type of information needed by each of those units.

Executive Policymaking   Initiative is the strength of executive policymaking. As discussed in Chapter 1, the executives of public policy are governors, or the president, or high-ranking officials who, in the national government, compose the president's cabinet. In the private sector these are corporate presidents or executive officers. In theory, the legislature makes law, the judiciary determines its constitutionality, and executive policy is made as law is implemented. In practice, however, the executive often initiates a policy process. The executive

TABLE 2.1 | POLICY DECISION-MAKING UNITS
AND INFORMATION NEEDS

Policymaking Unit	Decision-Making Environment	Type of Information Needed
Executive (presidency)	Single action, leadership	• Range of alternative policy situations • Dealing with policy substance
Legislative (Congress)	Negotiation, compromise	• Nature of group(s) affected (constituents, interest groups) • Who "wins" or "loses"
Judicial	Courts, very formal	• Legal aspects of policy • Litigation management
Administration	Staff meetings	• Policy-specific data • Program-specific data • Who "wins" or "loses" • Values involved
Policy transition	Negotiation	• Values involved • Processes
Policy execution	Day-to-day exposure to problems	• Program-specific data • Values involved • Settings for services

speaks with one voice. Consequently a clear message is communicated about what problems need attention and how they can be resolved. The executive is close to program implementation, and consequently is close to the problems. Because most policy is built on existing policies, and because the executive is charged with implementing policy, the executive is often forced to seek changes in policy or to initiate policy, rather than simply respond to it. This is particularly true of the president of the United States.

The political strength of the American presidency has varied over the nation's history. The U.S. Constitution defines exactly the powers of Congress, but it specifies only five powers for the presidency: (1) command the nation's armed forces, (2) authority to grant pardons for crimes against the United States, (3) power to make treaties, subject to Senate confirmation, (4) power to appoint Supreme Court justices and foreign ministers, and (5) the right to fill vacancies in the Senate. These five powers seem modest and almost irrelevant in comparison to modern government, which seems to place so much authority in the president. The stature now enjoyed by the American presidency in the exercise of domestic power is not a product of a strong institutionalized commitment to formal powers, but a result of the vagueness with which presidential power is defined. In short, the power of the presidency depends on the leadership ability of the individual president. John Kennedy complained of a "deadlocked democracy," but his successor, Lyndon Johnson, created public policy of enormous proportions. Richard Nixon was accused of initiating an era of "imperial" presidency, but under his successor, Gerald Ford, the phrase shifted to "imperiled" presidency. When Jimmy Carter was frustrated at every turn in attempts to achieve his policies, such as comprehensive welfare reform, his vice president called the presidency "the fire hydrant of the nation." President Reagan achieved outstanding legislative and administrative success that realized several policy changes of great magnitude.[2] The Omnibus Budget Reconciliation Act (OMBRA, 1981) and Reagan's Economic Recovery Tax Act (1981) both achieved significant new policy goals by cutting taxes and slowing the rate of growth of domestic spending. The 1981 OMBRA not only reduced domestic spending but also forced the consolidation of a number of domestic programs into block grants, thus transferring considerable authority to the states. In spite of his political popularity, President Clinton had little success with his showpiece legislation, health care. Clinton's leadership, however, is credited with initiating and sustaining the most significant period of American economic growth since World War II.

The quality of presidential leadership, therefore, is disguised by the institutional problems inherent in presidential policymaking. The president has virtually no control over the resources necessary to implement policy. For example, when President Eisenhower issued Executive Order 10557, requiring nondiscriminatory hiring practices in government contracts, he had no funds to establish an administrative organ to implement that policy. And although the presidency is the only political office designed to speak for all the people, it is fractured by competing interests and compromised politically in frequent contests with Congress. The system of constitutional checks and balances of power greatly restricts the capacity of the president to act decisively in policy matters. As administrative agencies continue to develop increased independence with Congress, presidential authority over the administrative bureaucracy continues to weaken. Perhaps even more significantly, Congress appropriates the funds needed to carry out all executive activity. Under such constraints, without strong leadership the presidency can quickly be gridlocked into inaction.

Executive policymaking requires special knowledge about the issues under consideration (Figure 2.1, stage 1). More than any other policymaking unit in the American system, the executive must take into account a comprehensive range of policy alternatives. Unlike legislators, who must represent varied interests, the executive is expected to represent the full range of public concern on any issue and consequently must take the very largest view of a problem and its solution. The executive is expected to lead, and therefore must have available the widest range of possible alternatives in order to minimize the institutional danger of deadlock when the time for decision making comes. The policy problems of the executive are illustrated by the pressure constantly brought on a president (or on a corporate executive) to take some position or make a stand—and by the frequency with which these positions must be abandoned. Not taking a position communicates weakness and uncertainty; yet sticking with a position that has proven defective after a period of public scrutiny gives an impression of inflexibility. However, abandoning a position may be seen as vacillation, which cuts deeply at the executive's leadership stature. Without knowledge of a full range of alternatives, and without systematic analysis to determine the best range of policy alternatives, executive policymaking degenerates quickly.

Legislative Policy   Unquestionably, legislation is the foundation of all social welfare policy. The product of legislation is statute law, the most forcible of all public policy. (In the private sector, articles of incorporation and corporate bylaws represent a somewhat similar consensus and force within the individual organization.) Statute law is the quest of ardent policy advocates. Legislators are, therefore, the center of most policy activity. But while legislatures possess considerable political power to make policy, the legislative process is a fragmented one. Legislators exist at the federal, state, and local levels of government. At the federal level, and in every state except Nebraska, legislatures are composed of two bodies chosen from diverse constituencies; both these bodies must agree before a position can become a policy. And legislators themselves are diverse. Repeated studies have shown that legislators who continue in office are likely to possess characteristics similar to the constituencies that elect them—a sobering revelation considering the diversity of American culture.[3]

Legislatures operate within both extremely formal and at the same time very informal structures. Hence, legislatures have developed extremely complex procedures. As suggested in Chapter 1, creating statute law is a time-consuming and complicated undertaking. Thus legislators frequently make policy by inaction. Because it takes so much power to steer an initiative through the legislative process, it is easier to defeat a proposal than to bring one into law. While much legislative energy emphasizes defeating legislation, compromise often is the alternative to defeat, giving most legislation its "watered down" flavor.

Legislators are handicapped by a formal structure. The U.S. House of Representatives is composed of 435 members, elected locally from districts of relatively similar populations. These representatives must consider wide-ranging policy proposals, and a majority of them must agree before a proposal becomes law. As most of us have discovered, it is hard to get a majority of three out of five ordinary people to agree on something controversial; it is virtually impossible for 435 persons, all attuned to the fine points of an issue, to meet in a single room and try to accomplish a task without some organization. Hence Congress and other legislative bodies observe very formal rules of order for final discussions and votes, and establish committees to do the preliminary work on proposals for legislation (bills). The committees are further divided into subcommittees, and staff members become very involved in moving things through this committee process. Thus although the floor vote may be the deciding event in legislatures, the policy-shaping work is done in the committee phase.

> Committees are the instruments by which Congress defines public problems and shapes policies. Here the political soundings are taken, the delicate compromises worked out and the technical language of the bills drafted and redrafted. Floor debate may illuminate problems and crucial questions may even be resolved in the clash of voting in the chamber. However, it is quite impossible for a large body of legislators to write a complex piece of legislation during floor debate.[4]

The committee process is like the tip of the iceberg; most of the whole cannot be seen. Even the public part of the process is often too dynamic to capture in a summary statement. Usually the public record of committee hearings provides only a general indication of the political forces at work in the committee process of shaping the proposals that become ratified (or are defeated) by floor votes.

Unlike the executive, which speaks with one voice, legislatures speak with many voices. Consequently, without leadership, either from within the legislature or from outside (as when a president provides leadership), the legislative process is likely to result in stalemate. The many voices of the legislature have varied origins, and the policy analyst must be aware of the different forces that shape legislative behavior. Legislators may act as delegates of the people, or as party members, or as statesmen. When acting as a statesman, a legislator may be acting from personal convictions about an issue, from personal preferences, or because he or she is motivated by a larger view of what would be best. Even though Americans tend to dislike the idea that legislators vote their own views about what is best, a strong case can be made for doing this, and most decisions are made on the basis of this concept of legislative independence.

A more popular view of legislative behavior suggests that the legislator acts on behalf of those who elected him or her to office. Legislators may identify their constituency as (1) the whole district from which she or he is elected, (2) the registered voters of the district, (3) those who actually vote in the district, or (4) the voters who voted for the representative. Legislative behavior can vary greatly depending on which of these "constituencies" seems most important at a particular moment.

Legislative policy development, in particular, must especially take into account legislative representation of special interests. Concerns about special interests are as old as the U.S. Constitution, and they were addressed frequently by James Madison.[5] For example, the Constitution was constructed to assure fair representation of the states in the federal union. But as the nation has grown, it has become increasingly difficult in more complex issues to separate public officials from their constituents' interests, and the contemporary proliferation of centers of interest—frequently called interest groups—has become a fundamental feature of democratic government as we know it in the United States. Special interests are represented in legislative decisions, most frequently through the influence of paid representatives of interest groups, known as lobbyists.[6]

It is through these interest groups that private-sector policy choices most frequently affect the public policymaking process. Preference for the rich and powerful, disfranchisement for the poor, single-issue politics, graft, deception, and callous disregard for the general welfare are a few of the evils inherent in interest-group politics. Often overlooked, however, are the advantages that interest groups can bring to the legislative process. Interest groups can translate private-sector problems into clear and fair recommendations for action. They can present, with great accuracy, the existing or desired policies of the citizens and organizations involved. This kind of information is extremely important to policymakers, and it is not likely to be obtained except through lobbyists. To represent private interests in an accurate way, lobbyists must provide solid and reliable information to support the position of the interest group. Hence the legislative process (or the policy analyst) is often supplied with a rich array of such information, which has to be sifted, evaluated, and reevaluated in terms of interlocking interests.

Interest groups also serve the legislative process by providing linkage between legislators and constituents. A legislator may find it difficult or impossible to remain in touch with large numbers of people. Interest groups represent what large groups of people are saying and thinking. The legislator, in turn, can respond to people through the interest groups, often through their newsletters.

Interest groups further assist the legislative process by helping adjust the differences in views among interest groups regarding policy outcomes. A legislator may play one interest group against another to promote further clarification of facts and issues. For example, the legislator may indicate that on a certain issue the position of the U.S. Chamber of Commerce is different from the position of the American Public Welfare Association. This leads to discussion between the two groups; one or both may then court sympathetic allies as a means of strengthening the case before the legislator. The Chamber of Commerce, for example, might seek and gain support for its position from the National Association of Manufacturers. Thus a coalition begins to build, helping the legislator resolve policy conflicts that may stand in the way of making a decision. Even groups with diverse orientations to an issue may form a coalition to support a particular policy proposal. This strategy may backfire, however; the legislative environment often prompts policy decisions based on marginal considerations that have more to do with satisfying claims of interest groups than with the substance of the proposal under consideration.

The context of legislative policy development—comprising a diverse group of people, a complex structure, and special ties with constituencies, usually through interest groups—dominates stage 2 of the policy process as shown in Figure 2.1. Legislatures, therefore, require special kinds of information to facilitate policy decisions. They need information about who is likely to be involved and affected in the policy choices under consideration. They need information about winners and losers with respect to alternative public decisions. They also need information about how the private sector is likely to respond to the possible public policies. They want information about how to balance competing interests in order to make a decision in the present, more than they need information about long-range policy implications. In other words, they are more concerned about the ability to make a choice than they are about the nature of the choice, more concerned about the substance of making a decision than about the substance of the decision itself.[7]

Administrative Policy   Regulation and program design are the policy development responsibilities of administrative agencies. Next to statute law, administrative policy attracts the most public attention. Because administrative agencies are charged with converting policies into useful social products, and because useful social products are expected to be carried out in certain ways to achieve their purposes, administrative agencies have been responsible for fashioning a form of policy development well known today. As such, administrative agencies engage in complex policy analysis tasks, which use social science knowledge and social science research. Administrative policy development exists in both the public and private sectors and is likely to be concentrated in the transition phases of the policymaking process (Figure 2.1, stages 3 and 4).

A brief review of administrative theory is necessary in order to understand the complexity of administrative activity alluded to by "policy transitions." To understand administrative policy development, one must first understand the administrative activities of the public bureaucracies and the complexities that such administration creates in the American system of governance. Public administrative agencies as we know them today were completely unforeseen by the founders of American government; so the system of constitutional checks and balances was designed without taking them into account. The institutional checks on administrative behavior that now exist have developed through ever-changing political alignments with the other branches of government. Because public administrative agencies have no constitutional basis, clear theories of administrative policymaking have been difficult to develop.

Administrative agencies emerged in their present form as part of the professionalization of social science, and as a way of applying science to the acts of governance. In 1887, Woodrow Wilson published an essay on the newly recognized field of public administration. This incisive essay sought to explain how the rationality characteristic of the new social sciences could be brought to bear on the rapidly expanding activities of the executive branch. "Public administration," he stated, "is detailed and systematic execution of public law."[8] This scientific approach to government administration developed around the beginning of the twentieth century, contemporaneously with professional planning, industrial management in the private sector, and the social and political reform movement.

Public administration matured after World War II, as both public- and private-sector management became influenced by the rediscovery of Max Weber's political and social explanations for the development of modern bureaucracy. Herbert Simon in particular provided a synthesis between the new science of management and the earlier Wilsonian science of administration through his emphasis on the rationality of both. He established a foundation for the classic definition of both public- and private-sector administration: "scientific, . . . value-free activity isolated from the surrounding politics of government activities." Simon understood formal organizations as human enterprises characterized "by a high degree of rational direction of behavior toward ends that are objects of common acknowledgement and expectation."[9] In his analysis, administration was a means of achieving agreed-on goals. Thus Simon distinguished between policymaking and implementing policy, and he studied the two as different, yet rational, activities. Simon's work reinforced the dichotomy between politics and administration that had been suggested by Wilson so many years before. Simon deepened the distinction by arguing that rational decision-making and rational administration, as in public administration, were the expression of the new social sciences, whereas politics (at its best) was an expression of art. Implicit in this view, however, were (1) the belief that public administrative agencies, through the election of the executive, were clearly under popular control, and (2), in accord with Wilsonian tradition, an understanding that administration merely carried out decisions made in the political process.

This orthodox view of public administration was seen by others as ill-suited to the realities of administration in the years after World War II. In 1949, Paul Appleby observed that public administration was clearly a political process.[10] Shortly before that, Dwight Waldo had illustrated the value-laden, culturebound, nonrational, incremental character that public administration took on in actual practice. He was particularly dismayed by the distinction that had developed between politics and administration, and he advocated an integrated understanding of administration. "Any simple division of government-and-administration," he wrote, "is inadequate [because] it carries with it the idea of division, depicting an antagonism."[11] Thus the orthodox view of public administration as a form of scientific management was gradually abandoned as public administration came to be recognized as a part of the political process that exercised discretionary power of its own. In a classic study published in 1953, Robert Dahl and Charles Lindblom demonstrated that public administration was in fact deeply engaged in value choices, often outside the controlling authority of the elected executive.[12] Wallace Sayre wrote that public administrators develop autonomy and express political power "much as Presidents, senators and Congressmen, party leaders, and interest group leaders make their respective claims . . . achieving levels of self-direction satisfying even to their own aspirations."[13]

Although an agreed-on political theory of administration has yet to emerge, it is increasingly clear that the administrative bureaucracy plays a semiautonomous role in American governance, and is even sometimes referred to as the fourth branch of government. Like other political institutions, bureaucracies are powerful and give up power grudgingly. The administrative bureaucracy has become integrated into the fabric of checks and balances characteristic of the American system of governance. But unlike its counterpart branches of government, where authority, power, and the limitations on both are spelled out, the power necessary to carry out administrative work, as well as the limitations on that power, derive from political interactions, not from constitutional forces.

In this view, the political behavior of the administrative bureaucracy is not dissimilar from the political behavior of other horizontal institutions of American governance.[14] At the center of this behavior are activities designed to accumulate sufficient power so that the administrative bureaucracy can carry out its governmental responsibilities. As the primary agent of policy implementation, then, the administrative bureaucracy must have sufficient independent power and authority to carry out its tasks, and this authority derives from bureaucratic political exchanges with the legislature as well as the executive.

> The modern administrative bureaucracy has power assets needed by both the legislature and the executive in the form of information, expertness, and responsibility for connecting policy products with those who consume them. Information is the primary power asset of administrative bureaucracies. As part of its policy implementing activities, administrative bureaucracies obtain, store, and disseminate considerable amounts of information. Administrative bureaucracies know how much money is spent on what kinds of activities that are of benefit to which kinds of people. The information gathering and disseminating activities are essential to effective policy implementation, and the use of information processes is one way that administrative agencies capture political power necessary to develop autonomy. In this respect administrative bureaucracies often act as guardians of policy information. Neither legislatures nor executives have sufficiently independent information necessary for them to make informed policy choices, and both must depend on the bureaucracy to provide information critical to the policymaking process.[15]

Bureaucracies are also a source of expertness on policy questions. Bureaucracies collect, obtain, and utilize policy experts, who understand a wide range of issues that attend particular policy questions. Seldom do legislators develop sufficient expertness on their own staffs capable of challenging bureaucratic expertness, and executives, presidents, and governors are stretched too thin to be policy experts themselves. Bureaucracies possess effective power when substantive, technical advice, rather than political advice, is needed in policy development. In most cases the administrative bureaucracy actually sets the policy agenda for the executive, rather than the other way around, based on its policy expertness.

Administrative bureaucracies, finally, are the link between a policy and the consumers. Whereas both legislators and executives may promote themselves as authors of a particular policy, the consumer's experience with the policy comes through the administrator by way of the program provider. Neither executives nor legislators hire and train the persons who link the policy with the user, and the worth of the policy product is usually judged by both the provider and the consumer in the field. This bureaucratic power is far from insignificant, having the capacity to transform the very purpose for which the policy was created in the first place. As Thurgood Marshall observed some years ago, the administration of welfare often deprives clients of their "social citizenship," which the welfare policy was designed to create and protect in the first place.[16]

Interest groups often operate to confer additional power to administrative agencies. John Wright, for example, discusses the political leverage that interest groups give bureaucracies. "[Interest groups] help bureaucrats build coalition support for programs in Congress, and they provide information and electoral support for legislatures. Legislators, in turn, create programs for the bureaucrats, and bureaucrats administer their benefits to the [interest] groups." [17] The very separation of powers among governmental branches also works to confer power to administrative agencies, opening the door for administrative autonomy. In most instances the legislature creates the administrative agencies placed at the disposal of the executive, while legislation once enacted is usually passed to a designated administrative agency by the legislature, not by the executive. In like manner the executive has the use of the administrative bureaucracy to communicate with the legislature.[18] B. Guy Peters puts the matter this way: "Thus we can view the bureaucracy as being in a powerful position in competition with its ostensible masters. Having control of information and of the instigation of policy alternatives, having an expert knowledge of the subject matter, and having a ministerial or departmental ideology concerning the manner in which the subject matter should be treated, the bureaucracy can control decisions actually adopted by the partisans at the top." [19] Charles Barrilleaux captures a similar sentiment when he observes that "in the current context of American state politics . . . bureaucracies may prove to be important guardians of the status quo. The inherent inertia of American government that is so important to its daily operations and continued peaceful existence receives substantial support from the system of administration in place in the states." [20]

This digression into the origins of the activities of administration as we know them today is intended to highlight the most delicate problem in the processes of administrative policymaking in both the public and private sectors: a lack of consensus over the appropriate balance between making policy and carrying it out. The rationality of administrative policymaking activities remains a vigorously defended tenet, but few today would disagree that administration has been used to achieve political objectives, independent of strictly reasoned outcomes. To attempt to understand administrative policymaking in any other way than through this paradoxical view both oversimplifies and distorts the expectations placed on policy analysis in administrative settings.[21]

Although it is tempting to distinguish between two groups of administrators in the administrative context, for example, the "technocrats," experts in a particular field, and the "bureaucrats," who maintain the political balance of an organization, this simplification too may only cloud our understanding further. The whole of the administrative policymaking process is involved in balancing the two, in reconciling the rational administration of the technocrats with the bureaucrats' demands for political products such as fairness, representation, and conflict resolution. To accomplish this, the administrative policymaker needs a complex blend of information.

Most students of social welfare policy will likely work in or for an administrative agency, and these professional people must provide the administrative policymaker with a wide range of alternatives for consideration as part of the process of rational choice. These alternatives include both "rational" and political outcomes. Administrative policymakers require considerable factual information in order to project the effects of different outcomes. They are also concerned about the marginal utility of various alternatives, in order to support their decisions when the time comes for review or approval by the executive or legislature. Administrative policymakers are often forced to choose a less preferred policy that has greater potential for adoption, and their policy analysis must provide enough information to explore the entire range of policy possibilities.

Judicial Policy   Case law, as judicial policy is often called, is often obscured by the complexity of the overall judicial process. In a certain sense courts may not initiate policy; usually they are involved in sorting out policy differences created by others. Yet, informally, courts "invite" policy debates, as when a grand jury is created, or when the U.S. Supreme Court signals whether it will or will not become involved in litigation, as it did in the case of the 2000 presidential election. When the U.S. Conference meets, it sets a broad agenda for litigation, and when the U.S. Supreme Court issues a decision in a case, this may also suggest future likely decisions. The structure of the judiciary suggests that its policy role may in fact range across the entire policymaking process in both the public and private sectors.

Judicial policy is made at the federal level, at the state level, and locally. Each of these units of governance has courts that make legal judgments on matters that fall within the purview of the specific unit of government authority. Thus the federal courts, including the U.S. Supreme Court, make judgments on national legal matters, state courts make judgments on matters that pertain to states, and so forth.

Judicial processes are complicated by "standing," meaning whether or not it is possible for a matter to receive attention in a particular court of law. Certain matters must be brought before certain courts; for example, some cases must be heard in state courts. Sometimes, however, plaintiffs who wish to bring a case before the courts have options. Depending on which issue of law the plaintiff chooses to engage, a choice of court may be possible. This targeting process, usually called "litigation management," may be based on points of laws that would be more favorable to the plaintiff or to the defendant, and represents a form of political choice.

The politics of litigation management most frequently involves choices between state and federal courts. State courts have traditionally been most sympathetic with state government and related agencies, but they have limited jurisdiction over public social issues except for issues relating to property. Historically, federal courts have generally been involved in matters of dispute between states and the federal government, but in recent years, since the Warren court (Earl Warren, chief justice, 1953–69), they have become more responsive to social issues, particularly issues of personal rights and protection. Consequently, contemporary public policy has been more deeply influenced by judicial decisions than might have been the case fifty years ago.

Litigation management provides an important means to seek policy changes through the use of the various courts. Litigation management not only involves framing an issue so as to have it heard in the most favorable court system, but also carefully choosing a plaintiff, skillfully building the facts of the case, and structuring the case to fit the existing legal theory. Litigation management may thus be the key political issue in the policymaking role of the courts. One commentator has stated that "the federal courts have always (and correctly) been perceived by political leaders as a major instrument for control over the substantive content of public policy." He also observes that "it may make a considerable difference to the parties whether a case is to be tried in a state or national court."[22] Anyone who tracked the judicial proceedings in the 2000 presidential election has a good perspective on the role litigation management plays in determining policy outcomes.

Presidents Ronald Reagan and George Bush (Sr.) had unprecedented opportunity for changing the ideology of the U.S. Supreme Court as it developed during the past twenty years. With the appointment of new justices, many with conservative social views, the role of the U.S. Supreme Court is undergoing a period of political change. Given the philosophy that seems to emerge from the current Rehnquist court, those who would seek an expanded role for the federal government in social policy have begun to steer clear of judicial policymaking altogether. *Gilliard v. Craig* provides a fine example of litigation management in policy development.[23] In a class action, Daisy Gilliard sued the state of North Carolina for back welfare payments. Her son, Samuel, had been receiving Social Security checks from his father; her other children had a different father. In calculating the family's AFDC benefit, the state had considered Samuel's Social Security money as a resource available to the whole family. Gilliard believed this to be unfair; even though Samuel lived with the family, it seemed he must be entitled to the Social Security benefit regardless of the financial status of the other family members.

The federal district court in Charlotte, North Carolina, had developed a reputation for sympathy in civil rights matters. The state courts, however, were very conservative in matters that affected state government agencies. Gilliard argued that the case should be heard by the federal court, as the action of the state welfare agency had deprived her of due process under the 14th Amendment. The state, on the other hand, argued that the case should be heard in the state courts, because the issue involved the personal property of Samuel and, as such, was not appropriate for the federal courts. Gilliard prevailed. The case was heard in the federal court, and Justice James MacMillian ruled in her favor, ordering the state to pay her, and all others like her, whatever back monies were due to them because of this budgeting practice.

The judicial role in welfare policy development has been cautious, suggesting that the direction of welfare development is a legislative responsibility. This position was first affirmed when the constitutionality of the original Social Security Act was challenged in 1937. The constitutional question turned on the narrow consideration of whether taxing and spending for Old Age Insurance and Unemployment Insurance constituted taxing and spending for the general welfare, as allowed under Article 1, section 8 of the Constitution, or whether such taxing and spending constituted a specific form of welfare. Writing for the Court, Benjamin Cardozo confirmed the constitutionality of the act, recognizing that "the spending power advocated by Hamilton . . . has prevailed over that of Madison," yet also that "the line still must be drawn between one welfare and another, between general and particular": "Where this shall be placed can not be known in advance of the event. There is a middle ground or certainly a penumbra in which discretion is large. This discretion, however, is not confined to the courts. The discretion belongs to Congress, unless the choice is clearly wrong, a display of arbitrary power, not an excess of judgement." [24]

Since the federal courts affirmed the constitutionality of the Social Security Act in 1937, they have continued to shape welfare policy into today's familiar forms. The 1954 school desegregation case, *Brown v. Board of Education,* was perhaps the landmark case, since its ruling not only struck down school segregation, but in so doing opened the courts for welfare litigation as well. According to the *Yale Law Journal,* section 1983 of the U.S. Code required administrative fair hearing procedures that could be substituted for judicial review of federal and state law, thus prohibiting wholesale individual challenges of public welfare programs.[25] *Brown v. Board of Education* challenged the validity of administrative review procedures and made it possible for individuals to petition the federal courts for redress of public welfare grievances under the 1st and 14th Amendments to the Constitution, as did Mrs. Gilliard. Both amendments deal with issues of personal rights as they intersect with public sector policies. The 1st Amendment guarantees freedom of religion, speech, and press. The 14th Amendment guarantees equal protection under the law for all citizens. Both these amendments offered a wide latitude for the Supreme Court's involvement in policymaking once *Brown v. Board of Education* opened the door.

Three cases, in particular, changed the character of welfare considerably. *King v. Smith* (1963)[26] established the right of a dependent child to assistance regardless of whether the child's mother was living with a man who was not the child's father. The court held that Congress meant by the term parent an individual who owed the child a state-imposed duty of support, and a state could not disqualify a child from receiving assistance on the basis of a "substitute father" who had no such duty.

Shapiro v. Thompson (1969) struck down residency laws in the states. The Court held that denying assistance to individuals who had not lived in a state for one year challenged the right of interstate movement and violated both the equal protection and due process clause of the 5th Amendment to the Constitution.[27] Finally, the Court's decision in *Wyman v. James* (1971) struck down the practice of "night raids," often used to determine whether clients were violating state rules by harboring men in their homes overnight. The court held that "home visits" were legal when they did not constitute "snooping" and when they were used reasonably as an administrative tool, as long as they did not unnecessarily intrude on the beneficiary's rights in her own home and were appropriate to the objectives of welfare administration.[28] After the restrictions placed on home visits by the Court, their use has been seriously reduced. These and other rulings, as important as they are, suggest the measured approach the courts have taken toward welfare in general.

From the brief review of these cases it is clear that judicial policymaking requires rather specialized information. Attorneys as well as judges need information not only about the legal aspects of any given policy and the methods by which the judicial system operates, but also about the substance of the policy subject. Information about judicial politics and judicial issues and methods may be marginal to the policy issue, but information about the policy itself and how it fits into that specific policymaking process (the legal aspects of the policy) is central to judicial policy analysis. The legal parameters of a policy question exist whether or not the policy has the force of law, including formally executed administrative policy. Hence all policy analysis, of both the public and the private sector, must be sensitive to the legal constraints that will affect any policy choice.

Though policy analysts do not need to have legal training in order to analyze a policy issue, they often seek the advice of legal experts to clarify the legal elements of a policy problem. Policy analysts would do well to carefully investigate any questions that seem to require specialized legal information; the dividing line between a legal issue and a substantive policy issue is seldom clear.

Policy Transitions — Stages 3 – 4

The transition phase in the policy process is hard to describe because so little attention has been devoted to understanding it. Obviously a great deal happens between the time a law is passed, an executive decision is made, or a court decision is reached, and the time that a policy is transformed into a program. The transition that takes place involves many forms of analysis and policy development (sometimes not specifically recognized as decision making but referred to as "good common sense") and the final choice of a specific program. So while formal policy analysis may not be evident, policy choices are made by persons who have responsibility for moving the process of policymaking from a policy statement, such as a statute law or a court decision, to the next stage, a specific program that can be used by those who need the products of the policy.

Usually administrative agencies play a lead role in the policy transition phase. The administrative agency usually has the task of blending varied viewpoints heretofore involved in policymaking, as well as reconciling these views with policy actors who will be influenced by the policy as it becomes implemented in the form of a particular program. If policy is made on the federal level, for example, transitional activities must take into account how states will respond to the policy if and when they themselves become part of program administration. Additionally, administrative agencies may themselves be seeking specific policy outcomes, based on their own policy views.

Thus getting from public policy to public programs requires considerable policy skill. Often the federal administrative agency functions as mediator between federal expectations, as set out in statute law, the specific problems raised by citizen advocacy groups, and the specific circumstances found in states and localities. These different agendas constitute major features of American federalism, and it is up to administrative bureaucracies at both the federal and state levels to adjust federal policy, often developed for the general case, to the specific needs of those that the policy addresses.

A good example of how the administration attempts to balance the diverse expectations for policy outcomes can be found in the federal Child Support Enforcement (CSE) program. Developed in 1975 from earlier efforts of the federal government to ensure legal parental support for children, the 1975 legislation offered generous federal funding to improve flagging efforts in states to establish child support orders and to collect on them. Consistent with Social Security Act Title IV programs, Child Support Enforcement was crafted as a grant-in-aid program that provided rich financial incentives to states in exchange for very little modification of ongoing state activities. In particular, states were permitted to keep 75% of everything they collected from absent parents whose children were receiving AFDC. The federal government also provided $3 for every $1 that states spent on program administration. The 1975 federal law that amended Title IV of the Social Security Act slipped through Congress as the second, generally unnoticed, part of a major undertaking to create the first social services block grant.

The 1975 CSE legislation was passed on to states who already had statutory power to require parents to support their children, thus creating some discontinuity between existing state practices and this new federal program. Thus while the CSE statute set a national policy, its transition to a specific program rested on the ability of the federal administrative agency to make it fit with the ways states were already operating child support programs. The federal administrative agency, the Department of Health and Human Services (DHHS), continued to prod states to improve their collection efforts, but states showed little motivation to do so. Part of the reason was the design of CSE policy itself. While Congress saw CSE as an important way to reduce federal spending for the AFDC program, other policy actors saw the program as a way to improve the financial well-being of children. Thus rich financial rewards for collecting child support from welfare cases went to the states, while child support collected on behalf of nonwelfare children went directly to those children. States preferred to spend their energy on the former rather than the latter collection efforts.

But the creation of a new federal initiative did not resolve the problem of nonsupporting parents. According to the Bureau of the Census, by 1985 about 39% of all women who cared for children parented by an absent father were never awarded child support, and 60% of poor women were without child support awards. Only 50% of women who had a child support order were receiving the amount of money specified in the support order. Approximately $26.6 billion in child support was owed by noncustodial fathers, of which about $20 billion was uncollected. Thus the program resulted in collections of slightly less than $2.5 billion, roughly 10% of that which could be paid. The share of that $2.5 billion that could be attributed to the efforts of the 1975 law was not clear, nor was it clear what share would have been collected without the program. After fruitless efforts to improve the overall performance of this program, the federal Office of Child Support Enforcement (OCSE) decided to present Congress with a legislative package incorporating changes that would be required of states to make the CSE program effective. This legislative package was presented to Congress and signed into law August 16, 1984, PL 98-

378, as the 1984 Child Support Enforcement amendments to Title IV-D of the Social Security Act.

Still the implementation of the 1984 amendments was difficult. Twenty-two new, different program requirements were produced by the legislation. While some states had some of the new requirements already in place, many states had to make changes in their programs. Some of these requirements could be implemented by changes in a state's administrative practices, but others could be implemented only through state-enacted legislation. The amendments also carried significant fiscal penalties for states that failed to comply. In this environment, states were given a full two years after the final regulations were published to implement the amendments.

But even so, more than two years after the federal regulations were published, and at the deadline established by Congress, only nine of the requirements were implemented in all states, and none of the states had implemented all of the requirements. Of the nine requirements implemented in all the states, 20 states were operating their program with most of these "new" requirements already in place before 1975. Eventually the federal administrative agency had to grant states waivers for regulations they failed to implement, for without doing so the states' programs would have been out of compliance and would have had to be shut down completely.

Following the implementation of the regulations, child support collection performance actually declined rather than improved. By 1992, 35 states were performing below the national average of $3.99 total collections for each dollar of administrative expense, and 11 states actually spent more money to collect child support owed to AFDC recipients than they collected. Because the federal government provided funds to administer this program, the savings to the public went from $202 million in *savings* in 1979 to $173 million in *losses* in 1992. This program designed to save money actually ended up costing more.[29] The 1996 welfare reform legislation continues to seek improvements in collections by tightening regulations placed on the states.

With constant efforts the Child Support Enforcement program has become more effective in collecting child support monies, yet the savings in collections does not yet exceed the administrative costs associated with collecting them. This example serves to underline the difficulties of transforming policies into workable programs, and the important role the administrative agency plays in this process. When programs do not meet policy expectations, the administrative agency seeks to involve other policy actors to revise the policy, in this case asking Congress to create the 1984 policy changes. But if programs still fall short of expectations, the administrative agency finds ways to modify programs to make them more effective. Thus, there is a constant process of policymaking throughout the life of program implementation. Policy transitions involve harmonizing the expectations of policymakers at the federal level, as well as harmonizing federal expectations with the realities faced by the states and localities. Administrations play a crucial role in this balancing activity.

Conflicts over values regarding how resources are used are addressed and to some extent resolved during the policy transition process. To the extent that there are legitimate differences about what goals policy should meet, and how specific programs should achieve them, the policy transition phase provides an environment for resolving these conflicts, a characteristic of policy development discussed in Chapter 1. Thus policy transitions are not a mechanical translation of policy mandates into public programs, but a process that adjusts different views about how a policy should address a problem, harmonizing these views into useful products for those who need them.

Chapter 3 presents a full discussion of the intergovernmental environment in which administrative agencies undertake their mediating activities in policy transitions. Frustrated by the growing role of government, particularly "government by administration," Congress is undertaking efforts to simplify the transitional phase of policymaking by consolidating programs and sending funds to states in "blocks" rather than on a program-by-program basis. While block grants seem to hold the promise of avoiding the need to reconcile federal policy with exigencies of the states ("turn the matters over to the states and let them decide" remarked Majority Leader Dick Armey in the 1996 welfare reform debates), different, often conflicting, viewpoints between the federal government and the states are inherent in the American system, and only time will tell whether efforts to minimize these differences are more productive than efforts to mediate them.

Policy Implementation: Professional People and a New Policy Cycle: Stages 4–5

The final product of the policy process is usually a program or a commitment that directs the accomplishment or fulfillment of the policy in a particular way. Policy implementation focuses committed resources, such as money, personnel, equipment, and supplies, at the problems the policy addresses. Policy implementation usually takes place within an organizational context, such as a housing authority, an environmental protection agency, a department of social services, or in a not-for-profit business. Professional people are responsible for directing the resources provided by the policy at the problem for which the policy was created. Beneficiaries of the policy can be identified clearly at this point, and the policy's ineffective or unintended consequences may become apparent.

Professional people execute the policy through programs. Doctors, social workers, lawyers, nurses, and many other professionals must understand the relationship between the programs they use and the normative contexts from which the policy was developed, because the programs continue to carry values with them, and these values are implemented as part of the policy. For example, it would be difficult for a doctor or social worker to implement a planned parenthood program if the social worker found the values inherent in planned parenthood programs offensive.

The way professionals implement policy may also become a form of policymaking. Sometimes professionals are given discretion in the way a program is provided, and when this happens they are expected to shape the policy as it is reflected in the program. Often a program is the product of several policies, and it may be plagued with various inconsistencies or inadequacies. Here again, professionals must understand the normative contexts of the policies they execute in order to harmonize them into a usable product for the beneficiaries. Professional people are there to provide the beneficiaries with the products of the policies, and therefore policy analysis and policymaking become professional responsibilities among the range of professional activities.

Sometimes a program may not address the exact problem the professional faces, making it important that the professional understands what problems the policy was created to address. Rather than viewing the entire program itself simply as inadequate, the professional might selectively use those program features that fit the problem at hand, recognizing how the underlying policy needs to change in order to develop programs that will provide better assistance. Thus, professional people are often advocates for policy change, since they see firsthand what issues need to be dealt with. But, when professionals try to use a program to alleviate problems that the policies were not designed to address, the client is often placed in the difficult position of using resources inappropriately. These professional concerns suggest the kinds of knowledge professional people must have to play their part in the policy process. As policy executors, professional people must be extremely sensitive to the mandates of the policies that created the programs they implement, and not attempt to translate any program into something it was not meant to be, but rather, work to make the policies and their programs more effective.

An excellent example of the policy knowledge that professional people need is evident in the Elderly Nutrition Program, administered under Title III of the Older Americans Act. The program was initially developed in response to public concern that many older people had less than adequate nutrition because, living alone, they did not prepare proper meals. In that sense the program was created from a normative orientation that sought to serve older people by improving their nutrition. It provided free lunches to older people in a congregate setting and offered the beneficiaries a program of nutrition education as well. However, it was not too long before professional people became more concerned about the lunch than about nutrition, and they began to question why older persons of some financial means could come and have a free lunch, when poor people might be turned away for lack of available meals. People of means did not "need" a free lunch, they argued, while many of the poor did. The policy behind the lunch program supplies a solution to this uncertainty. The nutrition program policy addresses nutrition, not financial need, and the program must be provided consistent with that policy. Other programs have to be created to provide meals for the needy.

Policy implementation, therefore, often becomes the point at which additional normative issues are uncovered and new policy recommendations are initiated. New policies are most commonly implemented through existing agencies and organizations. Accommodating these new policies often requires agencies to change the way they do things. An inability to adjust may result in considerable slippage between the programs prescribed by the new policies and the actuality of their execution. Until 1980, for example, public child welfare agencies placed heavy emphasis on finding stable foster-care homes for children who were difficult to adopt, children who were older, perhaps handicapped in some way, or of minority heritage. Over many years, it became clear that substantial amounts were being spent to keep these children in foster homes when many of them could be in more permanent home environments. Title IV-E of the Social Security Act was created in 1980 to encourage states to shorten foster placements, accelerate adoptive placements, and otherwise find permanent homes for children. This change in policy caused considerable difficulty for many child welfare agencies that formerly had provided service to children by keeping them in foster homes, rather than by getting them out.

Policy implementation also requires monitoring and evaluation. Monitoring and evaluation in turn require a decision about what will be measured. Policy products typically have been measured by elements suitable for counting— for example, the numbers of people served, the proportion of total beneficiaries who use the program frequently, or who use only one of several services offered, and so forth. Less tangible results of the policy—for example, whether children get a better education, or whether public housing residents are more satisfied with their lives—are harder to measure. Choosing an appropriate strategy for monitoring and evaluating these intangible effects is an especially important, and difficult, aspect of policy execution. (A full discussion of policy analysis and evaluation is presented in Chapter 4.)

CONCLUSION

The policymaking process is far-reaching in the time it takes to develop a policy, in the range of institutions involved in that development, and in the diversity of activities that take place within this process. Policy analysis is thus not a single act, but a series of actions that take place frequently over a policy cycle and at various points within that cycle. This activity is defined by the kind of information that is needed at a particular point in the process. Just as there is no exact center for policymaking, there is no single method for policy analysis.

Policy may be made at any of the multiple points in the policy process. To be useful, policy analysis must be specifically sensitive to the particular policy process it serves. The products of policy analysis, from oral summaries to formal published reports, may also be wide-ranging and often must serve overlapping objectives. For example, a briefing paper analyzing a particular proposal for a legislator can seldom be longer than one to one and one-half pages, whereas analysis of the same issue by the Congressional Budget Office may run to one hundred pages. Both may have to deal with overlapping objectives. It is crucial that the analyst understand exactly what is being requested and adapt the analysis accordingly.

Policy analysts often see themselves as generalists, but the model of welfare policymaking discussed in this chapter does not conform to this view. According to the model presented here, policy analysis and those who perform it need specialized knowledge and skills in two areas: knowledge and skill regarding the specific policy analysis unit in which they are working, and knowledge of and skill in the subject they are working with. In this view a competent legislative policy analyst, for example, might not be as effective in an administrative bureaucratic setting. The two units go about policy analysis in different ways, and the kind of information needed in the former may be useless in the latter. In the same way, a policy analyst with expertness in transportation policy may have great difficulty analyzing welfare policy.

The policymaking model discussed in this chapter and the policy analysis caveats it suggests fit closely with the Multiple Stream approach to policy analysis proposed some years ago by John Kingdon (see Chapter 4).[30] In particular, it conforms with Kingdon's notion that policy development takes place in an environment of ambivalence, rather than one of uncertainty, and "attention to a particular issue is a function of opportunity, bias, formal position in an organization or government, and the number of issues competing for the policy maker's attention."[31]

The "policy windows" that open are not only time limited, as Kingdon suggests, but are related to either a focus on a problem or a focus on existing political forces, or both, underscoring the idea of different policy units acting separately or together. This and other policy analysis issues are explored further in Chapter 4.

QUESTIONS FOR DISCUSSION

1. Discuss the difference between a policy and a program. What are some of the actions that have to take place in order to move from policy to program?
2. What is the most desirable form of public policy? Defend your conclusion.
3. What is the role of professional people in the development of public welfare policy?
4. Identify several present-day social problems and discuss how social programs have addressed them. Discuss whether we have policies and programs that address these problems. Why do you think we have problems for which there are no present policies and programs?

3

C H A P T E R

POLICYMAKING AT THE SUBNATIONAL LEVEL

Although the policymaking model discussed in Chapter 2 offers a general picture of the policy development process, policy analysis in subnational policymaking activities requires some special attention. Just as policymaking links public and private sectors, it also links state and local policymaking in an intergovernmental environment. As suggested in Chapter 2, policies made by the federal government often require complementary activities by state and local governments in much the same way that policies made by the national office of the Boy Scouts of America require policy adjustments by local Boy Scout troops across the country.

It is tempting to suggest that the policymaking model presented in Chapter 2 is hierarchically organized. In other words, it may seem that problems or issues become labeled as policy topics when they receive sufficient national attention, and that the policy process then spins down to the local level. In a hierarchical model, policy processes that span policy and program development and their transitions would take place at the federal level, whereas implementation, or the policies of execution, would occur at the local level—in counties and municipalities. To some extent this is a true picture of the policy development process. For example, as discussed in Chapter 2, after growing nationwide concern about the inadequate amounts of child support that noncustodial parents were paying, Congress passed and President Ford signed into law amendments to the Social Security Act creating the Child Support Enforcement Program (Title IV-D). States were required to develop state laws and administrative procedures if they wished to take part in this new program, and the federal program and the state policies were in turn passed on to counties that developed further policies to help parents collect child support for their children.

However, even though some policymaking is hierarchically organized, a considerable amount takes place at state and local levels, independent of significant policy activities at other government levels. This independent policymaking activity is possible because state and local governments have independent, constitutionally guaranteed bases of political authority, a fundamental element in the American system, just as private organizations have independent spheres of action.

The United States has one national government, but it also contains over 80,000 other semiautonomous governments, including the fifty states, more than three thousand counties, and thousands of towns and cities, townships, special districts (such as school districts), and public authorities (such as housing, port, and airport authorities). Add to this the hundreds of thousands of private organizations with independent policymaking authority within their own spheres of activity, and it becomes quite apparent that the amount of policy made at the federal level constitutes a minute portion of all the public policy created in the United States in any given year. States collectively pass more than 200,000 new laws each year, and no estimate is possible of the number of local ordinances enacted by municipalities, not to mention the number of state and local regulatory and procedural policies, along with the policies made by state and local courts. These examples make it clear that the public policy analyst needs to find some context for understanding policymaking at local and state levels of government responsibility.

THE PECULIAR CONTEXT FOR SUBNATIONAL SOCIAL WELFARE POLICY DEVELOPMENT

The public context of policymaking outlined in Chapter 2 carries into policymaking at the state and local levels, but with a few important exceptions. Executive, legislative, judicial, and administrative policymaking takes place within state and local units of governance in a manner similar to federal and state patterns. Unfortunately for the policy analyst, however, in much local-level policymaking activity additional levels of complexity are added by (1) the atomized nature of local political structures, (2) ambiguities in policymaking power and authority, and (3) the lack of formality. When these are combined with overlapping jurisdictional authority and a certain amount of independent policymaking authority, subnational policymaking becomes almost too complex to analyze.

Thus, the whole of social welfare policymaking defies understanding unless three facts about the complex American system of governance are understood. First, the federal government has almost no constitutional authority to develop and implement social welfare policy. A mere thread of constitutional authority was "discovered" by associate justice Benjamin Cardozo when the Social Security Act was found to be constitutional in 1937, as discussed in Chapter 2. The other social welfare litigation after 1937, summarized in the previous chapter, generally limits what states can and cannot do, rather than developing a constitutional foundation for American social welfare activities.[1]

A second characteristic of the American system that determines how welfare policy develops is that most social concerns are matters for the states. Almost all legislation that defines the context for social welfare is found in state laws. Child support, abuse and neglect, adoptions, foster care, day-care requirements, nursing and rest home standards, school attendance, motor vehicle operation, housing standards, and many other social welfare subjects are defined variously by the states. The development of social welfare in the United States became clear toward the end of the nineteenth century as states asserted their authority over scattered and fractured social welfare activities. This foundation of state policy preceded the development of any federal social welfare activity as we know it today.[2]

The third characteristic of American social welfare development concerns localities and their relationship to their respective states. Local governments are creatures of their respective states. County governments, municipalities, and various authorities, such as airport authorities—all those units of local governance listed above—come into existence through a legislative action by their respective states, making them "incorporated areas" and granting them specific legislative, executive, and judicial powers. In exchange, states require local units of governance to carry out functions as the state may prescribe. For example, a cluster of neighborhoods may petition the state legislature to become incorporated as a municipality under a given name. If the request is granted, the new municipality is given specific powers, like law enforcement, but it must meet certain requirements as well, like levying taxes or performing specific services that the state may require.

Taken together, the limited federal constitutional authority for developing social welfare, the concentration of social welfare authority in the states, and local units of governance that exist at the pleasure of the states present a striking contrast to the frequently mistaken notion that American social welfare policymaking is a product of the federal government. With this broad picture in mind, the significance of subnational social welfare policymaking becomes much more apparent.

Local Policymaking

The structural context for local policymaking was established by the legal doctrine pronounced by Justice Douglas Dillon, often referred to as Dillon's rule: "Local governments are mere tenants at the will of the legislature." This 1868 court decision held that states may "sweep from existence all municipal corporations of the state."[3] Some years later the U.S. Supreme Court held that local governments "are the creatures, mere political subdivisions of the state" and may "exert only such powers expressly granted to them."[4] Thus localities are themselves products of federal and state policies. States create local government by granting them charters in much the same way that private corporations are chartered (also by state authority). Within these charters the responsibilities, obligations, and powers granted to local governments are clearly specified. Still, great variation exists in the ways local governments carry out such obligations.

Overlapping Jurisdictional Authority   A wide variety of local governmental units have come into existence. Counties, townships, municipalities, and city governments have been created to provide local governance within established geographic boundaries; many of these units now have, or share, school districts, special districts, and authorities that deal with special issues of governance, such as schools, airports, transportation, solid waste disposal, and similar public concerns. These later forms of local governance almost always overlap the older ones, usually by design, creating the first complication in local policy-making: overlapping jurisdictional authority.

Independent Policymaking Authority   If a clear legal doctrine of local govern-ment exists, defining local governments as creatures of the state, political doc-trine gives local governments independent authority in much the same way as states themselves are independent of the federal government. This political doc-trine derives from Article 10 of the U.S. Constitution, which reserves all undefined constitutional powers to the states "and to the people." Thus indi-viduals possess a form of constitutional power that they are free to exercise within their own organizational arrangements, including their local govern-ments. This doctrine of "popular sovereignty" has given sufficient political au-thority to local governments so as to prevent states from exploiting their legally defined authority over the local governance they create. In practice, therefore, states define local governments and vest them with power to do specific things, but leave them free to decide for themselves how they will do these things and whether they will do other things in addition to what the state specifically em-powers them to do.

Examples of this independence are abundant. One common instance is provision of the Medicaid program, created in 1965 as Title XIX of the Social Security Act to assist poor people in obtaining medical services. The federal government required states to generate plans for the kinds of services that would be provided, subject to federal guidelines. Most (but not all) states re-quire in turn that their counties administer the Medicaid program as outlined by the individual state's guidelines and that the counties contribute to the cost of the Medicaid program through their own tax revenues. In 1978 the federal government decided that, except in unusual cases, it would no longer provide funding for abortions under the Medicaid program. As a result, several states stopped paying for abortions for low-income women. Some states, however, re-sorted to the use of state monies to make sure the policy and program of publicly funded abortions continued. In still other cases, states let counties do whatever they chose to do, and some counties supplied their own funding for these ser-vices. Counties frequently make policies to provide other wide-ranging services to their populations, independent from implementing state-required programs. For example, many counties fund emergency shelters for victims of spousal abuse. Local governments have considerable independence in policymaking, which often exceeds their legal arrangements with states. They not only engage in policymaking activities within their own areas of geopolitical authority, but frequently enter into policymaking activities with other public governmental and private organizations. Therefore, rather than being a centralized activity, local policymaking becomes atomized as local units struggle to work together.

One of the most interesting types of collaborative policy activity occurs when local governmental units become engaged in policymaking somewhat independently of the state's jurisdiction. For example, under Title II of the Higher Education Act, the federal government may provide funds to local school districts that experience high rates of poverty, called "impact aid." In these cases, local school boards develop policy directly consistent with federal funding guidelines, independently of state activity. The War on Poverty programs of the Kennedy-Johnson years were characterized by federal initiatives that sought to bypass states and develop policy alliances exclusively with local governments.

Another example of local-federal patterning, discussed at greater length in Chapter 7, is that almost all policy relating to housing is essentially locally oriented. Housing codes are, for the most part, creatures of local governmental activity. Zoning, which determines the kind of housing that can be built and where it is permitted, is a local responsibility. Federal public housing policy, as in the implementation of low-income housing or rental assistance, requires not only local decisions about where such housing can be located, but also coordination with policies of the federal government. Private housing policies, such as bank mortgage policy, likewise interlock with local public policy decisions. Like housing policy decisions, policy decisions about transportation, health, public safety, sanitation, and other issues that directly affect most people's day-to-day lives have significant roots in local policymaking activities, many of which are not expressly mandated by the state government. Each local policymaking unit will probably produce policy that is unlike that made by neighboring units. And if this varied policymaking tapestry at the local level reflects beautifully the complexity of life throughout localities across the nation, its variety also creates a completely atomized context for examining local policymaking.

Ambiguities of Scope and Jurisdiction   Ambiguities in the scope of local policymaking abound. The legal scope granted to local governments by state charters barely provides the outlines of policymaking authority in those units. At best this legal structure determines what must be done in a few instances and what cannot be done in most other instances, but it leaves everything in between to the discretion and initiative of local policymakers. The lines of authority among local policymakers themselves are also ambiguous. For example, most municipalities are governed by an elected board of aldermen or a city council (the local legislative equivalent) and a mayor (the local executive equivalent), but in most cases the councillors and mayor deliberate policy matters together. Consequently lines of decision are blurred. Municipalities and counties hire managers (the local administrative bureaucracy equivalent), who often are the only officials who manage the entire budget process for the locality and hence must confront policy issues constantly. Municipalities also have justices, usually magistrates, who deal with only the most routine issues of local justice, for example, traffic offenses. Addressing these issues are seldom considered policymaking activities; however, they require policy decisions from a variety of local governance units.

The scope of local policymaking is made even more ambiguous by overlapping policymaking structures. Special-purpose structures often overlap the older, geopolitical structures. For example, it is not unusual for a school district or a housing authority to serve both a municipality and a county. In such a case, the school district's operating budget in large part probably comes from local tax levies and hence has to gain favorable approval by both the municipality and the county. Similarly, the housing authority may have to comply with building code requirements and zoning regulations in both a county and a municipality. In these situations it is often impossible to determine which unit has primary authority, the special-purpose unit or the geopolitical unit. The school board may have authority to set tax rates, for example, but the rates must be consistent with those set by the county and/or the municipality.

A lack of clear lines of authority complicates strictly geopolitical policymaking as well. For instance, counties and cities both may have policy authority for health care. Suppose that people in an outlying county area request health care from a central municipality that has developed more extensive services; the county accordingly offers to pay the municipality for access to these services until the county can develop comparable services. Once the county services catch up, and the county withdraws its support from the municipal health services, the municipality may find itself in a financial crisis.

These lines of authority are blurred even further by the rapid proliferation of both incorporated and unincorporated nonprofit organizations. The policymaking ability of these organizations often surpasses that of the public policymaking structures at the local level. For example, a city council or a board of county commissioners cannot direct the local United Way to use its funds to support specific social programs the county may need. The local United Way can choose to support social services and thus challenge the credibility of public services, or on the other hand a United Way may be courted to encourage it to support existing public social services. In either case, funding for public and private services becomes commingled, and it becomes difficult to tell who, indeed, is in charge of making policy about these services, the public body or the private organization.

The fact that both public and private social welfare organizations exist in the same locality, often providing similar if not the same services, has led to efforts to identify distinguishing characteristics of each. An earlier model of private nonprofit and public social welfare organizations proposed that private welfare organizations were innovators, charting new directions for the development of social services. With the increased flexibility offered by block-grant funding, public social organizations now contract with private social welfare organizations to provide services that would usually be provided by the public agency. But private social welfare agencies that desire contractual relationships with public agencies must agree to abide by the regulations set down by the public agencies. Thus while contracting for service delivery has energized the private sector, it has done so at the cost of removing whatever distinctions might have existed between the two types of social welfare organizations, and has made each dependent on the other for the development of social welfare policy at the local level.

In recent years, as local policymaking units have matured in number and scope, multijurisdictional coordinating and planning organizations have been developed to help coordinate and focus policymaking authority at the local level in the face of increasing ambiguity. The most widely recognized multijurisdictional organization is the council of governments (COG). As its name implies, a COG is the creation of two or more local governments, under a charter issued by the state, in which the different local governments collaborate in efforts to reach policy positions that will find acceptance throughout all participating areas. The Triangle J Council of Governments, for example, which covers the region in and around the Research Triangle Park in North Carolina, includes representatives from 6 counties and 27 municipalities within those counties and also interacts with other joint policymaking bodies in the same geographic area.

Multijurisdictional planning and coordinating bodies constitute one of the most unusual features of the policies and programs of the Older Americans Act (see Chapter 9). Called Area-wide Agencies on Aging (AAAs), these organizations are required to coordinate services for older people across local governmental jurisdictional lines. They are administrative structures created by states, and because COGs are the most prevalent multijurisdictional form of local government, AAAs are likely to be colocated with COGs and sometimes operate as administrative units under them, as, in fact, is the case with Triangle J. Like the COGS, AAAs have limited policymaking authority that is likely to be further compromised by the authority of other individual units of local governance.

Informality of Policy Decisions   Finally, local policymaking is characterized by informal policy decisions. Partly because local policymaking structures are atomized and policymaking authority is ambiguous, many local policy decisions are made informally, or even outside structures of governance. These informal decisions may be "ratified" by a local government unit, but the decision process takes place somewhere else. This sometimes lends an aura of mistrust and deceit to local policymaking activities, but the nature of local policymaking often demands such an informal process. Take the following example.

A small, local, private nonprofit agency serving older people saw the need for day-care services for about 50 older people who were unable to stay at home alone during hours when their children worked. The agency director decided to investigate funding sources for such a program, which she estimated would cost about $75,000 a year in additional funds. Space was available in the agency for the program, and the agency already served lunch to older people. The director talked with a private foundation that seemed interested in providing some of the funding, but only for a short period of time, as a start-up grant. The agency director presented the matter to her board of directors, who adopted a policy of expanding the agency's services to include adult day care.

Because the foundation would commit only seed money to the project, both short-term and long-term financial commitments had to be found. The county welfare department had funds that could be directed to day care, as did the state aging office through the AAA that served the local jurisdictions in which this agency was located. The state was willing to commit the money only if old people from the whole multijurisdictional region could be included in the services, subject to the agreement of the AAA director. The county did not want to commit its funding to the project unless the service was provided only to its poor older people. The director of the agency did not want to use the agency's facilities to provide service to these populations if it meant that the people usually served by the agency (people of all incomes, but only those who lived in the municipality, not the whole multijurisdiction) might be excluded from the services. The foundation would not give the seed money until the issues were resolved.

The agency director renegotiated the policy entirely. The agency would be exclusively responsible for deciding who got adult day care. Service would be restricted to the county (part of the AAA's area of responsibility). Half of the spaces would be reserved for people who were eligible for county aid, whether they were receiving county aid or not at the time they applied for day care. The county would therefore pay 50% of the cost. The state would pay 25% of the cost, which would be an amount equal to providing day-care support to this portion of the AAA's multijurisdictional area. The foundation would pay the balance for two years, at the end of which the amount would be made up from fees paid by day-care users who were not in the county's quota of poor people. The balance would be made up from the general operating budget of the agency. The foundation agreed to make a small annual contribution to the agency's operating budget after the second year, by an amount roughly equal to the amount the service would require after fees, county support, and state aid were calculated.

Complex? Extremely. The county commissioners approved the policy at one of their meetings, as did the state agency office and the local agency's and private foundation's boards of directors. The policy itself was made in an informal process for which the agency director took responsibility, and in which persons not usually in policymaking positions reached agreements that were formalized by the appropriate public and private local units. The policy was the composite agreement of each local unit. No single unit "owned" the policy process. The policy that governed the provision of service was written, but the full policy, reflecting the financial commitments, was not part of this written policy. Instead, the local agency, which ultimately provided the service, had separate letters of funding agreement with the county, the state, and the foundation. In other words, not only was the policymaking process informal, but the whole of the policy was not represented in a single policy document.

This example is not unique. Local policymaking often emerges through complex processes that span the fragmented authority of several public and private policymaking units. Because no two situations are likely to reflect the same dimensions of the problem, and because no two local units are likely to participate similarly in the complexity of local policymaking structures, this particularistic policymaking process is essential to the provision of local services.

LOCAL POLICYMAKING IN
THE BROADER POLITICAL CONTEXT

Subnational policymaking is difficult to understand without an appreciation of the broader political boundaries that give it some definition. These boundaries are (1) the mechanics of American intergovernmental relations and (2) the fiscal constraints posed by the federal system itself.

Intergovernmental Relations

Relationships among different governmental units operate in the United States through frequently changing patterns of interaction among the national government, the states, and local governmental units. Unlike in other federalized systems—for instance, Canada and Australia, where the governmental relationships among different units are fairly well established constitutionally or legislatively—intergovernmental relationships in the American system have been left to develop as the times and issues may dictate. Hence scholars of American government have had to struggle to identify patterns of intergovernmental relations that change over time. The difficulty in these changing relationships is evident in some of the descriptive phrases attached to intergovernmental relationships over the years: "layer-cake federalism . . . marble-cake federalism," and, perhaps the clearest metaphor of all, "rainbow marble cake" with a "mingling of differently colored ingredients."[5]

Deil Wright, a well-known contemporary scholar of American intergovernmental relations, has moved from metaphor to a six-part alliterative scheme to characterize the relationships among the federal government, the states, and localities: conflict (1930s and before), cooperation (1930–50), concentration (1940–60), creativity (1950–60), competition (1960–70), and calculation (1970–present). One feature of the current "calculative" period of intergovernmental relations has been the "increasing tendency to estimate 'costs' as well as the 'benefits' of getting a federal grant."[6] Changes in funding relationships, increased federal regulatory authority, and increased litigation over expanded regulation have led to a more cautious and discriminating approach in cooperative endeavors among the governmental partners. The important feature of Wright's scheme is that he sees patterns in intergovernmental relations that change over time. Accelerated during the Clinton administration, intergovernmental relations of the early decades of the 21st century, it appears, will be characterized by shifting more domestic decision-making to the states through increased use of block grants.

In practice, however, the interaction among the federal government, the states, and local governments is not as patterned as Wright portrays it to be. Why? Because each governmental subunit, and its accompanying "branch of government," interacts in different ways with other "branches." In other words, state governments do not interact as a whole with local governments. Rather, for example, state administrative agencies interact with their local counterparts, and so on. Interactions are also likely to differ depending on the policy area involved. Though there are formal arrangements that link fragmented governmental counterparts, most policy interactions take place outside these formal structures. For example, the National Governors Conference provides formal linkages among governors, and the National Conference of State Legislatures links legislators. But a particular policy issue usually requires a circumscribed pattern of interaction among the branches and levels of governance. Congress may pass a law that requires the federal administrative bureaucracy to issue policy that is communicated to a state governor, who in turn may ask his or her administrative bureaucracy to produce policy that a local city council may have to deal with legislatively (in an ordinance) before the local program agency can develop policy that will connect a product with the people who need it. These constantly shifting patterns are difficult to pinpoint as occurring in stages, and the patterns are likely to be different for different policy subjects. Yet policymaking goes on at all these points in the process. In other words, the linkages among intergovernmental partners in health policy, driven, for example, by the federal Medicaid program, will likely be different from intergovernmental linkages in welfare driven by TANF block grants.

Wright's own research suggests how difficult it is to capture intergovernmental relations in static descriptions. On examining the kinds of interactions state administrators had within the intergovernmental framework in 1978, he found that contact with other intergovernmental officials is quite widespread. Moreover, he found state-level patterns vary from one functional area to another. For example, of the units he surveyed, heads of human resource agencies had their greatest intergovernmental contact with similar agencies and clientele, as well as significant contact with federal regional office personnel and administrators of similar agencies in other states. Heads of natural resource agencies, by contrast, had most contact with similar agency personnel, and significant contact with county and city officials. Even more striking differences exist between the contacts of governors and those of state legislators, but again, all these actors are involved in making policy.[7]

Thus although the intergovernmental environment sets some boundaries for state and local policymaking activities, intergovernmental relations are so dynamic that little or no practical value may come from pursuing an enhanced understanding of the intergovernmental system as a whole. However, it is possible to specify the intergovernmental policy boundaries for the five policy sectors examined in Part II of this book: income maintenance, health, housing, child welfare, and older adults.

TABLE 3.1 | INTERGOVERNMENTAL POLICY ENVIRONMENTS FOR FIVE POLICY SECTORS

Policy Sector	Intergovernmental Units with Greatest Policy Authority			
	Federal			
	Exc	Leg	Jud	Adm
Income maintenance	X	X		X
Health	X	X		X
Housing	X	X	X	X
Child welfare	X	X	X	X
Older adults	X	X		

Policy Sector	State			
	Exc	Leg	Jud	Adm
Income maintenance		X		X
Health		X		X
Housing	X			
Child welfare		X	X	X
Older adults	X			X

Policy Sector	Local*			
	Co	Mun	SpD	SpA
Income maintenance	X			
Health	X		X	
Housing		X		X
Child welfare	X		X	
Older adults		X		

Abbreviations: executive (Exc), legislative (Leg), judicial (Jud), administrative (Adm), county (Co), municipality (Mun), special district (SpD), special authority (SpA).

*Executive, legislative, and administrative functions have limited distinguishing characteristics at the local level.

Table 3.1 shows fairly consistent locations for policymaking authority for these sectors at the federal level. Notable by comparison are the variations at the state and local levels. For example, the executive, legislature, and administration are all involved in policy development in all five policy sectors at the federal level. But at the state level the major actor is the administration. Counties carry the intergovernmental program burden at the local level.

Federal Fiscal Constraints

Money is the glue that holds subnational policymaking together. Bounded by fiscal constraints inherent in the federal system, the federal government may spend money directly only for policy purposes that are consistent with federal powers granted by the U.S. Constitution; these are limited, and touch only obliquely on the policy sectors that are discussed in this book. Otherwise, most of the federal government's authority to spend directly comes from its authority to regulate activities among the states and to manage the economy. Spending on transportation, environmental concerns, and communication derives from this federal interstate authority.

Federal funding for social programs, therefore, has to take a circuitous route. The most familiar paths are the grant-in-aid and its cousin the block grant. (The federal government also funds some programs by subsidies, interest-free bonds, and tax incentives; all of these strategies, for example, are particularly significant for funding housing policies.) The grant-in-aid and the block grant were developed as ways to distribute federal funding for specific public policies and programs. Essentially, both these mechanisms offer funds to the states if states will provide certain programs and carry out policies in ways generally promulgated by the federal government. For purposes of discussion, we might say that the chief characteristic of federal government funding mechanisms is that they give considerable latitude to states as to the standards and procedures by which the programs and policies will be carried out. The chief difference is the amount of flexibility delegated to the states; grants-in-aid are much more restrictive than block grants. (See Table 3.2.)

Originally in 1935 when the present welfare structure was created, a method of spending federal money on public welfare had to be available. The foundation for federal spending in 1935, as it is today, was the Morrill Act (1862). To meet the demands of states for technical assistance in farming and, to a lesser extent, manufacturing, Congress created the system of land grant colleges through the Morrill Act. Under this act Congress agreed to give a portion of its public lands to each state, permitting the state to sell these lands and use the proceeds to create colleges dedicated to teaching agriculture and mechanical arts. The act was amended in 1890 and in 1907, expanding the gifts of land and adding federal monies to the grants. Not only did this early legislation propel the federal government into matters not specifically assigned to the federal government by the U.S. Constitution, but it also established the grant-in-aid, a creative mechanism for the distribution of federal funds.

The grant-in-aid has become the most ingenious mechanism of American governance. The grant-in-aid permits the federal government to set national priorities and policies without violating state sovereignty. Essentially the federal government offers a grant to states, if states will use the money (or the land in the 1800s) for the purposes specified by the grant. States are free to refuse the grant should they choose not to undertake the purpose of the grant. In this arrangement the federal government is not administering any programs, leaving that to the states. Rather, the federal government's role is to "explain,"

TABLE 3.2 | CHARACTERISTICS OF MAJOR FEDERAL FUNDING PATTERNS

Degree of Funding Flexibility

Very restrictive			No restrictions at all
0% Flexibility - 100% Flexibility			
Payments to individuals	Grants-in-aid to states	Block grants	Revenue sharing
Examples:			
Social Security payments SSI payments Earned Income Tax Credits	Day-care services Child abuse services Child Support Enforcement	Welfare: TANF Social service Block grant	Unrestricted monies to states and localities (discontinued in 1980)

sometimes "interpret," the specific terms of the grant, so as to award the funds within the framework set forth by the grant, and to ensure that federal funds are spent consistently with their purposes.

The grant-in-aid and the block grant are the carrot and stick of American intergovernmental relations. It is extremely unlikely that states will refuse to accept a federal grant, particularly if the grant provides funds for purposes the state is undertaking anyway. However, accepting the grant means the state must make sure that the way its purposes are carried out is consistent with the grant, and usually this means making some changes in the way the state would normally administer its program. The grant-in-aid thus not only makes large sums of federal money available to states, but it also provides a way for all levels of governance to have some role in the development and implementation of domestic programs, thus providing some harmony for a system of welfare that otherwise would be singing different songs. The great functional separations between what the federal government might seek as national social welfare policy (but is unable to accomplish), and what the states are involved with, are brought together through this ingenious funding mechanism.

Experience with the grant-in-aid over nearly 70 years of welfare history has uncovered its disruptive influences on American governance. Grants-in-aid for welfare purposes have expanded well beyond their modest use in 1935. In fact it has been extremely convenient for Congress to create numerous grant-in-aid programs, to the extent that a broad range of domestic special interest groups develop and seek special legislative treatment. With respect to public welfare, Congress has created one grant-in-aid here, another there, until today there are over 300 grant-in-aid welfare programs. Thus a network of poorly connecting, sometimes overlapping programs proliferate federal public welfare initiatives, and the special interest groups the programs serve are loath to permit combining, or refocusing programs. Whereas the grant-in-aid and the block grant are the least controversial mechanisms for the federal government to fund domestic social programs, politically they have contributed considerably to the development of social programs not always well focused on the nation's most significant problems.

Since only states have sufficient statutory and constitutional authority to operate welfare programs, grant-in-aid and block-grant funding contribute to welfare policy fragmentation. Yet without this carrot and stick American welfare programs would be in even greater disarray. The policy significance of grants is two-sided. On the one hand, both grants-in-aid and block grants pass considerable policymaking authority from the federal government to the states and to localities. This devolution greatly complicates the policymaking process, because, as described above, no exact or specific unit in the state and local intergovernmental structure ever dominates the policymaking process. For example the AFDC program (Aid to Families with Dependent Children) had operated as a grant-in-aid until it was replaced by TANF (Temporary Assistance to Needy Families) in 1996. Under AFDC the federal government offered funds to a state if the state would implement programs that appropriately distribute financial support to dependent children and their adult caretakers as the federal government decreed. When the AFDC program was reformed into TANF, broad flexibility was given to the states in how welfare money could be used. So, while the federal government set the broad framework for TANF programs, states and localities now have considerable authority to develop social welfare policy that fills in and makes the broad policy conditions operational. In particular under TANF, states and localities determine who will get welfare benefits and what levels of financial support there will be. Such activities constitute large policymaking responsibility.

The other side of this grant mechanism exerts a narrowing effect on local policymaking. Participating states must move within the policy as funded, and not elaborate its purposes. For example, though states set the payment levels for present-day welfare programs (TANF), they do not set all financial eligibility conditions, nor do they set financial eligibility standards for other programs that are funded exclusively with federal funds, such as Supplemental Security Income (SSI) and Social Security. (See Chapter 5.) And though states may exercise discretion in the types of health services offered under the Medicaid plan— for example, a grant-in-aid program—states have no authority to determine which foods mothers can buy with their food stamps, a program operated by the federal Department of Agriculture. This narrowing of subnational policymaking discretion, as determined by funding mechanisms, helps to target more specifically which state and local officials are likely to participate in policy decisions once the topics of policy are known. County commissioners will most certainly be involved in shaping income-maintenance policy; municipalities will be involved in shaping public housing policies, usually through their housing authorities and zoning ordinances; states will be heavily involved in the development of health programs, such as Medicaid; while the federal government, alone, will shape the Social Security program. (See Table 3.2.) The cost of this narrowing of policy authority, however, is a wide range of social programs that do not fit together very well.

In 1981 the federal government began a major refocusing of its funding; 80 social welfare, grant-in-aid programs were reorganized into 9 block grants. (See Table 3.2.) Policy and program support for areas ranging from education to social services were affected by this change. Although a full evaluation of the impact of this change has not been made, a study by the federal General Accounting Office, published in 1985, documented a clear shift in policymaking authority from the federal government to states and local governments. The study did show, for example, the boundaries that different policy sectors set on intergovernmental policymaking activities. In general, state policies to implement the new block grants were "either derived from or intertwined with basic allocation decisions made during the states' normal budgetary or decision-making process." However, in policy areas where states had had little prior policymaking responsibility, such as community services and support for energy savings, states felt the changes from policy development more acutely.[8]

Another study of the social service block grants also suggests that block-grant funding lessened intergovernmental policymaking, putting more focus on state and local policymaking. In many situations after the federal shift in 1981, specific social services formerly provided by states under the grants-in-aid were no longer offered. In most states the actual number of different services decreased. In some states such long-standing services as day care for children were no longer being provided under the authority of the block grant, even though they had been regularly provided under the authority of the grant-in-aid.[9] Recently, Charles Brecher and Colin Chellman of the Robert Wagner School of Public Service, New York University, noted that "President [George] Bush appears to be setting a new pattern for growth in his allocation of funds for grants to states and localities."[10]

Categorical Grants versus Block Grants (Efficiency versus Effectiveness)

Categorical grants-in-aid, the most restrictive grant funding provided for social welfare programs, permit targeting of funds to deal with very specific issues, thus making this kind of funding effective at dealing with the subject for which the program was created. However, this targeting often leads to less efficiency in the use of funds, since money is directed at narrow populations. Specialization is likely to take place, narrowing the population further and often raising the unit cost of service. Inasmuch as there is considerable variety in the populations served, both from state to state and within states, grant-in-aid funding leads to funding programs category by category, often referred to as "categorical funding." Thus grant-in-aid funding leads to developing additional categories, or, as is more often the case, using the funding for populations that only marginally meet the categorical requirements (i.e., trying to make people fit the program).

Block grants are a form of grant funding without narrowly defined categories. Block grants may not be as effective as categorical grants because the funds can be used for a broad group of activities, but they may be more efficient since they provide sufficient flexibility to adjust the use of funding for exigencies as they may exist in the local community. Because block-grant funds can be used broadly, it is more difficult to monitor their use. Moreover, because there are fewer experts involved in program development, and less administrative oversight in programs funded by block grants, appropriate use of these funds is highly dependent on the character of those who are administering them. These persons are likely to be local administrators. Knowledge of what needs to be accomplished in each community becomes essential, since there are few directions or guidelines accompanying block grants.

States may decline to accept federal social welfare funds, but the advantages of accepting are greater than the disadvantages of "attached strings" in either categorical or block-grant funding. Since most social welfare authority rests with the states, states are forced to respond to social problems, one way or another. The ability to get $2 or even $9 for every $1 a state would normally spend is a powerful incentive for states to use federal funding to support social needs. In the case of block grants, there is often no matching requirement at all. Block grants appear to save states and local communities money, but savings may not be realized due to the following circumstances.

States and localities are forced to comply with the political pressures that categorical grants sometimes stir up. Since certain groups are helped by certain programs—for example, the elderly in senior centers—these groups develop into constituencies that lobby directly and indirectly for programs offered by the federal government. Satisfying these constituency demands is a politically valuable activity. Refusing these demands risks political misfortune. Thus the flexibility of the block grant may be limited by constituency pressures stirred up by previous categorical funding.

Administrative agencies usually respond positively to categorical programs because implementing this kind of funding requires a certain amount of administrative capacity. The more narrow the category of the grant, the more administrative activity is required to make sure the administration of the grant complies with federal expectations. Moreover, narrowly focused categories require program experts, often highly sophisticated program applications, and training necessary to ensure staff are able to carry out increasingly specialized activities. Thus administrative agencies often work in subtle ways to preserve and expand previous categorical programs within the framework of block-grant funding.

POLICY EVALUATION

Evaluation of policy outcomes is extremely important in the policy development paradigm such as set forth in Chapter 2. (See also Chapter 4.) However, as the above discussion suggests, policy evaluation depends on where the evaluation takes place. A particular program in a particular county may be evaluated quite highly, while the same program in another place may be a failure. Thus the complexities of subnational policymaking contribute heavily to the success or failure of social welfare policies.

Policy funding patterns also contribute to policy evaluation outcomes. Particular program outcomes become more difficult to evaluate unless allowances are made for how funding patterns may affect expected outcomes. For example, categorically funded social programs may be appropriately evaluated for their effectiveness (Did those who received service change in any measurable way?), while more broadly focused block-grant programs may be more appropriately evaluated for their efficiency (Did we get good value for the monies that were spent? Were certain social problems in the community adequately addressed?). The former evaluation is focused on specific client outcomes, while the latter is focused on outcomes of community change.

Both types of evaluations are outcome-based (What changes can be attributed to the use of monies?) rather than process-based evaluations (How quickly was the staff able to get the program up and running?). While outcome evaluation under categorical funding focuses on the effective use of funds, evaluation of block-grant funded programs focuses on efficiency outcomes. An effective categorically funded program must examine the following: (1) Did the funds go to the right people? (2) Did the people served (clients) get their benefits in a timely manner? (3) Did the clients use the resources as they were supposed to use them? (4) Were matching funds provided in accordance with the grant-in-aid formula? On the other hand, an efficient block-grant program must examine the following: (1) Were the right people involved in deciding the use of funds? (2) How well were resources directed at each community's most significant problems? (3) What kind of ongoing community involvement ensures appropriate use of funds? (4) Are funds being used to replace funding that might be otherwise available? (5) Is good value being received for funds being spent (i.e., how do unit costs compare with spending in other sectors?), or are there too many or too few options being offered for the amount of funds available?

By reviewing the policy development paradigm presented in Chapter 2, one sees that evaluation is necessary to complete the policy development process, and this chapter suggests that such evaluations must take into account subnational policymaking complexities as well as the way policies are funded. There are other "marginal program benefits" that represent outcomes also requiring evaluation. "Marginal" in this sense does not mean "unimportant," but rather refers to those program benefits that may not be of central concern, such as better educational performance of children. A full discussion of marginal policy analysis questions is presented in Chapter 4. Not only does shifting funding patterns place greater responsibility on localities for policy development, but increased block-grant funding will force localities to undertake different kinds of policy development activity, like program evaluation, that have not been previously expected of local policymaking.

CONCLUSION

Examining subnational policymaking centers and processes gives greater breadth to our understanding of the whole of the policymaking process, but it also makes general observations about the policymaking process itself more difficult. Several factors clearly complicate local and state policymaking processes: the confusions between the legal and political autonomy of local governmental units; the great variety and number of local units, which make policy individually and collectively; and the as yet unclear patterns of interaction among governmental units within the framework of American federalism as shaped by different funding patterns. The lack of one clear center of power in the American system suggests that there is no clear center of policymaking, either. Even though some policymaking sectors are more appropriate for specific governmental units, in the completion of a policymaking process all centers can become involved, and frequently most do. When private-sector policymaking is added to this complexity, the final policymaking picture truly becomes the "black box of politics," as one commentator has quipped.[11]

Under such circumstances it is not surprising that most studies of policymaking continue to focus on case studies; general principles are difficult to develop. Research by Randall Ripley and Grace Franklin has offered some hope of detecting order in the chaos. After a first investigation of bureaucratic policy within the federal system, they and their colleagues suggested that the structures of state and local policymaking units have an important influence on the roles the agencies play in policymaking. In particular, an agency's maturity, the characteristics of its personnel, and its internal decision-making processes not only determine how it becomes involved in policymaking, but also suggest what the policy outcomes might be.[12]

In later work Ripley and Franklin refined some of their structural theories and devised an interactional framework for understanding policy development. A chief characteristic of this framework is the activity of what they call "subgovernments": "clusters of individuals that effectively make the most routine decisions in a given substantive area of policy. . . . Since most policymaking is routine most of the time, subgovernments can often function for long periods of time without much interference of control from individuals or institutions outside the subgovernment."[13]

> Not only are the lines between governmental and nongovernmental institutions blurred by the norm of open, continual access during policymaking, but there is also a constant flow of personnel between governmental and nongovernmental institutions that further blurs the distinctions. This flow of personnel enhances the importance and stability of subgovernments, and the magnitude of this type of personnel interchange is so large that subgovernments have also been called "incest groups."[14]

These observations and the discussion throughout this chapter suggest once again the importance of identifying exactly where in the complexity of the policymaking process a particular request or need for analysis is located. Seldom will a policy analysis be requested that will span the entire range of the policy-making process. Without this focus the policy analyst cannot produce a product that will be useful. The discussions of policy analysis models that follow, in Chapter 4, are offered from the perspective that different approaches are required for each journey into the labyrinth of the policymaking process.

QUESTIONS FOR DISCUSSION

1. To what extent are the various governments in the United States independent of each other? How do they come together in the development and execution of welfare policy?
2. What are the advantages and disadvantages of block-grant and grant-in-aid funding patterns?
3. What are the similarities and differences between process and outcome evaluations? When is one evaluation type rather than another used?
4. Given the fragmented nature of policymaking at the subnational level, would it be better to have one national program, such as Social Security, to provide all the welfare benefits to all who need them? Defend your answer.

A FRAMEWORK FOR
POLICY ANALYSIS
AND DEVELOPMENT

The close association between policy analysis and social research often confuses the purpose of policy analysis with the methods used in it. The purpose of policy analysis is to provide reliable information to policymakers about a problem they must consider, in order to guide policymaking activities to appropriate conclusions. This information may include detailed assessments of a problem, careful comparisons of alternative proposals, and projections of costs against benefits to identifiable population groups, as well as suggestions about the larger social and political consequences of various proposals. The phrase "policy research" is often substituted for "policy analysis" because policy analysis draws heavily on the methods of social science research. However, although policy analysis uses the products of social science research to build the information it produces, policy analysis does not have the same purpose as social science research. Whereas social science research is free to range wherever the facts may take it, policy analysis is sought within an environment of public choice. Policy analysis is scientific, but it is not social research.

THE SOCIAL SCIENCE FRAMEWORK

Social science research, especially that which requires statistical analysis of behaviorally defined information, is often called "empirical" research. A dictionary definition of *empirical* shows that it may mean basing conclusions on experiment and observation, or it may mean a disregard for science, relying solely on practical experience. The origin of the word is Greek, *en peria*, meaning "in trial"; the same root, *peri*, occurs in "experience" and "experiment." Empirical research has been called "the investigator's experiences with the person, objects, or events of the real world. In other words, the raw materials from which scientific knowledge is derived are systematic observations of reality."[1]

An understanding of the revolution in science that ushered in our modern world helps put the purposes of policy analysis in proper perspective to social science research. Science as we know it today began in the seventeenth century, when Galileo publicly confirmed Copernicus's theory that the sun, not the earth, was the center of the universe. Science and religion became polarized into two camps: the discoverers and the believers. Copernicus had believed that the earth revolved around the sun. Galileo, however, had proved the theory by his repeated observations, made possible with tools not available to Copernicus. It was his assertion of this proof, derived empirically, that provoked Galileo's trial for heresy; under threat of death, he recanted. The furor that continued (to this day, in fact) was not over the conclusion that he had reached, but the way in which he had reached that conclusion. Before, truth about the world was presumed to be revealed to man by God. After Galileo, truth about the world could be discovered by man without God. Out of this came modern science, an understanding of the world through knowing, rather than believing. This differentiation between faith and science has remained a challenge to Western thought.

Auguste Comte laid the foundations of what he called "positive philosophy," in which he "discovered" a law of three stages that explained the whole of social interaction. Comte and those who followed him were so convinced that science, or systematic discovery, was the key to understanding that they frequently urged the methods of science for studying the entire range of human problems. This movement of science through the world of social thought was "an attempt to transfer to the study of social and human phenomena, the methods and concepts of the natural sciences in the belief that human phenomena, like physical phenomena, obey certain laws of nature which can be inductively discovered by the empirical examination of successive events."[2]

The new social science found its first and most lasting synthesis in blending with biology. Charles Darwin's *Origin of Species* (1859) posited the idea of natural selection: species fitted to their environment survive and reproduce. Offspring vary in their characteristics, and because of certain characteristics some survive to reproduce more successfully than others. In this way species may "evolve" or change. Darwin posited in *The Descent of Man* that our present human species evolved from another animal form—a scientific idea that creationism continues to debate. Fortified with Darwin's ideas and well read in Comte's social positivism, Herbert Spencer, a contemporary of Darwin, devised what have since been called "fantastic comparisons between biological organisms and societies."[3] Spencer argued, for example, that like species that could not adapt to the natural environment, individuals who did not adapt to the social environment would not survive. He also held that government, specifically, had an obligation to avoid any activities that would interfere with these laws of nature. From this arose the social doctrine of *laissez faire:* "let things alone." The world is self-regulating. Spencer's social application of "survival of the fittest" soon became an accepted truth.

This digression into the origins of social science provides a background for considering appropriate uses of social science in policy analysis. In its most fundamental application, social science relies on the ability to predict events on the basis of experience with present events, assuming that a regularity, or a pattern, exists with respect to the observable events. The key words are *regularity, observation,* and *pattern.* Three presuppositions are fundamental to social science methodology. First, a pattern must be assumed. The social scientist must infer through assumption, previous experience, or previous research that some patterns exist between eating breakfast, for example, and doing well in school. If no presumed pattern existed, if the two events were seen as random, without association or order, there would be no need for the social scientist to collect information about them for scientific purposes.

Second, social science requires a systematic approach to the process of observation. A conclusion is reached by assuming that the regularity observed is systematic and consequently applies in all situations. Social scientists also try to define their observations clearly, so that they can be counted. For example, suppose you, as a scientist, decided to test the assumption that children who eat breakfast are better students. After deciding what was meant by "breakfast" and "better students," you would observe what students actually did, both at breakfast and at school. The observations would have to be gathered regularly, by some system, so that all observations could be trusted to fit the presumed patterns of association between the two sets of events. For example, all the observations of each activity (breakfast or schoolwork) would have to be made at the same time of day; the same kinds of performance would have to be observed (not reading one day, math the next); and separate records for breakfast-eaters and non–breakfast-eaters would have to be kept. Whatever observable pattern occurred could be attributed to the association of the two events—providing they were not due to chance.

Third, therefore some mechanism is required that will enable scientists to assert that an association existing between sets of events is not due to chance. An association of events can never be certain; scientists can only refine their estimates of certainty. The greater the amount of certainty desired, the greater the number of observations necessary. Suppose you as a scientist kept records on 90 out of 100 second-graders at one particular school and discovered that all 90 ate breakfast and also did well in school. You might fairly predict that at least 9 of the 10 remaining second-graders who ate breakfast would likewise do well. You might also have cause to believe that in a similar group of children the same association of events would prevail. However, if out of 100 children only 20 were observed, even if all 20 children ate breakfast and did well in school, projecting that association to the group of 100, or to other groups of students in a similar situation, could not be done with much confidence. Thus a system for collecting sizable amounts of quantified information is an essential part of the scientific method.

THE POLICY ANALYSIS FRAMEWORK

Though policy analysis draws heavily on social science knowledge and social science research methods, and may also contribute to social science knowledge, it has its own essential elements. These include (1) identifying, understanding, or clarifying the problem; (2) identifying the location for policy decision; (3) specifying possible solutions (alternatives); and (4) estimating or predicting the impact (outcomes) of these solutions on different populations.

Problem Identification

Policy has a number of purposes, but a primary one is to resolve problems. (See also Chapter 1.) A problem may be recognized to exist, but putting some boundary around the problem may prove difficult. The way a problem is defined usually determines how it will be resolved. Any of several definitions may be appropriate for understanding and subsequently resolving the problem. Problem identification requires:

1. Specifying the problem's origins. Learning the problem's history, including previous attempts to deal with it. Specifying the origin of a problem isolates who thinks this is a problem and why.
2. Determining the problem's scope. Clarifying who is affected by the problem. Determining the scope of a problem clarifies the groups that interact with the problem. Some are disadvantaged; some benefit.
3. Sketching the pervasiveness of the problem, and determining its implications for other sectors of society. Sketching the pervasiveness of the problem identifies the social institutions that may presently be engaged with parts of the problem.
4. "Framing" the problem within these conditions intentionally limits the scope of the problem for which a policy is sought. This framing may also set the conditions under which the problem will be analyzed.

Locating the Focus for Policy Decision

As previously discussed, policy analysis takes place at various locations during the policymaking process, and the character of that analysis differs depending on where it is located. Moreover, each specific element of policy analysis may differ depending on what actor or set of policy actors makes the policy decision. Problem identification, for example, may be quite different among executives than in courts, even when the subject matter is the same. Each set of policy actions has its own policymaking environment in which it operates.

Determining Alternatives

Determining the alternatives available for choice is an essential part of the policy analysis process. Generally, alternatives are thought of as different ways of achieving the same objective; in policy analysis, however, the alternatives themselves frequently have policy implications of their own. The task for the analyst is to explore the alternatives and make clear any further consequences they might have if ultimately chosen as policy.

Frequently, alternatives are discussed and debated as choices, not so much because they are really different ways of doing the same thing, but because the alternatives themselves address normative issues inherent in the problem. For example, the United States has struggled for years to reduce poverty, particularly among children. Several alternatives for achieving this objective are incorporated into Title IV of the Social Security Act, for example. TANF provides cash to families with financially dependent children; Title IV-B and Title IV-E provide foster care and adoption services for poor children who have no natural homes. Title IV-D provides services to help collect child-support payments. Each of these sections of Title IV states an alternative for reducing poverty among children, yet each is seen as a policy in its own right. Each offers a different normative solution for resolving poverty among children. TANF provides money for children when they need it. Title IV-B and Title IV-E offer alternative homes to children who need them. Title IV-D requires absent parents to pay for their children's support. These policies do not form a unified collection of alternatives, consisting of different ways of doing the same thing. Rather, they legitimate different and sometimes conflicting normative approaches to poverty. Thus, in practice, these alternatives may pull against each other rather than pulling together; they may not act as "alternatives" as the word is generally used.

Predicting Policy Impacts and Unintended Effects

The real impact of a policy alternative may be significantly different from the expected one for several reasons. Because there is always the possibility that the projected pattern will not continue, or will continue in a different way from what was expected, prediction is risky. In order to make predictions, social science depends on observations that confirm assumptions about identical situations, but it is impossible to find truly identical situations in the social world. What might seem to be a probable outcome may not turn out to be so at all. In other words, there is no certainty that any future state of affairs can be predicted.

The actual impact of a policy also may differ from the predicted impact because values conflict and normative views differ. As discussed in Chapter 2, deliberation over values may subvert the entire effort of the analysis. Much as problems are understood from normative orientations, the potential effects of alternative solutions are understood in terms of existing, not future, circumstances. Sometimes a policy analyst may truly prefer a particular outcome and consequently may strive to develop an alternative that achieves specific normative consequences. In other cases, the context of the problem itself may have changed, and the consequences are different simply because the circumstances are different.

The ambiguity about whether alternatives are a means to achieve policy or an independent form of policy in themselves contributes to the unanticipated consequences of policy choice. Inadequate policy analysis often leaves the policymaker uninformed about the impact a particular alternative may have in other policy sectors. Perhaps no better example can be found than the unintended consequences of the 1996 welfare reform. (See Chapters 1 and 5.) The statute (Personal Responsibility and Work Opportunity Act, PRWOA) was designed to provide benefits to families even though the parents might be working. But states, and the general public, saw this welfare reform as a way to reduce the number of persons receiving welfare by putting them to work. Many states went so far as to require family heads to register for work *before* they could apply for assistance. In North Carolina, for example, the reformed welfare program was called Work First.[4]

Another example of unintended policy consequences arose in 1981 when President Reagan faced a depressed economy and a federal deficit. Reagan's budget established across-the-board reductions, but congressional implementation of this policy had consequences that reached far beyond reductions in funds. To lessen the impact of the reductions, Congress agreed to the administration's proposal to group a large number of programs into block grants—a more general form of program implementation. The financial allocation for all the programs in that group could then be reduced; the states in turn could decide which specific programs they would reduce or, again alternatively, supplement with state funds. The unintended consequences of implementing the block-grant policy began to appear as states passed along to local program administrators reduced funding for established public programs that had long been important for addressing a number of domestic issues at local levels. For example, reductions in federal funding for environmental programs not only curtailed efforts to clean up toxic dump sites but limited state-level inspection activities. Shifting additional authority to states also created a fragmented and inconsistent social service system, in which program benefits and eligibility began to range greatly from state to state.[5] In some cases, reductions in funding even discouraged welfare recipients from working.[6] One researcher has claimed that cutbacks in prenatal care programs "contributed significantly to the [increase] in infant mortality by weakening national policies . . . for the care and protection of pregnant women," greatly increasing future medical costs.[7] The "ripple effect" of these policy outcomes continued for several years.[8]

THREE CAVEATS FOR POLICY ANALYSIS

As suggested in Chapter 2, and also in the remarks above, policy analysis has a very broad scope. Almost any social science research has "policy implications." The diverse purposes that public policies serve, as well as the multiple centers that exist for policy decisions, propel policy analysis into far-reaching activities. Three caveats, or cautions, apply to policy analysis that do not apply to social science research. Attention to these caveats will help the analyst apply an appropriate method of analysis.

First, only problems and policy alternatives that are in the public domain should be examined. To the extent that policy analysis is concerned with the examination of public problems and the use of public resources, this restraint seems prudent. Policy analysis is less useful for the examination of private issues when those issues do not interlock with public concerns. For example, a private family counseling center, such as a family service association, may decide not to provide service to drug users without analysis of the policy decision about whom the agency wants to serve. The same family service association might conduct a policy analysis and consider an alternative to its refusal to treat drug users if local churches would agree to provide the counseling, but this alternative is not in the public domain either. Other radical alternatives could be suggested, but analyzing obscure or inventive alternatives that are so far-reaching or so questionable that they appear "best" only because nothing much is known about their implications is not consistent with policy analysis.[9]

Second, different centers of policymaking require different kinds of policy analysis. Policy analysts usually are on the staff of such centers or are members of organizations directly related to them. The analyst's task is closely related to the kind of information the decision maker needs. Each organization has a mission, and because its policy analysis is done within that organizational context, the scope of analysis, particularly the identification of alternatives, must be compatible with the mission. Thus many possible alternatives for policy choice may exist outside the realm of a particular policy environment. For example, an administrative staff charged with a policy analysis task cannot suggest new legislation as an alternative to administrative policy; the focus must remain on administrative alternatives.

Third, policymaking is a value-laden enterprise, and the analysis always takes place within an established context of values. Social values, organizational values, professional values, and personal values all limit policy analysis. Unscrambling the values that lie behind the definition of a problem, or the range of alternative solutions, is every bit as important as determining what type of information is most useful for examining the problem itself. The analyst must be appropriately cautious about values, but values guide the analysis. Most likely these values are not the personal values of the analyst, but the preferences and values that guide the operation of the organization. Policy analysis is not a political process as such, but because values are clarified in the process of analysis, it is part of the political process that maximizes value positions.

MODELS OF POLICY ANALYSIS

In recent years policy analysis and policy development have become a subspecialization in a number of academic disciplines such as economics, political science, and sociology. Additionally, many professions now devote considerable attention to policy analysis as part of their educational programs. Indeed, many universities now offer complete courses of study in policy analysis and development. Paul A. Sabatier, himself a well-respected public policy scholar, recently has collected a number of theories of the policy development process. Sabatier states: "Understanding the policy process requires a knowledge of the goals and perceptions of hundreds of actors throughout the country involving possibly very technical scientific and legal issues over periods of a decade or more when most of those actors are actively seeking to propagate their specific 'spin' on events." [10]

With the caution that policy analysts should be capable of applying several models of analysis, depending on the expectations placed on the analyst, a wide range of policy analysis models by distinguished policy scholars are presented in the following sections. Table 4.1 summarizes these and other approaches to policy analysis, which provide a range of policy analysis options the policy analyst might use.

As the models presented in Table 4.1 suggest, policy analysis uses various types of social science information. However, debate continues over what kind of information is best in what kinds of situations. Sometimes appropriate information already exists, and it can be applied readily in the analysis. Sometimes new information has to be generated by social research. In either case, that information must be organized to connect with the particular issue under consideration. Each policy decision requires a specific mixture of information presented in a specific way. Policy analysis requires reliable, useful, purposeful information. This information is likely to be some form of social science information, but the important point is that it be presented in a relevant form.

Three General Policy Analysis Models

Based on a study of different policy analysis approaches, it is possible to distill three general approaches to policy analysis. These three models are the *behavioral,* or "rational," the *incremental,* and the *criteria based* (see Table 4.2). To some extent they also identify three points along a continuum of policy analysis. At one end of the continuum, in the behavioral model, the analyst requires information that likely must be obtained through traditional social science methods of research. At the other end, where information for policy choice is least likely to depend on social science data and research methods, and most likely to depend on the analysis of values, the incremental model is most useful. An incremental policy analysis is sometimes called a "political analysis" because the alternatives considered seem more oriented to the political realities of choosing than to the social realities of the consequences of the choice. The criteria-based model rests at some midpoint on the continuum. It balances the use of social science research knowledge with an emphasis on the marginal significance of criteria (values) that may be involved in choosing.

Table 4.2 describes these models in terms of procedure. In practice any analysis may contain or omit different features of the models; in some cases elements from different models may be combined. The actual task of analysis proceeds as the requirements for information become clearer, depending on the problem under consideration and who is making the policy decision. The following discussion of the models should be tempered by our understanding that no two policy problems are the same. Just as the process of analysis varies with the kind of information necessary for a policy choice, the method of analysis in one situation may not be useful in another.

The Behavioral Model

The behavioral model of policy analysis represents analysis that requires the maximum amount of social science information and social research methods. The model has its origins in the work of Herbert Simon, a pioneer in the application of scientific principles to management and administrative decisions. Simon was a consultant with the Rand Corporation, a think tank that during the early 1950s was principally concerned with developing new technologies for making decisions. Thus the behavioral approach to policy analysis was developed from a context of how effective decisions should be made. More than any other, this model depicts an orderly process by which decisions take place. For this reason it is often called a "rational" model.

Defining the Problem in Objective (Behavioral) Terms   Defining the problem in objective (behavioral) terms is a critical first step in the behavioral model, and the rest of the analysis succeeds or fails on that basis. As discussed in Chapter 1, defining the problem presents a complex task for the policy analyst who uses this model, and considerable social science information is needed. The behavioral model makes no allowance for normative orientations toward problem identification. Instead it attempts to integrate all different problem definitions, producing a final definition that may have a number of subparts. This process often establishes a sense of hierarchy within the definition, particularly when complex problems are at issue. The subparts and hierarchical organization yield "alternative sets" of problem definitions.

Creating Sets of Alternatives   Just as definitions are objectified in this model, so alternatives are stated in behavioral, or measurable, or operational terms. One set of behavioral alternatives that could address the problem of hunger and poor nutrition would be to provide poor people with money; another set might be to provide poor people with food stamps; yet another would be to provide wages through employment; another would be to provide poor people with surplus food. These alternatives are called "sets" because each constitutes a distinct grouping of subfactors that must be considered together to build an alternative. For example, providing food stamps might be undertaken in a number of different ways: (1) provide $200 in food stamps per month to poor families with children under age 16; (2) provide $75 in food stamps per month to every undernourished person; (3) provide $100 in food stamps to poor mothers who are willing to purchase them at a 75% discount; (4) provide food stamps, up to the value of the poverty line, to all pregnant women. Efforts at problem definition would continue in this fashion to specify all the possible subsets for each alternative, until the list was exhausted.

The process of defining alternatives and their subsets may seem endless, but the usefulness of this model depends on having every possible alternative spelled out. Identifying all alternatives and all possible subsets for each is another way of defining the problem's conditions in more precise terms, thus eliminating the need to consider normative positions. In other words, defining *all*

TABLE 4.1 | MODELS OF POLICY DEVELOPMENT AND ANALYSIS*

Referent Name	Characteristics	Notations
Stages[1]	Agenda setting–Policy formation–Legislation–Implementation–Evaluation	Hierarchical, somewhat "top-down"
Institutional (rational choice)[2]	Interaction among existing institutions, e.g., legislative/administrative interaction to produce policy	Most widely referenced, many different variations
Multiple streams[3]	Problem stream; policy stream; politics stream; come together in windows of opportunity	
Equilibrium ("punctuated")[4]	Long periods of incremental change "punctuated" by brief periods of major policy changes brought about by exploiting multiple policy venues that are in constant play	
Advocacy coalitions[5]	Coalition of advocates influences "policy elites"	May include "grass roots" advocacy but probably not
Policy diffusion[6]	National policy filtered down to states and localities and adapted as it diffuses across the whole system	
Outcome analysis[7]	Policy outcomes dependent on existing economic, political, and social structures	
Cultural[8]	Policy an expression of cultural values, e.g., liberalism and individual choices	

Areas of power[9]	Policy concentrated in several "areas" (e.g., distributive, regulatory, etc.); certain policy characteristics for each "area"
Policy domain[10]	Within a given policy domain patterns of resource exchange developed in organizations to influence the outcome of policy events
"Garbage can"[11]	Characterized by no set framework; all random actions with very little rhyme or reason

*Condensed from Paul A. Sabatier, *Theories of the Policy Process* (Boulder, Colo.: Westview Press, 1999), 1–19.

1. James Lester and Malcolm Groggin, "Back to the Future: The Rediscovery of Implementation Studies," *Policy Currents* 9, no. 3: 1–10.

2. Fritz Scharpf, *Games Real Actors Play* (Boulder, Colo.: Westview Press, 1997).

3. John W. Kingdon, *Agendas, Alternatives, and Public Policies*, 2d ed. (New York: HarperCollins, 1995).

4. Frank R. Baumgartner and Bryan D. Jones, *Agendas and Instability in American Politics* (Chicago: University of Chicago Press, 1993).

5. Paul Sabatier and Hank C. Jenkins-Smith, *Policy Change and Learning: An Advocacy Coalition Approach* (Boulder, Colo.: Westview Press, 1993).

6. Frances Berry and William Berry, "Tax Innovations in the States . . . ," *American Journal of Political Science* 36 (August 1992): 715–742.

7. Thomas Dye, *Politics in States and Communities*, 7th ed. (Englewood Cliffs, N.J.: Prentice Hall, 1991).

8. Mary Douglas and Aaron Wildavsky, *Risk and Culture* (Berkeley: University of California, 1982).

9. Randolph Ripley and Grace Franklin, *Congress, the Bureaucracy, and Public Policy* (Homewood, Ill.: Dorsey Press, 1976).

10. Ronald Knoke et al., *Comparing Policy Networks: Labor Politics in the U.S., Germany and Japan* (Cambridge, England: Cambridge University Press, 1996).

11. Michael D. Cohen, James March, and John P. Olsen, "A Garbage Can Model of Organizational Choice," *Administrative Science Quarterly* 17: 1–25.

TABLE 4.2 | THREE MODELS OF POLICY ANALYSIS ON A POLICY ANALYSIS CONTINUUM

The Behavorial or Rational Model[1]

1. Define the problem in objective (behavorial) terms.
2. Devise sets of specific alternatives that would resolve the problem under prescribed circumstances.
3. Project the likelihood of achieving each set of alternatives.
4. Examine data appropriate to each alternative and determine which give the greatest benefit per unit of cost.
5. Calculate the benefits of each alternative in relation to feasibility of implementation.

The Criteria-Based Model[2]

1. Define the problem in objective (behavorial) terms.
2. Establish universal and selective criteria (values) for evaluating the alternatives (feasibility would be one of several criteria.)
3. Gather data appropriate to each alternative and determine which alternative gives the greatest benefit per unit of cost.
4. Weigh costs and benefits for each alternative against the universal and selective criteria.
5. Recommend an alternative that maximizes the criteria, or offer a range of alternatives that would maximize different values in different ways.

The Incremental Model[3]

1. Calculate the marginal benefits of current choices for dealing with the problem.
2. Initiate small choices toward a solution that would achieve measurable results.
3. Accelerate the choices that produce positive results; decelerate choices that produce negative results.
4. The combination of choices that work becomes the policy.

(left margin, vertical: Pure social science research — Policy implementation)

---

1. Herbert Simon, "A Behavorial Model of Rational Choice," in *The Making of Decisions*, ed. William Gore and J. W. Dyson (Glencoe, Ill: Free Press, 1964), 124–126.

2. Developed from the policy analysis model of the University of North Carolina Bush Institute. See James Gallagher and Ron Haskins, *Policy Analysis* (New York: Ablex Press, 1984), 87.

3. Charles Lindblom, "The Science of Muddling Through," in Gore and Dyson, *Making of Decisions*, 84–90.

the alternatives would capture all the normative definitions of the problem. In the behavioral model, however, the more extensively the problem is defined, the more likely the right solution to it can be found.

Projecting the Likelihood of Achieving Each Alternative Set   Projecting the viability of alternatives requires developing something like a hypothesis that can be tested to establish which alternative set is most likely to resolve the problem. The analyst must project, for example, the extent to which hunger might be reduced if families were given $200 a month in food stamps, if undernourished individuals were given $75 in food stamps each, and so on. Proposing which alternatives are most likely to alleviate a problem requires information (data) and a method to examine it (analysis). Information would be necessary, for instance, to determine how much of what kind of food is essential, and how much the food costs; one would also need to know how many individuals or families would be involved, depending on which alternative was chosen.

Because this phase of policy analysis requires a considerable amount of social science data, how much of what kind of data becomes an important consideration. The analyst must become familiar with the "policy sectors" that are relevant to the problem. To determine whether food stamps will assist in reducing hunger, for instance, the analyst must know something about food and nutrition as well as money management. Without substantive knowledge of the policy sectors involved, the analyst might consult data that are irrelevant and come to a false conclusion about the potential usefulness of the alternative under scrutiny. In 1967, for example, largely at the insistence of Senator Herman Talmadge (D-GA), the AFDC program was amended first to permit, then to require, that welfare recipients work when they were able. Although the Talmadge Amendment to the Social Security Act was considered by Congress for its marginal value, the analysis of the proposal focused on the impact of the proposed alternative—whether requiring work reduced the need for welfare. The analysis did not, however, consider relevant information about work. Data about the employability, health, literacy, and work skills of AFDC recipients were not considered. As a result, the Work Incentive (WIN) program, as this initiative was called, failed miserably to encourage welfare recipients to work, and failed, as well, to achieve its marginal goal of reducing welfare caseloads. This same scenario was repeated when Congress created its 1988 welfare reform, the JOBS program. The behavioral model was used for policy analysis, suggesting that JOBS was not the best way to "reform" welfare. But Congress chose the JOBS alternative anyway.

Establishing a Cost-Benefit Ratio and Calculating the Benefit   The data appropriate to each alternative set are examined in order to establish a cost-benefit ratio, and the benefit is calculated in relation to implementation feasibility. The objective in these two stages of policy analysis is to arrive at some practical ordering of alternatives, from the best to the worst. To achieve this ordering, the costs of each alternative are projected against the benefits the alternative would provide. The first phase in this process requires establishing some cost-benefit ratio. For example, after considerable research the analyst may determine that it costs, on average, a certain amount per year to keep a child adequately fed. Other data are then weighed to project the benefits resulting from such an expenditure; the analyst may discover that adequate nutrition has been shown to reduce the risk of several serious health problems, both during childhood and in later life. These benefits might be judged not only worthwhile for the child, but also as a savings in later welfare costs. On these terms a ratio of cost to benefit is established.

The term *cost-benefit* implies a ratio with cost as the numerator, benefit the denominator. Strictly speaking, the lower the cost-benefit ratio, the better. All other things being equal, it seems clear that a ratio of 1 to 5 would provide benefits more cost efficiently than a ratio of 1 to 2. Once a cost-benefit ratio is established for each alternative, the analyst begins to consider the feasibility of implementation. Providing $200 in food stamps to every poor family might be calculated to cost $2 billion and result in improving diets up to the minimum nutritionally acceptable level, as determined by an earlier analysis. Another alternative, providing food stamp supplements up to the poverty level for pregnant women, might be calculated to cost only $1 billion. The supplement given to pregnant women would reach only about 10% of the people with nutritional needs. Nevertheless, good nutrition is extremely important for those women, because undernourished women are likely to have low-birth-weight babies who will be vulnerable to serious medical problems. Moreover, because of budget restrictions (a common issue in implementation) it may be more feasible to implement this second alternative set than the first, even though from a cost-benefit perspective the first one is more desirable. (Note that both alternatives represent tacit agreement on a number of normative issues about the problem.)

Data Analysis   The behavioral model is deceptively simple. By the time the final phase of analysis is completed, all the alternative sets might be ordered as presented schematically in Table 4.3. Once the alternatives are stated and the data are examined to determine which alternative sets best meet the conditions of a problem, a best alternative is apparent. Table 4.3 shows alternative sets ranked from A (high feasibility, high cost-benefit ratio), downward to P (low feasibility, low cost-benefit). This is a schematic representation; in actual analysis the matrix might run to many more slots than 16, or to many fewer, and cover more or fewer gradations from high to low.

It is in the later phases of analysis that the behavioral model begins to raise perplexing questions. Examining alternatives in terms of their relative costs indirectly introduces values into the analysis. Benefits are often projected in terms of human goods (such as adequate amounts of food), whereas costs are calculated in dollars. Simon himself recognized this dilemma: "The classical theory does not tolerate the incompatibility of apples and oranges." [11] In other words, it is probably impossible to place a dollar value on the benefits of an adequate diet or any other human good, even though it may be possible to add up how much it would cost to provide it. Assessing costs in dollar terms and benefits in some value context may not yield a true cost-benefit ratio. If, for example, poor people do not know the basics of good nutrition and consequently do not use food stamps to buy food appropriately, the real costs of the policy may well be much higher than its estimated dollar cost.

Presenting Alternatives to Policymakers   The final action in the behavioral model is to see that this amassed information is given to the particular decision makers who have requested it in a form that they will be able to use conveniently and meaningfully. The policy analyst does not make a recommendation,

TABLE 4.3 | A RANKED ORDERING OF ALTERNATIVE SETS A-P AS DETERMINED BY THE BEHAVIORAL MODEL OF POLICY ANALYSIS

Feasibility	Cost-Benefit Ratio			
	High	Medium	Medium	Low
High	A	B	C	D
Medium	E	F	G	H
Medium	I	J	K	L
Low	M	N	O	P

as such, because the model assumes that the best alternative has become evident through the analysis, that clear evidence will have emerged that a single alternative will best resolve the problem. In Table 4.3, this choice would be alternative set A.

Despite the widespread use of this model of policy analysis, its effectiveness is limited by its highly theoretical orientation. In theory all situations must be identified and explained if one is to be able to discover the best solution. In practice this course is never followed, and even Herbert Simon, the person most closely associated with this model of policy analysis, was obliged to offer a major compromise in the model for the sake of applicability. According to Simon: "In most global models of rational choice, all alternatives are evaluated before a choice is made. In actual human decision-making, alternatives are often examined sequentially [and] when alternatives are examined sequentially, we may regard the first satisfactory alternative that is evaluated as such as the one actually selected." [12]

Simon suggested further modification to the model by contrasting "feasibility" with "optimality":

> In theory and practice the distinction is commonly drawn between computations to determine the feasibility of a program and the optimal program. An optimal program is one of the feasible programs which maximizes a greater pay-off function. If, instead of requiring that the pay-off be maximized, we require only that the pay-off exceed some given amount, then one can find a policy . . . by methods of feasibility testing. . . . For all practical purposes, this procedure may represent a sufficient approach to optimization, provided the minimum required payoff can be set reasonably." [13]

But if there is no unique "best" alternative in practice, how can one be sure that the best alternative produced by the analysis is really better than other alternatives that may be presented? Simon calls this uncertainty "limited rationality," and given uncertainty, the model loses much of its authority. Because there may be no such thing as a unique best alternative, the policymaker is free to choose among alternatives and argue that one is the "best" in that it is most feasible, so long as it meets the minimum payoff level. Hence values that were not formally considered in the model may end up determining the best alternative, and the analysis itself may lose some of the authority it purports to add to the decision process.

If the analyst who uses this model lacks strong authority from the strength of the analysis itself to assure the policymaker that the alternative set A (as in Table 4.3) is the best alternative, the best policy choice may really be F, G, J, or K. Because the model is designed to be value-neutral, there is no way to consider directly the normative orientation of the problem or the normative issues inherent in the possible alternative solutions. And because there probably is no such thing as a value-neutral problem or solution, if this rational model cannot reveal a clear best solution for the problem presented, the decision maker ultimately will be apt to evaluate the alternatives offered by the model in terms of his or her own values.

Despite these major drawbacks, the behavioral model is an extremely important tool of policy analysis. It generates a considerable amount of factual information, and it orders this information into systematic clusters that permit the analyst and the decision maker to see clearly the outlines of a problem. Moreover, the essential elements of the model, such as data collection and examination, are frequently used in all policy analysis activities; in this way, the behavioral, or rational, model provides a prototype for all policy analysis work. Regardless of the organization in which analysis takes place, elements of this model are likely to be useful, and facility with the model will help the analyst irrespective of the kinds of analytic products that are expected.

The Incremental Model

The incremental model emphasizes the marginal considerations of the policy problem and its alternatives. It represents the opposite end of the policy analysis continuum from the behavioral model, not so much because of the limited way in which it uses social science information, but because it seems to begin with the solution rather than the problem. It is called the incremental model because, in contrast with the behavioral model, it identifies and certifies small increments of policy choices until the right combination is found, the problem is satisfied, and the result becomes the policy.

"Marginal values" is one of the key phrases in understanding the incremental model. Although "marginal values" implies the values are unimportant, the phrase is not used in this way. The phrase is imported from social science research and applied to policy analysis to explain how incremental policy analysis is undertaken. Often social science data are analyzed by looking first at the totals or subtotals of data before looking at the individual data themselves. This use of "marginality" is common when talking about taxes—for example, when referring to "marginal tax rates." Or when speaking about economic issues, someone may refer to "marginal economic benefits." The idea, then, behind the use of the phrase "marginal values" is not that such values are unimportant, but that they represent a summarized form of values. Marginal values in the incremental policy analysis model represent a summary, or partial summary, of sets of values, rather than individual, single values that are under consideration.

The incremental model is most commonly associated with Charles Lindblom, who has called its process "the science of muddling through." [14] Like a number of policy analysts, Lindblom distinguishes between social science research and policy analysis. In fact, he and his colleague David Cohen have argued that social science research sometimes gets in the way of policy analysis: "Information and analysis provide only one route [to policymaking], because a great deal of the world's problem solving is and ought to be accomplished through various forms of social interaction that substitute action for thought, understanding, or analysis." [15]

The distinction between the positions represented by the behavioral and incremental models is important. Because policy analysis has formed such a close alliance with social science research, many analysts tend to reject the incremental model as not sufficiently scientific to be worthy of serious consideration. Lindblom and Cohen have confronted this criticism with an apt rejoinder:

> Policy-makers attack specific problems in light of a general framework or perspective that controls both explanatory hypotheses and a range of solutions that they are willing to consider. . . . [For example,] it appears that policy-makers [once] share[d] a framework of . . . academic psychology. They subsequently abandoned it only to take up in its place another that is represented by academic sociology. . . . Hence, even if policy-makers do not turn to [social science knowledge] in many of the ordinarily expected ways, for specific data, evidence, or policy evaluation, they may take the whole organizing framework for their work from the academic social sciences. [16]

Calculating the Marginal Benefits of Known Choices   Investigating choices that are already known may seem to be a contradictory point for beginning a policy analysis. Yet the incremental model deliberately begins with alternatives that appear to be available for resolving the problem at hand and lets comprehensive problem definition rest until these alternatives have been explored. This means that the alternatives under consideration are usually modest and limited, as the full scope of the problem and all its ramifications have not yet been made clear. The incremental model begins this way because of its normative orientation toward problems and their solutions. It assumes that the normative configuration of the problem as a whole is really a representation of a variety of "marginal values" that are difficult to unscramble (a subject discussed in Chapter 1). Lindblom argues that, paradoxically, the only practicable way to disclose relevant marginal values, even to oneself, is to describe the policy one chooses to achieve them.

It is important to recognize that marginal values are not unimportant values. For example, in both WIN, JOBS, and TANF welfare reform policies mentioned earlier, getting people off welfare was the central value in each policy. There were other values policymakers expressed, such as "getting tough" with welfare recipients, as well as providing adequate amounts for public assistance and providing work training. These were important values, even though they were not examined in the policy analysis process. These marginal values represent the starting point of the incremental policy analysis process because, the model argues, most people understand "the problem" through their own value lens, rather than in some "objective" way.

Marginality dominates the incremental model, and it is important to understand the idea behind it. As mentioned earlier in this chapter, values are an inherent part of policymaking, and many of the most influential values at work in any policymaking process are not those specifically acknowledged in the policy, but other values, personal and more general, that arise from or become attached to the policy as it develops, as a kind of "fallout." Accommodating these marginal values, absorbing the useful ones and sidestepping the troublesome ones, enables the policymaking process to move forward practically. Table 4.4 is a schematic representation of how an analyst might perceive the incremental process and proceed through it.

Suppose that "the problem" is generally stated as poverty, and suppose that improved nutrition is a policy goal or objective. This total concept is signified at the lower right of the table as the sum of several alternative objectives (here simplified as alternatives W + X + Y + Z, not ranked, unlike alternative sets A–P shown in Table 4.3). The combined alternatives (W + X + Y + Z) represent marginal values, but which are the most important in each case is not yet known. As the incremental process moves forward, these values and their relative importance can be gradually defined. To begin with, however, the analyst may assume a hypothetical weight for the sum of all of them and set it down as a numerical score in the lower right corner, along with the total cumulation of alternatives (in the table this total sum of marginal values has arbitrarily been set as 16). When the four alternative sets are broken down into paired sets (W + X, Y + Z; and W + Y, X+ Z), as shown in the right-hand column and bottom row of the table, these permutations likewise sum to 16, although it is not yet clear exactly how. In other words, in whatever order the alternatives are pursued, the ultimate result will represent the maximized values.

Note that the matrix in which the individual alternative sets W, X, Y, and Z are laid out resembles that for Table 4.3, a scheme for ranking alternatives in terms of cost-benefit ratio and feasibility. (Like the matrix for that model, this matrix too could be expanded to incorporate more alternative sets and more gradations from "high" to "low," depending on the needs of the analysis.) If the analysis were to proceed according to the behavioral model, as in Table 4.3, alternative set W would be the obvious best choice. However, the incremental approach may begin at any point, probably with one alternative set, but perhaps with two or more, and then go on, adding new alternatives, perhaps dropping an alternative that did not work. As experience accrues, the analyst can begin to assign relative weights to the marginal values associated with the alternatives. These can be adjusted to greater or lesser scores as the picture becomes clearer. The emphasis given to the alternatives associated with these values could be adjusted accordingly.

TABLE 4.4 | MARGINALITY IN THE INCREMENTAL MODEL OF POLICY ANALYSIS, BEGINNING PHASE (NUMERICAL SCORES FOR MARGINAL VALUES AS YET INDETERMINATE, BUT TOTAL 16)

Feasibility	Cost-Benefit Ratio		Cumulative Marginal Values
	High	Low	
High	W	X	W + X
	(?)	(?)	(8? + 10?)
			(Constituency support)
Low	Y	Z	Y + Z
	(?)	(?)	(8? + 6?)
			(Little support)
Cumulative	W + Y	X + Z	W + X + Y + Z
marginal	(8? + 10?)	(8? + 6?)	(16)
values			(Reducing poverty)

Note: The number 16 represents the desired goal, reducing poverty. The goal is a combination of policy choices (represented by W, X, Y, and Z) that is presently unknown. Because we want to reach a final goal of 16, we need to go through a process of trial and error to see which combinations produce the best results. W + X, for example, may represent strong constituency support, W to reduce welfare payments, X for food for children. W + Y may represent good cost-benefit ratios, W to reduce welfare payments, Y for good child nutrition. Different marginal values are "tried out," as represented by the numerical values designated by question marks.

Initiating Small Changes That Affirm the Choices That Achieve Marginal Benefits For most people the incremental model seems like working backward from the solution to the problem. The analyst becomes engaged in efforts to discover a combination of values (or choices) that will achieve the overall goal (W + X + Y + Z). More than any other, this phase of the model requires considerable skill on the part of the analyst to keep the analysis from becoming simply a trial-and-error exercise. In order to pinpoint and implement the choices that do clarify what it takes to achieve the policy goal, the analyst must know about (a) values, or normative positions reflected in or by the alternatives; (b) the substantive elements of the policy itself (the subject matter); and (c) information and data relevant to understanding how the small changes might operate.

The values inherent in normative orientations to problems and potential solutions are a focal point of the model. In fact, the whole model is concerned with values:

> Suppose an administrator is given responsibility for formulating policy with respect to inflation. He might start by trying to list all related values in order of importance, e.g., full employment, reasonable business profit, protection of savings, preventing

a stock market crash. Then all the possible policy outcomes could be rated as more or less efficient in attaining a maximum of these values. This would, of course, require a careful inquiry into values held by members of society and an equally prodigious set of calculations on how much of each value is equal to how much of each other value.[17]

The analyst must be able to identify and account for the values represented by the alternatives, even though it may not be possible to calculate how they relate to each other. This requires facility with the policy sector under consideration. A history of how present policy has developed, including an assessment of which kinds of problems have been important to which people, will shed considerable light on the normative issues involved. For example, the proper treatment of mental illness is a long-standing mental health problem. A history of mental health policy reveals that there has been a consistent tension between two basic solutions to the problem: treating patients in mental hospitals and treating them outside formal institutions in social centers in their own communities, a strategy that originated in Dorothea Dix's work in the 1850s. Drug treatment, mental health clinics, halfway houses, and many other community-based mental health policies that have evolved over the years all reflect values based in deinstitutionalized care. Thus it is safe to assume that any acceptable mental health alternative would have to include some attention to deinstitutionalization in order to gain any public acceptance.

To assist initiation of small, marginal choices, the policy analyst needs substantive knowledge of the policy field. An analyst who uses the behavioral model may learn about the policy environment while engaged in problem definition, but the analyst who uses the incremental model requires an explanation of the makeup of the problem when he or she begins operating within the specific policy field. Without substantial preliminary knowledge, the analyst would be unable to suggest which choices would or would not maximize benefits, and the whole incremental process would deteriorate into a meaningless trial-and error process.

Finally, data are essential to the initiation of small steps that affirm the policy choice. The analyst simply must have some knowledge of the status of the people who will be affected by the policy, and of how they will be affected. In particular, the analyst must discover which policy choices would combine values for different groups of people. For example, efforts to release the currently hospitalized mentally ill may place a heavy strain on local community resources for housing and other life management activities; on the other hand, developing mental health services in community-based agencies may not tax federal resources as heavily. Information about the people who are particularly affected by a policy is necessary to understand how small marginal choices might connect and produce an overall policy. For example, if most people in a community's mental hospitals are more than 65 years old and have no family ties, a policy emphasis on deinstitutionalization would yield very different results than if these patients were mostly working-age males with prolonged stress reactions from prior military service.

Accelerating the Choices That Have Produced Positive Ends and Decelerating the Negative Choices   Lindblom's orientation to policy analysis is again instructive:

> Making policy is at best a very rough process. Neither social scientists, nor politicians, nor public administrators yet know enough about the social world to avoid repeated errors in predicting the consequences of policy moves. A wise policymaker consequently expects that his policies will achieve only part of what he hopes and at the same time will [not] produce unintended consequences he would have preferred to avoid. If he proceeds, through a succession of incremental changes, he avoids serious lasting mistakes.[18]

Lindblom calls this approach one of "successive limited comparisons," because a policy is achieved in increments as small elements of it are adopted and modified to fit the circumstances. Here again, policy analysis has a more significant role than might at first appear. This is not a random, trial-and-error effort, where the analyst suggests one option, then another. Rather, successful analysis requires consistent monitoring and evaluation at each step to assess the extent to which the incremental changes do, in fact, achieve the expected results.

The policy analyst may engage in small social research projects during this part of the process to ensure that the positive choices stay on target and the negative choices are eliminated. As this phase progresses, the marginal values become clarified. In Table 4.4, which represents the process at the outset, the marginal values are left unspecified. The W + X figure could be, say, 8 or 10; the Y + Z figure could be 8 or 6; W + Y could be 8 or 10; and X + Z could be 8 or 6. Suppose (see Table 4.5) that during the adjustment process the marginal value of W + X can be pinpointed as 10. This means that the figure for Y + Z must become 6. In this manner the cumulative marginal values gradually become clarified, and in turn it becomes possible to see what weights can be attached to values associated with individual alternative sets W, X, Y, and Z. Notice, too, how the cumulative marginal values determine limits for weights of the values that can be proposed for the individual sets. In Table 4.5 the weight for either W or X cannot be greater than 10 (because W + X has an associated weight of 10), and if the score for X is 10, the values for Y will have to be scored as 0, in which case (now adding downward rather than across) the score for Z would have to be 10 as well. The scores in Table 4.5 are midrange numbers filled in to give an impression of how the cumulative choices, once determined, force the choices in the individual cells; they are not absolute numbers that would apply across the board in real applications of the model.

Suppose that the incremental combination of W + X, Y + Z seemed to be working in the right direction. Further incremental choices could be made accordingly in terms of the individual alternative sets. In the end, in the hypothetical case shown in Table 4.5, X would turn out to have the greatest weight as a single alternative set, even though it has a less advantageous cost-benefit ratio than W. Hence X would become a main thrust of policy, despite its less than "ideal" configuration in terms of the behavioral model—a not uncommon situation in public policymaking. Under the incremental model, however, the

TABLE 4.5 | MARGINALITY IN THE INCREMENTAL MODEL OF POLICY ANALYSIS, LATER PHASE (WITH POSSIBLE ARRANGEMENT OF SCORES FOR VALUES)

| Feasibility | Cost-Benefit Ratio | | Cumulative Marginal Values |
	High	Low	
High	W	X	W + X
	(4)	(6)	(10)
	(Breakfasts)	(Reduced welfare costs)	(Breakfasts or reduced welfare costs)
Low	Y	Z	Y + Z
	(2)	(4)	(6)
	(Food stamps)	(Increased welfare payments)	(Food stamps or increased welfare payments)
Cumulative marginal values	W + Y	X + Z	W + X + Y + Z
	(6)	(10)	(16)
	(Breakfast or food stamps)	(Reduce or increase welfare)	(Reducing poverty)

final policy choice becomes a product of finding the right combination of choices that maximizes marginal values.

Combination of Choices That Produces Incremental Results Consistent with the Goal Becomes the Policy   The policy becomes evident as it is put in place, gradually, piece by piece. Table 4.5 demonstrates that theoretically alternative set X would be the best policy with high feasibility and less than optimal cost-benefit ratio; W might be chosen, even though its value is less, in order to provide both high feasibility and high cost efficiency. Hence it may happen that, as with the behavioral model, ultimate choice in the incremental model may not lie with the alternative that is apparently the "best" in theory. Lindblom explains why this may be true:

> If [direct] agreement on policy as a test for best policy seems a poor substitute for testing the policy against its objectives, it ought to be remembered that objectives themselves have no ultimate validity other than [that] they are agreed upon. Hence, agreement is the best policy in both methods [the behavioral and the incremental]. . . . In an important sense, therefore, it is not irrational for an administrator to defend a policy as good without being able to specify what it is good for.[19]

The policy analyst must carefully monitor the progress of these incremental activities throughout this final stage of the incremental model. The analyst must also be able to present a clear statement of the policy; during the incremental process a number of policy elements will have been attempted, some discarded, some modified, as the final policy takes form. The ultimate policy may represent a large departure from the original position that prompted the first marginal decision. In the end, to recall our ongoing example, it may turn out that providing an adequate diet to people in poverty requires not just food stamps (in whatever way they may be allocated) but a program of education in nutrition.

The views of those affected by the problem, the views of those who make policy as well as of those who might carry it out, and the views of various groups that might have connection with the policy are all accommodated by the incremental model. The individual increments of policy choice test the strength of values inherent in different normative views of the problem against standards for policy choice such as feasibility and cost-benefit ratios. Policy choices are made marginally and are based on the strength of the values that operate; these choices are gradually adjusted to approximate an ultimate choice that meets the values and the standards demanded by the policy sector itself. And because this incremental process ensures agreement among concerned parties by the time the final policy is realized, the chosen policy by definition becomes (in Lindblom's view) the best policy. By contrast, in the behavioral model the best policy is, in theory, the policy objectively determined, even though in practice the best policy may be reached less rationally. In any event, the culmination of the behavioral model is the designation of ranked alternatives; the policy choice itself still has to be made and implemented. Policy generated under the incremental model may have superior appeal or utility because it becomes implemented as it is being made.

Consider an example from the Temporary Assistance to Needy Families program (TANF). A *behavioral* policy analysis would probably reveal that poverty among many TANF families is due to inadequate child-support payments; the resulting policy would encourage strong efforts to implement support collections. An *incremental* policy would probably reveal that unemployment among TANF mothers causes their poverty; work-training and work-placement policy would be developed from the incremental model. The work-training program would have high feasibility but high cost; it would be implemented as part of the policy analysis. The child-support collection policy, derived from a behavioral analysis, would have high feasibility and high cost, but on implementation it would probably conflict with values of various interest groups, such as non-supporting fathers. If chosen as a product of the behavioral model, it might not be implementable. Hence the ultimate policy choice of the behavioral model might, in reality, be relatively closer to that of the incremental model. This combination of "trade-offs" is exactly what underlies the drastic welfare policy changes inherent in the 1996 welfare reform (TANF). (See Chapter 5.)

Policy analysts often compare the incremental model unfavorably with the behavioral model, preferring the behavioral model for its more systematic approach to analytical tasks. The incremental model also receives negative criticism for its apparent trial-and-error approach and its emphasis on marginality. On the positive side, the incremental model manages the difficult problem of addressing values, which in most policy development are likely to be the basis for choice even when an analysis purports to be "value-neutral." And because the incremental model approximates the policy implementation, it provides significant guidance for decision makers, particularly when only small differences exist among alternatives.

For example, in 1994, Congress and President Clinton had difficulty coming to agreement on a budget—a not uncommon situation in federal government. The budget issues were many and diffuse. They basically reflected "political" (ideological) differences over spending. In 1996, however, there continued to be differences over the budget, but the issues had become narrowed and focused. Everyone was in relative agreement about acceptable alternatives, and the choices at hand did not represent major ideological differences. All parties agreed that the deficit should be reduced, and that Social Security benefits should be protected. The disagreements were over the degree of choice, not the choices themselves. Review of additional data may have given greater clarity to the issues, but it was only by small changes, represented by shifts in value positions over how much to control which areas, that enough agreement was reached to achieve a budget.

Criteria-Based Model

If the behavioral model and incremental model of policy analysis represent opposite ends of a continuum, the criteria-based model marks a midpoint. This model offers the analyst both a full consideration of possible alternatives and, at the same time, engagement with dominant value positions. The model is developed from the methods of policy analysis used by the Congressional Budget Office and refined by the Institute for the Study of Child and Family Policy at the University of North Carolina during the 1980s. (See Table 4.6.)

Defining the Problem with Respect to Available Policy Alternatives   Like the incremental model, but unlike the behavioral model, the criteria-based model begins with a limited range of analysis. The problem-definition stage is concerned only with available alternatives for resolving the problem, rather than all alternatives that are theoretically possible. Framing the problem in this way may limit problem definition, but the procedure quickly brings into focus the problem's normative orientation and channels consideration toward those elements of the problem that seem possible to resolve. For example, only about 40% of all children living in single-parent, female-headed families receive the mandated amount of child support from their absent fathers. Consequently, many such children are poor. Theoretically, an unrestricted definition of this problem might lead to consideration of such alternatives as limits on procreation, or even infanticide. On the other hand, defining the problem at the outset in terms of tightening enforcement of court orders, improving collection mechanisms, and establishing the paternity of all children limits the way the problem is defined but sets out the major normative themes. The tightened range of alternatives focuses the problem's normative orientation. In this example (see Table 4.7) it is well known that high value is placed on an absent parent's responsibility to support his or her children.

Establishing Universal and Selective Criteria for Ordering the Alternatives
Once the normative positions in the problems are clarified by alternatives, the value positions become apparent. The model engages three types of values, universal, selective, and efficiency, in the process of analysis. These values are called criteria. Universal criteria represent value positions that should receive consideration in all problem definition and social policy analysis. Selective criteria represent value positions with particular relevance for the problem at hand. Thus, for example, to the extent that child support is defined as an issue of collecting support payments from absent parents, parental responsibility becomes one of the selective values in the policy analysis. A full configuration of criteria and possible alternatives is suggested in Table 4.7.

The analyst's knowledge about the policy environment greatly aids the successful completion of the first two stages in this analytic model. This knowledge helps suggest the alternatives that frame problem definition, and it also determines the selective criteria against which the alternatives will be analyzed. Knowledge of the policy environment also clarifies the meanings that attach to the universal criteria. For example, the universal value of personal preference has a different meaning in child-support policies than in mental health policies. In child-support policy, "personal preference" may refer to how money is obtained; in mental health policy, the term may refer to a patient's choice of whether or not to accept treatment. Thus, even though they must be considered in every analysis, universal criteria have specific connotations that must be carefully defined in relation to the particular problem at issue.

Gathering Data Gathering data is necessary to determine the costs, benefits, and feasibility associated with each alternative. This data gathering proceeds along the lines of the behavioral model. But in contrast to the behavioral model, where all subsets of each alternative are examined, analysis in the criteria-based model examines only the data that are relevant to each criterion. For example, in the first column of Table 4.7, the cost of increasing welfare benefits to unsupported children and the feasibility of achieving that increase are examined (first item) to determine whether one proposal would promote one value (criterion) of equal treatment for affected parties, "horizontal equity." The number of unsupported children might be counted, and the amount of dollars to provide them with at least a poverty level of living would be projected. The resulting information would determine whether the alternative (increased welfare payments) could be expected to maximize the value (equal treatment). A similar set of data would be collected and examined for all the criteria under each of the alternatives.

Weighing Costs and Benefits of Each Alternative Against the Criteria The cumulative results of this analysis give a comparative view of the extent to which a particular alternative would maximize all or some of the criteria. For example, in Table 4.7, data may indicate that increased welfare payments would be a very efficient but not very equitable way of improving child support; in contrast, improving child-support collections might enhance parental responsibility but be less efficient in providing funds to unsupported children.

TABLE 4.6

TABLE 4.6 | AN EXAMPLE OF THE CONGRESSIONAL BUDGET OFFICE'S CRITERIA-BASED POLICY ANALYSIS MODEL

Selected Characteristics of Recipient Households in Current Major Housing Assistance Programs, 1977[1]

Household Characteristics	Section 8 New Construction Substantial Rehab.	Section 8 Existing Housing	Public Housing	Section 235 Original Program	Section 235 Revised Program	Section 236	Rent Supplements
Average family income[2]	$4,376	$3,506	$3,691	$8,085	$11,532	$6,285	$3,544
Annual family income (as % of all households)							
Below $3,000	27.7	37.3	35.4	NA	NA	NA	NA
$3,000 to $4,999	39.0	38.6	32.6	NA	NA	NA	NA
$5,000 to $6,999	21.6	16.0	15.4	NA	NA	NA	NA
$7,000 to $9,999	10.0	7.0	9.6	NA	NA	NA	NA
Above $10,000	1.7	1.0	6.9	NA	NA	NA	NA

Percent of all households with some welfare income	16.2	26.7	42.6	NA	NA	NA	NA
Percent with minority head	27.7	29.8	62.9	NA	23.0	NA	NA
Percent of elderly head	42.9	33.4	35.8	NA	2.1	26.0	31.0
Percent with handicapped member	2.0	2.3	1.2	NA	NA	NA	NA
Household size (as percent of all households)							
Single person	43.1	36.0	33.3	NA	NA	NA	NA
2–4 persons	50.9	53.3	45.2	NA	NA	NA	NA
5–6 persons	5.4	8.4	14.6	NA	NA	NA	NA
7 or more persons	0.6	2.3	6.9	NA	NA	NA	NA

Source: U.S. Congress, Congressional Budget Office, "Alternate Approaches for Housing the Poor" (Washington, D.C., 1978), 87.

[1] Data for Section 8 are as of June 1977; data for public housing, the original Section 235 program, and rent supplements are as of September 1977; data for the revised Section 235 program are as of December 1977.

[2] Figure reported is the mean family income for the original Section 235 program, Section 236, and rent supplements. Median family income is reported for Section 8, public housing, and the revised Section 235 program.

TABLE 4.7 | THE CRITERIA-BASED MODEL

Policy Criteria	Selected Policy Alternatives			
	Increase Welfare Payment	Collect More Child Support	Establish Paternity	Incarcerate Nonsupporting Fathers
Universal criteria				
Equity				
Horizontal	low	high	high	high
Vertical	high	high		medium
Efficiency criteria				
Nonstigmatizing	high	medium	low	low
Personal preferences	low	medium	varies	low
			varies	low
Selective criteria				
Parental responsibility	low	high	high	high
Adequacy of funds	medium	high	high	high
Ranking (1 = highest)	2	1	4	3

High: alternative maximizes this value

Low: alternative minimizes this value

Medium: alternative neither maximizes nor minimizes this value

Varies: impact varies among population subgroups

Table 4.7 permits the use of a weighing system that could provide marginal totals for policy decision-makers: a high, low, medium, or variable weight is assigned to each criterion under each alternative, as determined by the analysis. Or, as the Congressional Budget Office frequently does, dollar amounts could be placed in the cells, weighing the alternatives against the actual costs of alternatives.

Recommending the Alternative That Maximizes the Criteria The criteria-based model permits the analyst to point out which alternative maximizes the greatest number of values; it also allows the analyst the option of presenting several alternatives that variously maximize the values that the decision maker favors. For example, in Table 4.7 the analyst may point out that if the policy-maker wants to apply a particular criterion (that is, maximize a particular value), a particular alternative could be selected. In this way the policymaker can review several possible alternatives in terms of both cost-benefit relation-ships and value-maximizing positions.

The criteria-based model represents something of a compromise between the behavioral and incremental models with respect to both problem definition and value management. Using criteria (values) to limit the examination of al-ternatives is consistent with a normative examination of problems and their consequences. The model also allows decision makers to see clearly the costs, benefits, and feasibility of maximizing particular values. Thus a policymaker has a good picture of the consequences of a particular choice, but the choice it-self is not directed by the analysis. This feature circumvents the problem of fric-tion that often develops between analyst and policymaker when the behavioral model is used as an analytic tool, friction that is often resolved in the applica-tion of the incremental model by giving very limited authority to the analyst.

The criteria-based model also encourages decision makers to examine their own biases about alternatives and to review a number of alternatives that might more effectively maximize their values. For example, some policymakers might insist that putting parents in jail is the only way to resolve the problem of non-support. But Table 4.7 shows that this alternative has very weak potential for dealing with the fundamental issues of child support. If, however, the policy-maker continues to insist that parental responsibility only comes about by in-carcerating parents (a value position), the policymaker can still maximize this value (responsibility) and choose an alternative that has better potential for dealing with the problem, such as improving child-support collections.

The criteria-based model further makes it possible to focus the analysis, de-pending on the intergovernmental framework for policy implementation. As pointed out in Chapter 3, categorical grants and block grants differ consider-ably with respect to the conditions that influence how they are carried out. Categorical grants are more tightly targeted, while block grants provide greater implementation discretion. The criteria-based model offers the opportunity to consider implementation differences by specifying the extent to which policy will be analyzed with a focus on universal criteria, efficiency criteria, or policy-specific criteria, as policies implemented categorically are more sensitive to ef-fectiveness outcomes. Block grants, on the other hand, suggest a greater empha-sis on efficiency criteria, as policies carried out under block-grant authority are more sensitive to efficiency issues, such as getting the job done quickly for the least cost.

SUMMARY

The three methods of policy analysis and the methods of social research inter-sect frequently, but they are different activities used for different purposes. The models in some ways represent a summary of the many theories of policy analy-sis presently under development. To operationalize the policy analysis process, it is necessary to include a few factors that influence the information that is available to use in the models.

INFORMATION AND DATA FOR ANALYSIS

Chapters 2 and 3 discussed the range of the policymaking processes and suggested that tasks of analysis differ depending on where information is requested within the process. To the extent that the three models described provide different kinds of information, the analyst may find it useful to apply different models in different policymaking settings. For example, the incremental model is well suited for policy analysis work in legislatures; the criteria-based model is more useful when administrative agencies are asked to make policy that takes the form of regulations.

Determining the Kind of Information That Will Be Used

Determining the kind of information that will be used in the analysis becomes clearer as the policy activities are identified. Sometimes, particularly when an analyst is working with the behavioral model, new information must be developed because existing information about the variables is inadequate. In most cases, however, policy analysis uses existing information. Gathering and using this information is discussed in detail below. Knowledge of the policy area under consideration is critical in choosing the kind of information needed for the analysis.

When Necessary Information Exists

Aggregate data are among the richest sources of information but among the most difficult to use. The best and most familiar aggregate data are those collected by the U.S. Bureau of the Census. What is now known as the Department of Commerce was one of the original administrative departments in the fledgling American government, and it conducted the first national census in 1790. This and subsequent censuses were required by the U.S. Constitution as an enumeration of citizens for the purpose of apportioning the seats in the U.S. House of Representatives according to the state population.

The idea of compiling social statistics began with Herbert Spencer (1820–1903). In his highly influential work *Social Statistics* (1850), he envisioned amassing all sources of social knowledge together under a single authority. Influenced by the growing interest in social information, the decennial census enumeration began to collect more elaborate demographic information, and in 1878 the Bureau of the Census published the first *Statistical Abstract of the United States*. This document, now published at regular intervals, provides standard summaries of demographic and statistical data and various forms of social and economic information from several hundred reporting sources.

The censuses, along with a wide range of other sources of aggregate data, offer a vast source of information that is extremely helpful for policy analysis. Somewhat in contrast to survey data, which provide information on particular cases, these aggregate data bring together distinct elements into a general picture in which the individual case can no longer be found. For example, distinct personal characteristics, such as age, race, and gender may be brought together into a whole that describes all persons in poverty, but a single poor individual may be quite different from the general picture of impoverished persons represented by this whole. Thus, although aggregate data by themselves or in coordination with other aggregates may contain extensive information that far exceeds that obtainable by other information-gathering techniques, they may not always define a specific problem accurately, and consequently they are difficult to use.

Because they represent a total picture, built upon a synthesis of numerous distinct elements, aggregate data may not provide sufficient detail for developing adequate policy alternatives. For example, although aggregate data on poverty give a picture that poverty is concentrated among children in single-parent, female-headed households, many poor children live in two-parent families. Many old people are poor, too, and many working adults of both genders are poor. Thus the aggregate picture often has to be broken down into its respective parts, to be "disaggregated," in order to be more useful. Disaggregation may be difficult or impossible because of the way the data were originally collected. The original collection design may not have distinguished, for instance, between working and nonworking families, so that backtracking for that purpose is futile.

Because so many aggregate data exist on so many subjects, several sets of aggregate data can often be used together in a policy analysis. For example, data on poverty and data on employment may be used together to provide more detailed information about children and poverty. Beyond the most elementary comparisons, however, combining data sets may be difficult, because similar elements in the data sets are usually not truly comparable. For example, data on poverty may count persons under age 18 as children, whereas data on employment may count persons 16 years and older as adults in the labor force. To use these two sets of data reliably in a close comparison, they would have to be broken down and reconstituted in some way that dealt with the 16- to 18-year-old age group consistently. This might not be possible if the data were not originally collected by distinctive (one- or two-year) age groupings that could be retabulated.

The problems involved in using these aggregate data may explain, in part, why these data are infrequently used in policy analysis. Data generated by the Bureau of the Census are used extensively, but secondary analysis of the many other data sets that exist is uncommon. Rather than disaggregating such data, policy analysts and other researchers often prefer instead to develop information that is specific to the problem at hand. They are usually very generous in sharing this new information as it accumulates. The Institute for Research in Social Science at the University of North Carolina, Chapel Hill, like similar centers at most major research universities, has more than 500 public-use data sets as part of its holdings, and through a consortium of academic institutions it can obtain electronic access to many other such collections. The Bureau of the Census itself lists more than 700 sources of aggregate data routinely collected by governmental agencies. Because of the unusual and presently untapped potential that aggregate data have for policy analysis, special attention is given to the use of secondary analysis in a later section of this chapter.

Social indicators provide another form of information useful in policy analysis work. The idea of social indicators was developed during the 1960s as a way of providing social planning information, much as economic indicators—developed by the Council of Economic Advisors—had already been developed to provide economic information as a means of monitoring the nation's economic activity. The idea was drafted into a useful form in 1966 by Mancur Olson, who served as deputy assistant secretary for social indicators in the Office of Planning and Evaluation of the Department of Health, Education, and Welfare. These early social indicators were designed explicitly for policymakers, to lend greater visibility to pressing social problems and to provide insights about the accomplishments of various public programs. The first systematic effort to use social indicators in policy analysis, which appeared in 1969, stated its purpose in part: "Social reporting cannot make the hard choices the nation must make any easier, but ultimately it can help insure that they are not made in ignorance of the nation's needs." [20] Social indicators were originally proposed as a standardized database of information pertinent to specific policy subjects. For example, social indicators might be developed for national health and include data about births, deaths, illnesses, time lost from work, and personal health practices such as doctor visits. These data could then be examined to reflect the status of the nation's health at a particular point in time, either as a whole or on particular issues. Later the same indicators could be reviewed, and changes in the nation's health status could be determined.

Most early advocates for the use of social indicators argued that such information also could be used to evaluate programs, on the assumption that social programs would and should affect the problem that was first measured by the set of indicators. For example, it was assumed that an expanded Medicare program would influence the health status of older people, with results that could be measured by health indicators over time.

Because social indicators were proposed as a means of monitoring changes in social conditions that were influenced by the existence of various public programs, they became a popular source of information for policy analysis work. Policy analysts of the 1970s suggested that by demonstrating changes already induced by various programs, a form of program evaluation, this type of review could lead to recommendations on policy for further changes or for different kinds of programs. However, social indicators have not been able to continue to provide the kind of information that is generally useful in policy analysis. Although there is certainly a relationship between public programs, public policy, and social conditions, the exact relationship is not clear, and the associations may not be exactly the same in all situations.

While the Department of Health and Human Services (DHHS) was struggling with various welfare reform options during the early 1990s, a new interest in social indicators emerged, and Congress created the Welfare Indicators Act of 1994 (PL 103-432). Under this act, the DHHS is required to develop social indicators that measure the extent of welfare dependency and economic dependency for the purpose of predicting future welfare dependency and recommending how dependency can be reduced. Over 70 indicators have been created that show welfare dependency trends, generally, and specifically in three social program areas, while over 20 indicators are used to predict the future dependency on these programs. The welfare programs subject to this analysis are TANF, SSI, and Food Stamps. (See Chapter 5.)[21]

Deciding which data should be used to establish the indicators is also an imprecise activity. When the normative elements of a particular social condition are recognized, the development of viable social indicators is made more difficult by the necessity of accounting for value positions along with factual data.[22] Hence social indicators may provide useful information for policy analysts, but their development and application may be too complex for direct application in most forms of policy analysis.

Experiments and demonstrations, when used as part of social science, provide important ways of obtaining very reliable information, but often at high costs. Much information has accrued in recent decades from many small-scale social experiments. To obtain useful information for policy analysis, however, experiments and demonstrations would often have to be conducted on a scale that is costly and thus difficult to implement. Because policy decisions affect large populations, experiments and demonstrations designed for direct use in policy analysis might require the collection and assimilation of huge amounts of information. Secondary analysis, that is, reanalysis of information obtained by prior experiments and demonstrations, both those conducted for policy analysis and those done for strictly scientific purposes, considerably expands the use of these data for a variety of policy analysis work.

Demonstrations are usually applications of specific research techniques to specific groups or geographic populations, without attempts to control for any exogenous outside factors. They are designed to field-test policy options, to determine how far these options may actually resolve certain problems, with an eye toward showing how something can be done. Because circumstances vary from place to place, demonstrations usually have limited applications. They do, however, generate information that policy analysts may find useful for fine-tuning programs after basic policy decisions have been made. They can be very useful aids to the incremental model of policy analysis.

Experiments, on the other hand, test policy applications in controlled environments. They are designed to generate information that can show whether hypotheses or assumptions about causative factors can be verified. Because the innumerable social factors that impinge on policy problems are so difficult to identify completely, much less to control, most social experiments are forced to restrict the scope of their explorative activities. Unrestricted social experiments are extremely costly and time consuming. For example, a series of guaranteed-income experiments that was initiated in 1963 in two experimental cities in New Jersey and Pennsylvania required additional control groups in two North Carolina counties. Collecting and preparing the information obtained from the experiments in a form that could be useful to policy analysts took nearly five years. Follow-up studies designed to confirm elements of the initial experiments were conducted ten years later (1973) in Seattle and Denver. Even though the policy questions that provoked these experiments have long since been settled, these data provide a source for further study.

Demonstrations and, especially, experiments have had only modest use in policy analysis, and some social researchers believe that this form of information gathering may even inhibit policy choices. It has been observed that "none of the innovative social programs [tested by social experiments between 1968 and 1975] has yet been implemented although at least preliminary results from all these studies have been available for some time."[23] Costs, time factors, and difficulty of translating findings into useful policy may explain partly such reservations about social experiments. Some of the incompatibilities between social research and policy analysis, as discussed in Chapter 2, may also explain the limitations of experimental information in policy research.

Nevertheless, at least 36 large-scale social experiments were conducted between 1965 and 1985, at an estimated cost of more than $1 billion. These experiments have generated considerable data on important policy issues.[24] With careful secondary analysis, those data could have long-range usefulness to policy analysis, even though their use has been modest to date.

When Necessary Information Does Not Exist

Surveys are the most frequently used method for gathering additional information. In their most fundamental form, surveys provide a general view of the variables under consideration. For example, a survey of housing in a community may point up the general characteristics of housing and who lives where. Surveys also can be used more selectively to gather detailed information about specific factors of a general subject. For example, more specific information about the general subject of housing conditions might be obtained by surveying certain groups of people, perhaps couples with young children, to determine how housing conditions affect them. In such cases, when surveys are used to elicit discrete information, care must be taken to define the specific focus of the survey. For example, if the survey is to cover couples with young children, the analyst must decide whether all such couples should be surveyed, or only particular kinds of couples, such as families in which both parents are employed.

Thus any survey that moves beyond collection of general information must be concerned with the selection of a smaller population, or a sample, as it is usually impossible to survey the entire population of persons involved. A sample can be thought of as a piece of the whole population, but it is more properly considered as representative of the whole. As such, it may be a general representation or a specific representation. In a general representation, the sample surveyed represents the total population with respect to the information sought; this sample would probably include all types of householders in the community. In a specific representation, the sample surveyed represents a particular part of the whole with respect to the information sought—for instance, leaseholders as opposed to homeowners, or elderly householders as opposed to younger families. Care must be taken to assure that a general representation is composed of randomly selected cases and that a specific sample is carefully controlled, or balanced, so as to include only cases that match the selected characteristics.

Surveys often involve interviewing, or person-to-person exchanges between the surveyor and individuals in the sample. Because interviewers must collect exactly the same information from everyone in the sample, they usually conduct each interview according to a standardized form or questionnaire on which information can be systematically collected for later compilation and analysis. Considerable care must be taken to prepare a questionnaire that will elicit all the necessary information; if something relevant is omitted, the entire survey may be less useful than planned, or even seriously compromised. Hence questionnaires are often pretested before interviewing officially begins, to ensure that they are adequate.

Survey information is most useful when very little is known about the subject under analysis or about some of its parts. Surveys are time consuming, however, and usually expensive. Moreover, it is essential that all contacts be made as planned. Particularly in surveys that require interviewing, response rates must be large enough to ensure that the information generated does reflect reliably the characteristics of the population under examination. Repeated follow-up efforts are often necessary to obtain the information required by the survey.

When a good deal is known about a subject, surveys may not produce enough additional information for analysis, even when narrowly focused on selected populations. Other means of information gathering may be more appropriate. Surveys are more likely to provide useful information in applications of the incremental model, in which general information about the effectiveness of small choices can help guide the policy analysis process and marginal values often are not clear in the initial phases of policy development.

Need assessments are a popular but often abused form of collecting information for policy analysis. They are based on the idea that problems are produced by deficiencies. Something essential is presumed to be lacking. By discovering that deficiency, a need assessment attempts to suggest what might be supplied and how the deficiency might be corrected, thereby eliminating the problem. The abuse of need assessments has arisen from a tendency to assume that the circumstances that define a need are causally related to whatever problem is under study. For example, poverty is often associated with the need for jobs. Clearly there is a need for jobs. But more than half the households in poverty have at least one member employed at least part-time. Thus, although jobs are needed, the lack of jobs does not necessarily cause poverty, and more jobs may not reduce poverty.

Need assessments also suffer from lack of clarity over normative issues. Perceptions of need vary from person to person, even under identical circumstances. In other words, need is a personal impression, and comparisons of need from person to person are difficult. Given this limitation, efforts to define need in aggregate forms useful to policy analysis may be fruitless. Moreover, if preset questions are used that standardize definitions of need—such as questions about whether a person is employed or employable—an additional normative element may be added, and the replies might well be too biased to be useful analytically.

Despite these limitations, need assessments may be useful, particularly when undertaken with surveys, as a way of providing added dimensions to general information collected about a problem or a population. For example, a housing survey might be enriched by extra data about what renters identify as their housing needs, in addition to the general descriptive information amassed.

The *delphi technique* was developed out of the Rand Corporation's research into the process of reaching decisions.[25] It is a technique for obtaining information from experts in a field in which information is being sought. The experts are assembled and asked to brainstorm the subject under consideration. The thoughts generated through this process of freely thinking about the subject are then collected in some written form. No thought is rejected, and the experts are encouraged to let down all barriers toward discussion, so that no possible view will be lost.

Once the thoughts are collected in a written form, an effort is made to organize them. As discussion proceeds, general categories become focused around similar thoughts, duplicate ideas are combined, meanings are clarified; specific ideas may be discussed briefly to establish their relation to the overall picture. Once the thoughts are understood better, the assembled group is asked to rank the thoughts with respect to some criterion, usually their relevance to the subject under consideration. Ranking can be done by category or by subject. Then each expert's rankings are summarized and condensed, and out of the process comes a hierarchy of statements about the subject under study. This hierarchy, with its overall ranking, then becomes the foundation of information about the subject:

The delphi technique develops information on a basis that is quite different from the information obtained, for example, by surveys. It provides a refinement of extensive information, integrated and harmonized by the experts themselves. The information thus obtained may be useful at several stages of the policymaking process, not necessarily only at the beginning.

The delphi technique is closely associated with the behavioral or rational model of policy analysis (which also has a strong history in the Rand Corporation), as both the model and the technique seek the widest possible range of views about the subject under consideration. The delphi technique is limited by the knowledge and expertise of the persons assembled. Complete information can be obtained only if that information is available somewhere among them. If those assembled do not represent the complete range of information, the conclusions reached through the delphi technique may actually misrepresent the information the analyst uses.

Although not thought of as a delphi technique, more routine consultation of experts to review a subject and provide information about it is often undertaken during policy analysis. Expert opinions not only help to clarify normative positions, as, for example, when congressional committees hear the testimony of expert witnesses, but also may provide important information about the dimensions of a problem and the likely impact of various policy choices on affected populations. Thus despite the limitations of the delphi technique for obtaining information, every model of policy analysis offers some opportunity where at least a modified version of it would be useful.

CONCLUSION

It is not necessary to demonstrate causal relationships in policy analysis. Establishing the likelihood that certain alternatives will produce certain results takes precedence over efforts to establish causal relationships. Most policy analysis accepts a "necessary but not sufficient" criterion as the standard for policy recommendations. For example, if policymakers want to improve the quality of high-school education, policy analysis may establish that it is necessary to improve the quality of teachers and teaching. But improving teaching may not be sufficient by itself to improve education, since many other factors, including out-of-school experiences, have an influence on the quality of education. Critics of a particular policy may sometimes want to establish the harsher standard of "necessary and sufficient." But even though that standard may be appropriate to some conditions of social science research, it has little usefulness in policy analysis because it would be almost impossible to achieve.[26]

The choice of a policy analysis model plays an important part in determining what kind of information is needed and how it will be analyzed. The behavioral model, for example, may call for information from experiments or demonstrations, whereas the incremental model may require surveys. Similarly, analysis of information produced under the behavioral model may require complex statistical analysis, whereas information acquired by examining secondary data sources may lend itself to more descriptive methods. The information necessary to satisfy analysis using the incremental model may rely on surveys and even the delphi technique.

A policy analysis must clarify the normative issues of a problem, isolate the important variables for study, develop the information necessary to understand how the variables operate with respect to the problem, and, finally, examine this information in such a way as to suggest meaningful policy alternatives. The entire process cannot be prescribed in advance. The numerous ambiguities, drawbacks, and dilemmas in policy analysis and decision making mentioned in these first four chapters should reinforce awareness that policy analysis is as much an art as a science.

The framework of these four chapters has been intended as a guide to the background and general processes of social policy development. By understanding how policy is analyzed, the student is able to come to a better understanding of the social welfare policies that are in place and how these policies might be modified to become more effective. The chapters that follow examine major policy subjects by discussing each in terms of the elements of the policy-making process already described.

QUESTIONS FOR DISCUSSION

1. What are unintended policy consequences and how are they likely to come about in the policy development process?
2. What are the differences between social science research and policy analysis?
3. What are the basic similarities and differences between the behavioral (or rational) policy model, the incremental model, and the criteria-based model? What are some likely applications of each?
4. What sources of information would be most useful to a policy analyst who is asked to analyze a policy that would end welfare benefits for women who give birth to children out of wedlock? Defend your answer.

POLICY ANALYSIS
APPLIED

Technical ability alone is not enough to conduct a useful policy analysis. Part I notes that understanding the particular policy sector that is the subject of the analysis is an essential part of the analysis. The chapters in Part II are designed to provide the student of social welfare policy with background information in five sectors of social welfare policy: income maintenance, health, housing, children, and older adults.

These five areas have been selected for several reasons. First, each has a national policy significance that stimulates policymaking across the full spectrum of policy decision-making. For example, housing policy has a comprehensive national policy framework, as contrasted with education policy, which has a very small national policy framework because most education policy is local policy developed within the states' educational expectations. Second, the policy areas selected for review in Part II exercise at least some policy authority over almost all social welfare policy in the nation. Depending on what is included, policies in these five sectors govern almost 90% of all public domestic spending and almost 60% of public spending at state and local levels. Thus the reach of these five policy sectors is extremely wide. Third, these five policy sectors were selected because there is considerable definition, or agreement, about their scope. Each has been the subject of public attention for many years.

The selection of any policy area for discrete study immediately raises questions of boundaries: where does this area end, and another begin? As discussion proceeds in Part II, questions may arise as to why, for instance, policies that seem to deal with children are treated under the topic of income-maintenance policies, or why policies directed at older people and housing seem to overlap. Sometimes the choice is simply a matter of judgment—deciding which policies fit best with which policy sectors.

But on closer examination it is possible to talk about two major streams of social welfare policy in the United States. One stream deals with specific populations. The other deals with special issues. Table II.1 gives a general

TABLE II.I | INTERSECTING POLICY SECTORS, HORIZONTAL AND VERTICAL

Policy by Populations

	Aged	Children	Sick	Poor	Middle Class	Rich
Income maintenance	▓	▓	▓	▓		
Health	▓	▓	▓	▓		
Housing	▓	▓	▓	▓		
Other						

▓ = Major social welfare areas for study

scheme showing how these streams overlap. Policy for the aged crosses income-maintenance policy, health policy, housing policy, and other special-issue policy sectors; income-maintenance policy crosses policies that are developed for special populations. The main focus of analysis in Part II is the social policy sectors that deal with vulnerable populations—the shaded areas of the table.

Part II begins with an examination of income-maintenance policy (Chapter 5), then moves to health policy (Chapter 6) and housing policy (Chapter 7). Chapters 8 and 9 review policy for two special groups: children and older adults. Curiously enough, no clear policy sectors exist specifically for the "poor." Policies directed at this group are highlighted repeatedly in discussion of all five policy sectors.

Another reason for selecting these five policy sectors for study is that each has a distinctive national (federal) legislative framework from which policy and programs have been developed and continue to develop. Each of these legislative frameworks has a distinctive normative orientation or way of looking at the issues addressed by the legislation. Figure II.1 shows in graphic form these major federal legislative frameworks, and the general kinds of services that are provided as a result of policies created from these legislative frameworks. The chapters that follow in Part II discuss the major programs in each sector in some detail.

The Social Security Act of 1935 holds a special place as the foundation for modern American social welfare policy. More than any other policy document, the Social Security Act has become central to the development of American so-

FIGURE II.I

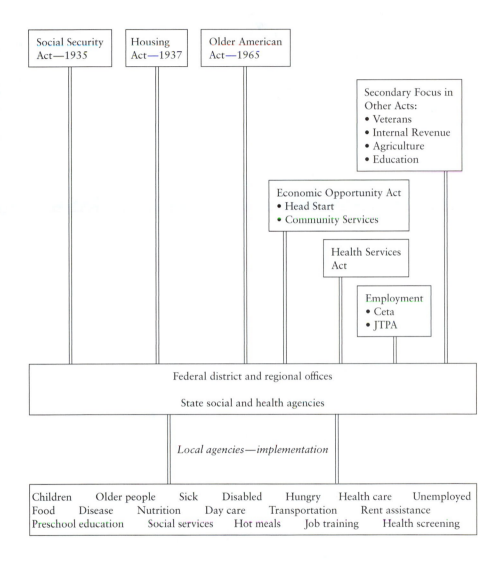

cial welfare policy. The Social Security Act is a complex document, containing many titles, or sections, most of which have been changed, redeveloped, modified, and improved on usually every year since 1935. The most recent welfare reform, Temporary Assistance for Needy Families (TANF), has been re-created from the Aid to Dependent Children's program that was part of the original Social Security Act. Today's Social Security (retirement) program likewise has gone through many changes and modifications. Thus, welfare policy as developed under the Social Security Act represents incremental policymaking at its best, something Gilbert Steiner called "tireless tinkering" some years ago. The

FIGURE 11.2 | THE DEVELOPMENT OF THE SOCIAL SECURITY ACT, 1935–2000

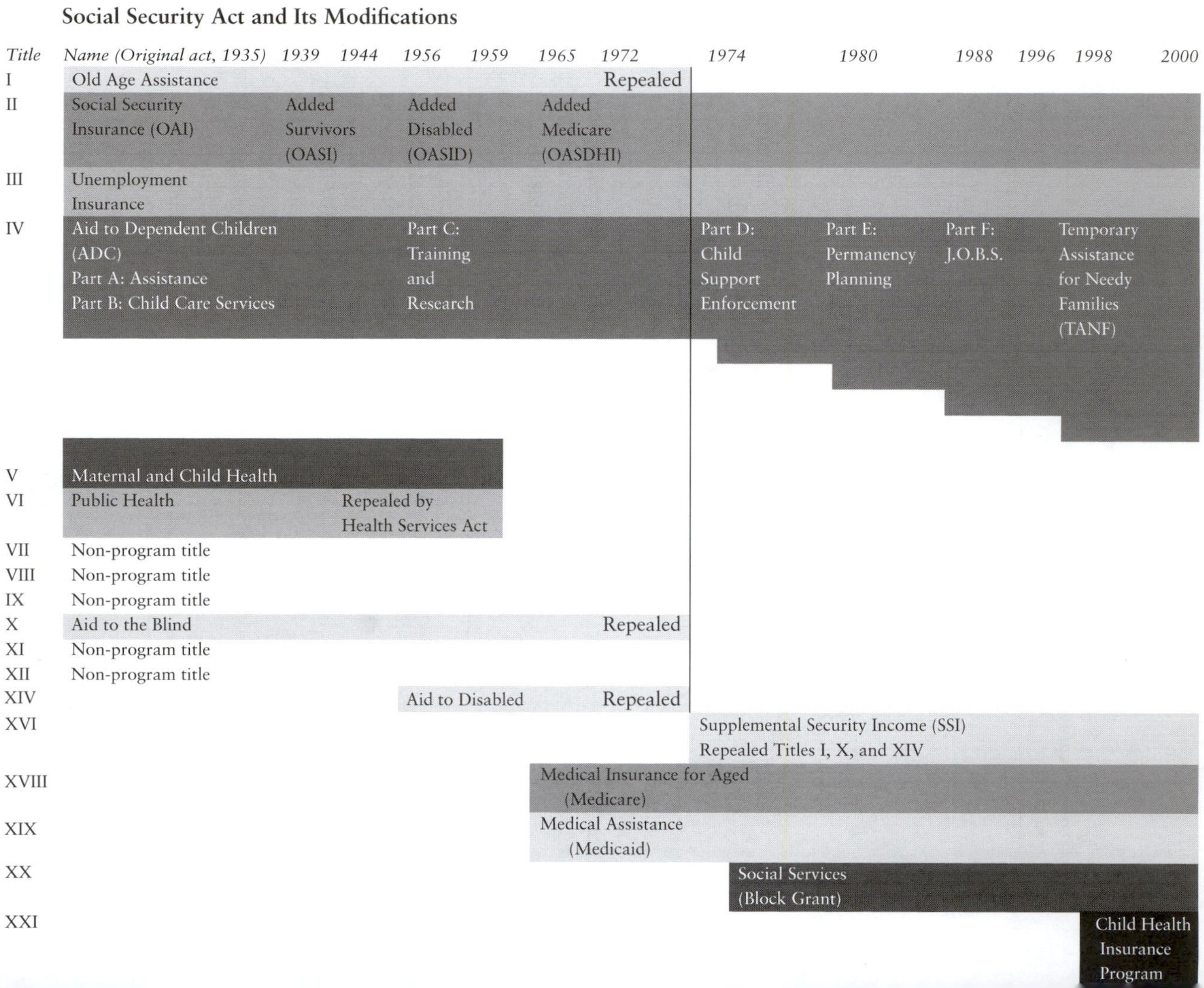

Social Security Act and Its Modifications

Title	Name (Original act, 1935)	1939	1944	1956	1959	1965	1972	1974	1980	1988	1996	1998	2000
I	Old Age Assistance						Repealed						
II	Social Security Insurance (OAI)	Added Survivors (OASI)		Added Disabled (OASID)		Added Medicare (OASDHI)							
III	Unemployment Insurance												
IV	Aid to Dependent Children (ADC)			Part C: Training and Research				Part D: Child Support Enforcement	Part E: Permanency Planning	Part F: J.O.B.S.	Temporary Assistance for Needy Families (TANF)		
	Part A: Assistance												
	Part B: Child Care Services												
V	Maternal and Child Health												
VI	Public Health		Repealed by Health Services Act										
VII	Non-program title												
VIII	Non-program title												
IX	Non-program title												
X	Aid to the Blind						Repealed						
XI	Non-program title												
XII	Non-program title												
XIV	Aid to Disabled						Repealed						
XVI								Supplemental Security Income (SSI) Repealed Titles I, X, and XIV					
XVIII						Medical Insurance for Aged (Medicare)							
XIX						Medical Assistance (Medicaid)							
XX									Social Services (Block Grant)				
XXI													Child Health Insurance Program

TABLE 11.2	POLICY VARIETY FOR PROGRAMS ADMINISTERED UNDER SOCIAL SECURITY ACT	
	Federal Administered	**Federal–State Administered**
Not Needs-tested (Universal entitlement)	1. OASDI (Social Security retirement), Title II[a] 2. Medicare (hospital insurance for aged), Title XVIII[b]	3. UC (Unemployment Compensation), Title III[a] 4. CSE (Child Support Enforcement), Title IV-D (for all who apply)[b] 5. Permanency Planning, Title IV-E[b] 6. MCH (Maternal and Child Health), Title V[b,c] 7. Social Services, Title X[b,d]
Needs-tested (Entitlement based on law)	8. Supplemental Security Income (SSI), Title XVI[a]	9. TANF (Temporary Assistance to Needy Families), Title IV-G[a] 10. Child Welfare Services (foster care, adoption), Title IV-C[b] 11. CSE (Child Support Enforcement), Title IV-D[b] (restricted to TANF recipients)[b] 12. Medicaid (medical assistance for low income), Title XIX[b] 13. CHIPs (Child Health Insurance Program), Title XXI

[a] Income-support program—cash; [b] In-kind program—services, no cash; [c] Funding transferred to Health Block Grant; [d] Funding transferred to Social Services Block Grant.

major welfare changes reflected in this most comprehensive policy document are represented in Figure II.2, and the most significant of them are discussed in the following chapters.

Chapter 10 brings the discussions in both Parts I and II together with a critical examination of the development of social welfare policy in the United States. The striking feature of American social welfare policy is its overlapping nature, its fragmentation, and its limitations. American social welfare policy is not a coherent body of programs such as exists in Western European "welfare states." Instead it far too often stops short of comprehensive welfare goals.

Thus many pressing problems remain unaddressed by American social welfare policy, and Chapter 10 attempts to explain why this is so.

Finally, Table II.2 arranges the Social Security Act's programs based on the variety, or types, of welfare policy the programs seek to realize. Some programs are administered based on need, while others are available regardless of economic need. Some programs are administered by the federal government alone, and others are administered cooperatively with the states, as discussed in Chapter 3. These distinctions are represented by Table II.2 and discussed further in Chapter 5.

The information in the following chapters, as detailed as it may be in some sections, leaves plenty of room for further exploration and understanding by social welfare specialists. Hopefully the chapters that follow will lay a groundwork for such further exploration.

INCOME
MAINTENANCE

CHAPTER 5

INTRODUCTION

In the broadest sense, public policy for income maintenance covers all efforts to protect and ensure a steady flow of income for all Americans. From this perspective, earned income (usually wages) and unearned income (usually rents, dividends, and gains on capital) are subjects for income-maintenance policy, as are government-sponsored income-transfer programs. Income-maintenance policy consequently overlaps with tax policy, employment policy, and wage policy, among other sectors of public policy. But income-maintenance policy in the social welfare context is more narrowly focused and is most concerned with income maintenance for the poor.

The whole idea of income-maintenance policy has been emerging slowly in America. It was less than 70 years ago that the United States developed an income-maintenance policy when it passed the Social Security Act. What fragments of income-maintenance policy that existed before we had the Social Security Act were initiated by states in localities providing varied amounts of money to needy persons, under widely varied circumstances. Money to the aged, the unemployed, the dependent child, the blind, and the sick was highly dependent on the whims of those who provided it.

The Great Depression, a period between 1929 and 1935 when as much as one-third of the labor force was unemployed, signaled the need for a change. Local agencies had no funds to distribute to the destitute, and states themselves were facing bankruptcy. Only the federal government had the capacity to intervene effectively to reverse the flow of the depression, and correspondingly, provide financial support to the millions caught up in it. The architecture of today's income-maintenance policy, found in the Social Security Act of 1935, emerged from the environment of the Great Depression (see Figure II.1). Since 1935 the Social Security Act has been the keystone of America's social welfare efforts and the cornerstone of America's income-maintenance policies.

The income-maintenance policies created by the Social Security Act, however, fall short of any comprehensive income-maintenance policy. Indeed the Social Security Act best resembles a patchwork of different programs: some for children, some for the aged, some for the unemployed, and so forth, all stitched together by a single piece of legislation to resemble an income-maintenance tapestry. For almost 70 years the Social Security Act has been reworked into a more coherent whole, and the creation of an income-maintenance block grant under the authority of the 1996 welfare reform statute (Personal Responsibility and Work Opportunity Act, PRWOA, otherwise referred to as TANF) continues to give further definition to America's constantly changing income-maintenance policy. But even after years of refinements, this income-maintenance policy retains its piecemeal character, and the pieces are constantly being reassembled.

This chapter examines the income-maintenance pieces and in so doing provides a context for an income-maintenance policy analysis. Though it is difficult to separate the social welfare part of income-maintenance policy from other income-maintenance policies some would call "welfare for the rich," this chapter explores income-maintenance policy that deals with the problems of the poor, the near poor, and those who would probably be poor if not protected by existing income-maintenance policy. This limited treatment seems justified in the American political and economic climate, which places a high value on economic freedom, individual self-reliance, and a market economy. The history of American (relatively) free enterprise suggests that although markets do operate effectively most of the time, for most of the people, sometimes they fail for everybody, and more frequently for some portions of the population. Because market failure wreaks havoc on individual lives, there have been many public attempts over the years to remedy the negative consequences of market failure. This body of policy, often discussed as forms of income transfers, or income redistribution, has been an enduring focus of social welfare policy since the Great Depression and the passage of the Social Security Act (1935). The legitimacy of various forms of income-maintenance policy is challenged constantly by changing public attitudes about the appropriate political balance between government activity and the American economic system. Over time, and in different sectors, government interaction with established economic institutions has promoted income-maintenance policy; at other times this interaction has resulted in a seesaw effect on income-maintenance policy— sometimes providing support for income-maintenance policy, at other times undermining it. The discussion of the 1996 welfare reform that follows is a good example of the uneven consequences of government efforts to link economic and welfare policy.

NORMATIVE ISSUES: THE UNEVEN TERRAIN OF INCOME MAINTENANCE

Income-maintenance policy is constantly confronted with a series of beliefs that shape the debates over income-maintenance issues. For example, what causes poverty? Why do people need welfare if they work? How is the need for welfare related to work? Should women work or be responsible for maintaining a family, or both? These and many other questions dominate contemporary debates over income maintenance. Beneath these questions a protracted debate smolders over equitable and/or equal income allocations. *Equality* refers to evenly proportioned shares of income or other benefits, based on some measure; equality promotes like treatment of like persons in like circumstances. *Equity*, on the other hand, aims at fairness; for example, fair income maintenance would provide greater financial support to larger families. Equity may promote equality, but it often calls for an unequal treatment of persons; equity is often considered a central measure of justice, although Americans seem to prefer income-maintenance policies that achieve equality.

Income Measurement Issues

In the United States, income is not distributed equally, nor would one necessarily expect it to be. In Table 5.1, which shows actual distribution of income in the United States over 30 years, it is obvious that each 20% of the population does not receive 20% of the total national income.[1] Table 5.1 leads to several more observations. First, though unequal distribution of income might be accepted as inevitable, a distribution in which the highest fifth of the population receives almost half of all the income and almost 14 times the amount of income received by the lowest fifth does not seem fair (equitable.) (See Table 5.1.)

Second, the relative shares of income have not changed much over a 40-year period, but the changes that have occurred shift more income from the poorest to the richest, while the middle remains about the same. This does not seem fair either, since, as Table 5.2 shows, poverty rates have remained relatively constant over the past several decades. An income-maintenance policy of any significance will have the overall effect of shifting the distribution of income. That is why equity and equality are such strong features of debate in income-maintenance policy. To be equitable requires greater equality, and greater equality will require a redistributed income profile in America.

On the surface at least, equality is measurable—that is, it is amenable to statistical monitoring—but equity is not. Equal income maintenance would mean providing the same amounts to people in the same circumstances. However, measuring equality of income is complicated by the different units of "income" that can be used in the measurements. One common measure is the flow of income, as in monthly earnings or in income from investments. But

TABLE 5.1 | PERCENTAGE OF TOTAL NATIONAL INCOME

Portion of Population	1969	1979	1989	1998
Lowest fifth	4.1	4.2	3.8	3.6
Second fifth	10.9	10.3	9.5	9.0
Third fifth	17.5	16.9	15.8	15.0
Fourth fifth	24.5	24.7	24.0	23.2
Highest fifth	43.0	44.0	46.8	49.2

Source: U.S. Census Bureau, "Income Inequality (1967–1998)," table 2, www.census.gov/hhes/income/incineq/p60204

FIGURE 5.1 | EXAMPLES OF DIFFERENT WAYS TO MEASURE INCOME

Wage income	Interest income	Welfare income
——————————— OR	——————————— OR	———————————
Number of families	Numbers of individuals	Number of households

subsidized medical care, gifts, disability allowances, fringe benefits, reduced taxes, and similar goods can excite extensive debate among policymakers about the type of income that should be counted—the numerator of income measurements. Defining the denominator can have similar far-reaching implications. Individuals, couples, households, children, adults, and families may all serve as units of measure. Determining equality of income statistically thus requires many choices, not only about the monetary units that reasonably may be applied but also about the units of population to which they might apply. (See Figure 5.1.)

Many fundamental normative issues have been raised as a means of harmonizing tensions over issues of income equity, since equity often seems opposed to equality. To be fair to those in poverty, for example, often means redistributing income to them, and those who pay for this redistribution often complain that they are treated unequally by tax laws. In the case of poverty, equity is usually valued over equality. But in other matters of income policy, like taxes, equality may be valued over equity. Though very important, these equity/equality concerns are not always visible as open issues in debates on income-maintenance policy. For example, policies that advance equity become less sustainable when the issue is poverty versus work, even though questions about

TABLE 5.2 | DISTRIBUTION OF THE POOR BY RACE, 1975–1999 (NUMBERS IN THOUSANDS)

Year	Total Number	Total Percent	White Number	White Percent	Black Number	Black Percent
1999	32,258	100.0	21,922	68.0	8,360	25.9
1998	34,476	100.0	23,454	68.0	9,091	26.4
1997	35,574	100.0	24,396	68.6	9,116	25.6
1996	36,529	100.0	24,650	67.5	9,694	26.5
1995	36,425	100.0	24,423	67.1	9,872	27.1
1994	38,059	100.0	25,379	66.7	10,196	26.8
1993	39,265	100.0	26,226	66.8	10,877	27.7
1992	38,014	100.0	25,259	66.4	10,827	28.5
1991	35,708	100.0	23,747	66.5	10,242	28.7
1990	33,585	100.0	22,326	66.5	9,837	29.3
1989	31,528	100.0	20,785	65.9	9,302	29.5
1988	31,745	100.0	20,715	65.3	9,356	29.5
1987	32,221	100.0	21,195	65.8	9,520	29.5
1986	32,370	100.0	22,183	68.5	8,983	27.8
1985	33,064	100.0	22,860	69.1	8,926	27.0
1984	33,700	100.0	22,955	68.1	9,490	28.2
1983	35,303	100.0	23,984	67.9	9,882	28.0
1982	34,398	100.0	23,517	68.4	9,697	28.2
1981	31,822	100.0	21,553	67.7	9,173	28.8
1980	29,272	100.0	19,699	67.3	8,579	29.3
1979	26,072	100.0	17,214	66.0	8,050	30.9
1978	24,497	100.0	16,259	66.4	7,625	31.1
1977	24,720	100.0	16,416	66.4	7,726	31.3
1976	24,975	100.0	16,713	66.9	7,595	30.4
1975	25,877	100.0	17,770	68.7	7,545	29.2

Source: U.S. Bureau of the Census, "Current Population Survey," Poverty and Health Statistics Branch/HHES Division.

FIGURE 5.2   DISTRIBUTION OF FAMILY INCOME, 1998
              (BY PERCENTAGE OF FAMILIES)

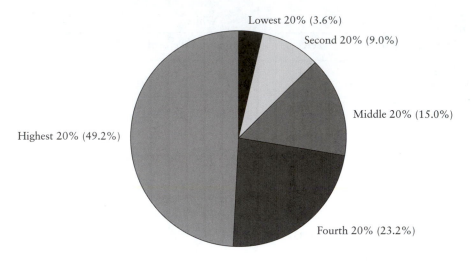

Source: U.S. Census Bureau, *Income Statistics*, table 2, August 24, 2000, www.census.gov/hhes/income/incineq

equity still lie just beneath the surface of debate. If a person does not work, the fairness of income maintenance becomes confused with the fact that the person does not work. Wage earners often ask, "Why should I support them if they do not work to help themselves?" This question ignores the problem of fairness to people who, though willing to work, cannot find jobs or must consent to take work that pays too little to be economically worthwhile. The lack of fairness in income distribution is easily seen in Figure 5.2.

Income-Maintenance Policy Issues

Although issues of equality and income fairness (equity) constitute fundamental questions that define the income-maintenance policy environment, most debates over income-maintenance policy choices involve more transparent policy issues. The capitalist ideology drives most of the normative debates over income-maintenance policy in the American system, and capitalism values hard work as the means to economic independence. The work ethic is valued highly in America, and this ethic often suggests that low income and poverty are the result of not working or not working hard enough. This is why it is difficult to analyze income-maintenance policy in the normative context of equality and equity without a specific focus on the relationship between income maintenance and work.

The following are the most significant normative issues associated with income maintenance for poor people.

Issues Defining Income—Determining When Income Maintenance Is Needed

1. Measurement of the poverty level. Should a mathematical measure be established, or should the need for income maintenance be defined in relation to individual conditions?
2. Elements of the income-maintenance products. Should in-kind benefits and nonwage income (for example, Social Security) be included in the measurement, or should only earned income be included?
3. The form of income maintenance. Should both cash and in-kind benefits be distributed, and, if so, in what proportion?
4. The unit of distribution. Should income maintenance be made available to the family or to the individual? How should a family be defined?
5. The distribution of the income-maintenance burden. Should it come from general revenue taxes or from other contributions (such as Social Security), and, if both, in what proportion?

Income Maintenance and Work Issues—Work versus Income Maintenance

1. Work and welfare. Should income maintenance be provided to people who work but do not earn enough by working?
2. Work in place of income maintenance. Should welfare be used to enforce work and discourage dependency?
3. Work incentives. Should incentives, such as child care, be given to support some kinds of workers? All work? Should these work incentives be counted as forms of income maintenance?
4. Family roles and work. Who is expected to work, and who determines this? For example, should mothers be expected to work?
5. Availability of work. Should people be required to work at low-paying, dead-end jobs that have little social usefulness?
6. Work and other values. Should rewards be given to those who do work, such as retirement benefits, paid vacations, free medical care?

Many of the above issues that direct the development of income-maintenance policy emerge from the political economy of American capitalism, and they have become institutionalized in American economic activities. Since American economic ideology places a high value on work, no income-maintenance policy can be proposed without taking into account the value placed on work. Nor is it possible to discuss income-maintenance policy that does not account in some measure for the range of differences in the way income is defined. In other words, it is quite unlikely that American income-maintenance policy would ever treat all forms of income the same way when considering the need for income assistance.

EXAMINING NORMATIVE ISSUES

Determining When Income Maintenance Is Necessary

First, defining what constitutes income is complicated by several issues. "Earned" versus "unearned" income, the value of in-kind benefits, and the establishment of standards to judge income adequacy are difficult issues. A distinction is made between "earned" and "unearned" income. Earned income usually comes from wages and provides the base for most income measurements. Income from investments and annuities, including Social Security and retirement income, government transfers (welfare), and gifts and savings as liquid and nonliquid assets (wealth), constitutes unearned income. Unearned income is extremely important to some groups of people, particularly older adults, even though it is not usually part of the way income is measured.

An important paradox emerges when these forms of unearned income, such as dividends and private insurance premiums, are used to calculate eligibility for public programs, such as Supplemental Security Income (SSI). Because earned income is more likely to be used in income measures, people that rely more on unearned income may seem less well off financially than they actually are. On the other hand, people with a lot of unearned income may be, practically speaking, worse off than those who have little earned income when applying for income-maintenance programs since some forms of unearned income are not available for everyday living purposes.

A second complication of determining when income maintenance is needed results from the difficulty of assigning value to in-kind, or nonmonetary, social products. What is the value of housing, medical care, or day care? And, because these products substitute for income, should they be considered as income for purposes of income-maintenance policy? Older people who own their homes may be considered to have a form of income substitute. Similarly, workers who are given health-care benefits by employers conserve personal funds they otherwise might spend for these purposes.

In-kind benefits are distributed very unevenly throughout the population. For example, total federal government spending for all social programs, including cash and in-kind programs, when added together is more than enough to raise the poor above the present poverty index. In 1993 the Congressional Research Service compiled information regarding cash and in-kind income-maintenance programs using information from the U.S. Census Bureau, the *Budget of the United States,* and various sources of agency expenditure reports, from both federal and state government. In this report only 23.9% of all income-maintenance benefits were provided in cash for the FY 1992 reporting period. The remaining 76.1% of needs-tested income-maintenance spending was through various in-kind programs. When resources, whether in cash or in-kind, are provided to persons based on some standard of need, these distributions are often called needs-tested or income-tested resources, based on the idea that persons "need" a certain amount of income in order to come up to a defined income standard. For example, an income standard for Supplemental

TABLE 5.3 | COMPOSITION OF NEEDS-TESTED BENEFITS

Forms of Aid	FY68	FY73	FY78	FY83	FY88	FY92
Medical	29.8%	29.3%	29.0%	33.2%	38.4%	46.2%
Cash	46.7	37.6	29.1	26.8	26.6	23.9
Food benefits	5.5	10.4	11.1	14.8	12.4	11.8
Housing	4.9	9.1	8.7	9.8	8.6	7.1
Education aid	5.3	4.9	5.1	6.0	6.8	5.5
Jobs/training	4.7	2.7	11.6	3.6	2.2	1.9
Services/other	3.1	6.0	5.1	4.2	3.8	2.9
Energy aid	0.0	0.0	0.3	1.6	1.2	0.6
Total	100.0	100.0	100.0	100.0	100.0	100.0

Source: Vee Burke, "Cash and Non-Cash Benefits for Persons with Limited Incomes: Eligibility Rules, Recipient and Expenditure Data" (Washington, D.C.: Congressional Research Service, 1993).

Security Income (SSI, see pp. 152–153) may be $512 per month per individual. If the person has only $400 in monthly income, funds are added to bring the amount up to $512. Thus SSI is a needs-tested, or income-tested, program.

About 93% of all poverty families receive some form of income-tested income-maintenance support in both cash and in-kind programs, with medical expenditures leading the list with 46.2% of all means-tested welfare expenditures. The share of cash expenditures as a portion of all income-maintenance expenditures has been decreasing over the past 25 years, while the share of in-kind benefits has been increasing. Table 5.3 shows these trends.[2] Similar comparisons are not available for more recent years, but there is strong evidence to suggest these trends continued. The U.S. Department of Health and Human Services reports that in 1998, 13.5% of all persons received some or all of their income from means-tested programs. Almost 30% of non-Hispanic Blacks received some or all of their income from means-tested programs.[3]

The Earned Income Tax Credit (EITC) has become the greatest source of cash benefit for both male- and female-headed poverty families, but the value of this cash benefit varies for both family types. The various forms of income-maintenance cash and in-kind benefits provided to male- and female-headed poverty families by type of program clearly indicate the value of in-kind income-maintenance assistance.

Third, a discussion of the value of in-kind benefits and reports that they are usually combined with forms of cash assistance raise questions as to what proportion of each type of benefit should contribute to an overall income-maintenance formula, could one be established. Combining the benefits in some proportion raises further questions of adequacy. What may be adequate for one person in one place is not necessarily adequate in another context. In general, determining adequacy of income represents an effort to combine nonfiscal re-sources with fiscal products. Measures of adequacy may vary greatly depend-ing on who is asked to apply them. Standards for adequate income as applied by a social worker, the businessman, and the welfare recipient would probably vary considerably and vary according to what kinds of in-kind benefits were in-cluded in the package.

In 1993 the Congressional Research Service estimated that 6.2 million fam-ilies with children had pretax cash income (including income from AFDC and General Assistance and Supplemental Security Income) but 21.1% of families still remained below the poverty line. If the value of food stamps, free and re-duced school lunches, rent subsidies, and Medicaid were counted as cash, the poverty rate would drop five percentage points to 16.1%. Of the approximately 35.7 million poor persons in 1991, 73% lived in households that received some form of income-maintenance cash or in-kind benefit. Accordingly, the value of all benefits for all persons would reduce the overall poverty rate for all persons to 9.2%.[4]

Fourth, units of income-maintenance distribution must be considered. Whether benefits should be distributed to the individual or to the entire family is a significant policy issue. For example, the current TANF program allows payments to "child only" cases. These are cases where, for a variety of reasons, all family members are not included in determining the benefit payment. Yet the benefit to the child is likely to be absorbed into the total income package of that family unit of which the child is a member. If that unit is quite well off, finan-cially, should the child still receive a benefit?

But cash distributions and in-kind distributions are difficult to equate in in-come-maintenance policy analysis. They represent separate distributional choices; some people are benefited by one, others by another. Most in-kind pro-grams are restricted to specific groups of people. Public housing, for example, is reserved for the poor who need housing, but not for the homeless. The Food Stamp Program is available to households, not necessarily to families. At first, low-income households were required to purchase stamps with cash, at which time they were given "bonus stamps." But very poor large families frequently did not have sufficient cash to make the purchase, and consequently they tended to avoid using the stamps. This example of selectivity of in-kind programs lim-its their usefulness as alternatives to income maintenance. Spurred by the 1996 welfare reform (TANF) changes (see pp. 143–150), food stamps are moving to-ward becoming a direct cash supplement.

Cash benefits are praised for their flexibility and the autonomy they allow recipients. In-kind programs target the use of resources and often contribute to the national stock of the benefit being used; for example, providing housing as a means of maintaining income requires that housing exist or be created so that it can be provided. Special tax treatments likewise have a targeting influence on public benefits. The tax law that permits homeowners to deduct mortgage in-terest from their federal tax liability was designed to stimulate private home ownership; exempting older adult homeowners from property taxes encour-ages them to maintain an independent (noninstitutionalized) lifestyle.

Finally, questions about implementation also arise in debates over who the distributing agent should be: the states and localities or the federal government or some combination of public and private agencies? Chapter 3 discussed the structural, political, and economic complexities inherent in America's vertical policy framework. Because of the limited federal authority for public spending, income-maintenance policy is particularly sensitive to vertical distributional bottlenecks. Exclusively federal income-maintenance policy has been confined to social insurance programs, while federal/state cooperative income-maintenance policy depends on a grant-in-aid funding mechanism. The social insurance programs receive their authority from the federal government's constitutional right to tax citizens for the special, precise purpose of creating a government-backed insurance program. These revenues are credited to special funds and must be used for the exclusive purposes of unemployment, retirement, medical care, permanent disability, and unemployment. They cannot be used for other purposes. Thus it is important to remember that the complete elimination of these programs would not help reduce the national debt or assist federal support to other programs because if these insurance programs were discontinued, so would the special taxes that fund them.

Issues of equality and equity are enmeshed in distributional questions. To the extent that the federal government is the distributor, and the states to a lesser extent, equality becomes the norm, and equity is more difficult to achieve. The social insurances are a good example of the application of the principle of equality. Workers are taxed in the same ways, and their benefits are determined by the same standards. A form of equity has recently been interjected into Social Security as benefits are determined by weighing more heavily the first portion of individual earnings. But equality challenges equity in the broader sense, for the very richest retirees still collect Social Security and at a very high rate even though their benefits are taxed.

Equity is more easily obtained when choices about distribution are closest to the users. It is easier to decide what is fair when considering a particular person, in a particular situation, at a particular time. Thus, the new TANF program enhances income-maintenance equity. Nevertheless, efforts to achieve equity in this manner have often caused mischief, as some particular situations have been decided not so much on the basis of what was fair, but in terms of achieving compliance with ideologically based behavioral norms. The history of income-maintenance policy development so clearly illustrates the problems inherent in obtaining equity that equality and, consequently, federal standards have most commonly become the basis for distributional decisions.

Work and Income-Maintenance Policy

First, work is a primary measure of personal value in American society. "What do you do?" is often the first question asked of a new acquaintance, and the answer may determine the future course of the friendship. Work also establishes a dividing line in income-maintenance programs. In the United States, 6 of the 11 most costly welfare programs are available to people who work or have worked.[5] The other 5 are available to people who do not work or have not worked. Furthermore, considerable effort has been devoted to finding answers to questions of whether welfare discourages people from working and whether work eliminates the need for welfare. Empirical evidence from one of the most comprehensive social experiments ever undertaken shows that adequate income maintenance does not significantly discourage people from working.[6] But even though this and other evidence is clear, the contrary normative view prevails. Most people still believe that income maintenance erodes the recipient's willingness to work.[7]

Income-maintenance policy is often criticized by those who think that welfare payments replace work. Yet the vast majority of those in poverty are already working or are too young, too old, or too sick to work. Depending on how poverty is measured, about 70% of all persons in poverty who are not presently working are unable to work. Even so, half of those who do not work have at least one family member working at least part-time.[8] Thus there is no strong empirical evidence that income maintenance comes at the expense of work initiative.

There are several important permutations of the work/welfare issues. The appropriateness and type of work, the value of work incentives, and the treatment of women are important work-related questions that affect income-maintenance policy.

First, the poor often prefer work to welfare, even when wages are worth less than an income-maintenance package. Those who do not work are faced with constant pressure to seek work whether it is appropriate work or not. Inappropriate work often includes jobs for which people are poorly educated, jobs that are not economically feasible, and jobs that have no future. People in poverty who are not working usually have limited skills and poor motivation, whereas most of the jobs that are available usually require some skill and strong motivation. Hence most of the jobs that are available are not appropriate for most welfare recipients. Job creation and job training for low-income people can be expensive undertakings. Capital investment of $10,000 to $15,000 to develop a single position may take as long as five years to begin to show profit. Training for the job can cost another $5,000 to $10,000 over a five-year period. Jobs that do exist for low-income people are often dead-end jobs: seasonal work, part-time jobs, or "spot" employment opportunities. Moreover, taking or keeping many of these jobs may be too expensive for a poor person. Lacking in medical and fringe benefits, requiring transportation to and from worksites, and usually devoid of arrangements or subsidies for child care, these jobs may not pay enough to make them worthwhile.

Putting a poor person to work also requires difficult and costly supporting policies, perhaps more costly than providing income maintenance. Before income-maintenance policy could incorporate a work policy, considerable development in employment policy would be necessary. The Family Support Act (welfare reform in 1988) that created the Job Opportunities and Basic Skills (JOBS) training program proposed to put welfare recipients into jobs, but required millions of dollars up front for basic education before job searching could even begin. Sharply increased work participation among welfare recipients was expected after the 1996 welfare reform (Temporary Assistance to Needy Families, TANF, see below), but as Table 5.4 shows, labor force attachment for this group of persons is very weak. Establishing a livable minimum wage, ensuring fair-employment opportunities for all, creating and maintaining public-sector jobs, protecting the authority of organized labor, and reforming the tax laws to protect the wages of the low-income workers all are necessary before a synthesis between work and income maintenance could be achieved. For example, a working mother with two children would have to earn approximately $7.16 per hour at a full-time job to stay out of poverty. These earnings would not cover work-related expenses such as child care and transportation. Present minimum wage is $5.15 per hour.

The quality of work plays an important role in income-maintenance decisions. If jobs do not pay enough, if jobs include no possibility for advancement, if jobs have little or no social value, should people be expected to work at them? One of the great failures of the 1996 welfare reform (TANF) has been that it has not helped income-maintenance-dependent people understand some of the intrinsic values associated with work. Without appreciation of these values, the work available to most low-income people loses much of its quality.

Second, although the major incentive for working is its immediate financial reward, nonmonetary rewards can provide powerful work incentives. Nonmonetary rewards help to define higher quality work: medical and child-care benefits, paid vacations, employer-sponsored recreation opportunities, attractive working environments, employer-subsidized travel. Nonmonetary rewards may equal or even surpass money income as considerations for accepting a particular job. The most powerful work incentive may be income protection in retirement through employer-subsidized pension plans, personal savings, and Social Security (employers are required by law to pay half their employees' Social Security taxes). These forms of work incentives are completely consistent with institutionalized capitalism, and for the most part they reflect an American compromise between equity and equality. But work disincentives are more likely to enter discussions of income-maintenance policy. Punishments, in the form of reduced benefits to people who do not work, seem to prevail when public income-maintenance policies are proposed, in contrast with the positive work incentives that encourage people to work as promoted in the private sector.

Third, family roles, particularly the role of women, have greatly complicated the relationship between work and income-maintenance policy. In both single-parent and two-parent families, mothers are expected to provide primary care for children, but in low-income families and particularly in single-parent families, women are also expected to provide primary financial support for their children as well. To such women, work presents a serious ideological conflict. On the one hand, Americans generally believe that work should be an option for women with children, but for a large number of women, and for all poor women, work outside the home for wages is a necessity. In all these cases,

| TABLE 5.4 | WORKERS AS A PROPORTION OF ALL POOR PEOPLE, 1978–1999 (NUMBERS IN THOUSANDS) |

| | | Poor People Age 16 and Over | | | |
| | | Worked | | Worked Year-round Full Time | |
Year	Total	Number	%	Number	%
1999	21,382	9,113	42.6	2,499	11.7
1998	22,256	9,133	41.0	2,804	12.6
1997	22,753	9,444	41.5	2,345	10.3
1996	23,472	9,586	40.8	2,263	9.6
1995	23,077	9,484	41.1	2,418	10.5
1994	24,108	9,829	40.8	2,520	10.5
1993	24,382	10,144	40.8	2,408	9.7
1992	23,951	9,739	40.6	2,211	9.2
1991	22,530	9,208	40.9	2,103	9.3
1990	21,242	8,716	41.0	2,076	9.8
1989	19,952	8,376	42.0	1,908	9.6
1988	20,323	8,363	41.2	1,929	9.5
1987	20,546	8,258	40.2	1,821	8.9
1986	20,688	8,743	42.3	2,007	9.7
1985	21,243	9,008	42.4	1,972	9.3
1984	21,541	8,999	41.8	2,076	9.6
1983	22,741	9,329	41.0	2,064	9.1
1982	22,100	9,013	40.8	1,999	9.0
1981	20,571	8,524	41.4	1,881	9.1
1980	18,892	7,674	40.6	2,644	8.7
1979	16,803	6,601	39.3	1,394	8.3
1978	16,914	6,599	39.0	1,309	7.7

Source: *Statistical Abstracts of the United States* (2000), table 14.

child care must be arranged if the mother is to work, but child-care resources are scarce, costly, and unappealing, often making work outside the home seem even more unattractive. As with work incentives, income-maintenance programs that are directed at working women, such as the Temporary Assistance to Needy Families (TANF) program, penalize mothers for not working even though mothers in upper-middle-class families are often praised for staying home with their young children. Income-maintenance policies that continue to pressure low-income women to work will only create greater class divisions among American families.

Confusion over women's roles is at the heart of many work-incentive issues, warranting an expanded discussion. After World War II, social values strongly supported women as wives and mothers who created and maintained a home for their husbands and children. These values protected the option that mothers with dependent children could choose to remain at home or to seek employment. But a gradual alteration in the value of women as homemakers, the increase in single-parent, female-headed ("nontraditional") families, and an increase in out-of-wedlock births combined to change attitudes toward women in general and led to punitive treatment of low-income and African American women in particular. As various work-enforced programs were appended to the AFDC program under Title IV of the Social Security Act, poor women were no longer given an option to stay at home and care for their children. Growing evidence suggests that few women have role options anymore, and poor women in particular are forced to play the dual roles of homemaker and breadwinner. The Congressional Research Service predicted that by the year 2000, 70% of children with two parents will also have a mother in the labor force.

Fourth, confusion over the role of women is particularly evident in single-parent families headed by a woman. Highly vulnerable to poverty and consequently likely to need income maintenance, these women are required to work under the 1996 TANF law if they expect to receive financial aid. The 2000 census shows a continuing increase in single-parent female-headed households with children. The District of Columbia leads the list of states by far, with over 53% of all families with children headed by a single parent; 47% of these families are headed by a single female. Also high on the list are Mississippi (28%), New York (26%), Michigan (26%), Florida (25%), and New Mexico (25%). In New Hampshire, 8 out of 10 (81.19%) of all single-parent families with children are likely to be poor, followed by 78.78% in North Carolina, and 78.59% in Maine. Unquestionably, single-parent families are likely to be poor families, giving rise to increased pressure on women to work, even though, with poor work skills, these women may make better use of new resources staying home caring for their children.

Conclusion

Many of the normative issues that are associated with the above discussions of work and income-maintenance policy are really not income-maintenance issues at all but issues inherent in the American economic system. For example, if earned and unearned income were treated in the same way, or if work were appropriate, with adequate income and equal treatment of women and families, then income-maintenance policy could be developed for those who were not part of the existing economic system. As it now stands, the intersection of work issues with income-maintenance issues confuses attempts to develop a clear income-maintenance policy. Only when work is not a normative issue in the debates, as with respect to Social Security (see pp. 135–139), do we have sufficient clarity in the development of income-maintenance policy.

Income-maintenance policy, then, is layered with overlapping normative issues that often find explanation in conflicts between equity and equality. The range and complexity of these many normative issues greatly complicate the task of policy analysis, since policy decisions are often made on the basis of normative issues that cannot be easily analyzed. For example, the question of whether mothers should work or stay home and care for children would be difficult to answer in terms of empirical information, and more likely would be decided on the basis of attitudes about mothers. Normative decisions about what is considered income, or what levels of existence constitute poverty, similarly must often be made without empirical guidelines.

Because so many value choices must be made about income-maintenance policy, income-maintenance policy analysis must account for a wide range of marginal decisions that may direct which course the analysis takes, as well as that of subsequent decision making. Because these normative questions require complex political choices, rather than straightforward "rational" or "scientific" choices, the incremental model may offer the best framework for analyzing income-maintenance policy. The major normative questions would become the criteria against which different alternatives could be examined. (See Table 5.5.)

THE BACKGROUND OF
INCOME-MAINTENANCE POLICY

Based on the assumption that income-maintenance policy changes in the past provide insight into the policy choices likely to be considered in the future, some understanding of the history of income-maintenance efforts in the United States is important to policy analysis work.

Since about the middle of the nineteenth century, debates over the normative issues relating to income maintenance have fixed with some certainty the public responsibility for income-maintenance policy. Presently, "poverty" is officially defined or bounded by a poverty index based on income, most likely from wages. Public responsibility for the portion of the population that is not eligible to work—namely, children, older people, and the sick—begins at the level of the poverty index (the "poverty line") and moves down the scale, in most situations, to bring the recipient up to that level. At present, income-maintenance policy generally treats in-kind benefits as a separate question, although in some cases their cash value is taken into account, thus blurring the distinction. Income-maintenance policy also equates work with rising out of poverty. When this equation does not work well in particular cases, as with working mothers, a different understanding of poverty often emerges.

The poverty index is one measure of income used in income-maintenance policy discussions. This measure counts cash income from earnings, interests, and rents, and, by calculating what a family needs to live on, establishes a line that says if a family has less than this amount, it is a poor family. Table 5.6 pro-

| TABLE 5.5 | NORMATIVE ISSUES AND POSSIBLE ALTERNATIVES IN INCOME-MAINTENANCE POLICY |

Normative issue	Income Type		Work			Distribution	
	Cash	In-Kind	Required	Incentives	Training	Federal	State/Local
Income-maintenance policy:							
Management issues							
Elements of measurement							
Form of income maintenance	X						
Units of distribution							X
Distribution of the burden						X	X
Income-maintenance and work:							
Work and welfare				X			
Work instead of welfare			X				
Work incentives							X
Ability to work					X		X
Availability of work							X
Work and other values						X	

Note: Using one criteria-based policy analysis framework set forth in Chapter 4, the matrix would be filled in by the policy analyst. X reflects choices inherent in 1995 welfare reforms.

vides information about the poverty index for previous years. Each year the poverty index is adjusted for increases in costs of living. From this information it is possible to see that even in applying such modest income levels to determine who is poor, about 17% of all Americans have incomes below those set forth in Table 5.6 and are therefore considered to be living in poverty.

Most income-maintenance policy has generally become the responsibility of the federal government, and most is authorized by the Social Security Act, first legislated in 1935. The broad federal income-maintenance authority granted in 1935 presented a sharp contrast to earlier public attitudes, stated eloquently by President Pierce as early as 1854, which held that all income-maintenance and other social policy was the exclusive responsibility of the states.

The Social Security Act recognized the difference between those who could work and those who could not. Somewhat in contrast with today, in 1935 there was good reason to believe that once someone found a job, the job

TABLE 5.6 | POVERTY GUIDELINES, 2001

Number in Family	Annual Amount	Monthly Amount
1	$8,590	$715.83
2	11,610	967.50
3	14,630	1,219.17
4	17,650	1,470.83
5	20,670	1,722.50
6	23,690	1,974.16
7	26,710	2,225.83
8	29,730	2,477.50
Over 8, for each person add	3,020	251.67

Historic Poverty Index for Four-Person Family:

2001	$17,650.00
2000	$17,050.00
1999	$16,700.00
1995	$14,800.00
1993	$14,350.00
1992	$13,950.00
1990	$12,650.00
1989	$12,100.00

Source: *Federal Register*, vol. 64, no. 52, March 18, 2001, pp. 13428–13430.

would generate enough income to keep the worker out of poverty. This presumption gained greater support as the original Social Security Act was changed during the next fifty years and as the income-maintenance program authorized under the act matured. Specifically, Social Security and unemployment insurance, legislated in 1935, and medical insurance for the aged (Medicare), legislated in 1965, were designed to reward employment by establishing universal, government-administered programs to protect participants in the labor force against involuntary loss of wages. These programs are often called *insurance programs*. Income-maintenance programs for those unable to work, often called *assistance programs*, were also authorized in 1935 through Aid to Dependent Children (later AFDC), Aid to the Aged, and Aid to the Blind, and, in 1950, through Aid to the Disabled. These latter three programs were merged as Supplemental Security Income (SSI) in 1972, and Aid to Families with Dependent Children (AFDC) was converted into Temporary Assistance for Needy Families (TANF) in 1996. (See Table II.2.)

In addition to the Social Security Act, significant income-maintenance policy has been established under income tax laws that provide special tax treatment for low-income families with children and families with elderly or disabled people in the home. The Earned Income Tax Credit, too, has become an important form of income maintenance for family members who are employed at below minimum wages. Income tax laws also provide a large tax deduction to people who own their homes, but these beneficiaries are usually middle-income working people well above the poverty level. Thus implementation of income-maintenance policy through tax laws may more generally help people who live above the poverty line than those who live below it.

The Social Security Act's assistance programs divide program responsibility between the federal government and the states. States are given great flexibility in administering these income-maintenance programs for nonworking populations. Under federal authority, assistance programs were funded by the categorical grant-in-aid, and subsequently "entitled" everyone to receive financial aid (such as Aid to Families with Dependent Children) if they met the eligibility criteria. Through the creation of an income-maintenance block grant under the 1996 TANF program, nonworking populations are subject to uncoordinated changes in eligibility criteria from state to state and are no longer "entitled" to assistance when the pool of block-grant funds is spent.

The major income-maintenance programs under the Social Security Act are presented in summary form in Figure II.2. Although income-maintenance policies and programs have changed considerably over the years, the normative issues that have shaped them remain. Many of the work and nonwork income-maintenance policies have been modified to bring their implementation into closer alignment with present-day understandings of those original normative issues, but few policy changes have been made to address new normative issues. For example, income-maintenance programs today continue to take form in terms of a distinction between poverty and work. They fail to take adequately into account the large number of working poor.

THE PROGRAMS

Social Security (Insurance)

Title II of the Social Security Act is its largest and most comprehensive income-maintenance program. In fiscal year 1999 Social Security paid out $286 billion in monthly benefits to more than 44.6 million beneficiary units. Only 62% of these units (with 63% of these payments) were retired workers (see Table 5.7). Social Security also provides benefits to disabled workers, wives and husbands of retired workers, and children, widows and widowers, and parents of workers. Between 1983 and 1992 both the number of beneficiaries and the payments increased for widows and widowers, reflecting a demographic shift in the characteristics of the older adult population. Social Security truly is a comprehensive income-maintenance program for workers and their families.

TABLE 5.7 | OASDI BENEFICIARIES IN CURRENT PAYMENT STATUS AND NEW AWARDS, DECEMBER 1999

Type of Beneficiary	Current Beneficiary Payments (in Thousands)	%	Average Monthly Award	New Awards	Average Amount New Award
Retired workers	27,775	62.3	$804	1,690	$795
Wives and husbands of retired workers	2,811	6.3	411	276	338
Children of retired workers	442	1.0	373	100	351
Disabled workers	4,879	10.9	754	620	783
Wives and husbands of disabled workers	176	0.4	189	46	207
Children of disabled workers	1,468	3.3	216	378	212
Widowed mothers and fathers	212	0.5	566	42	569
Widows and widowers	4,745	10.6	775	440	715
Disabled widow(er)s	199	0.4	500	30	502
Parents	3	a	674	b	888
Special age—72	1	a	209	b	101
Totals and averages	44,596	100.0	731	3,917	654

Source: Office of Research, Evaluation, and Statistics, Social Security Administration.

[a] Less than 0.05 percent.

[b] Fewer than 500.

There has been much criticism of the Social Security Trust Fund and the wisdom of transferring large sums of money from present workers (young people) to retired workers (older people). However, the program is dynamic enough to be adjusted as these concerns become more compelling. Social Security taxes are paid into a fund that can be used only for Social Security insurance purposes. Congress decided as early as the 1940s that the Social Security Trust Fund need not hold the full contribution of each worker to his or her retirement account. In fact, such a strategy would have created a severe economic crisis for the country because if the trust fund were to grow to full maturity, the government rather than the private sector would hold massive and disrupting amounts of capital.

While it might not be fruitful to go into detail about the economic dangers of a large Social Security Trust Fund, the debate about how large the trust fund should be was given a bit more clarity by Alan Greenspan recently when he testified before Congress. Holding large sums of private monies in government accounts may not be wise, he stated:

> The continuing unified budget surpluses currently projected imply a major accumulation of private assets by the federal government. . . . I have noted in the past, that the federal government should eschew private asset accumulation because it would be exceptionally difficult to insulate the government's investment decisions from political pressures. Thus, over time, having the federal government hold significant amounts of private assets would risk sub-optimal performance by our capital markets, diminished economic efficiency, and lower overall standards of living than would be achieved otherwise.[9]

For this and other reasons the Social Security program became a pay-as-you-go program and an intergenerational transfer program many years ago. In other words, younger people pay the retirement costs for older people and have done so throughout the entire life of the program. However, although the ratio of persons 65 years old and over to persons 18 to 64 years old had remained relatively constant since the 1940s, it is now beginning to change. In 1960, there were 17 older people for every 100 younger people of working age. By 2000 this had risen to 31 per 100; the relative burden across generations has increased, though not unreasonably. This ratio will become critical as the "baby boom" generation ages. Estimates range as high as 35 or more retirees for every 100 working-age younger people by the year 2005.

The Social Security program is effective. It distributes 68% of all income-maintenance funds of the federal government (excluding veterans' benefits). The trust fund is maintained by mandatory contributions (taxes) adjusted each year to keep the fund solvent. The tax rate itself is comparable with that of other countries. The present tax rate, equally shared by employee and employer, is approximately 15.3%, rising from 10.4% in 1972 and 14% in 1985. In 1999 about 97% of households with an aged householder collected Social Security payments. From 1983 to 1993 approximately 23% of all families received some Social Security, including 31.8% of white and 21.4% of African American female-headed families. Benefits are distributed via monthly checks mailed to the recipient. Social Security operates to some extent on a basis of equity, since benefits are calculated in part on the basis of previous earnings. Social Security is also efficient. Administrative costs as a portion of total program costs have remained constant at about 1.2% per year since the early to mid-1940s.

At present, Social Security is considered to be income. It is now taxed. It is also computed as income for determining eligibility for means-tested programs such as Supplemental Security Income (SSI) and for a variety of in-kind benefits, particularly Medicaid. All these in-kind programs are extremely important for Social Security recipients. For example, if the value of in-kind benefits is not counted as part of their resources, one-quarter of all people over age 65 live below 12.5% of the poverty level. When in-kind public support such as food, housing, and medical benefits is taken into account, this rate drops to as low as 7.7%, depending on how the benefits are valued. (Medical benefits for Social Security recipients are also considered separately in Chapter 6.)

The adequacy of Social Security benefits is frequently questioned. Because these benefits vary with work history and are not based on need, many people who live on Social Security are also forced to rely on other forms of income maintenance. The average monthly benefit payment for 1999 was $731. The average benefit for retired workers was $804; for wives or husbands of retired workers it was $411 (see Table 5.7). For the average person in 1999, the average benefit of $731 per month calculates to $8,772, or 10% more than the poverty threshold. In comparison, for the average person in 1983, the average Social Security payment amounted to $517 a year, or about 8% more than the poverty threshold.

Social Security may seem more adequate when the Social Security benefit is compared with preretirement earnings. In general, Social Security was originally expected to replace about one-third of preretirement income. Two-thirds were expected to come from the worker's savings and company pensions. Social Security provides a greater share of preretirement income for low-income people than for high-income people, but still, by itself, without in-kind benefits, particularly medical benefits, Social Security alone is inadequate for most recipients. Social Security never was intended to carry the full income-maintenance load for retired people, and its present adequacy must be evaluated against its original intention.

Work incentives play an important role in Social Security benefits. Benefits are determined by a complicated formula that is based on average wages and the amount of time the worker was employed during which Social Security contributions (taxes) were paid. Hence both in theory and practice, stronger attachment to the labor force provides greater benefits. Effective January 1, 2000, Social Security benefits can be paid while recipients continue to work for wages, without a reduction in benefits. However, Social Security benefits are taxed as other earnings are. Full Social Security benefits are paid at age 65, and partial benefits can be received at age 62. These age limitations will increase gradually over the next decade.

The adequacy and equity of Social Security are especially problematic for women.[10] A person becomes eligible for Social Security retirement in two ways—on the basis of his or her own work record, or as the spouse of an eligible person. In the latter capacity a recipient is entitled to benefits equal to 50% of the spouse's benefits. This may seem reasonably equitable, but it may not be adequate as financial support. On the other hand, because women's wages in employment covered by Social Security have traditionally been about 50% of men's wages, a woman's benefits, if established on the basis of her own work, are usually considerably less than a man's, raising questions about both adequacy and equity. Moreover, women are likely to have sporadic work histories, having taken time off to remain at home rearing children; this also results in lower benefits. Several proposals (discussed later in this chapter) have been made for correcting these problems. Current modes of distribution have also raised some protest; if a wife accepts 50% of her husband's benefit as her rate of benefit, the combined monthly benefits for the couple are disbursed in a single check, made payable to the husband.

There is presently a strong debate about whether part of the Social Security program should be "privatized" by permitting workers to invest part of their Social Security payments in the private sector. President George W. Bush has appointed a task force to study this issue, and the task force has issued an equivocal report on the subject. In spite of continued anxieties over the way Social Security dollars are managed, and the repeated proposals for changing this program ever since 1942, it appears that the Social Security program will continue to operate similarly to how it has operated in the past.

Unemployment Insurance and Workers' Compensation (Insurance)

Unemployment insurance and workers' compensation were also original programs of the Social Security Act. Like Social Security, these programs were developed for those who were working to ensure an income during periods of unemployment. Unemployment insurance provides benefits when a worker in employment covered by the program becomes unemployed through no fault of his or her own. Workers' compensation provides benefits for workers who become injured or disabled on their jobs. Both programs operate under federal laws, but they are administered by the states. To fund unemployment insurance, the federal government collects taxes from employers on the basis of the amount of unemployment they report, and it keeps these funds in accounts earmarked for each state. States then determine the exact benefit payment when someone becomes unemployed. Benefits are distributed directly to the unemployed, through weekly checks.

Unemployment insurance raises several issues of equity. Most significantly, it is available to less than half of the unemployed population. In 1993, for example, when unemployment officially stood at 7.2% of the labor force, only 2.8% of the unemployed received unemployment benefits. In 2000, when the unemployment rate was 4.2%, only 1.8% received benefits. The explanation for this limited coverage can be traced to eligibility rules and differences in the states' administration of the program. Only workers in "covered" employment are eligible for benefits, and many jobs in which low-income people are likely to work are excluded from program coverage—for example, part-time jobs, jobs with few employees, and most types of agricultural work. (See Table 5.8.) Moreover, because the states have administrative responsibility for the program, different state policies govern when benefits begin, the duration of the benefit payment period, and the status of the recipient during that period.

Because unemployment experiences vary from place to place, benefits paid to workers can differ considerably. In 1999, for example, the average weekly unemployment payment in the United States was $213 per week, ranging from a high of $288 per week in Massachusetts to a low of $156 per week in Mississippi. In general about 44% of the unemployed received some unemployment benefits in 1999.[11] This lack of equity is a serious problem, as a different

TABLE 5.8

MONETARY QUALIFICATION REQUIREMENTS FOR
MINIMUM AND MAXIMUM WEEKLY BENEFIT
AMOUNTS AND MAXIMUM TOTAL POTENTIAL
BENEFITS, 1999[1]

State	Required Total Earnings in Base Year			
	For Minimum Weekly Benefit	For Maximum Weekly Benefit	For Maximum Potential Benefits[2]	Minimum Work in Base Year (Quarters)
Alabama	$2,136	$9,096	$14,819	2Q
Alaska	1,000	26,750	26,750	2Q
Arizona	1,500	7,293	15,209	2Q
Arkansas	1,350	14,612	21,918	2Q
California	1,125	9,542	11,958	
Colorado	1,000	30,888	30,888	
Connecticut	600	14,480	14,480	2Q
Delaware	966	13,800	13,800	
District of Columbia	1,950	12,051	16,068	2Q
Florida	3,400	10,725	28,598	2Q
Georgia	1,872	10,752	23,294	2Q
Hawaii	130	9,256	9,256	2Q
Idaho	1,657	8,613	23,039	2Q
Illinois	1,600	14,079	14,079	2Q
Indiana	2,750	6,750	21,914	2Q
Iowa	1,230	6,871	18,642	2Q
Kansas	2,100	8,430	22,039	2Q
Kentucky	1,500	20,561	21,561	2Q
Louisiana	1,200	8,063	20,704	2Q
Maine	3,120	17,082	17,082	2Q
Maryland	900	9,000	9,000	2Q
Massachusetts	2,000	11,460	31,833	
Michigan	3,084	11,840	20,720	2Q
Minnesota	1,250	10,758	25,818	2Q
Mississippi	1,200	7,600	14,820	2Q
Missouri	1,500	8,250	17,160	2Q

State	Required Total Earnings in Base Year[1]			
	For Minimum Weekly Benefit	For Maximum Weekly Benefit	For Maximum Potential Benefits[2]	Minimum Work in Base Year (Quarters)
Montana	1,440	23,700	23,700	2Q
Nebraska	1,600	5,850	16,068	2Q
Nevada	600	9,675	19,350	2Q
New Hampshire	2,800	28,500	28,500	2Q
New Jersey	2,020	12,067	21,117	2Q
New Mexico	1,430	7,085	9,707	2Q
New York	1,600	14,580	14,580	2Q
North Carolina	2,904	12,090	25,116	2Q
North Dakota	2,795	16,900	21,632	2Q
Ohio	2,640	10,680	13,884	2Q
Oklahoma	4,280	9,450	16,575	2Q
Oregon	1,000	26,320	26,320	2Q
Pennsylvania	1,320	14,920	14,920	2Q
Rhode Island	2,060	11,266	25,061	2Q
South Carolina	900	8,931	17,862	2Q
South Dakota	1,288	8,924	15,132	2Q
Tennessee	1,560	11,440	22,880	2Q
Texas	1,702	10,360	26,959	2Q
Utah	1,800	11,076	27,348	2Q
Vermont	1,723	12,375	12,375	
Virginia	3,000	11,300	22,600	2Q
Washington	2,200	10,250	36,900	
West Virginia	2,200	28,600	28,600	2Q
Wisconsin	1,590	8,460	18,330	2Q
Wyoming	1,750	7,563	20,082	2Q

Source: U.S. Department of Labor.

[1] Based on benefits for total unemployment. Amounts payable can be stretched out over a longer period in the case of partial unemployment.

[2] Based on maximum weekly benefit amount paid for maximum number of weeks. Total potential benefits equal a worker's weekly benefit amount times this potential duration.

real value is attached to unemployment insurance depending on the state in which one resides. The program itself, however, is highly efficient. Administrative costs are higher than for Social Security because the program also offers employment counseling services to its beneficiaries. The cost of unemployment insurance is quite reasonable, averaging about a 2.5% tax per year on wages, levied on employers.

Only earnings from work are calculated in determining eligibility for unemployment benefits. A person could become unemployed, receive income from interests and rents, receive some in-kind benefits, and still receive unemployment benefits. Considering that unemployment benefits amount on average to less than 40% of average weekly wages, it is no surprise that in-kind benefits are very important to the unemployed. Because unemployment benefits are so inadequate when compared with regular earnings, food stamps and medical benefits under Medicaid can be especially important resources.

Work incentives are an integral part of unemployment insurance. To be eligible for benefits, an unemployed person must have worked in covered employment and must be willing to go back to work if a suitable job becomes available. Moreover, that person must have worked in covered employment for a certain number of weeks, not just for a short while, and the unemployment must have resulted from circumstances other than the person's performance on the job—such as a plant's closing or layoffs. Under such conditions, women are at a great disadvantage. They are often employed in uncovered positions, especially part-time work, and hence ineligible for benefits. If they do qualify, their weekly benefit payments will probably be quite low, since they also typically make lower wages than men.

Aiding Families and Financially Dependent Children (Assistance)

For many years "welfare" meant Aid to Families with Dependent Children (AFDC). As one of the programs that originated with the Social Security Act, income maintenance for children and their families has undergone many changes in the past sixty years. Income maintenance for children and their families has been one of the most controversial of all income-maintenance efforts. In one way or another, this income-maintenance effort has touched on almost all the normative issues that underlie income-maintenance policy. Originally called Aid to Dependent Children (ADC), these income-maintenance efforts rested on the idea that financial assistance had to be made available to children when there were no wage earners available to support them. In 1935 the prevailing assumption was that women were responsible for caring for children at home, and men were responsible for supporting the home and family financially. In 1935 and immediately thereafter, and particularly during World War II, it was not uncommon for men to die while still quite young, leaving their wives and small children with no easy means of support. It was presumed that in most cases employed men would be covered under Social Security and that if they died while their children were still in their maturing years, these children would receive Social Security benefits. Thus the original ADC program was planned as a small and temporary income-maintenance initiative.

But the United States has changed considerably since 1935. Traditional family patterns changed in the postwar era. Women were no longer expected to remain at home, but were seen as wage earners as well. Divorce became more frequent, and out-of-wedlock births increased. African Americans migrated to urban areas, leaving the protection of small communities and local farms, and urbanization required formal programs of income maintenance to replace informal, although often inadequate, systems of financial aid. In 1959 Aid to Dependent Children was expanded to include all family members and became Aid to Families with Dependent Children (AFDC). And in the 1960s the massive movement toward equal civil rights for all minorities swelled these welfare programs.

One stunning consequence of these changes was the increased number of dependent children who had living fathers who were not supporting them financially. Instead of representing a solution to the problems of poverty, AFDC came to be seen as a cause of poverty. Critics argued that the program encouraged loose sexual behavior and work irresponsibility, thus placing the issue of work versus welfare at the center of the debate. In 1964 the program was expanded to include an effort to collect child support from absent and nonsupporting parents.

AFDC operated as a state-administered, state and federally funded, means-tested, "entitlement" program that paid a monthly benefit to dependent children and their adult caretaker(s), usually their mothers. Benefit levels were determined according to a standard of need established by the state in which the child resided. In no state was this standard of need based on a fixed standard like the federal poverty index, and no state had provided a benefit that matched or exceeded the poverty index. Hence from the standpoint of equality, not only were children and adults treated differently from state to state, but within each state AFDC recipients were treated differently with respect to the definition of their needs. The standard of need set by each state ranged from 13% of the poverty threshold (Mississippi) to 79% of the poverty threshold (Alaska).[12]

Over the years this basic income-maintenance program has been changed to strengthen the relationship between work incentives and provision of benefits. In 1967, women who did not have preschool children at home were encouraged to work, and in 1969 they were required to work before they would be granted benefits. The 1988 welfare reform legislation (JOBS) required that all able-bodied adults who are included in an AFDC household work or receive job training and/or education, but by 1993 only about 20% of the AFDC families participated in this program.

In 1996 Congress created the Personal Responsibility and Work Opportunity Act (PL 104-193), replacing the 61-year-old program of Aid to Families with Dependent Children (AFDC) with a new welfare program, Temporary Assistance to Needy Families (TANF). By early 1995, many governors had pressed for a cash welfare block grant to free them from AFDC rules. TANF gave states welfare monies in the form of a fixed block grant that they could use for temporary and work-conditioned programs of their own design.

> TANF combined into a single block grant peak-year federal funding levels for AFDC benefits and administration and two related programs—Emergency Assistance to Needy Families (EA) and the Job Opportunities and Basic Skills Training Program (JOBS). TANF entitles each State to an annual family assistance grant equal to the largest yearly amount paid by the Federal Government to the State for AFDC benefits and administration, EA, and JOBS during the fiscal year 1992–95 period. From their own funds, States are required to spend on needy families at least 75% of their "historic" level, defined as fiscal year 1994 spending on programs replaced by TANF, including AFDC-related child care. This is known as the maintenance-of-effort (MOE) rule.[13]

TANF differs from the older AFDC program in several important ways:

1. *Entitlement.* TANF expressly denies entitlement to individuals. Under AFDC, states were required to aid all families eligible under state income standards. Under TANF, states determine who is eligible for welfare.
2. *Funding.* TANF law appropriates a fixed family assistance grant to each state. States may not reduce their own spending by more than 20–25%. States may use these funds as they see fit to aid low-income families.
3. *Time limit for benefits.* TANF sets a five-year limit on federally funded aid, with a 20% hardship exemption. AFDC had no time limit. States, of course, may provide payments for longer periods of time, but these payments would have to be composed entirely of state funds.
4. *Work.* TANF requires work (defined by the state) after a maximum of two years of benefits. AFDC had no work requirement. TANF also requires a specified and rising percentage of the total caseload to engage in work activities as required in the law.
5. *Eligibility.* TANF allows states to decide what categories of families to aid. AFDC required states to aid all families that fell below the state-established minimum.

Two basic program features of AFDC were retained by TANF. States decide how needy families must be to receive aid, and states establish benefit (payment) levels.

The legislative purpose of TANF is to increase flexibility of states in operating income maintenance designed to provide assistance to needy families so that children may be cared for in their own homes or in the homes of relatives. TANF also seeks to end the long-term, intergenerational dependence of needy parents on government benefits by promoting job preparation, work, and marriage. TANF also seeks to prevent and reduce the incidence of out-of-wedlock pregnancies, and it establishes annual numerical goals for preventing and reducing the incidence of these pregnancies, and it encourages the formation and maintenance of two-parent families.

States may use their family assistance (TANF) grant "in any manner reasonably calculated" to promote any of the above goals. States also make limited transfers of TANF funds (totaling 30%) to the Child Care and Development Block Grant (CCDBG) and the Social Services Block Grant (SSBG, Title XX). While TANF monies must be used for "assistance," broad latitude is given to states in determining what constitutes "assistance." Food, clothing, shelter, utilities, household goods, personal care items, and general incidental expenses, as well as supportive services such as transportation and child care for families who are not employed, all are considered forms of assistance. Thus, in many ways, the TANF welfare reform is more than a new way of providing welfare benefits; it acts as a funding stream for a variety of state-determined welfare purposes.

Although TANF does not require states to reduce their caseloads, it is assumed that by requiring recipients to work, and by setting a five-year time limit on benefits, caseloads will decline. Thus TANF offers states an incentive for reducing their caseloads. For each percentage point drop in the caseload not attributed to state policy changes, the required work rate each state must meet is lowered by one percentage point. Two exceptions to this rule are allowed. First, if a TANF recipient is the only parent or caretaker relative of a child under age six, she need work only 20 weekly hours; and second, if a TANF recipient is a single teen household head or married teen without high school diploma, she or he may receive work credit by maintaining satisfactory high school attendance or, for an average of at least 20 hours weekly, by engaging in schooling directly related to work. Special rules apply to two-parent families. They must work at least 35 hours weekly, with at least 30 hours in high-priority activities. (The two parents may share the work hours.)

State caseloads dropped so sharply between fiscal year 1995 and fiscal year 1997 that all states exceeded their adjusted all-family required work rates. Fiscal savings due to caseload reductions remained with the states, and states were required to maintain existing spending levels. Thus the use of all TANF monies—federal and state—had to be spent on TANF-eligible families, suggesting a large amount of funds are available to assist some families with intensive services. Even with the emphasis on work, in 1998 only 33.6% of TANF adults were engaged in some type of work activity or subsidized or unsubsidized employment. (See Table 5.9.)

Conclusion   The TANF program appears to have no better result in satisfying some of the bothersome questions underlying U.S. income-maintenance policies. While the number of welfare cases has declined significantly, from approximately 4.4 million cases in 1996 to approximately 2.2 million cases in June 2000, the reductions are likely due to the vigorous economic growth during the latter half of the decade. As the economy slows, welfare caseloads are beginning to grow again. The U.S. Census Bureau argues that the welfare policy changes brought about by TANF have had little impact on the reduction in the welfare population; rather, strong demands for labor account for welfare reductions. By 2000 the caseloads as a percentage of the population had been reduced to levels comparable with those in the early 1960s. (See Table 5.10.)

TABLE 5.9	PERCENTAGE OF AFDC/TANF ADULTS ENGAGED IN WORK OR JOB PREPARATION ACTIVITY, FISCAL YEARS 1994–1998

	1994	1995	1996	1997	1998
Some activity	19.1	20.4	22.4	24.7	5.3
Unsubsidized employment	8.3	9.3	11.3	13.3	22.8
Subsidized employment	1.4	1.2	1.7	2.4	5.5
Job search	4.0	4.1	4.7	5.3	4.0
Education	3.6	3.9	3.5	3.0	3.6
Other [1]	2.7	2.8	2.4	2.3	2.7

Source: Congressional Research Service tabulations of the fiscal year 1998, Emergency TANF Data Report sample, and fiscal year 1994–97 AFDC-QC files.

[1] Includes activities that states conduct under pre-TANF waivers from AFDC/JOBS rules.

TABLE 5.10	TEMPORARY ASSISTANCE FOR NEEDY FAMILIES (TANF), PERCENTAGE OF TOTAL U.S. POPULATION, 1960–1999

Year	Recipients	U.S. Pop.	% of Pop.
1960	3,005,000	180,671,000	1.7
1961	3,354,000	183,691,000	1.8
1962	3,676,000	186,538,000	2.0
1963	3,876,000	189,242,000	2.0
1964	4,118,000	191,889,000	2.1
1965	4,329,000	194,303,000	2.2
1966	4,513,000	196,560,000	2.3
1967	5,014,000	198,712,000	2.5
1968	5,705,000	200,706,000	2.8
1969	6,706,000	202,677,000	3.3
1970	8,466,000	205,052,000	4.1
1971	10,241,000	207,661,000	4.9
1972	10,947,000	209,896,000	5.2
1973	10,949,000	211,909,000	5.2
1974	10,864,000	213,854,000	5.1
1975	11,165,185	215,973,000	5.2

Year	Recipients	U.S. Pop.	% of Pop.
1976	11,386,371	218,035,000	5.2
1977	11,129,702	220,239,000	5.1
1978	10,671,812	222,585,000	4.8
1979	10,317,902	225,055,000	4.6
1980	10,597,445	227,726,000	4.7
1981	11,159,847	229,966,000	4.9
1982	10,430,960	232,188,000	4.5
1983	10,659,365	234,307,000	4.5
1984	10,865,604	236,348,000	4.6
1985	10,812,625	238,466,000	4.5
1986	10,996,505	240,651,000	4.6
1987	11,065,027	242,804,000	4.6
1988	10,919,696	245,021,000	4.5
1989	10,933,980	247,342,000	4.4
1990	11,460,382	249,913,000	4.6
1991	12,592,269	252,650,000	5.0
1992	13,625,342	255,419,000	5.3
1993	14,142,710	258,137,000	5.5
1994	14,225,591	260,372,000	5.5
1995	13,652,232	263,034,000	5.2
1996	12,648,859	265,284,000	4.8
1997	10,936,298	267,636,000	4.1
1998	8,770,376	270,029,000	3.2
1999	7,202,639	272,690,813	2.6
June 2000*	5,780,543	275,130,000	2.1

Source: HHS Administration for Children and Families.

Note: Unless noted, caseload numbers are average monthly.

*Most recent available

The full income-maintenance impact of TANF, however, is difficult to determine. There are a multitude of studies on various aspects of this most recent welfare reform (Table 5.11 lists long-term studies of TANF). It has been almost impossible, however, to develop a comprehensive understanding of TANF, since each state, and in many places each county, has considerable discretion to administer welfare as it sees fit. Questions about welfare adequacy, the relationship between work and welfare, and the roles of women all have not been

TABLE 5.11 | LONG-TERM, ONGOING TANF EVALUATIONS

Agency/Organization	Evaluation Focus
U.S. Census Bureau	Survey of Income and Program Participation (SIPP). Longitudinal data on income, patterns of welfare receipt, and condition of children.
U.S. General Accounting Office	State welfare program structures, challenges, and program outcomes. 50 state overview and 6 in-depth state studies.
Urban Institute	"Assessing the New Federalism." Monitor and assess how states handle welfare devolution. Evaluation of policies, administration, and funding of social programs to determine the effects of devolution on the well-being of children.
University of Chicago Poverty Center	Review of administrative data to determine how its quality can be improved for further research.
Nelson A. Rockefeller Institute of Government	"State Capacity." Study of TANF implementation to determine the capacity of state governments to operate complex programs.
Mathematica Policy Research	Develop a "microstimulation" model for projecting welfare costs, caseloads, and other welfare-related issues.
U.S. Department of Health and Human Services	Ongoing research into children's issues by the Administration for Children and Families into the effects of welfare reform.

Source: Douglas Besharov, Peter Germanis, and Peter Rossi, *Evaluating Welfare Reform* (College Park, Md.: School of Public Affairs, University of Maryland, 1997) (http://www.welfare-reform-academy.org).

answered by TANF. Thus many of the normative questions raised earlier in this chapter are addressed differently by different TANF administrative units. For example, some states and localities may be more generous in providing TANF benefits than others, resulting in greater or lesser time spent on welfare. Or states and localities report postwelfare earnings differently, some based on individual earnings, some based on family earnings, some based on monthly earnings, some based on quarterly earnings, and so on. States have fashioned their TANF programs so as to maximize specific goals: so, for example, some states might emphasize work readiness while others might emphasize developing cohesive and functional families. Thus there are so many variables that receive different treatment in the administration of TANF that it is very difficult to project whether TANF, as the most recent welfare reform, deals with normative income-maintenance issues any differently than its predecessor welfare programs administered under Title IV of the Social Security Act.

Perhaps the most ambitious effort to evaluate the policy consequences of TANF has been undertaken by the U.S. Department of Health and Human Services, Assistant Secretary for Policy and Evaluation (ASPE). The ASPE funded comprehensive studies of those who left welfare in 10 states and 3 large metropolitan counties to attempt to determine whether those who left welfare had steady jobs with sufficient income for their families, and whether they suffered hardships of hunger and homelessness. Since these studies, like others, were so variant in their findings, the Urban Institute attempted to draw out general conclusions from the studies. In general, this synthesis of studies offered the following conclusions about those who left the TANF program.[14]

1. *Employment.* Half of those who left welfare worked in the first quarter after leaving welfare. This percentage showed little change over time as people cycled in and out of jobs. Overall, between 35 and 40% of those who left welfare worked in all four quarters after leaving TANF.

2. *Earnings.* Earnings ranged from $2,400 to $3,200 per quarter, resulting in approximately 90% earning less than poverty wages. Average work was 35–39 hours per week. Earnings of the postwelfare worker were combined with other household earnings in 60% of the cases. Less than 30% of the postwelfare workers were receiving child support.

3. *Health insurance.* Only 32% had health insurance in the first quarter of employment, but this increased to 53% for those who held jobs for two to three years.

4. *Returning to welfare.* Between 25 and 28% of those who left welfare returned to welfare within the year, reflecting welfare "cycling" characteristic of the predecessor AFDC program.

5. *Dependence on other social programs.* Food stamps were needed by 80–90% of welfare leavers in the first quarter, dropping to 67% during the first postwelfare year. Seventy-eighty percent used Medicaid; 18–24% needed some form of housing assistance, while only 40–50% received Earned Income Tax Credit.

6. *Hardship and homelessness.* Twenty-four to forty-four percent reported they often did not have enough food; as many as 44% reported receiving food donations; as many as 41% reported being behind on their rent, and up to 21% reported they had to move. Still, over 80% reported that they were much better off, or at least better off, as a result of leaving welfare. Only about 20% reported they were worse off after leaving welfare.

These conclusions, as general as they are, are similar to those reported by the 1999 study by the National Conference of State Legislatures of 19 state-initiated studies of TANF recipients who left welfare.[15] Most families in these studies said they were better off, although still struggling to get by. A similar study of all postwelfare recipients in a small North Carolina county produced similar conclusions. In this study 23% of those who left welfare said the only reason they would go back on welfare would be if they lost their job and had no other options available to them, leading to the conclusion that "a long reported characteristic of welfare recipients [shows] that they would prefer to work rather than receive welfare."[16] Thus we could conclude that TANF might have changed welfare administration by giving states unprecedented autonomy in spending federal welfare dollars, but it did little to change welfare for those who are forced to receive it. The normative issues that established the pre-TANF welfare context continue to dominate welfare administration under this most recent welfare reform.

The experience with work incentives in both the AFDC and TANF programs demonstrates how difficult it is to resolve normative issues about work incentives in general. Most data suggest that welfare with companion work programs has been ineffective at getting people off welfare and making them more attractive employees. Appropriate jobs for poorly educated and poorly trained people are very difficult to sustain at rates of pay that will offer sufficient incentive to choose work over welfare. They pay poorly, usually have no fringe benefits, tend to be harsh forms of work, and more than likely are temporary. To obtain such work a woman must find child care and carry out other household duties, in addition to working. The rewards are seldom greater than the costs of going to work. Moreover, social science research suggests that mandatory work-training programs may have a negative effect in helping people get work. By contrast, when well-paying jobs are accessible, people are eager to work. Yet with all these well-known caveats, ideas persist that income-maintenance policies should be linked with work.

The experiences with welfare and work requirements further suggest that, in spite of their political popularity, a work/welfare paradigm does not provide a realistic policy environment for significant welfare reform. In spite of the fact that TANF forced recipients to work in one of the most favorable economic climates America has enjoyed since the end of World War II, many of those who left welfare were unable to earn enough to stay out of poverty, and continued to depend heavily on other social programs for their existence. In spite of the robust economy, poverty did not decrease even though the welfare caseloads did. Thus while it may be appropriate to expect that everyone who is able will be working, it is not realistic to expect that everyone will be able to earn enough to stay out of poverty. Thus "safety net" welfare, together with collateral income maintenance and other programs discussed below, will continue to be necessary to provide a realistic income-maintenance policy framework in the future.

Child Support Enforcement (CSE) Program

The Child Support Enforcement (CSE) program was created by Congress in 1974 because of growing concern over the large number of parents who were not supporting their children financially. Complete discussion of this program is reserved for chapter 8, which is devoted to child welfare policy. But because this program has important income-maintenance functions and because it is part of Title IV, an income-maintenance section of the Social Security Act, it also deserves recognition here.

TABLE 5.12 | CHILD SUPPORT PAYMENTS DUE AND ACTUALLY RECEIVED, BY GENDER

Characteristics	Custodial Parents	Custodial Mothers	Custodial Fathers
Custodial parents due child support payments:			
Total (thousands)	7,006	6,331	674
Mean payments (dollars):			
Due	$4,152	$4,172	$3,965
Received	$2,440	$2,503	$1,856
Deficit	$1,712	$1,669	$2,109
Aggregate payments (billions of dollars):			
Child support due	$29.1	$26.4	$2.7
Child support received	$17.1	$15.8	$1.3
Aggregate child support deficit	$12.0	$10.6	$1.4
Percentage of aggregate due actually received	58.8	60.0	46.8

Source: U.S. Census Bureau, "Current Population Survey," April 1998

CSE is available, through the parent under whose care the children live, to children who are not presently receiving child support, whether they receive TANF or not. Because almost two-thirds of all single-parent households live in poverty and many more live close to the poverty line, better child support from absent parents could dramatically lift the income status of these families. In 1998 there were 10,900,000 single-parent families, about 32% of all families in 1998 compared with 13% of all families in 1970, and 16,624,000 children under age 18 living in these families. Of the 11.6 million custodial mothers of children under the age of 21 whose father was not living in the household, only 7.1 million, or 61%, had a child-support award and were owed child support. About one-third of the 4.5 million custodial mothers without awards chose not to pursue a child-support award. In other cases, custodial parents were unable to locate the noncustodial parent, had a nonlegal agreement with the noncustodial parent, or the noncustodial parent was unable to pay. About 72% of whites had child-support awards, compared with 45% of African Americans and 47% of Hispanics.[17]

However, only 75.2% of those entitled to child support actually received any, and the average amount of child support per year was only $2,995. About $26 billion in child support was owed by noncustodial parents in 1989, and only $5.2 billion was collected.[18] By 1998 $29.1 billion was owed and collections had reached $17.1 billion. (See Table 5.12.) Obviously, optimal use of the program would have significant consequences for government income-maintenance efforts. CSE maximizes equity, is efficient, and could provide adequate income maintenance for many families.

Supplemental Security Income (SSI) (Assistance)

Supplemental Security Income (SSI) was created in 1972 under Title XVI of the Social Security Act by lumping together the original programs of Aid for the Aged (formerly Title I), Aid for the Blind (formerly Title X), and Aid for the Disabled (created in 1950 as Title XIV—see Figure II.2). These three public aid programs were income-tested assistance programs and, like AFDC, were administered by the states. SSI continues the tradition of income-tested assistance programs for the same groups of people, but it shifted program administration to the federal government, which now "guarantees" a basic monthly benefit to every aged and disabled person who meets federal criteria of eligibility. Because the federal benefit level is so low, states may decide to supplement this benefit. Even though there is a maximum allowable SSI benefit, actual SSI benefit payments may not always reach this level due to the ways states supplement SSI, and due to financial resources that may be counted in determining the SSI payment. Table 5.13 summarizes the SSI program through 1999. Because payment levels increase each year, in 2000 the maximum allowable SSI payment for an individual was $512 per month and $679 per couple. The average SSI payment, however, was only $368 per individual per month, because most SSI recipients have other forms of income, Social Security in particular. Overall, SSI provides income support at about 75% of the poverty level, and 79% of the poverty level when a Social Security payment is included.

SSI raises many questions about equity because it overlaps with Social Security. Both Social Security and SSI provide benefits to adults who are unable to work because of age or disability. In the case of Social Security, however, the benefits are paid because the recipient "earned" the right to benefits by working. SSI becomes available when an individual's financial resources are not sufficient to raise him or her above the SSI eligibility level. Because Social Security benefits are considered as income for determining eligibility for SSI, many Social Security beneficiaries find that their Social Security benefit disappears when they begin to receive SSI.

Table 5.14 displays how SSI creates a problem of equity for Social Security beneficiaries who have low benefit levels. The older person in this example essentially loses the value of private retirement income and the value of Social Security, with the exception of $20 per month that the Social Security Administration "passes through" (does not count as income). Ironically, the SSI recipient ends up still on the edge of poverty. Certainly the $440 total approaches the average Social Security payment mentioned earlier in this chapter. But 89% of all SSI recipients are also receiving Social Security; in these terms, their years in the labor force have no value when compared with other beneficiaries who are receiving SSI independently of eligibility for Social Security. In a perverse way, the work-earned benefits of Social Security are used under this policy to pay the un-

| TABLE 5.13 | NUMBER OF PERSONS RECEIVING FEDERALLY ADMINISTERED SSI PAYMENTS, TOTAL AMOUNT AND AVERAGE MONTHLY AMOUNT, BY SOURCE OF PAYMENT AND CATEGORY, DECEMBER 1999 |

Source of Payment	Total	Aged	Blind[1]	Disabled[1]
Number of persons				
Federally administered payments	6,556,634	1,308,062	79,291	5,169,281
Federal payment only	4,115,152	687,801	43,173	3,384,178
Both federal and state supplementation	2,159,555	515,255	30,406	1,613,894
State supplementation only	281,927	105,006	5,712	171,209
Total federal payment	6,274,707	1,203,056	73,579	4,998,072
Total state supplementation	2,441,482	620,261	36,118	1,785,103
Amount of payments (in thousands)[2]				
Federal payments	$2,290,591	304,775	26,347	1,959,469
State supplementation	$283,428	79,579	6,246	197,603
Total	$2,574,019	384,354	32,593	2,157,072
Average monthly amount				
Federal payments	$341.86	249.36	350.72	364.24
State supplementation	$110.92	125.90	167.64	104.52
Total	$452.78	375.26	518.36	468.76

Source: Social Security Administration, Office of Research, Evaluation, and Statistics, Division of SSI Statistics and Analysis.

[1] Blind includes approximately 19,200; disabled, 690,400 persons aged 65 and older.

[2] Includes retroactive payments.

earned benefit of SSI. SSI also has many of the same problems with equality that TANF does, since states still set standards for benefit payments by choosing how they will supplement SSI; despite some standardization, SSI benefit payments vary considerably from state to state.

There are no work incentives associated with the SSI program. Whoever meets its financial eligibility standards receives assistance. Largely for this reason, the program raises few questions of equity and equality in treatment of women.

TABLE 5.14 | EXAMPLE OF SSI BENEFIT CALCULATION

SSI benefit payment	$512.00
Less Social Security benefit	$350.00
Less private retirement	$70.00
Net SSI benefit payment	$92.00
Plus Social Security "pass through"	$20.00
Total SSI payment	$112.00

Earned Income Tax Credit (EITC), Homeowner Mortgage Benefits, and State "Homestead" Exemptions

Tax credits are not usually thought of as income-maintenance programs, but they must be considered in this context for purposes of policy analysis. Tax credit programs differ from those previously discussed because they provide a subsidy indirectly, through the tax codes. EITC is a direct cash subsidy and works like a negative income tax: families whose incomes fall below $26,928 (1999) are entitled to a tax "refund," even though they may have paid no tax to begin with. For example, a family with an income of $12,460 in 1999 and two children could have received $3,816 in 1999. (See Table 5.15.) This amount may also be distributed prospectively—that is, the payments can be included in a worker's monthly paycheck, equaling a nice supplement to monthly earnings. EITC has become a very important source of income maintenance for low-income workers.

Mortgage credits and "homestead" exemptions are based on policy for housing and for aging, and hence might seem unrelated to the present discussion. However, like CSE, they have some significance as income-maintenance mechanisms that should be mentioned here. Homeowner mortgage credits were established in the 1930s deliberately to stimulate private-sector housing development by permitting a tax credit against owners' taxes on the basis of the interest paid on the mortgage in owner-occupied homes. In 1993 the value of these tax and mortgage benefits totaled $41.7 billion on average. The value of home mortgage benefits for a family earning between $50,000 and $75,000 per year amounted to $1,179 on average for each family. Over 85% of the estimated mortgage deduction is received by approximately 25% of taxpayers with incomes over $50,000. Hence such benefits most commonly accrue to upper-income people, usually in amounts greater than the average stated above. Conversely, low-income people are not likely to own their own homes, and those who do may not have generated enough related expenses to be able to use these

TABLE 5.15 | EARNED INCOME CREDIT, 1996–1999
(DOLLAR AMOUNTS UNADJUSTED
FOR INFLATION)

Calendar Year	Credit Rate (%)	Minimum Income for Maximum Credit	Maximum Credit	Phase-out Rate (%)	Phase-out Range	
					Beginning Income	Ending Income
1996:						
No children	7.65	4,220	323	7.65	5,280	9,500
One child	34.00	6,330	2,152	15.98	11,610	25,078
Two children	40.00	8,890	3,556	21.06	11,610	28,495
1997:						
No children	7.65	4,340	332	7.65	5,430	9,770
One child	34.00	6,500	2,210	15.98	11,930	25,750
Two children	40.00	9,140	3,656	21.06	11,930	29,290
1998:						
No children	7.65	4,460	341	7.65	5,570	10,030
One child	34.00	6,680	2,271	15.98	12,260	26,473
Two children	40.00	9,390	3,756	21.06	12,260	30,095
1999:						
No children	7.65	4,530	347	7.65	5,670	10,200
One child	34.00	6,800	2,312	15.98	12,460	26,928
Two children	40.00	9,540	3,816	21.06	12,460	30,580

Source: United States Congress, Joint Committee on Taxation, 2000.

credits against their taxes. Mortgage benefits and dependent allowances can also have important income-maintenance consequences for independent older people, many of whom have borderline financial stability.

A number of states add to these tax credits through a series of property-tax exemptions specifically for older people. Sometimes referred to as "homestead" exemptions, they relieve older people of all or mostly all of the state tax liability on their homes. These state policies represent considerable savings for many older people and consequently are meaningful income-maintenance policies. The exemptions permit many older people to continue to live in their own homes and communities when increased taxes might otherwise force them to sell and move away to cheaper and less amenable quarters.

Other tax incentives that serve income-maintenance functions for all tax-payers, such as mortgage credits and deductions or exemptions for maintaining dependent children or older adults in the taxpayer's home, similarly offer minimal benefits that may be critically important to low-income families. However, they do not serve traditional welfare purposes as discussed at the beginning of this chapter, since these various tax benefit programs were created for purposes other than welfare.

INCOME-MAINTENANCE POLICY ANALYSIS

The development of income-maintenance policy provides a classic example of incremental policy building. Even though many of the individual programs seem to conflict with one another, the policies that exist offer a general normative consistency. Because these policies have been shaped over more than half a century (since 1935), normative issues have been addressed by creating new programs to overlay the old; in this way, complex value-related questions have been resolved, but at the expense of a coherent set of programs. For example, Social Security addresses work issues, but efforts to make it a more equitable income-maintenance program have compromised the principle of work-related benefits.

Income-maintenance policy continues to develop marginally in order to resolve constantly changing value conflicts. For example, developing income-maintenance work incentives in the face of their continued overall ineffectiveness represents efforts to realize contemporary values through income-maintenance programs despite the fact that, by objective criteria, they fail to satisfy larger income-maintenance objectives such as adequacy. Thus constantly emerging new values contrast with the values around which programs were originally created.

A successful income-maintenance policy of the future must identify and organize normative positions and suggest which values might be maximized by adjustments to the formidable array of policies and programs that already exist. The incremental model offers the best guidance to policy analysis in this sector. In order to frame the policy analysis, it is important to review, in summary fashion, the major normative (value) issues and the costs and benefits of the major income-maintenance alternatives that presently exist (step 1 in the model described in chapter 4).

To condense the discussion, it might be stated that the major existing normative issues surrounding income-maintenance policy are the following:

1. Work (labor force attachment) is highly valued.
2. Adequate benefits are valued.
3. Reasonable, straightforward program administration (i.e., efficiency) is valued.
4. In-kind benefits important to target resources (i.e., effectiveness) are valued.

TABLE 5.16	COSTS AND BENEFITS OF MARGINAL VALUES IN INCOME-MAINTENANCE POLICY	

Program	Costs	Benefits
Social Security	Very expensive Unequal treatment of women Not means-tested	Comprehensive coverage Related to work initiative Not means-tested Fits nicely with tax schedules
Unemployment insurance	Equality issues Federal money, but state administration	Related to work initiative Adequate benefits

Temporary assistance	Very poor benefits
	Poor interface with
	  other programs
		Partially related to work
		State administration for equity
		Necessary for dependent
		  children given today's
		  family structure

SSI	Poor benefits Unequal treatment of recipients	Universal administration Guarantees an income floor
Tax credits	Not targeted on poor Expensive	Improves work initiative

5. Equitable (i.e., fair) treatment for everyone, including women and minorities, is valued.
6. Direct payments are valued, more than forms of tax credits.

Referring back to the incremental model in Chapter 4 (see Tables 4.4 and 4.5), income-maintenance policy analysis would proceed along the following lines. First the normative issues represented by existing programs are condensed. These issues are then reorganized as marginal values of cost-benefit considerations. (As Table 5.16 suggests, any program has both costs and benefits that must be considered in the formation of policy.) Then the condensed cost-benefit values are placed into the incremental model as items a through f. (See Table 5.17.) Through a trial-and-error approach, various programs (numbers 1–5) are tested for their ability to satisfy the marginal values. These programs are identified in cells A, B, C, and D. Because we have considerable experience with the income-maintenance programs identified in these cells, the specific programs are assigned to the specific cells. For example, Social Security is assigned to cell A, representing cost-benefit and high feasibility. Without this experience the analysis would "shift" programs from cell to cell and eventually come up with the best "fit," as discussed in Chapter 4. In this analysis, Social Security and Unemployment Insurance would best satisfy income-maintenance

TABLE 5.17 | AN INCREMENTAL SCHEME FOR INCOME-MAINTENANCE POLICY ANALYSIS

| | | Cost-Benefit Ratio | | Cumulative Marginal Values |
		High	Low	
Feasibility	High	**A** (1) Social Security	**B** (5) Tax credits	Equitable for benefit distribution
	Low	**C** (1) Social Security or (2) Unemployment	**D** (3) Temporary Assistance to Needy Families (4) SSI	Reasonable economic costs
Cumulative Marginal Values		Relationship to work Adequate benefits	Inadequate Inequitable	(a) Related to work (b) Adequate (c) Reasonable administration (d) Connects with in-kind benefits (e) Equitable for women (f) Direct payments

issues, and thus would become the programs that, if adjusted, would improve the whole of income-maintenance policy.

RECOMMENDATIONS

On the basis of the data presented earlier in this chapter about the present operation of income-maintenance programs, the normative issues, and the model represented in Table 5.16, it is possible to offer some recommendations for modifying income-maintenance policy by adjusting these programs.

Social Security could be expanded in its coverage and made more equitable in its allocation of benefits. Social Security is already positioned to come closest to the overall income-maintenance values sought. The fact that about half the poor are working at least part-time, but without benefits such as Social Security or unemployment insurance, minimizes job attachment for this group of people and suggests that job attachment alone will not provide them with sufficient income protection to prevent them from dipping in and out of poverty. Expanding Social Security for the marginally employed would enhance all marginal values. Efforts to bring other groups into coverage, such as federal employees, suggest the need to expand Social Security even further.

Expanding Social Security coverage to employees who work less than full-time would also help minimize some of the inequitable treatment of women. Approximately 30% of all employment in the country is work that is less than 35 hours per week, and most of these jobs are held by women. Consequently, women are less likely to establish adequate Social Security benefits on their own; they might establish no independent benefits at all. Better coverage for women would diminish the dramatic inequities in benefit distribution.

Unemployment insurance could be expanded for the same reasons. The percentage of unemployed who are unable to collect unemployment insurance would strongly indicate that those at the lower end of the work force, who may need assistance the most, are apt to find it inaccessible. In this sense, adequacy, equity, and labor force attachment are undermined by restrictions in the program. Expanding both insurance programs—Social Security and unemployment insurance—would also guarantee a base of income to the most vulnerable workers without a serious increase in tax rates, and general program adequacy could be maintained without serious tax adjustment.

Temporary Assistance to Needy Families (TANF) and its predecessor AFDC programs have been viewed as income-maintenance failures for many years. The federal role in these programs will continue to shrink as they become programs of state initiative. Still, over 7.3 million children will continue to need financial support. Thus modifying programs that provide specifically for children (see Chapter 8) may have sufficiently greater advantage than modifying TANF-type income-maintenance programs. From a programmatic standpoint, eliminating the federal role in the income-maintenance AFDC program by establishing the TANF block grant that turns responsibility over to the states might improve program efficiency, but the history of AFDC suggests that such a step might make other marginal values—such as adequate benefits—even more unreachable. Thus TANF-type welfare programs might be improved by considering them within a children's policy environment.

Supplemental Security Income, like TANF, has become inequitable and inadequate as a base of income-maintenance policy development. Yet the number of persons served by this program continues to decline significantly. At present there are about 4 million SSI recipients, 89% of whom are also collecting Social Security. If Social Security were improved, the SSI program could be reduced even further. Almost two-thirds of all SSI recipients are disabled workers who have achieved at least some coverage status under Social Security. Conceivably, by expanding Social Security and reducing the federal income-maintenance responsibility of TANF and SSI, a federal block grant for financial assistance could be large enough for the states to provide general assistance to people not covered by the federal income-maintenance programs. If these alternatives could be harmonized with improved programs directed specifically at children (see Chapter 8), considerable policy reform could be achieved.

SUMMARY

Income-maintenance policy has been focused less on the subject of income than on a series of substantial normative issues that are at the heart of American policy debates in general. Issues such as work, the treatment of women, what counts as income, and which groups should benefit from policy all come to rest around what may be the most highly valued product of American society: money. Hence consideration of policy that protects income is crisscrossed with a great variety of nonmonetary issues.

The role of the states with respect to federal policy has been a particularly thorny one in income-maintenance policy. The federal government has the capacity, which the states lack, to fund income-maintenance programs. But the federal government has severe constitutional limitations on how it can spend those funds. The whole history of income-maintenance policy development and implementation has thus given to state political structures a great influence over the development and administration of income-maintenance programs. This latitude accounts for a great variation in program implementation from state to state, which has inevitably led to inequality. There are advantages to state administration, but these are more obvious in policy areas other than income maintenance. To this extent, expansion of Social Security, and of federal insurance programs in general, would also help to shrink state-generated inequality in income maintenance.

The difficulty of connecting income-maintenance policy with other policies created to assist the three most economically vulnerable populations—the aged, children, and the sick—has become an important issue in itself. Income-maintenance policy must not be thought of simply as a broad, horizontal policy that assists everyone, but instead must be directed at the poor, if it is to be effective within the American system.

Consistent with the picture of policy intersections suggested by Table II.1, the following chapters discuss health and housing policy as horizontal policy issues, that is, policy developed to help everyone. Then, the aged and children are discussed as vertical policy issues, that is, policies that deal with specific vulnerable populations.

QUESTIONS FOR DISCUSSION

1. What variety of income-maintenance policy and programs are you likely to find in the Social Security Act?
2. What are the characteristics of income distribution in the United States? How do you explain this income distribution?
3. What are the strengths and weaknesses in the way poverty is measured? What are the implications for setting poverty standards for the administration of income-maintenance programs?
4. How have issues about work played into the development of income-maintenance programs? Illustrate your discussion with reference to specific programs.

5. Some years ago welfare policy analysts discussed a proposal to give every-one a basic income-maintenance payment. Called a "demogrant," the proposal would ensure that no family or individual would be without a basic floor of income. What are the advantages and disadvantages of such a welfare policy? Do we have any income-maintenance programs today that reflect the principles of a "demogrant"? If so, what are they? Defend your answer from your understanding of the issues discussed in this chapter.

6

C H A P T E R   HEALTH

INTRODUCTION

By 1998, Americans were spending more than $1 trillion a year for health care—13.5% of the gross national product (GNP)—almost doubling expenditures over the previous ten-year period. (See Table 6.1.) Consumer health and health care have become a national preoccupation, from those whose medicine chests are bulging with prescriptions and over-the-counter medications, to those whose pantry shelves are equally jammed with health foods and "natural" products, reflecting a different approach but equal concern, while many others cannot afford to buy their prescription drugs. In spite of the high level of expenditure and heightened public interest, the nation's health has not shown dynamic improvement. The death rate has remained relatively unchanged since the early 1960s, and the infant death rate has slowed its decline and even shows signs of a slight increase.

Health policy is as laden with normative issues as any sector of public policy, and in many respects health policy is intertwined with all social welfare policy. Health policy has become enmeshed in a complex web of public issues that shape both public perceptions of health and the current debates over health policy itself. For example, the relationship between high health risks and current environmental conditions is well known, yet health policy continues to develop as a reaction to environmental effects rather than as a prevention of such effects. This and other ambiguities in health policy raise questions about whether a relationship exists at all between the amount of money spent on health care and the factors most frequently associated with good health.

NORMATIVE ISSUES

Defining Health

A number of well-worn normative issues cloud efforts to analyze health policy, and current definitions of health top the list. "Absence of illness" is a necessary but not sufficient definition of health for contemporary policymakers. The elements of a full definition of health today range from good medical care to genetic engineering, from adequate health insurance to adequate means to afford basic health services. The variety of normative issues covered by contemporary definitions of health cannot be accommodated within the scope of any single policy analysis. Understanding the underlying problems of how Americans define health is essential background knowledge for all health policy analysis.

David Mechanic, a well-known medical sociologist, sets a definition of health in a broad context: "In all ideas of health and disease—whether specific or more general—is some concept of normal fitness and behavior. But concepts of health, fitness, and acceptable behavior, as well as those of disease and disability, depend on the state of health institutions and health science on the one hand, and the social and cultural context within which human problems are defined on the other."

In one sense, diseases are easily recognized because they do not align with assumptions that people make about the state of good health, which "has been seen as a condition of equilibrium."[1] This idea of equilibrium, so important in the early days of medical theory and practice, remains a crucial element in present-day efforts to understand health as a balance, not merely as the absence of disease.

In such a comprehensive framework it is almost impossible to define health from a normative position without thorough examination of the entire social structure in which people interact with their environments. The most straightforward approach for policy analysis would be to assume that health policy is a composite effort to maintain or to restore equilibrium, so as to prevent or remedy disequilibrium, usually understood as disease. Thus, invariably, most definitions of health deal in one way or another with the idea of disease.

This focus on disease as a key element in the definition of health is compounded by normative approaches to dealing with disease itself. For example, most definitions of health care emphasize treatment rather than prevention of disease. Accordingly, public efforts to restore sick people to a state of healthy equilibrium have far outweighed efforts to prevent disequilibrium from occurring in the first place. Preventing disease, however, is much more effective and much more cost-effective than treating it. Medical history of the past two centuries, especially of more recent decades, offers many dramatic examples. Most severe childhood diseases have been eradicated; smallpox, cholera, and yellow fever are almost unknown in the United States and have greatly diminished worldwide; emerging technological knowledge may permit biological alterations that would in time eradicate the more common genetically linked diseases, such as sickle-cell anemia.

Efforts to prevent disease are based on a different set of values from those that underlie efforts to treat disease. Prevention requires a commitment to the future over the present, a willingness to adjust and change certain patterns of behavior, and a dedication to improved living standards at public expense. These values may require a restructuring of individual freedoms. The values that support treatment of diseases, on the other hand, reflect more personal concerns. Treatment is more individually focused and more consistent with values based in America's traditional ideals of individualism and self-sufficiency. Though the public may financially support the research necessary to determine appropriate preventive measures, it is often unwilling to accept the constraints on individual behavior that would implement such policy. For example, mass immunization programs remain voluntary, rather than mandatory, and even though it is well documented that the use of seat belts decreases injury during automobile accidents, the public fails to fully support seat belt laws on the basis that individual choice should determine whether they are worn.

The preference for treatment over prevention has led to an emphasis on cure rather than care. The normative definition of health as the absence of disease encourages medical emphasis on repair and restoration to a state as close as possible to a person's condition before the illness occurred. Determining this prior condition is often an important measure for establishing a treatment goal and gauging its success. "Baseline" medical data generate a framework that is necessary and helpful for later medical intervention. "This is normal for you" or "This is normal for a person with your age and history" are phrases that provide guidance to treatment, starting points to look back to, and, if possible, to return to.

The idea of care, on the other hand, makes no claim for repair or restoration. The focus of care is continued maintenance at the present functional level with as much support and comfort as possible. While not in opposition to cure, care tends to emphasize adjustment to current circumstances. Care may be just as individualized as cure; in many circumstances it is more appropriate than cure. But the emphasis on cure has persisted to the point that in current usage the term "health care" usually means a series of efforts to effect a cure.

Although these normative positions on basic definitions of health and health care remain latent in policy debates, the American approach to health policy is fairly consistent. Specifically, American health policy (1) defines health as an absence of disease, though permitting considerable latitude in the definition of disease, and (2) enhances both prevention and treatment of disease, with the greater emphasis on treatment. Too often prevention carries with it restrictions on individual freedom, a price most Americans are unwilling to pay. Health policy oriented toward treatment supports much greater emphasis on cures than on care.

Figure 6.1 depicts an American health paradigm. The American emphasis on care represents a small commitment of resources, while the major emphasis is on treatment and cure. As both Figure 6.2 and Table 6.1 show, most health spending, both private and public, focuses on various forms of treatment and cure.

FIGURE 6.1 | THE FRAMEWORK OF HEALTH-CARE POLICY

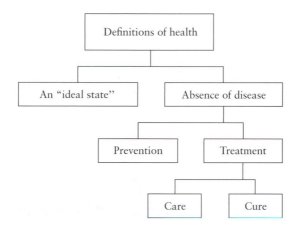

FIGURE 6.2 | PUBLIC SPENDING FOR HEALTH

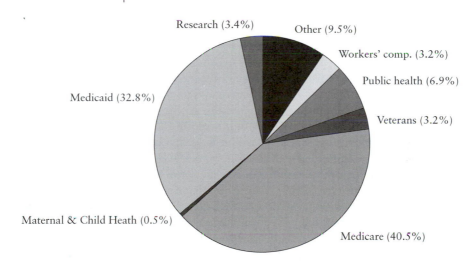

Source: HCFA, 1999.

Health-Care Products

Although considerable agreement exists among Americans on a definition of health care, the provision of that care can still raise difficult issues of equity, equality, and freedom of personal choice. Throughout the remainder of this chapter the common term "health care" is used to refer to health care and cure as stated above. Using the various criteria discussed in Chapter 4 (see Table 4.7, for example), a better analysis of health-care policy and various health-care options becomes clear.

Equity is often debated in terms of the quality of medical care received. For example, do the poor get the same quality of care as the wealthy, and should they? Equality is especially troublesome when considering access to health services. For example, the poor, who often do not have private physicians, may be obliged to accept emergency rooms as a primary source of care.

The various forms of public and private health insurance have evolved in an effort to deal with issues of both equity and equality by placing a third party between the patient and the health system. Under this scheme, the patient deals directly with the health-care provider for the service, and the provider and the patient deal with the third party to pay the cost. This separation of the individual patient from direct responsibility to the provider for the cost of services rendered has been blamed for the escalation of medical costs in recent years (a topic considered in greater depth below), but it has helped to enhance both equality of access and equity of medical care for Americans.

Preference satisfaction is a pervasive issue in health care. At one level health-care providers' preferences may underlie their reluctance to move toward more efficient approaches to health care. The private general practitioner and the doctor–patient relationship remain the central focus of America's health-care system, even though in many situations other medical professionals may be more appropriate providers and supervisors of primary and secondary health care. For example, most medical workups for routine physical examinations are done by the nursing staff, physician assistants, and laboratory technicians. Pharmacists know more about dispensing drugs than the average general practitioner. And medical engineers are often more qualified than doctors to administer complex diagnostic and treatment procedures, maintain the complex equipment used for these procedures, and monitor and interpret the results.

From the patient's point of view, the choice of a physician to manage the requested or required care clearly maximizes personal preference. Moreover, personal choice also dictates what kind of medical interventions are necessary and desirable. Preference satisfaction becomes expensive, however, when the choice of services is removed from direct responsibility for paying for them, as is the case with health insurance. In other words, if people can choose whatever health care they want, without much concern for what they may have to pay, they may choose services that are not medically justified. Such choices accelerate the use of existing services, create demands for new services, and quickly contribute to rising costs in health care.

Preference satisfaction also may be market sensitive: if more people want certain products, those products become scarcer and their prices rise to a level that balances demand with resources. Policy pressures toward equality—that is, aimed at equal access—have created an insurance system that has kept the relative costs of health care (as measured by what it costs the user) exceptionally low. On average, the individual user pays only about 9% of the full cost of services received; public and private insurance covers the rest. In this environment, market forces can exacerbate inflationary pressures on medical care: "The patient and his agent, the physician . . . can elect the most expensive (and presumably the best) services available—more expensive than they might elect if third party payments did not exist."[2]

Unrealistically low consumer costs for health care have been complicated by public efforts to increase the supply of health-care products so that cost alone does not prevent equal access or yield inferior services. Important public policy milestones have made public funds available for constructing local hospitals and educating doctors, and publicly supported reimbursement systems (Medicare and Medicaid) have kept high-quality care within the reach of the whole population, regardless of the individual's ability to pay. Such policies both stimulate supply and increase demand, in an environment of third-party contracts that preserves personal preference by keeping prices to the consumer artificially low. This combination of normative choices, made in health policy over the decades since 1940, lies at the center of today's concerns over health policy and provides the basis for current policy analysis.

The Boundaries of Public Responsibility for Health Care

A clear distinction between public responsibility and private choice is an important normative issue in all policy sectors, but it has particular importance for the analysis of health-care policy. Government supports the idea of private enterprise in the provision of health-care services while at the same time supporting public responsibility for health care if all citizens are to reap the benefits of a healthy society. Through its public expenditures, mostly in the private sector, the federal government exerts considerable influence over the provision of health products in the private sector. Table 6.1 summarizes the division between public and private responsibility for expenditures for certain types of health services over the past two decades.

In 1998, 54.6% of total national health-care expenditures were paid by private sector consumers (a 3.5% reduction in the past decade), but total direct out-of-pocket expenditures were only 17% (a decrease from 24% in 1980). The remainder, about 45.5% of national health-care costs, was paid from public funds. Most public funds come from two federal programs, Medicare and Medicaid, both of which showed significant percentage increases in the past five years. This picture affirms the strong presence of the federal government in the provision of health-care services and financial support for health care, almost all of which is provided in one way or another by the private sector. Government coverage and private-sector insurance payments together came to about 73% of total expenditures. The picture that emerges here is not one that says we are not providing enough public funding for health care, but that we are not spending our public dollars very well.

Figure 6.2 offers confirming evidence that health policy is inclined sharply toward treatment rather than prevention, toward cure and restoration rather than care. Excluding medical research, only about 3.2% of all health-cost expenditures in 1998 was directed toward prevention (see Table 6.2, line for government public health). Table 6.2 shows that over $1.1 billion, almost 97%, of

TABLE 6.1 | NATIONAL HEALTH EXPENDITURES BY TYPE, 1980–1998 (IN BILLIONS OF DOLLARS)*

Type of Expenditure	1980	1985	1990	1993	1994	1995	1996	1997	1998
Total	247.3	428.7	699.4	898.5	947.7	993.3	1,039.4	1,088.2	1,149.1
Annual percentage change[1]	14.9	9.9	12.2	7.4	5.5	4.8	4.6	4.7	5.6
Percentage of gross domestic product	8.9	10.3	12.2	13.7	13.6	13.7	13.6	13.4	13.5
Private expenditures	142.5	254.5	416.2	513.2	524.7	537.3	559.0	586.0	626.4
Health services and supplies	138.0	248.0	405.9	501.3	513.0	526.3	547.5	572.7	613.4
Out-of-pocket payments	60.3	100.7	145.0	167.1	168.2	170.5	178.1	189.1	199.5
Insurance premiums[2]	69.8	132.8	239.6	306.8	315.3	324.0	334.9	346.7	375.0
Other	8.0	14.5	21.4	27.4	29.5	31.8	34.5	37.0	38.8
Medical research	0.3	0.5	1.0	1.2	1.3	1.3	1.4	1.5	1.6
Medical facilities construction	4.2	6.0	9.3	10.7	10.5	9.6	10.1	11.8	11.5
Public expenditures	104.8	174.2	283.2	385.3	423.0	456.0	480.4	502.2	522.7
Federal percentage	68.7	70.7	68.9	71.5	71.2	71.5	72.3	72.3	72.1
Health services and supplies	97.6	164.3	268.9	368.2	404.3	436.2	460.0	480.7	500.4
Medicare[3]	37.5	72.1	111.5	148.7	166.9	185.3	199.4	211.3	216.6
Public assistance medical payments[4]	28.0	44.4	80.4	126.8	140.1	151.6	159.5	165.2	175.5

Temporary disability insurance[5]	0.1	0.1	0.1	0.1	0.1	0.1	0.1	0.1	0.1
Workers' compensation (medical)[5]	5.1	8.0	16.1	18.5	18.6	17.9	17.7	17.5	17.0
Defense Dept. hospital, medical	4.4	7.5	11.6	13.3	13.2	13.4	13.3	13.4	13.6
Maternal & Child Health programs	0.9	1.3	1.9	2.2	2.3	2.4	2.4	2.5	2.6
Public health activities	6.7	11.6	19.6	25.3	28.2	29.8	31.3	34.6	36.6
Veterans hospital, medical care	5.9	8.7	11.4	14.3	15.3	15.6	16.5	16.5	17.1
Medical vocational rehabilitation	0.3	0.4	0.6	0.6	0.7	0.7	0.7	0.8	0.8
State and local hospitals[6]	5.6	7.0	10.8	11.8	12.0	11.9	11.5	11.2	11.8
Other[7]	3.1	3.3	5.0	6.6	7.1	7.5	7.5	7.7	8.7
Medical research	5.2	7.3	11.3	13.3	14.6	15.4	15.7	16.4	18.3
Medical facilities construction	2.0	2.6	3.0	3.8	4.1	4.4	4.7	5.2	4.0

Source: U.S. Health Care Financing Administration, *Health Care Financing Review* (Winter 1999).

* Includes Puerto Rico and outlying areas.

[1] Change from immediate prior year.

[2] Covers insurance benefits and amount retained by insurance companies for expenses, additions to reserves, and profits.

[3] Represents expenditures for benefits and administrative cost from federal hospital and medical insurance trust funds under old-age, survivors', disability, and health insurance programs.

[4] Payments made directly to suppliers of medical care, primarily Medicaid.

[5] Includes medical benefits paid under public law by private insurance carriers, state governments, and self-insurers.

[6] Expenditures not offset by other revenues.

[7] Covers expenditures for Substance Abuse and Mental Health Services Administration, Indian Health Service; school health and other programs.

TABLE 6.2 | NATIONAL HEALTH EXPENDITURES BY OBJECT, 1980–1998 (IN BILLIONS OF DOLLARS)*

Object of Expenditure	1980	1985	1990	1993	1994	1995	1996	1997	1998
Total	247.3	428.7	699.4	898.5	947.7	993.3	1,039.4	1,088.2	1,149.1
Spent by:									
Consumers	130.0	233.5	384.6	473.9	483.5	494.6	513.0	535.7	574.6
Out-of-pocket	60.3	100.7	145.0	167.1	168.2	170.5	178.1	189.1	199.5
Private insurance	69.8	132.8	239.6	306.8	315.3	324.0	334.9	346.7	375.0
Government	104.8	174.2	283.2	385.3	423.0	456.0	480.4	502.2	522.7
Other[1]	12.5	21.0	31.6	39.3	41.2	42.7	46.1	50.3	51.8
Spent for:									
Health services and supplies	235.6	412.3	674.8	869.5	917.3	962.5	1,007.5	1,053.5	1,113.7
Personal health-care expenses	217.0	376.4	614.7	790.5	834.0	879.1	924.0	968.6	1,019.3
Hospital care	102.7	168.3	256.4	323.0	335.7	347.0	359.4	370.2	382.8
Physician services	45.2	83.6	146.3	185.9	193.0	201.9	208.5	217.8	229.5
Dental services	13.3	21.7	31.6	39.5	42.4	45.0	47.5	51.1	53.8
Other professional services[2]	6.4	16.6	34.7	46.1	49.6	53.6	57.4	61.5	66.6
Home health care	2.4	5.6	13.1	23.0	26.2	29.1	31.2	30.5	29.3

Drugs/other medical nondurable	1.6	37.1	59.9	76.2	81.5	88.6	98.0	108.6	121.9
Vision products durables[3]	3.8	6.7	10.5	12.3	12.6	13.3	14.1	15.1	15.5
Nursing home care	17.6	30.7	50.9	66.4	71.1	75.5	80.2	84.7	87.8
Other health services	4.0	6.1	11.2	18.0	21.9	25.1	27.6	29.2	32.1
Net cost of insurance[4]	11.9	24.3	40.5	53.7	55.2	53.6	52.1	50.3	57.7
Government public health	6.7	11.6	19.6	25.3	28.2	29.8	31.3	34.6	36.6
Medical research[5]	5.5	7.8	12.2	14.5	15.9	16.7	17.2	17.9	19.9
Medical facilities construction	6.2	8.5	12.3	14.5	14.6	14.0	14.8	16.9	15.5

Source: U.S. Health Care Financing Administration, *Health Care Financing Review* (Winter 1999).

* Includes Pueto Rico and outlying areas.

[1] Includes nonpatient revenues, privately funded construction, and industrial in-plant.

[2] Includes services of registered and practical nurses in private duty, podiatrists, optometrists, physical therapists, clinical psychologists, chiropractors, naturopaths, and Christian Science practitioners.

[3] Includes expenditures for eyeglasses, hearing aids, orthopedic appliances, artificial limbs, crutches, wheelchairs, etc.

[4] Includes administrative expenses of federally financed health programs.

[5] Research and development expenditures of drug companies and other manufacturers and providers of medical equipment and supplies are excluded from research expenditures but are included in the expenditure class in which the product falls.

all expenditures in 1998 were for personal health services and supplies. More specifically, $1 billion (88.7%) went toward personal health care, in large proportion to hospital and physician services. Health expenditures other than services and supplies constituted only 6.3% of the total (see Table 6.2, lines for government public health, medical research, and medical facilities). Expenditure shares have shown increases toward treatment activities over the past five years.

Public responsibility for intervention in private-sector activities is usually justified when markets are not efficient, as when the full price of a product is not reflected in the market price (economists attribute the differential to "externalities"). When the poor cannot get needed medical services in private markets, government intervention is justified, either through direct service programs or by providing funds so that services can be purchased. In that sense, social externalities would define situations in which the marginal costs of services must be paid by the general public for private-sector health products (services and materials) when it would be difficult and unwise to deny them to anyone. For example, it would be difficult and unwise to deny anyone police and fire protection and waste disposal, just as it would be unwise or impossible to deprive a portion of the population of a clean and toxin-free physical environment. In similar terms, victims of AIDS or newly recognized diseases may agitate for government relief for costs of specific medicines, which are exceptionally expensive because recently developed or salable only to relatively small populations; arguments vary over whether the government should cover the loss to the manufacturer or subsidize individuals' payments for such medications. Even under such circumstances, however, public-sector spending for health care that constitutes half of all health-care spending is bound to upset the usual forces of private market checks and balances.

Because health care is clearly a private market activity in the United States, public activity focuses on efforts to help those who are unable to purchase adequate medical care. Medicare and Medicaid constitute about 30% of all health spending. Both programs are designed to allot money to citizens to allow them to buy essentially privately determined health products. Some would argue that public responsibility should be taken a step further—that health care should be, overall, a public rather than a private responsibility. This normative position is justified to the extent that it would eliminate "externalities" as described above. However, under such conditions the public interest would be more inclined to support preventive activities, since it would cost less to supplement the private market with private funds, as is presently the case. On the other hand, to assert that financial support for health services should be an entirely public responsibility, despite the private nature of the current health-care market, fails to take into account the limitations that should be placed on the use of public funds. For example, should someone have the same access to public funding for cosmetic surgery as access to emergency services after an accidental injury? Except in unusual cases involving fiscal accountability or political liability, such as publicly funded abortions, the dividing line between public and private responsibility for providing health care has not been clearly discussed in the development of present-day health-care policy.

The lack of clarity about the public role in health care has become more pronounced as government efforts have stimulated the supply of resources. For example, to answer increased demand after World War II, the Hospital Construction Act of 1946 (the Hill-Burton Act) provided federal funds to construct community hospitals. These hospitals were required to serve low-income people. Although most hospitals constructed under the act were forced to budget some funds consistently toward services to low-income patients, no exact formulas were established, and similar policies were not included in related government efforts, such as federal funding for the education of doctors and other health professionals. Thus, without a clear policy on public responsibility for health care, the increase in supply of medical resources, combined with increased demand for the resources stimulated by public funding, has not only caused continuing cycles of rising costs but also left public health-care policy to drift toward accommodating whatever individual preferences seemed to emerge. In a curious twist of capitalism, individual choice is no longer controlled by the market, but nurtured by apparently unlimited public support. This drift might be compared with a public policy to provide cash supplements for individual recreation, which, though intended to promote better physical conditioning, would also permit people to buy tickets to football games if they preferred.

The recent effort on the part of the Clinton administration to reform America's health-care system unexpectedly confronted a number of these discussed ambiguities. The Clinton health-care reform effort was initiated only four days after the president took office, and was headed by someone without credentials in the health-care field. Just weeks after the appointment of the Task Force on National Health Care Reform, the initiative was in trouble. Composed of fifteen subgroups comprising health-care experts, congressional staff members, and six cabinet members, and consultations with more than 500 groups that had interests in health-care policy, the process quickly bogged down in wrangling, with the "big business" players, most notably insurance and pharmaceutical companies, targets of verbal exchanges.[3] But perhaps the real reasons behind this failed reform was the idea of a comprehensive health-care system directed by the federal government. Without clear perspective on the specific role the federal government could play in a sharply divided health-care system, the task force presented Congress with a 1,300-page bill (H.R. 3600, S. 1757), which because of its uncompromising effort to create a uniform health-care plan was largely ignored when presented to the 104th Congress.[4] President Clinton's health-care reforms at first sought to regulate health-care market activity as government regulates other sectors of private enterprise. But unlike other private-sector activity, government has a legitimate role in providing, or ensuring, the provision of health services, just as government has responsibility to see to the provision of other public utilities such as highways and airports. The failure to clarify exactly what constitutes a legitimate public responsibility—immunizations, for example—distinct from private responsibility for health care—such as cosmetic surgery—led to unprecedented confusion and eventual erosion of any support for comprehensive health-care reform.

METHODS OF IMPLEMENTATION

Health-care policy directed toward treatment has been implemented primarily through insurance programs that reduce the risk of large financial expenditures for individuals by spreading the costs among participating groups and doing so over relatively short periods of time when compared with other kinds of insurance. Other kinds of insurance—for example, accident, fire, or life—pay out benefits to the user; under health insurance, however, control of benefits rests not with the user, but with the insurance company and the health-care provider. In other words, as a way of protecting individuals against high medical costs, health insurance has created a health-care system in which the provider treats the patient but collects from the insurer. The user no longer controls either the cost or the product. Health insurance is thus essentially a funding mechanism, and really not insurance at all. As such, health insurance presents several limitations to health policymakers. The central issue at stake is cost control. Because insurance so dominates health policy, it is important that the analyst have a clear understanding of its basic operations.

In reality, two health insurance systems operate in the United States—private and public—and health-care policy is extremely difficult to control through either. About 81% of Americans are covered under some type of health insurance. The other 19%, according to most studies, are people in a borderline state of poverty not eligible for income-maintenance programs and related public health insurance, yet not well enough employed to be eligible for employer-sponsored private coverage, which generally is offered only to full-time workers. These uninsured people can receive health care at free public health agencies that have outpatient clinics or at hospital emergency rooms. Many receive no health care at all. The Reagan administration unsuccessfully sought to restrict public Medicaid funding, and as eligibility for income-maintenance programs has also been tightened, the number of people without adequate health care has increased sharply in the 1990s. The Clinton administration sought to set cost controls on the insurance industry, only to have the providers, consumers, insurance companies, in short, everyone, raise objections.

The Private Insurance System

The private health insurance system is usually characterized by an employer-sponsored health-care plan in which employee, employer, and (where applicable) unions participate in financing the plan and determining the benefits. Over 140 million people are covered under such plans. For many years the major private health insurance carrier was Blue Cross/Blue Shield (BCBS), but in recent years a vast array of competitors have entered the business.

The prototype for the Blue Cross system was founded in 1929 by Justin Kimball at Baylor University for schoolteachers in Dallas, Texas.[5] The idea arose because so many of the teachers had unpaid hospital bills. Under Kimball's original plan a premium of 50 cents would cover expenses for twenty-one days of hospital care in a semiprivate room. Ten years later, after Blue Cross had become an established hospital insurance plan, the California Medical Association established a similar insurance scheme to cover payment of doctors' bills. This system gained much acceptance among physicians and was added to the Blue Cross programs as Blue Shield. By the mid-1970s there were about 70 BCBS plans in the United States, with a total enrollment of nearly 85 million "subscriber" units.

The seeds of present policy dilemmas, those faced by the private insurance programs as well as by Medicare and Medicaid, were sown in these early phases. Three important founding principles still affect the operations of health insurance today. Reforms that do not account for these early problems, which have become locked into the structure of American health insurance, will fail to satisfy present-day policy. Similarly, the use of health insurance as a primary tool in the development and reform of health-care policy is severely limited by the continuing existence of these principles.

First of all, it must be recognized that health insurance does not provide cash benefits (indemnities) in the sense that accident or fire or life insurance does; it provides service benefits instead. Certainly the subscriber still receives a pro forma statement of costs absorbed by the insurer, but in effect what the subscriber has gained is not an indemnity but the service itself, such as emergency treatment or a hospital stay. For these benefits, as with forms of traditional insurance, the subscriber pays an advance subscription, or premium, at regular intervals. Premiums for traditional kinds of insurance are calculated on the basis of actuarial tables that can project fair prices against future payoffs with considerable accuracy. Estimating the need for future service benefits as in the case of health insurance is a more difficult task because the actual services and their actual costs are not known. This difficulty is compounded when public policy continues to stimulate the development of new health products, both services and materials, that are strongly desired by the consumers (patients). Adjusting for these discrepancies is the role of "managed care" as discussed below.

Second, Blue Cross began as an aid to payment of hospital bills. In fact, it functioned more as an insurance program for hospitals than for patients. In the early days, hospitals accepted the Blue Cross payment even if the payment did not cover the full cost of care. If Blue Cross did pay the full cost of covered hospital services, that cost was often discounted by hospitals in exchange for the certainty of receiving payment for services rendered. Blue Shield began with the same objectives—a method for guaranteeing payment of doctors' bills—and it too offered service in place of indemnity. Unlike Blue Cross, however, Blue Shield's service benefit concept was more difficult to establish, since the price for services was often based on negotiations between doctor and patient. Efforts to standardize rates for physicians' fees were essential to the fiscal integrity of the program. "Usual, customary, and reasonable" (UCR) rates were determined, but these could only be implemented if physicians agreed. Thus control of Blue Cross's costs rested with hospital administrators, and control of Blue Shield's costs rested with the doctors.

Third, because BCBS provided more protection to providers than to health-care consumers, participation was at first limited, usually to people with modest incomes. Blue Cross costs and benefits were developed specifically for hourly wage earners on the assumption that salaried employees would be able to afford better care without needing insurance. Blue Shield plans at first were limited to employed people who earned less than $3,000 per year. The per-unit-of-service reimbursement to physicians on the basis of UCR standards was acceptable to doctors who were expected to give care to this group of people anyway. Individual physicians usually covered their real costs by charging the wealthy more to balance the difference.

To make matters worse, advances in medical technology soon began to undermine the fiscal integrity of BCBS plans. Medical subspecialization proliferated as new technologies developed, producing a shift in the location of service providers. Because most new technology could not be purchased by the individual physician, hospital-based services took on a new dimension. Services of hospital-based physicians in specialized disciplines such as radiology and anesthesiology could now be included in costs covered under Blue Cross. This form of reimbursement made the hospital into an umbrella organization that established its own service systems, which in turn placed additional burdens on BCBS funding. Hospital services now ranged far beyond bed care, as hospitals continued to invest in expensive equipment that could only be paid for as the costs were written off against forms of insurance like Blue Cross. For example, new equipment costs were built into comprehensive costs of hospital care, whether or not the individual patient/subscriber had actually used the new equipment. These higher hospital and physician costs put financial pressure not only on the insurer but also on uninsured patients, although insured patients did not have to face these rising costs directly.

In 1947 the Supreme Court ruled that employee benefits, including health insurance, had a legitimate place in bargaining between labor and management. This ruling opened the door for enrollment of salaried workers as well as others who had hitherto been restricted from joining BCBS. These new subscribers pressured for more and expanded health coverage, placing even greater fiscal strain on the health insurance system. By the time Medicare and Medicaid were developed in 1965, BCBS had developed elaborate methods for absorbing the increased financial pressures. Limitations on service benefits surfaced between BCBS and physicians and hospital administrators. The age-old fear that nonmedical people, in this case, hospital administrators and insurance companies, would be telling physicians what to do, emerged in full force.

In 1978 Blue Cross and Blue Shield merged, reflecting nationwide pressures from states and the federal government toward standardization of health insurance benefits and reimbursements. The merger marked the end, for practical purposes, of the surrogate role BCBS had played for hospitals and doctors, and put the corporation in the position of a true third party in the triangle of medical care, a party with legitimate rights to negotiate both costs and benefits. However, the surrogate attachment remained latent in the concept of service benefits, which, in the climate of rapid technological advancement in medical care and universal availability of insurance, contributed significantly to increased costs. In this environment both Medicare and Medicaid were bound to add inflationary pressure by making more funding available for services when they were established in 1965. Efforts to contain costs by restructuring benefits proved generally ineffective as long as benefits remained in the form of services, and as long as reimbursements for them were protected by the providers.

The Public Insurance System

The public insurance system consists of two elements: Medicare and Medicaid. Both were created by amendments to the Social Security Act in 1965 and originally administered by the U.S. Department of Health, Education, and Welfare (later reorganized in 1980 as the Department of Health and Human Services). A separate agency, the Health Care Financing Administration (HCFA) was created in 1977 to administer the Medicare and Medicaid programs. HCFA was reorganized July 1, 2001, into the Centers for Medicare and Medicaid Services (CMS), which now provides Medicare and Medicaid. The following discussion of both programs makes reference to both CMS and HCFA.

Medicare   Medicare is a government-financed system of health insurance for Social Security beneficiaries. Because Social Security extends to survivors of covered persons and to the disabled as well as the elderly, it is available to more than elderly subscribers. About 39 million people are covered by Medicare. Eighty-seven percent are aged, and the balance are disabled. The majority of disabled are children and working-age persons. Medicare is insurance, and it operates almost exactly the same as BCBS and similarly to other private insurance programs. By paying a monthly Medicare premium, the subscriber receives basic benefit coverage for hospital care and major medical and surgical expenses.

Medicare is administered in two parts. Part A is hospital insurance that pays for inpatient hospital care, nursing-home care, home health care, and hospice care, less a yearly deductible. It is provided as part of the Social Security benefit package, financed by the Medicare insurance part of the Social Security payroll tax. Nursing-home care, like in-hospital care, is limited and requires a deductible assessed for each of the first days of care per year.

Medicare, Part B, covers medical costs associated with illness, such as Blue Shield does. It is funded by a monthly premium (of about 25% of the cost, $45.00 in 2000) and by federal funds from general tax revenues (the remaining 75%). For the premium, 80% of service costs are then paid by Medicare. The other 20%, and any medical expenditures that Medicare will not cover, must be paid by the individual. Most participants buy other insurance, such as BCBS, to cover the deductible and uncovered expenses, causing increased complexity in efforts to clearly distinguish between private and public responsibility for health care. The costs and covered benefits change frequently from year to year. (See Table 6.3.)

Because Medicare is insurance, it is faced with problems that are inherited from private-sector programs: service benefits, with fees set by providers; inability to control costs; and a third-party status, but with inadequate authority

TABLE 6.3	MEDICARE BENEFITS BY TYPE OF PROVIDER, 1985–1999 (IN MILLIONS OF DOLLARS)

Distribution of Benefits by Type	1990	1995	1996	1997	1998	1999
Hospital insurance (Part A)						
Total	65,721	113,394	123,908	136,007	134,321	129,107
Inpatient hospital	57,012	80,881	84,200	88,292	86,998	85,259
Skilled nursing facility	2,761	8,761	10,636	12,561	13,630	12,361
Home health agency	3,295	15,851	17,250	18,012	13,806	8,764
Hospice	318	1,854	1,969	2,082	2,080	2,479
Managed care	2,335	6,047	9,853	15,059	17,807	20,243
Supplementary medical insurance (Part B)						
Total	41,498	63,491	67,176	71,133	75,815	79,187
Physician fee schedule	(NA)	31,110	31,569	31,960	32,341	33,184
Durable medical equipment	(NA)	3,576	3,785	4,112	4,108	4,146
Carrier lab[1]	(NA)	2,819	2,654	2,414	2,168	2,040
Other carrier[2]	(NA)	4,513	4,883	5,449	5,845	6,245
Hospital[3]	(NA)	8,449	8,720	9,293	9,056	8,520
Home health	(NA)	223	257	265	202	761
Intermediary lab[4]	(NA)	1,437	1,322	1,416	1,470	1,571
Other intermediary[5]	(NA)	5,111	5,632	6,330	6,492	5,823
Managed care	(NA)	6,253	8,353	9,893	14,132	16,897

Source: U.S. Health Care Financing Administration, unpublished data.

NA = not available

[1] Lab services paid under the lab fee schedule performed in a physician's office lab or an independent lab.

[2] Includes free-standing ambulatory surgical centers facility costs, ambulance, and supplies.

[3] Includes the hospital facility costs for Medicare Part B services, which are predominantly in the outpatient department. The physician reimbursement associated with these services is included on the "Physician fee schedule" line.

[4] Lab fee services paid under the lab fee schedule performed in a hospital outpatient department.

[5] Includes ESRD free-standing dialysis facility payments and payments to rural health clinics, outpatient rehabilitation facilities, psychiatric hospitals, and federally qualified health centers.

to direct policy. Hence, like private-sector programs, Medicare is biased in favor of the service providers. Under Part A, for example, Medicare emphasizes
in-hospital care, which is expensive. Current average hospital room charges per
day have risen to more than $525, not including the costs of medical services
required by the illness itself. Less expensive, nursing-home costs average nearly
$1200 per claim. Care at home, by contrast, costs less than 30% of nursing-
home care, and less than 1% of an average hospital stay. Since the great majority of Medicare subscribers are older people, the age group that has the highest
rates of hospital use, this emphasis on hospital coverage is essential. But it has
meant that expenses for long-term routine care of patients outside hospitals—
for instance, convalescents, invalids, and some of the terminally ill—are virtually unrecoverable. Part B has similar provider biases in its basic package: 77%
of its expenditures go to physicians, and less than 1% to care in the home.

Medicaid   Medicaid is not an insurance program, but it operates like one. The
program disburses federal funds to states, which use the money along with their
own funds to pay for health care for poor people. States operate Medicaid programs by administering them directly or by contracting with private insurance
agencies for administrative services. States set the conditions of eligibility and
establish the benefit package consistent with federal regulations. States must
provide medical care for people who are recipients of aid in federally supported,
means-tested income-maintenance programs. They may also provide medical
care to other low-income people who have such large medical expenses that they
would qualify for income-maintenance programs if those expenses were paid
from personal funds—a form of relief often called a medical "spend-down."
    As with private insurance and Medicare, Medicaid recipients choose their
own health-care providers and negotiate their own health care accordingly. The
allowable services rendered are paid for by Medicaid as if covered by insurance.
    About 28 million people are covered by Medicaid. Medicaid expenditures
amount to more than 10% of all health care and 25% of federal health-care expenditures. Current costs are about $142.3 billion annually, of which 60% is
funded by the federal government, and the remainder by state and local governments. Because Medicaid is available to income-maintenance recipients and
other low-income people who cannot meet their own medical expenses, it acts
as a supplement to Medicare for older people who need skilled nursing or intermediate care. In fact, about 11% of all Medicaid recipients are older people
whose Medicare benefits have been exhausted. Half of Medicaid beneficiaries,
however, are under age 18. Still, large segments of the population in poverty—
childless couples, marginal employees, and the unemployed under age 65—receive no public medical insurance because they are not eligible for income-
maintenance programs. In short, only about 41% of people who live below the
poverty line receive Medicaid. (See Table 6.4.)
    Like Medicare, Medicaid is driven by service providers' demands. Figure 6.3
shows the proportions of Medicaid spent on various forms of services. Hospitals
and various long-term care facilities absorb more than half of Medicaid expenditures. By contrast, forms of home care constitute only 8.4% of Medicaid

TABLE 6.4 │ SELECTED CHARACTERISTICS OF PERSONS COVERED UNDER MEDICAID (IN THOUSANDS)

		Race			Age			
Poverty Status	Total[1]	White	Black	Hispanic[2]	Under 18	18–44	45–64	65 & over
Persons covered, total	27,647	18,131	7,820	5,550	14,066	7,593	3,025	2,962
Below poverty level	13,996	8,470	4,659	3,170	7,784	3,836	1,372	1,003
Above poverty level	13,651	9,661	3,161	2,380	6,282	3,757	1,653	1,959
Percentage of population covered	10.2	8.1	22.4	17.6	19.7	7.0	5.2	9.1
Below poverty level	40.6	36.1	51.3	39.3	57.8	29.6	29.5	29.6
Above poverty level	5.8	4.8	12.3	10.2	10.9	3.9	3.1	6.8

Source: U.S. Census Bureau, 1999, *Current Population Reports*, P60-208, earlier reports; and unpublished data.

[1] Includes other races not shown separately.

[2] Persons of Hispanic origin may be of any race.

FIGURE 6.3 | MEDICAID EXPENDITURES,
             TYPE OF SERVICE

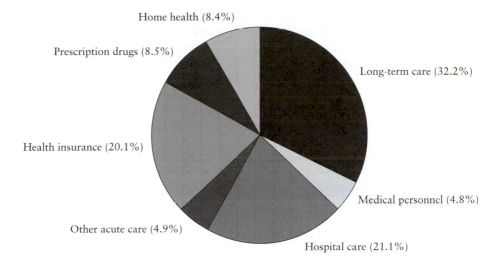

Home health (8.4%)

Prescription drugs (8.5%)

Long-term care (32.2%)

Health insurance (20.1%)

Medical personnel (4.8%)

Other acute care (4.9%)

Hospital care (21.1%)

expenditures. Indeed, expenditures for Medicaid are quite similar to those for Medicare, suggesting that both programs function to subsidize a medical care industry that is dominated by expensive institutional-related costs, with very little support for health care outside the existing medical structure. Hence as prices rise, public funding must increase, contributing to another rise in prices in a spiral of inflated medical costs. Notice the large increase in family planning expenditures in spite of the ban on the use of Medicaid funding for abortions.

State Children's Health Insurance Program (SCHIP)   Somewhat unexpectedly, Congress amended the Social Security Act to add a new title—Title XXI—in 1997 (PL 105-33), creating a special health insurance–type program for children, also administered by CMS. The purpose of SCHIP is to enable states to initiate and expand child health assistance to uninsured, low-income children through (1) a new program to obtain health insurance coverage that meets specific requirements or (2) expanding eligibility for children under the state's Medicaid program or (3) a combination of both.

Each state must describe standards and methods used to establish and continue eligibility and enrollment for targeted low-income children. The standards must cover lower-income children within a category of covered children before higher-income children and may not deny eligibility based on a preexisting condition. States also must include a description of screening procedures to ensure that only targeted low-income children receive assistance, and that Medicaid-eligible children are enrolled in Medicaid. A state must also describe procedures for outreach to families of children likely to be eligible for assistance under the plan or under other public or private coverage and to inform them of the availability of, and assist in, enrollment in these programs.

Although the SCHIP went into effect in October 1997, states have been slow to fully implement it. By 2000 only 41 states had implemented the program, and many of these programs were only partially implemented. Approximately 3.3 million children were being served in these programs, and since SCHIP allowed states to provide coverage of children who lived in families where incomes were as much as 200% of the poverty level, most states took advantage of this provision and were able to extend coverage to children who might not have been covered otherwise under their Medicaid programs (for the development of the SCHIP program, see http://www.hcfa.gov). As the program matures, more and more children in nonpoverty families will be covered, somewhat in contrast with the picture of Medicaid presented in Table 6.4, providing another example of policy creep discussed at the beginning of Part II.

CURRENT HEALTH POLICY OPTIONS

Cost-Containment Delivery Systems

For several years a number of efforts have been made to contain the costs of medical care. The first sought to reduce the growth in public spending in the Medicare and Medicaid programs. Proponents have reasoned that if costs could be contained and even reduced in these public insurance programs, the cost reductions would be spread to private insurance programs. This is not an unreasonable presumption considering the major role of public spending for health care. The Health Care Financing Administration (HCFA) first attempted to contain hospital costs by initiating a system of peer review for hospital care, to verify whether hospital stays and medical services were appropriate. This system monitored medical services by examining patients' records to ensure that hospitals would not keep patients beyond a period absolutely necessary merely to generate revenue for the hospital. Experience with this system during the late 1970s suggested that for the most part hospital and other medical services were appropriately handled. The peer review system itself was costly, however, and often excessively intrusive.

As a result of that experience, HCFA decided to modify its payment system from one that reimbursed for care already received (retrospective payments) to one based on established rates for specific services that might be needed (prospective payments); this was to be accomplished by creating a system of diagnostically related groups (DRGs). Under this prospective payment scheme, providers are paid a set amount for a particular problem that they have agreed to treat. If treatment turns out to cost less, the provider keeps the difference; if it costs more, the provider absorbs the additional costs. This alternative policy is still being implemented as existing diagnostic groups are being re-formed and new ones are being created. There is no evidence that costs can be contained or reduced as this policy continues to be implemented, and some critics fear that the DRG system will discourage providers from treating "unprofitable" medical problems. The Centers for Medicare and Medicaid Services (CMS) is considering yet further cost-containment policies that have not yet been publicly discussed.

Health Maintenance Organizations (HMOs)

Another effort to reduce public spending for health care, particularly medical care, has come through the increased use of health maintenance organizations (HMOs) as alternatives to prepaid insurance programs that emphasize medical care and treatment. To understand how HMOs operate requires another brief glance at the recent history of medical practice and health insurance.

At the time when BCBS plans were expanding, new structures of medical practice were also emerging that differed from the discrete units of doctor, patient, and hospital. By the late 1960s, five clear patterns for providing medical care had become standard:

1. In the traditional manner, the patient went to a physician, who organized a plan of medical care for the patient and provided services directly or through constituents.
2. The patient organized his or her own care, often with the result that the patient had several doctors, depending on the problems involved. This was partly a response to the rapid increase in physicians' specialization after World War II.
3. As hospitals increased in technological capacities and began to expand clinical services to outpatients, many people began to use outpatient clinics to receive medical care without dependence on any specific doctor or medical practitioner.
4. Because many low-income people had little access to ordinary medical care, they waited until medical problems became acute and then resorted to emergency rooms, which usually treat people first, assuming an emergency, and ask questions about payment later.
5. In a variation on the traditional doctor–patient pattern, and as a way of providing costly new technologies through private practice, physicians began to practice in groups.[6]

Physicians quickly recognized the advantages of group practice. Patients could be offered a variety of specialized services at the doctors' offices; operating costs could be shared; many supportive services, such as routine laboratory work, could be done at less cost to the patient and greater convenience to the doctors. Moreover, the patient could be seen in a more comprehensive environment, often including all family members; this encouraged provisional health maintenance services as well as more traditional treatment services. In many instances, however, it proved difficult to obtain insurance reimbursement for services provided by group practices. Splitting the fee in order to satisfy insurers' fee-for-service criteria was troublesome and sometimes impossible. Setbacks of this nature seriously limited the expansion of group practice.

Shortly after World War II, Henry H. Kaiser, the automobile manufacturer, launched a new and creative program for providing medical benefits to his employees. For the same amount as the usual insurance charge, the subscriber could receive comprehensive medical care in a group practice that he organized. All forms of care were made available to members, but the practice was designed to promote preventive medicine (health maintenance) in preference to treatment, on the assumption that it cost less to keep people well than to treat them when they became ill. The Kaiser plan quickly began to spread as a group practice option, setting the stage for the development of HMOs generally, and the Health Maintenance Organization Act of 1973.

The Kaiser Permanente model of medical care was an important development in the funding and organization of health care. First, it emphasized prevention and education to maintain a state of health. Second, each program was designed to integrate hospital and physician services by controlling both resources in a single program. To accomplish this, Kaiser Permanente programs usually constructed their own inpatient facilities, thus controlling overall health-care costs within each organization. Third, and no less important, the Kaiser Permanente plans substituted a "capitation" payment system for the fee-for-service system. Under capitation, the cost and reimbursement rates are based on the number of people served, not the services provided. By freeing group practices from the usual fee structures, Kaiser Permanente programs had greater flexibility to offer whatever services were appropriate. For example, health education, such as wellness classes during pregnancy, would be offered, rather than only services that were reimbursable, such as delivering a baby. It also made HMOs an attractive alternative for public funding of health care, and finally led to federal funding of HMOs and the encouragement of their widespread use.

At present there are about 230 officially recognized HMOs across the nation, serving about 12.5 million people. An HMO must meet certain criteria to obtain official recognition:

1. It must have an organized system of health care in a geographic area in which it assumes responsibility for providing that care.
2. It must have a defined and agreed-upon set of basic and supplemental health maintenance and treatment services.
3. Its subscribers must be voluntarily enrolled.
4. It must have certification as a group HMO or as an individual practice association (IPA). (Under the latter arrangement, physicians contract to see HMO patients on a capitation basis, but may also see their own patients on a fee-for-service basis.)

An approved (officially recognized) HMO is eligible to receive Medicaid and Medicare reimbursement on a person-by-person (capitation) basis as an exception to established Medicaid and Medicare regulations, and some private insurance companies similarly approve and reimburse insurance claims for services received through HMOs. The advantages of an HMO are the generally lower overall costs for total health services provided, even though individual cases may incur higher costs than normal. HMOs avoid the fiscal limits on health services that are created by insurance-based reimbursement systems, although HMOs limit sharply the services they will provide. HMOs, then, provide more comprehensive and health-oriented (rather than treatment-oriented) services. Capitation also makes it easier for HMOs to fund services for low-income people, and federal reimbursement for HMO services has enabled the expansion of "well-health" services into many traditionally lower-income urban centers.

Although it is not yet clear, HMOs may be victims of their own success. As health consumers begin to demand more health maintenance services, such as Pap smears and mammograms, traditional insurance programs have been forced to cover more of these "health" services in their basic package. At the same time, HMO patients were demanding many traditional treatment-oriented services often covered by health insurance packages, but not often available in the usual HMO. The HMO strictly limited the traditional treatment services it provided, thus "managing" the "care" a patient received. Most health-care consumers failed to recognize the organizational difference between the HMO and traditional health services available under traditional health insurance, and as demands for treatments increased, and as HMOs expanded to try to provide these services, they began to find themselves in financial difficulty. As a result, Kaiser Permanente, along with other HMOs, has closed many of its facilities.

The development of HMOs offered hope both for redirection of health-care policy and for containment of service costs. However, the gradual erosion of the classic HMO leaves most health-care decisions in the hands of insurance providers, suggesting that changes in forms of health services, in themselves, will not be enough to produce comprehensive changes in health policy. One element of the HMO experience that did seem to survive, however, was the idea of managing health care by setting restrictions on the type and amount of care that might be provided. Thus, the unsuccessful attempt to reform health care by the Clinton administration resulted in an acceleration of "managed care" principles as a way to control health-care costs. Under the threat of a "single payer" system, both hospitals and insurance companies began efforts to restructure their health-care products. The "single payer" would have required that hospitals, for example, not be reimbursed for services to John Doe unless John Doe received all his medical care from the same hospital. Thus hospitals began to acquire individual and group medical practices to expand the patient base of their services to include routine, nonhospital forms of health care so they could become a "single payee" and thus the "manager" of the health care the person received.

The "single payer" system originated from an experiment in Oregon in the late 1970s when Oregon sought to limit its public spending for health care by sharply restricting reimbursable medical services. To enforce these changes Oregon established a board that would "manage" reimbursements to be sure that only that which was agreed to would be paid for. For example, if Oregon agreed to three prenatal visits, and if the person needed a fourth, the fourth visit would not be reimbursable unless an exception was granted by the manager. Thus the generally unsuccessful Clinton health reform resulted in greater attention to and adoption of "managed care" as yet another cost-containment effort.

This latest effort in the cost-containment battle has added yet a fourth player in the provision of health care—the managed-care administrator, in addition to the patient, the doctor, and the insurance company. Essentially a managed-care organization oversees, or manages, several health insurance policies to make sure the proper service is provided as set forth in the insurance agreement. While many insurance providers had always managed their policies for appropriate compliance, the detailed monitoring by the managed-care organization purports to save insurance companies money while at the same time ensuring appropriate services for the client.

Thus Clinton's 1994 health-care reform effort brought about some subtle shifts in the provision of health-care products, even without legislation. There is great doubt, however, that these changes will do very much to reform health care, as they seem to give traditional providers of traditional services a level of protection in the highly volatile world of health-care policy.

Noninsured Health Care

Public support for health care provided without insurance reimbursement amounts to less than 10% of all health expenditures. The most important of such programs are (1) the Maternal and Child Health programs, (2) spending for local public health programs, (3) the U.S. Public Health Service, (4) special programs under the Health Services Block Grant, and (5) programs supporting medical research. There are also other programs that implement health policy even though their expenditures are not budgeted as health-related: environmental programs, for example, and the Special Supplemental Food Program for Women, Infants, and Children (WIC) are often considered forms of income-maintenance programs.

Maternal and Child Health (MCH)   Maternal and Child Health (MCH) began as an original part of the Social Security Act of 1935. The program transfers federal money to the states for the provision of pre- and postnatal health care to mothers and infants. This care centers on examination and screening for medical problems, monitoring pregnancy, well-baby checkups after birth, and considerable health education. In most cases MCH funds are channeled through local health departments, which generally provide a wide range of health maintenance services to a wide spectrum of the local population. Hence it is difficult to say exactly how many mothers and children benefit directly from the public funds spent specifically for the purposes of MCH. The MCH budget includes special funds for the provision of care and health services to handicapped children, which have been an extremely important source of fiscal encouragement for state and local health maintenance programs for such children. Many experts believe that the long-range steady decline in infant mortality rates and the decline in the number of low-birth-weight (premature) babies can be attributed to pre- and postnatal care provided by MCH and WIC.

Special Supplemental Food Program for Women, Infants, and Children (WIC) The Special Supplemental Food Program for Women, Infants, and Children (WIC) originated in 1975 as a program to identify women likely to bear children who would be vulnerable to medical problems. These women, who are also likely to be poor, are given a medical examination, monitoring during pregnancy, and special food supplements to ensure that they have an adequate diet throughout pregnancy and as long as they continue to breast-feed their newborn children. The program began with about 500,000 participants, but quickly expanded; it now covers about 2.8 million "high-risk" mothers. Along with MCH, WIC is highly valued for reducing the incidence of low-birth-weight babies, but it has also become an extremely important source of supplemental income for many low-income mothers. About 7.6% of all mothers give birth to low-birth-weight children, a ratio that almost doubles (14.6%) for teenage mothers, and soars to 32.8% for unmarried mothers. Thus WIC is well targeted on the most vulnerable.

Taken together, MCH and WIC implement one of the few publicly funded preventive health-care policies. This provides an unusual opportunity for comparing the relative costs for prevention and treatment. Children who weigh less than 2,500 grams (5 pounds, 8 ounces) at birth run a great risk of needing costly health care. The average cost of care during a child-bearing period is about $3,000, of which $750 is the average cost of prenatal care. Neonatal intensive care in hospitals averages $10,000 to $15,000 for each occurrence. Infants with low birth weight are highly susceptible to early childhood diseases and are also prone to develop severe respiratory problems during their first year of life. Nearly 250,000 such infants are born each year. C. Arden Miller, former dean of the University of North Carolina School of Public Health, estimates that for every dollar spent on prenatal care, $5.36 will be saved in medical costs in the twelve months following delivery.[7]

U.S. Public Health Service (PHS)   A variety of important programs are funded through and/or administered by the U.S. Public Health Service (PHS). The Public Health Service Act created the agency in 1944, and it has been recreated and modified many times since, as new health programs are launched and moved around in the federal bureaucracy. At present, the PHS includes the Centers for Disease Control (CDC), the Food and Drug Administration (FDA), the National Institutes of Health (NIH), the Health Resources and Services Administration (HRSA), and the Alcohol, Drug Abuse, and Mental Health Administration. Through research and regulation in their fields of activity, the CDC, FDA, and NIH provide a broad range of public health maintenance and protection services. The NIH has done considerable research in health maintenance and disease prevention through 11 research institutes and in a variety of public spending areas ranging from children to the elderly.

The HRSA administers professional training programs, funds for health planning, and funds for a few federally financed direct service programs. These programs include outpatient mental health programs, alcohol and drug abuse prevention and treatment programs, general funding for local public health services, and funding for service programs for special groups such as hemophiliacs. In 1981, under the Omnibus Budget Reconciliation Act, these programs were placed under the Health Services Block Grant, and their funds were given to states to spend as they see fit in these general program areas.

In summary, the public noninsurance programs are focused toward health maintenance, but they represent only a small proportion of expenditures for public and private health care. Some of these programs provide services directly to individuals; others are directed toward larger community issues of public health and protection from disease through long-range research and regulation. The services provided through these programs are likely to be closely associated with local public health agencies. Consequently they have come to play an important part in health care for low-income people across the nation.

POLICY ANALYSIS

Some analyses of health policy consider public and private health-care issues together, on the assumption that public spending for health has increased both demand and supply, forcing costs inevitably upward. This line of analysis seeks public, mostly federal, regulatory alternatives that will limit hospital and physicians' costs, the crucial factors in cost containment as discussed above. A recent analysis by the American Enterprise Institute takes a fairly typical stance along these lines:

> The central issue is not whether a system of government price and entry controls can succeed in decreasing [health care] costs, although success has so far proved elusive. The key question is what the health care delivery system will look like ten or twenty years from now if we squeeze providers through policies that do "work" in the sense of creating a slowdown of spending, but without changing the basic inequity in our health care financing system.[8]

This combined approach, however, does not address some of the crucial normative issues identified at the beginning of this chapter, particularly the entrenched bias toward treatment and cure in current conceptions of health and health policy.

Other analyses try to separate public from private health policy and focus on the high cost of federal spending, which is primarily directed at reimbursement for services performed in the private sector. Because this focus restricts the analyst to public-sector funding, assuming that the private sector is a world unto itself, it narrows considerably the range and scope of alternatives that may be presented to policymakers. For example, a recent study by the Congressional Budget Office states: "Major ways in which the federal government could bring market forces to bear upon medical costs include: altering the tax treatment of employment-based health insurance; offering Medicare beneficiaries a voucher to purchase a private health plan; and other adjustments in the Medicare reimbursement and benefit structures."[9]

In contrast with these approaches, the analysis suggested here attempts to examine the full range of normative orientations within a context of alternatives reflected by contemporary health programs. The criteria-based model in slightly modified form offers the best strategy for such a broad-scale analysis, precisely because the range of normative views is so wide that the normative issues cut across public and private health activities. A set of clear alternatives offers the opportunity for evaluating recommendations against normative criteria.

A summary paradigm of this analysis is presented in Table 6.5. The universal criteria and policy-specific criteria have been discussed as normative issues at the beginning of this chapter. The alternatives have also been mentioned in discussion above, and little needs to be said about them at this point, with the exception of "regulation against risks," which refers to policies (such as laws requiring the use of seatbelts and motorcyclists' helmets, or bans on smoking) that are intended to protect against health hazards. Policies of this nature apply equally to all concerned, and they are cost-effective, but they are difficult to implement because they restrict personal choices so severely. Relative values (high, medium, low) in Table 6.5 have been derived from preceding discussion of the criteria and the alternatives.

The paradigm presents no surprises. Insurance reimbursement plans rank highest in personal choice, preference satisfaction, and treatment, and low in cost containment and areas of prevention and care. The health services rank highest in universality, cost constraint, prevention, and public commitment, and low in personal choice, treatment, and preference satisfaction. Among insurance and reimbursement schemes the most appealing alternatives are Medicare and HMOs; public health clinics and mental health and drug treatment agencies look appealing among the service programs. The analysis affirms what seems to be the present status quo in health policy.

Use of medical care is difficult to determine accurately in terms of income and class. However, some surveys show evidence that the poor are less healthy and get less care than the wealthy. Between 1964 and 1974 there was a change in this general trend as a result of Medicaid and other efforts to bring the poor into the health-care system. For example, the poor began to see doctors at least as often as the nonpoor; poor women began to receive Pap smears and breast examinations almost as commonly as other women, and poor women who saw a physician during early pregnancy increased from 58 to 71%.[10] It will be interesting to see whether the SCHIP program improves health care for poor children in a similar manner.

However, it is possible to specify the mortality rate and then question whether the rates warrant an expanded discussion of policy alternatives. Table 6.6 reports the causes of death in 1995 and 1998. The major causes of death involve organ failure, an area that in recent years has received much attention in terms of medical research and technological advances in treatment. However, many of the leading causes of death could be prevented or delayed with a strong well-person approach. Most heart disease can be prevented. Diabetes,

TABLE 6.5 | PARADIGM OF HEALTH POLICY ANALYSIS, CRITERIA-BASED MODEL

Alternatives

Normative Orientations	Insurance/Reimbursements				Health Services				
	Public Health Insurance	Medicare	Medicaid	HMOs	MCH	WIC	Public Health Clinics	Mental Health Drug/Alcohol	Regulation Against Risk
Universal criteria:									
Equality (access)	Lo	Med	Hi	Med	Hi	Hi	Hi	Hi	Hi
Equity (quality of care)	Med	Med	Med	Med	—	—	Med	Med	—
Efficiency (cost containment)	Lo	Med	Med	Med	Hi	Hi	Hi	Med	Hi
Preference satisfaction	Hi	Med	Med	Med	Lo	Lo	Med	Med	Lo
Universality	Lo	Med	Hi	Med	Hi	Hi	Hi	Med	Hi
Policy-specific criteria:									
Maintain equilibrium (care)	Med	Med	Med	Hi	Lo	Lo	Hi	Hi	—
Restore equilibrium (treatment, care)	Hi	Hi	Hi	Hi	Lo	Lo	Med	Lo	—
Prevention	Lo	Lo	Lo	Med	Hi	Hi	Med	Lo	Hi
Personal choice	Hi	Hi	Hi	Hi	Lo	Lo	Lo	Lo	Lo
Public commitment	Hi	Hi	Hi	Med	Hi	Hi	Hi	Hi	Hi
	Hi = 3 Med = 2 Lo = 5	Hi = 3 Med = 6 Lo = 1	Hi = 5 Med = 4 Lo = 1	Hi = 4 Med = 6 Lo = 0	Hi = 5 Med = 0 Lo = 4	Hi = 5 Med = 0 Lo = 4	Hi = 5 Med = 4 Lo = 1	Hi = 3 Med = 4 Lo = 3	Hi = 5 Med = 0 Lo = 2

TABLE 6.6 | DEATH RATES BY SELECTED CAUSES, 1995 AND 1998

Cause of Death (Number/Percentage)	Year 1995	Year 1998
Total all deaths	2,312,100	2,338,100
Disease of the heart	32%	32%
Strokes	7%	7%
Cancers	23%	23%
Diabetes	3%	4%
Pulmonary diseases	4%	4%
Accidents	4%	4%
Suicide	1%	1%
Other (includes hepatitis, meningitis, and other infectious diseases	26%	25%
TOTAL	100%	100%

Source: U.S. Census Bureau, *Statistical Abstracts of the United States*, 2000, table 126.

which is on the rise, can be managed so as to prevent expensive medical complications, and even some forms of cancer can be prevented. Thus a shift in the health-care paradigm toward preventive measures may well have important consequences for cost containment.

RECOMMENDATIONS

When the alternatives are balanced against the criteria in the context of present-day experiences with health policy and the health profile of the nation, it becomes apparent that revision of some values might modify the weight given to certain alternatives. For example, health services seem to be at least as important as insurance programs in plotting a future health policy. Considering the health profile outlined above, a strong normative argument could be made that the effectiveness of present spending patterns for health care will have little long-term effect on health if a corresponding buildup of health services does not take place, particularly in the area of preventive services. The proportion of public spending devoted to such services does not suggest an even-handed development.

In general, the public insurance programs have brought low-income people closer to the mainstream of medical care, but at very great expense, as public insurances have sought equality of care perhaps at the expense of equity. Experience with private insurance systems suggests that it is impossible to control the escalation of costs that is almost certain to take place under such circumstances; consequently it is difficult to argue in favor of some form of nationalized health insurance program at this time. Cost containment and alternatives to medical care that are effective and cost-efficient (such as HMOs) must come from the providers.

The health services emphasize the very criteria that health insurance fails to deal with very well: maintenance and care. However, health services do not satisfy personal preference criteria in a way that public support for insurance does. In particular, public health efforts have a high degree of equity, but they rate comparatively low in terms of personal satisfaction, feasibility, and treatment. In practical terms, because individuality plays such an important part in health policy, efforts to achieve public health services, especially preventive health services, are apt to be extremely limited. Thus the feasibility of developing such services may remain low for years to come.

QUESTIONS FOR DISCUSSION

1. Provide a definition of health. How does this definition lead America to the development of health policy that seems to stress illness?
2. Assuming that one of the most significant health-care policy issues is containing costs, what efforts have been made at cost containment and how have those efforts turned out? Why are health-care costs so difficult to keep under control?
3. Discuss the interactions, if any, between the two most significant public health policies operating in America today.
4. What current public health programs are concerned with children's health care?
5. Considering that both private and public expenditures for health care are about equal, would it not be best to have one government-financed health-care program that would entitle everyone to a basic set of health services at public (taxpayers') expense? Defend your answer from your understanding of the issues discussed in this chapter.

HOUSING

CHAPTER 7

INTRODUCTION

Although finding a place to live is a trying experience for most Americans, the difficulties usually are limited to finding the kind of housing that suits personal tastes, rather than actually finding shelter. People may have to struggle to find the right style of housing in the right neighborhood at the right price, but in most cases they do find housing that satisfies their wants and needs. In other words, for most people, in most circumstances, housing policy in the United States is effective. But for others, particularly the poor and members of ethnic minorities, finding an adequate place to live seems almost unattainable; this need poses serious problems that erode the whole foundation of American housing policy. Thus housing policy, like health and income-maintenance policy, must be specific enough to deal with problems of the poor, but broad enough to satisfy the appetites of middle-class and upper-class Americans.

NORMATIVE ISSUES

Three general issues shape current housing policy: (1) housing standards, (2) developing the housing supply, and (3) housing subsidies and their distribution.

Housing Standards

Housing standards set the context for considering other normative issues. America does not tolerate "zero-standard" housing; squatter cities, tent towns, or cardboard communities would violate housing codes in every part of the nation. The vast slum housing that does exist in America is considered inadequate because it only barely meets, or fails to meet, local housing standards.

Several types of standards contribute to these norms. Land-use standards are usually applied by local governments, beginning with zoning laws that say what kinds of housing can be developed on what kind of land. Single- or multifamily housing, lot size, specialized land uses, and master land-use plans all set standards for housing development before building even begins. Construction standards center on building codes, which require that electrical wiring, plumbing, foundations, roofs, walls, windows, doors, and virtually every element of construction be undertaken in conformity with specific rules. Building codes usually reflect standards developed by national groups, often the federal government itself, but actual construction requirements may vary considerably from place to place. Moreover, zoning ordinances and building codes both interlock with standards set by insurance companies and lending institutions. For example, specific grades of roofing materials are required by fire insurance underwriters, and banks will not lend money toward the purchase of uninsured housing. Finally, trade unions may set work standards that affect how housing is developed. Different skilled tradespeople must be hired for different tasks— plumbers for plumbing, electricians for wiring, and so on—all of whom must abide by legal standards and may also have agreed-on standard procedures among themselves.

These formal standards, often expressed as requirements, contribute greatly to initial costs of housing, but they do ensure a certain quality of housing. Well-built housing lasts longer, which means longer replacement cycles and consequently lower overall housing costs. But questions are often raised as to which standards are necessary for quality and which exist for extraneous reasons. For example, are restricted lot sizes necessary for quality, or are they really forms of economic and racial segregation? Are some electrical and plumbing standards necessary for quality and safety, or are they appeasement to unions? Federal government regulations for housing that is developed using federal funds impose additional standards. For instance, grant proposals for funds under the Community Development Block Grant (part of the Housing Act) must consider and plan for historical property, floodplain management, wetland protection, noise, humanmade hazards, air and water quality, transportation, sewage and solid waste disposal.[1] These requirements raise housing costs, but can it be argued that they contribute to the overall value of housing as well?

Informal standards also contribute to housing costs. For example, land sold in certain neighborhoods may be bound by covenants that require development of housing within a special (usually high) price range or within certain criteria for size and appearance. Personal preferences also set informal standards. Even though the deplorable practice of housing segregation has been made illegal through fair housing laws at various levels of government, many whites still refuse to live in neighborhoods that have African Americans or other minorities in residence. Neighborhood amenities—schools, shops, public transportation, recreation, and cultural opportunities—all contribute indirectly to housing standards and cost.

Substandard housing is defined as the opposite of good-quality housing, again through the application of standards. Formal definitions of substandard housing are determined on the basis of violations of local building codes, such as incomplete plumbing, but housing may be substandard even when it is in conformity with formal standards. Much of the housing in inner-city slums meets formal criteria for standard housing, but most people, including many who live in it, consider it substandard. This creates a frustrating cycle. A particular building, for instance, may simply need one or two repairs, but because the community is considered generally substandard, there is little incentive for making the repairs; so they are left undone—contributing to a self-fulfilling prophecy of substandard quality. Ultimately, when considering housing standards, it is almost impossible to discuss the condition of housing without regard to its larger social and physical environment: the neighborhood of which it is a part.

Housing Supply

The relationship between housing standards and the neighborhood environment is intertwined with normative issues about the housing supply. Any housing policy must consider supply, because the population is expanding and because existing housing eventually wears out. That is, the need for housing increases geometrically in terms of both growth and replacement. The greater the population, the greater the supply of housing that must be created each year. Judging from these two standards alone, growth and replacements, a critical housing shortage already exists. Crises in housing supply are compounded by the time lag required for construction and the tremendous capital costs associated with development as a whole. Housing represents an immediate need, but also one that projects commitments into the future. Hence discussion arises as to how the housing supply should be created: by construction of new housing or rehabilitation of worn-out housing? If both, in what combination? And should housing be created by the private market or the government? And if both, in what balance?

New housing lasts a long time, and it can be constructed with current, "state-of-the-art" materials. Moreover, the costs of building new housing, as compared with rehabilitation of older housing, may be quite reasonable, particularly in the middle cost ranges. But new housing does not take into account the costs of housing amenities that go beyond the physical construction of a particular building. New housing is usually created in undeveloped areas outside cities or in the suburbs. Land in these areas tends to be cheaper, precisely because a community infrastructure has not been developed there. Roads and transportation systems may be incomplete, shopping resources scarce, schools and churches unplanned, even water and sewer systems may be available only in selected areas. This cheaper environment makes new housing economically competitive with more established housing on property that has already appreciated in value.

Rehabilitating old housing poses different problems. Old houses are usually in old neighborhoods, and rehabilitation of a few structures has little impact on the housing supply unless blocks, and sometimes whole neighborhoods, can be rehabilitated. Rehabilitation costs may be comparable with new construction costs, but overall there are fewer indirect costs associated with developing or renewing the service infrastructure. It is true that old neighborhoods often are plagued with high crime rates and deteriorated public amenities, but bringing neighborhood services into line with community expectations is less costly than developing them from scratch.

Choosing between new construction and rehabilitation may depend on whether it is more important to expand the existing stock of housing or to use what already exists more efficiently. Arguments for new housing derive from the housing needs of an expanding population: more people need more units. Arguments for rehabilitation derive from changes that take place within the population: young couples have children and add rooms to housing; older people with grown children may seek smaller homes or apartments; a family's home may need renovation to accommodate a disabled child or parent. Obviously both choices are desirable. The decision should depend on the expected use for housing in particular contexts.

Who should develop housing, the private or the public sector, is not as debatable as the question of who should ultimately own the housing. In practice, a "trickle-down" theory of housing development has undergirded American housing policy since the federal government first became involved in housing in the 1930s. This rationale assumes that new housing is built by people with capital to invest, and then gradually passed down through resale to those with less capital as it ages and becomes less valuable, until, in the end, zero-value housing is available to people with zero capital.

But in fact housing seldom approaches zero value, and consequently the poor have no chance of owning, or in most cases even using, housing that in theory should have become valueless. Thus, in order to house the poor, government must either build housing or pay housing costs for the poor or subsidize private housing so that the poor can afford it. No one debates the necessity of government intervention in housing markets as a means of aiding the poor. There is room, however, for considerable disagreement about the scope of this government intervention and the form it takes.

Housing Subsidies

The scope of government intervention in housing refers to its association with private industry to develop housing within the context of a free-market economy. Determining an acceptable scope of intervention is not easy. Government intervention on behalf of the poor is clearly acceptable, but as with policy for income-maintenance programs, it is difficult to define who the poor are.

Policy for publicly supported housing rests on an assumption that housing should consume 25% but not more than 30% of a household's after-tax income. This benchmark has received widespread acceptance not only as a threshold to eligibility for government-assisted housing programs but also in less restricted private-sector transactions such as approval of consumer loans for mortgages. Costs in excess of 25% of after-tax household income are often termed a "housing gap." This gap can be measured as the monetary difference between 25% of after-tax household income and the cost of housing available to the household. In theory, at least, government extends its intervention in the housing market to close the gap in order to provide housing that meets the 25% guideline when it cannot otherwise be achieved. Government might construct housing, charging no more for rent than 25% of each household's income, on an individualized sliding scale. Or it might supplement household income to make up the difference between the 25% guideline and the actual cost. Or it might supplement private builders, so that the housing constructed could be offered more cheaply, at prices consistent with 25% of people's incomes.

The problem with this formula lies in its application. If the 25% guideline is applied uniformly, many middle- and upper-income households also have a housing gap that may amount to several thousand dollars per year. Proponents of restricted government intervention would argue that efforts to close the housing gap should be applied only to those with very low incomes. Advocates of expanded government scope would counter that the housing supply is limited for middle-income households as well and that it is now almost impossible to find safe and sanitary housing for middle-income families because of a housing gap. In this view, government should act to reduce the cost of housing overall or should provide public subsidies to everyone with housing gaps regardless of income, until the market makes housing available to all at affordable prices.

In sum, normative debates over distribution of housing subsidies range over the type of subsidies that should be offered, who the recipients of the subsidies should be, and the amount of the subsidies themselves. The need for subsidies derives from the general understanding that government must be involved in housing markets. But governments should be involved unobtrusively, so as not to upset the capitalist market system. The most unobtrusive type of government intervention is to assist the construction of housing. Government may build housing itself, which competes with private markets, or help the private sector build housing, through various subsidy programs.

The way subsidies are distributed determines who benefits from them and how much the subsidy will be (see Table 7.1). Most opponents of housing subsidies agree that people who need housing, particularly those with low incomes, eventually benefit from subsidies, no matter who gets them originally. The most direct beneficiary of most housing subsidies is apt to be the developer or builder (see Table 7.2). Most housing subsidies take the form of tax credits rather than direct expenditures. By far the largest federal subsidy is the exclusion from capital gains tax that usually goes to developers, followed closely by the income tax deduction for interest on homeowners' mortgage payments. The larger the development, the higher the capital gain, and the greater the tax saving. The higher the mortgage payment, the greater the tax deduction. Thus

TABLE 7.1	FEDERAL HOUSING SUBSIDIES AND THEIR BENEFICIARIES

Form	Direct Beneficiary	Present Sources of Policy[1]
Reduction of interest rate	Developer/tenants	Secs. 235, 238
Increased loan coverage	Developer	Sec. 221
Payment of principal and interest on housing loans	Tenant/owner	Sec. 2; public housing
Payment of capital grant to developer	Developer	
Housing allowances to tenants	Tenant	Sec. 8
Housing allowances to owners	Owners	Sec. 2
Allocating housing for general income maintenance	Low-income tenants	
Allocating housing in public assistance	Low-income tenants	TAMF, assistance program
Tax deduction of mortgage	Owner/developer	tax codes
Interest and property taxes	Middle-income earner	
Accelerated depreciation	Developer	Sec. 236, tax codes
Reduction of local property taxes	Owner/tenant	Sec. 2
Reduction of land costs	Developer/owner	Community Block Grant (Housing Act)

Source: Anthony Downs, *Federal Housing Supplements: Their Nature and Effectiveness and What We Should Do about Them* (Washington, D.C.: National Association of Home Builders, 1972), 18.

[1] Section numbers refer to the Federal Housing Act.

higher-income persons are likely to receive higher benefits from these policies. Consequently present housing policy stimulates new construction and may have little benefit for people who need good-quality, affordable housing.

Low-income persons can and do receive housing subsidies directly through rental assistance programs (see Table 7.2) and indirectly through Public Housing programs and the housing allowance built into cash grants in need-based income-maintenance programs. About one-third of the cash grant in the TANF program, for example, is presumed to go toward housing. Yet subsidies for low-income persons are modest when compared with the total housing subsidy, and low-income persons are dependent on "trickle-down" housing to meet their needs. And even with the housing passed down to them, those with low incomes are likely to experience a housing gap.

The social value of housing subsidies may be understood better in terms of their different fiscal functions: some are intended to alleviate initial housing

| TABLE 7.2 | DIRECT AND INDIRECT (TAX CREDITS) FEDERAL HOUSING SUBSIDIES |

Direct expenditures

Housing assistance	7.95%
Mortgage credit and insurance	2.44
Community development	2.95
Regional development	1.92
Subtotal	15.26%

Indirect expenditures (tax credits)

Dividend exclusions	4.29%
Interest on consumer credit	11.28
Mortgage deductions	17.24
Property-tax deductions	6.47
Capital gains exclusion	18.53
Capital gains deferment (elderly)	0.58
Investment credits (rehabilitation)	16.35
Accelerated depreciation (rentals)	6.67
Corporate (housing) income	3.33
Subtotal	84.74%
Total	100.00%

Source: *U.S. Budget Receipts and Outlays, 1966* (Washington, D.C.: U.S. Government Printing Office, 1999).

debt; others are geared to closing the income gap.[2] Debt-tied subsidies include interest-rate reductions, modifications in loans, capital gains exclusions, and capital grants. Income-gap subsidies are rent supplements and housing subsidies that form part of need-based income-maintenance programs. Because they focus benefits on low-income households and provide housing more economically on a unit-cost basis, income-gap subsidies may seem to offer the best housing assistance to those who need it, but they may have several latent disadvantages. When housing costs accelerate more rapidly than incomes—for example, during periods of inflation—the costs of income-gap subsidies will rise proportionately. Moreover, costs of income-gap subsidies may be greater in the aggregate than debt-tied subsidies, even though unit costs may be lower, because they place demands on existing housing that is already in short supply and thus offer no incentive to keep housing costs low. Income-gap subsidies also require continuous administrative monitoring and supervision. The greatest disadvantage of income-gap subsidies may be that although they provide greater purchasing power to low-income persons, they contribute very little toward increasing the overall housing supply. Thus, direct government housing subsidies to low-income persons may end up costing more in the long run than debt-tied subsidies that create more housing for the poor.

Personal Preferences   The normative issues that drive housing policy span a wide range of topics, not all of them concerned with developing better and more affordable housing. Housing standards involve considerations about the kinds of communities people prefer. Decisions about where housing is built, and how it is built, cannot be made properly without attendant decisions about services infrastructure—schools, roads, transportation, health and social services, fire protection, and public safety. Housing policy also interlocks with local political decisions about taxes, land use, and the enforcement of housing codes. These are classic local policy issues that are discussed in Chapter 3.

Improving the housing supply requires not only projections of housing needs but also long-term political commitments to achieve targeted construction goals. For example, in an effort to close a looming housing shortage caused in part by the post–World War II "baby boom," Congress in 1968 set a goal of developing 26 million housing units by 1978. To achieve this goal, Congress created the Department of Housing and Urban Development (HUD) and gave it comprehensive program and funding authority to subsidize private housing development. But in 1973 President Nixon ordered a review of national housing policy, enforced a moratorium on housing development, and impounded funds already authorized by Congress that were necessary to achieve that goal. Private subsidized housing starts, which had averaged 1.75 million units per year during HUD's first several years, dropped gradually to 1.1 million in 1982. By 1992 the Government National Mortgage Association reported providing the capital to finance or refinance 1,135,000 units.

Thus government-subsidized housing continues to fall short of stimulating the development of housing to meet national goals, because the long-term funding commitment was not matched with political commitments to implement the policy through succeeding administrations. Government attention shifted in 1990 away from housing supply to the housing concerns of homeless persons and cumulated with the Cranston-Gonzales legislation that provided federal funds to localities to house the homeless. During the 1990s no housing targets were set and the Clinton administration had no housing policy, presumably because the vigorous economy seemed to suggest there was no need for one.

Finally, housing policy aimed at expanding the supply of housing has dramatic implications for the banking and construction industries. Not only is considerable individual wealth held in housing, but corporate wealth as well is heavily invested in all kinds of housing. Mortgages make up about 90% of all savings and loan companies' portfolios of assets, and housing-related loans constitute as much as half of all commercial banking activity. The entire construction industry, which ranges from the fabrication of building products to consumer products and home furnishings, from the tradespeople and their unions to the real estate salespeople who handle final transactions, is dependent on housing. This vast housing industry is extremely sensitive to policy changes that may affect any of its parts. Labor problems may disrupt construction or increase costs. Increased interest rates may dampen consumer demand and inhibit construction of new housing. Changes in direct housing subsidies or in tax laws that reduce special tax treatment of housing may cause investors to invest their capital elsewhere. Any of these changes can set in motion a chain of reactions that is difficult to reverse, particularly since housing policy requires such long-term commitments.

In such an environment, housing policy cannot be approached solely in terms of the development of housing units for low-income persons. Viable housing policy depends not only on how normative questions about housing the poor are answered but also on how other public concerns interlock with housing issues. From this perspective any analysis that focuses only on issues of developing housing for the poor is likely to be incomplete. On the other hand, approaching housing policy from the perspective of all the interrelated interests is much too comprehensive a strategy for most policy analysts. The analysis of housing provided later in this chapter tries to keep interlocking factors in mind while focusing on housing's most obvious social welfare problems.

THE CONTEXT OF AMERICAN HOUSING POLICY

Although the first national housing legislation was adopted in 1933, the basis of present housing policy was created with the Housing Act of 1937. This act was designed primarily to stimulate growth in private housing through various subsidies: loan guarantees, special tax treatments, and assurances for construction. The act (and its subsequent changes) did not place the federal government in the position of building housing, but rather made it a stimulator, guarantor, and insurer of efforts undertaken in the private sector. Nor did the federal government use this power to concentrate its efforts on the creation of housing for poor people. Rather, federal support of housing then and now continues to be directed primarily toward ensuring that private housing markets perform sufficiently well so that housing will eventually filter down to low-income citizens.

The context for American policy is thus the free-market mechanism of American capitalism. Indeed, economic analysts often use housing policy as an example of the efficiency of unregulated markets. There is, they say, a house for everyone at exactly the price that person can afford. This filtering or "trickledown" concept of housing development is a fundamental theoretical framework frequently used to dispute the necessity of public involvement in private affairs, and its operation with respect to housing bears closer examination.

In general, the theory argues that people who have capital to invest in housing put their money into new housing, usually in undeveloped areas where land costs and taxes are low. Once the housing is built and used for some time, its value (but not its market price) begins to decrease; to protect their capital, the owners sell, usually to people with less capital, as the value of the housing is now less. The sellers develop new housing somewhere else. The new owners hold the existing housing until its value declines to a point where they in turn decide to sell, again usually to someone with less capital to invest. Eventually the housing should reach zero value and thus be available to people who have nothing to invest. In the United States, the usual lifespan of housing (down to zero value) is calculated at approximately forty years. In practice, the market value of housing (resale value) is always greater than its "real" value, due to "market externalities."

Of course, this theory of housing does not operate as efficiently as its proponents argue, nor does it operate in such a way that low-income persons eventually get housing they can afford. Because housing development is so dependent on capital, slight fluctuations in money markets have immediate effects on housing production; larger fluctuations, such as 4 to 5% increases in interest rates, can disrupt the entire chain of housing production so seriously that it may take years to reestablish suppliers, builders, and other related businesses in a good balance. Moreover, the United States continues to experience a severe housing "shortfall" of about 2 million to 3 million units per year. If macroeconomic events, such as the 1981–83 recession or the 1990–91 high interest rates, continue to disrupt the housing chain, which is also bound by more and more stringent housing standards, this shortfall is likely to increase. The economic downturn of the late 1990s was first felt in housing markets, and action by the federal reserve, reducing interest rates, worked to stabilize housing markets and the American economy generally. In the present tight housing market, most low-income persons have been squeezed out of the private housing market, and private programs, such as Habitat for Humanity, have grown to take up some of the slack caused by a stagnant government housing policy.

Table 7.3 summarizes housing resources as they exist for certain population groups in the United States. Considering that there are approximately 105.4 million households in the United States (2000 census) and approximately 100 million occupied housing units, there exists an overall housing shortfall of approximately 5 million housing units. The distribution of housing units raises additional questions. Assuming 12.7 million African American households and approximately 12.1 million available African American occupied units, the housing shortfall among African Americans does not appear critical. But whereas 70.3% of white households own their own housing, only 45.2% of African Americans own their own homes. Hispanic households show a similar pattern to African American households. (See Figure 7.1.)

Table 7.4 shows that rental housing is overall more likely to have housing deficiencies, and less likely to have housing amenities. Housing deficiencies for African Americans and poverty households, both renters and owners, are three times as prevalent as housing deficiencies for all occupied housing units. Thus while there may be an adequate supply of housing for minorities and low-income persons, the quality of this housing may be quite inadequate and fail to meet standards of decent, safe, and sanitary housing. Notice, for example, that open cracks and holes and water leakage exist in about 2 million housing units occupied by persons in poverty (Table 7.4.) Given the slowdown in housing

FIGURE 7.1 | TYPE OF HOUSEHOLD HOUSING, BY RACE

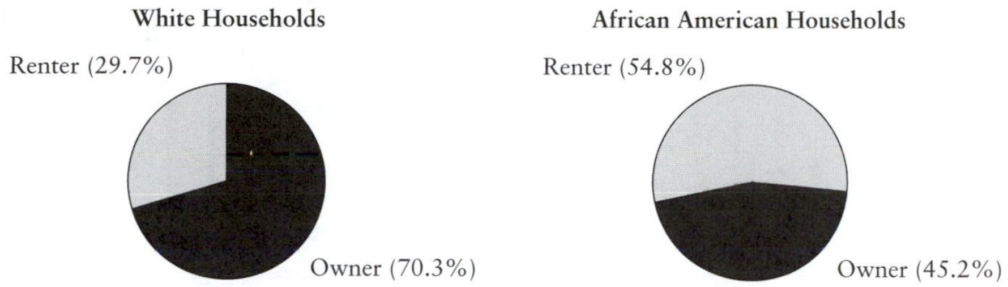

White Households

Renter (29.7%)

Owner (70.3%)

African American Households

Renter (54.8%)

Owner (45.2%)

TABLE 7.3 | OCCUPIED HOUSING UNITS, TENURE BY RACE OF HOUSEHOLDER, 1991–1997 (IN THOUSANDS)

Race of Householder and Tenure	1991	1993	1995	1997
All races [1]				
Occupied units, total	**93,147**	**94,724**	**97,693**	**99,487**
Owner occupied	59,796	61,252	63,544	65,487
Percentage of occupied	4.2	64.7	65.0	65.8
Renter occupied	3,351	33,472	34,150	34,000
White				
Occupied units, total	**79,140**	**80,029**	**81,611**	**82,154**
Owner occupied	53,749	54,878	56,507	57,781
Percentage of occupied	67.9	68.6	69.2	70.3
Renter occupied	5,391	25,151	25,104	24,372
Black				
Occupied units, total	**10,832**	**11,128**	**11,773**	**12,085**
Owner occupied	4,635	4,788	5,137	5,457
Percentage of occupied	2.8	43.0	3.6	5.2
Renter occupied	6,197	6,340	6,637	6,628
Hispanic origin [2]				
Occupied units, total	**6,239**	**6,614**	**7,757**	**8,513**
Owner occupied	2,423	2,788	3,245	3,646
Percentage of occupied	38.8	42.2	41.8	42.8
Renter occupied	3,816	3,826	4,512	4,867

Source: U.S. Census Bureau, *Current Housing Reports, American Housing Survey for the United States.*

[1] Includes other races, not shown separately.

[2] Persons of Hispanic origin may be of any race.

TABLE 7.4 | OCCUPIED HOUSING UNITS, HOUSING INDICATORS BY SELECTED CHARACTERISTICS OF THE HOUSEHOLDER, 1997 (IN THOUSANDS OF UNITS)

	Total Occupied Units	Tenure		Black		Hispanic[1]		Elderly[2]		Below Poverty Level	
		Owner	Renter	Owner	Renter	Owner	Renter	Owner	Renter	Owner	Renter
Total units	99,487	65,487	34,000	5,457	6,628	3,646	4,867	16,493	4,413	6,619	9,108
Amenities:											
Porch, deck, balcony, or patio	75,986	55,374	20,612	4,217	3,689	2,835	2,477	13,737	2,371	5,156	4,791
Usable fireplace	31,825	27,702	4,123	1,554	460	1,106	354	5,575	280	1,721	526
Separate dining room	39,077	31,411	7,666	2,805	1,635	1,555	917	7,269	749	2,696	1,690
With 2 or more living rooms or recreation	34,515	31,582	2,932	2,493	479	1,263	191	7,181	312	2,226	499
Garage or carport with home	58,027	47,488	10,539	2,903	1,173	2,566	1,543	12,208	1,210	3,754	1,969
Cars and trucks available:											
No cars, trucks, or vans	9,447	2,480	6,967	480	2,438	132	1,174	1,713	2,028	944	3,636

Internal deficiencies:

Signs of rats in last 3 months	920	425	495	78	154	68	180	79	42	92	211
Holes in floors	1,168	487	680	81	209	54	184	99	48	126	288
Open cracks or holes	5,748	2,719	3,029	387	78	229	493	420	212	342	1,010
Broken plaster or peeling paint (interior)	2,938	1,239	1,699	189	461	94	378	256	130	177	635
No electrical wiring	40	33	7	3	—	5	5	3	1	7	5
Exposed wiring	788	457	331	58	84	35	74	106	43	68	123
Rooms without electric outlet	2,122	1,160	962	119	238	88	181	281	106	190	323
Water leakage[3]	9,667	5,177	4,490	558	1,054	338	594	817	311	476	1,126

Source: U.S. Census Bureau, *Statistical Abstract of the United States*, 2001, table 1220.

— Represents zero.

[1] Persons of Hispanic origin may be of any race.

[2] Householders 65 years old and over.

[3] During the 12 months prior to the survey.

construction, the high interest rates for the early 2000s, and population increases as documented by the 2000 census, housing shortfalls in numbers are probably greater, reflecting about the same percentages found in Table 7.3. Public housing constitutes only about 1.5% of the nation's housing supply, for the 12% of households that live in poverty; 58% of all poverty households live in private rental housing.

The context of housing policy in America is framed by larger macro-economic concerns that shape money markets and the construction industry, and public efforts toward the development of housing must interlock with these traditional and powerful private-sector activities. Pressure for government involvement in housing thus comes from two sources: (1) from housing deficiencies that have developed from long-term policy based on the "trickle-down" principle and from attendant inequitable distributions caused by inefficiencies in the private sector; and (2) from the private sector's need for an adequate money supply, at attractive interest rates, to stimulate private capital investments in housing development at all levels. In other words, housing policy in the United States attempts both to satisfy redistributive concerns and to maintain an adequate housing supply for everyone.

This housing context has guided policy efforts to manipulate the housing market. Competition for scarce public resources has often bred antagonism over which of these positions should be maximized, but in reality the overall objective—decent, safe, and sanitary housing—is compatible with both. As a result of this tension, housing policy has evolved unevenly, sometimes concentrating on redistributive objectives, sometimes emphasizing efforts to support the present housing flow.

The Housing Act of 1937, the cornerstone of housing policy in the United States today, has gradually been molded into a leviathan that provides public support toward both these policy objectives. The housing legislation of 1933 committed government protection to housing lenders against financial losses during the Great Depression. The act of 1937 added to this the Public Housing program (a redistributive policy) and Federal Home Mortgage insurance, designed to stimulate lending for private-sector housing construction.

By the end of World War II a severe housing shortage was evident. A need for temporary shelter had arisen during the war itself for people who were relocated to defense plants, military bases, and other strategic locations. But few materials for permanent housing construction were available, and new housing starts dropped practically to zero. After the war, thousands of returning servicemen wanted to establish new households. To meet this need, the Housing Act was expanded to include the Veterans Administration (VA) loan program, which guaranteed mortgages to veterans, underwrote some of the share of interest, made it possible to extend the term of the loan, and subsidized the amount of down payment necessary to secure the loan. These changes in housing policy provided a tremendous boost to the housing industry. Largely stimulated by the VA loan programs, housing starts doubled from 1945 to 1946 and reached 1.9 million annually by 1950. More than 90% of these were single-family houses. Home ownership increased from its prewar level of 44%

of all households (in 1940) to 62% in 1960. The American housing dream was well within reach.

Interestingly enough, the Public Housing program was almost scrapped during this period, as an unnecessary effort, and no public housing initiatives were undertaken to respond directly to the housing needs of the poor. In fact, between 1945 and 1960, virtually no attention was given anywhere to subjects of poverty. The depression was history. The war had stimulated prosperity. Poverty supposedly no longer existed.

In 1949 further amendments to the Housing Act set a new course for housing policy by recognizing that housing development was a broader issue than a multiple of individual transactions in the housing market. Costs and benefits of housing affect residents in a community regardless of whether they are involved in current transactions, and the problems of housing "extras"—the need for roads, schools, and public services in new developments, and for improving slums and run-down neighborhoods in old developments—became a public responsibility. "Urban renewal" entered the vocabulary of housing policy in this 1949 legislation. By making federal funds available to local governments, the Urban Renewal program was intended to help cities revitalize areas "blighted" by "urban decay."

Urban Renewal supported local programs designed to eliminate deteriorated housing and replace it with new housing. Public Housing was promoted as the flagship of Urban Renewal programs. The 1949 Housing Act authorized the construction of 810,000 public housing units by 1955, but despite this commitment the fate of that program was questionable from the start. Initial lack of enthusiasm for public housing continued into and throughout the debate over the 1949 amendments, and only by linking the program with Urban Renewal was enough support gained to preserve Public Housing as part of the nation's housing policies. However, joining Urban Renewal and Public Housing in legislation and official policy was not sufficient to inspire the same results in redevelopment plans of local communities. Individual communities were not motivated to build public housing, and by and large Urban Renewal funding was used for other purposes, mostly rehabilitation and expansion of the middle-income rental housing supply.

The Housing Act of 1954 expanded Urban Renewal policy to include commercial redevelopment. Although Urban Renewal projects had spread rapidly as a means of revitalizing deteriorating urban residential areas, commercial redevelopment was an even more profitable scheme. By contrast, President Eisenhower's austerity budget held authorizations for public housing at a minimum. By 1960 only 250,000 public housing units had been built since the 1949 legislation was passed, bringing the national total to 478,200, well behind the 1949 policy goals. By 1980 the total had increased to only 1,281,900, about 1.5% of all occupied housing. By 1992 there were 1,323,000 public housing units, of which only 1,199,000 were occupied. The age of dwellings and years of abuse have taken a toll on America's Public Housing program.

Amendments to the Housing Act in 1957 permitted federal support for private housing rehabilitation as a means of keeping the focus of redevelopment on residential housing and of refocusing Urban Renewal toward its original emphasis on housing. This effort was too little, too late, and too unimaginative. Most existing housing in eligible areas was beyond rehabilitation, and the little that was worth saving often stood amid blocks and blocks of empty lots that had fallen to the bulldozers. The plan, which had called for revitalization (mostly of African American neighborhoods on property owned by suburban whites) but lacked the capacity to develop entirely new housing for residents of demolished buildings, was a dismal failure. Urban renewal became black removal. In many instances the vacant land was ultimately deemed economically unsuited for redevelopment in housing, and it was retargeted for commercial development as the only way to save local governments from huge financial losses from their original investments in Urban Renewal programs.

Housing policy met with further disappointments through the 1960s. The bitter experiences with Urban Renewal and the general lack of adequate housing for African Americans contributed significantly to urban unrest and rioting.[3] Criticism of Urban Renewal continued to undermine all efforts at residential redevelopment. Rehabilitation of the urban infrastructure became a more pressing aspect of the problem. Cities were not able to improve police and fire protection, area schools, or cultural and recreational opportunities, without massive public assistance. Thus the Housing Act was modified in 1968 to include funding for upgrading the infrastructure of Urban Renewal areas; this was the Model Cities program. That year also saw the creation of the U.S. Department of Housing and Urban Development; Robert Weaver, the nation's first African American cabinet member, was appointed its first head.

However, housing policy had again shifted in focus away from residential development. Once again the modifications provided too little support, after most of the damage of Urban Renewal had been done. Model Cities did little to reverse the growing housing shortage. A new interest-rate subsidy program (Section 235), designed to help low-income families become owners of their own homes, had even less success among the increasing numbers of people who were abandoning their properties in central city areas.

By 1970 the Senate Banking Committee had opened hearings to obtain information about the dearth of housing for the poor (particularly in the wake of urban riots). Concern focused strongly on the deterioration of the American city.[4] The hearings sorted out bitter complaints from all quarters. Public housing was in serious trouble. Too few units were available, and the occupants seemed to be all too representative of a subculture of poverty: African Americans and single mothers with young children. Public Housing was blamed for creating urban segregation, a reversal of the intention of the 1937 act. Urban Renewal was judged a failure, and some of the programs that it had bred—Section 235 and Model Cities—were condemned as compromises geared toward the middle and upper classes and far removed from the fundamental problems of decent housing.

Reformulation of housing policy emerged slowly from this public scrutiny, but finally, in 1974, Congress legislated modifications of the Housing Act that gave housing policy its present form. Unable to resolve all the conflicts that had developed over Urban Renewal and Model Cities, Congress acted in predictable fashion by turning all these functions over to the states through the much-heralded Community Development Block Grant program. The other programs under the Housing Act were preserved in their existing forms, and a new program, Rent Subsidy (Section 8), was added as a companion program to Public Housing. The Rent Subsidy program provided federal funds to local housing authorities to pay the difference between what would be a fair rent for housing and what a low-income person could afford to pay.

PRESENT HOUSING POLICY

In summary, present housing policy falls into four areas: housing programs, community planning, the Government National Mortgage Association, and solar energy and energy assistance.

Existing Housing Programs

Six housing programs are targeted to low-income persons: Public Housing, Section 8, Section 202, Section 235, Farmers Home Loans, and temporary shelters. Public housing is the most frequently discussed form of housing to aid low-income persons. Sometimes called "the projects," public housing is apartment-type housing constructed by local housing authorities using loans from the federal government. Because loans finance public housing construction, sufficient rents must be charged to repay the loans and to support maintenance. Thus the poorest of the poor are often refused public housing since large numbers of these families make it difficult for housing authorities to meet their financial obligations.

Begun in 1937, Public housing projects are now part of most local efforts to meet housing needs of low-income families. However, particularly in large metropolitan areas, public housing projects are in disarray and have become centers for considerable amounts of social pathology. This decay is due not only to fiscal constraints but to the behaviors of many of the people who live in this housing. These issues were well described many years ago by Alvin Schorr in *Slums and Social Insecurity.*[5] Recently the Department of Housing and Urban Development (HUD) has undertaken efforts to upgrade urban public housing projects through the initiation of its Model Projects program that provides funds to local projects for both physical as well as social redevelopment. The outcomes from this effort are not yet available.

Section 8 is more formally known as assisted rental housing. This program assists low-income persons with funds to make up the difference in rent between the cost of a standard rental unit and what a household can afford to pay (usually about 30% of net household income.) On receiving a certificate, the household head seeks out a suitable rental unit (it must pass inspection) and, if the landlord agrees, enters into a rental agreement that guarantees payment of rents by the housing authority should the client become delinquent.

The Section 8 program is not only poorly funded, but the rental housing market is not adequate for low-income households. Table 7.4 suggests that rental housing for this group of persons is likely to be substandard, and landlords are reluctant to spend the money to bring their units up to standard when they usually can receive the same amount of rent for their substandard units. Most housing authorities have a two-year or longer waiting list for those seeking housing assistance from this program.

Housing for the aged and disabled, known as Section 202, encourages the development of new housing and rehabilitation of old housing through subsidized loans to private, nonprofit organizations (or in some cases individuals) who wish to develop housing for this group of persons. Because construction loans are subsidized, the rents are regulated. But since rents are necessary, this program, too, fails to meet the needs of very low income individuals. Since most of these rentals meet established standard rents because of the subsidy, they are frequently used by those seeking Section 8 housing, providing they meet the criteria set for aged and handicapped.

Housing for middle-income households, Section 235, is also a program of subsidies to builders who in turn accept ceilings on the rents they charge. The subsidies are structured in such a way that these housing units are most likely to be used by middle-income households.

The Farmers Home Loan program has an interesting political history. First devised as a program to ensure that persons in rural areas could obtain housing loans, when there were few or no commercial lending institutions in these areas, the program gradually evolved into one that assists low-income persons in repairing their homes or in constructing new ones. Because the inability to obtain a loan from a commercial lending institution was the initial criteria for these subsidized loans, lack of income and/or collateral has now become the reason for the continued existence of this program. This program has been an important one for mostly low-income aged persons in rural areas who own their own homes: the homes are in dire need of improvement, but the homeowner has insufficient collateral in the home to obtain a conventional loan. Many of the older rural housing units lack complete indoor plumbing, for example, and Farmers Home loans have been available for these persons to upgrade their units to make them livable.

A temporary shelters for the homeless program was created in response to the public outcry in the late 1980s over homeless individuals and families. Congress amended the housing act to provide funding to local nonprofit organizations to create homeless shelters. Although slow getting off the ground, the McKinny Act has been able to provide funding for homeless in almost every municipality. In FY 1998, HUD provided $73.2 million to 372 shelters in cities to improve the conditions of shelters, sold or leased 2,400 properties to various nonprofit homeless providers, and extended Section 8 rental assistance for use of the homeless in Single Room Occupancy (SRO) facilities.

Community Planning

Community planning and development is carried out with Community Development Block Grants, which provide financial support to states for local rehabilitation projects, including private housing redevelopment and renewal and improvements to the infrastructure of local communities. These grants most recently have targeted rural communities, many of them low-income or minority communities, in order to improve community infrastructures such as water and sewer. They have also been used to create infrastructures that would make it possible to engage in various economic development projects, such as attracting new industries to the areas.

The Government National Mortgage Association (GNMA)

The Government National Mortgage Association (GNMA) and other loan programs such as "Fannie Mae" represent the fiscal arm of housing policy. These organizations manage the large loan portfolio of the government's support of essentially private-market housing programs. In 1984 GNMA had a budget of $6.2 billion. In FY 1992 it had a housing portfolio of over $72 billion in mortgages. By 2000 the portfolio was over $100 billion.

Energy Assistance

Active Energy Development funding supports efforts to develop alternative energy sources, mostly solar- and wind-generated energy. Low Income Energy Assistance block grants to states help low-income persons pay their utility bills and cope with energy-related housing problems. All types of energy sources, including coal, gas, oil, electricity, and wood, can be subsidized with these funds.

Federal programs called Weatherization provide block grants to states to fund local agency programs that assist low-income households in insulating their homes. All types of insulation work can be funded under this program, such as storm windows, underpinning, and minor structural repairs related to insulation problems.

Summary

How well these programs work toward meeting the primary objectives of housing policy is debatable. The above programs show that housing for low-income persons and the aged and disabled receives attention in several areas of housing policy. However, direct federal expenditures for all housing assistance to the poor constituted less then 10% of the annual federal housing budget in 1999. Table 7.4 reminds us that the shortfall of adequate housing for low-income persons is significant, and the history of housing legislation sketched above explains that incentives for local communities to construct public housing have been low, even when federal policy has offered the opportunity. If federal housing policy is regarded entirely in terms of aid to the poor, this is a dismal record indeed. But, as mentioned earlier, since its inception in 1937, federal housing policy has evolved amid the tension between two overall aims: assistance to those who cannot afford decent housing, and support of adequate housing for all. Because emphasis on either of these objectives alone tends to undermine the integrity of the other, evaluations of housing policies and programs are best approached through an understanding of the dual focus of housing policy as a whole. Thus government support of housing in general is aimed at reducing shortages that would create even greater competition for adequate housing for everyone, with the result that low-income households are gradually forced into even more desperate circumstances.

As it presently exists, housing policy spills into private-sector concerns in great volume, with macroeconomic implications only vaguely visible during periods of economic crisis. The "multiplier effects" of housing policy are difficult to determine even during normal economic cycles. For example, whether housing subsidies reduce housing costs or drive them higher remains an unresolved economic debate. It is also clear that housing policy straddles many such partly public, partly private issues. Even if analysis of housing policy could be confined to its possible effects on a clearly delimited public sector, such as the poor, normative issues surrounding distribution of benefits remain problematic. As a result of these economic implications, products of housing policy are distributed on an uneven geographic basis, rather than, for example, according to a nationwide standard of need.[6] Assisted housing, for example, tends to be clustered in urban areas, as opposed to rural areas; regionally it clusters in the Northeast and on the West Coast, as opposed to the Midwest and South. These patterns are a function of both spillover economic effects and factors indirectly related to housing, such as geopolitical administrative boundaries. Any analysis of housing policy, in sum, is apt to be severely compromised by latent and unforeseen anomalies within normative contexts.

POLICY ANALYSIS

The criteria-based model is especially helpful in analyzing housing policy because the values that surround housing policy as a whole are so diverse and because the programs have policy consequences that overlap in complex ways. The normative issues and the existing housing alternatives shown in Table 7.5 have been discussed above. Consequently the table contains no surprises. Tax incentives and mortgage guarantees maximize universal values, particularly for efficient, stigma-free housing of personal choice. They also contribute to expanding the housing supply, although not for low-income persons. Housing subsidies target resources better, particularly for improving housing and directing housing resources at low-income persons. Community development alternatives have very little relevance to selective or universal housing criteria. Public Housing and Section 8 subsidies have the greatest number of low evaluations on the table, even though these programs best target housing for low-

TABLE 7.2 | ALTERNATIVE POLICY AND PROGRAM APPROACHES FOR HOUSING (CRITERIA-BASED MODEL)

Alternatives

Normative Orientations	Housing Subsidies					Mortgage Guarantees	Community Development
	Tax Incentives	Sec. 235	Sec. 236	Public Housing	Sec. 8		
Universal criteria:							
Equity							
Horizontal	Hi	Lo	Lo	Lo	Lo	Hi	Lo
Vertical	Med	Hi	Hi	Hi	Hi	Med	Lo
Efficiency (low cost/high value)	Hi	Med	Med	Med	Med	Med	Lo
Nonstigmatizing	Hi	Med	Med	Lo	Lo	Hi	Lo
Preference satisfaction	Hi	Med	Med	Lo	Lo	Hi	Lo
Policy-specific criteria:							
Expand housing supply	Hi	Med	Med	Hi	Hi	Hi	Lo
Improve housing quality	Lo	Lo	Lo`	Lo	Lo	Lo	Hi
Improve housing supply	Hi	Lo	Lo	Hi	Hi	Med	Med
Protect financial markets	Lo	Med	Lo	Lo	Lo	Hi	Med
Stimulate the economy	Hi	Med	Med	Med	Med	Med	Med
Aid low-income households	Lo	Lo	Med	Hi	Hi	Lo	Med
	Hi = 7	Hi = 1	Hi = 1	Hi = 4	Hi = 4	Hi = 5	Hi = 1
	Med = 1	Med = 6	Med = 6	Med = 2	Med = 2	Med = 4	Med = 4
	Lo = 3	Lo = 4	Lo = 4	Lo = 5	Lo = 5	Lo = 2	Lo = 6

income persons. This evaluation of Public Housing and Section 8 programs confirms the historical development of housing policy: housing targeted for the poor, though a continuing issue, has never been a high priority. To state this in slightly different terms, policymakers who favor housing carefully targeted for low-income persons might do well to seek a different policy arena altogether, in which this value has greater potential for realization—such as income-maintenance policy, through which housing could be offered as a highly valued in-kind benefit. (See Chapter 5.)

CONCLUSION

Perhaps the major issue in all of housing policy is the duality of normative orientations toward the whole subject of housing. Certainly the normative issues outlined and discussed at the outset of this chapter present a complex orientation to housing in the United States that tends to deemphasize the government's direct creation of housing, particularly for the poor, preferring an emphasis on economic stimulus to housing in general. Nevertheless housing policy debates continue to raise the question of what *should* be the normative orientation to housing policy. For example, should housing policy be directed toward providing more units at government initiative, primarily for the poor, at the potential risk of driving up housing costs generally? Or should housing policy stress government subsidies and market stimulus strategies that would foster competition and some price control, but leave inadequate supplies, particularly for those who most need help with housing?

The analysis of housing policy presented in this chapter suggests two guiding principles that must be applied to any housing policy choice. First, the macroeconomic impact of any housing policy choice must be calculated. Housing policy operates in a vast nationwide environment of lending institutions, large federal, state, and local programs, the construction industry, and a complex network of related service industries. Even the slightest alteration in housing policy is likely to create ripples throughout these interrelated economic spheres. Second, developing and implementing housing policy requires prolonged "lead time." As in the docking of giant ships, housing policy moves slowly, and considerable leeway must be allowed for the execution of even the most modest maneuver. In this view, it may be wisest to insist that whatever course housing policy takes, staying on that course is more important than tinkering with the policy in order to achieve marginal objectives.

QUESTIONS FOR DISCUSSION

1. Why have most of the issues affecting the development of American housing policy reflected so little concern for problems of the poor and those who live in such poor housing?

2. Why has the development of public housing projects served only to intensify or make more severe the deplorable living conditions of many poor people?

3. What kinds of housing policy might be proposed to better accommodate the needs of the poor, given the present normative context for housing policy in America today?

4. Recently the United States Supreme Court found constitutional a federal housing statute that allows local public housing programs to evict entire families from a housing project if one member of the family is found guilty of dealing in narcotics, even if the narcotics violation took place off the public housing premises. What do you think of such a policy in the light of housing policy in general?

8 CHAPTER   CHILD WELFARE

INTRODUCTION

The welfare of children holds an exceptionally important place in American public policy. Until the Social Security Act established the contemporary framework for child welfare policy, children's concerns were met in a variety of ways. Even before the earlier reform movement of about 1890–1910, voluntary agencies and local communities had mobilized resources to protect and aid children. During the late eighteenth and early nineteenth centuries, children without parents (orphans) were placed in public homes or farmed out as apprentices in exchange for room and board. In 1853 the Reverend Charles Loring Brace founded an emergency "child-saving" movement with the formation of the New York Children's Aid Society, whose primary responsibility was collecting orphaned and deserted children from the streets of New York and other cities and transplanting them to farms of the American Midwest. Dorothea Dix's celebrated state-by-state visitation of county almshouses and local jails (1845–54) uncovered abusive treatment not only of the mentally ill but of children. The New York Society for the Prevention of Cruelty to Children was formed in 1870 after public outcry over the case of Mary Ellen, an abused child, who had less public protection than many of New York's animals. This first "child protection" agency was legitimated by the English and American legal doctrine *patens patriae,* which held that public courts have surrogate parental authority to protect the property rights (and now all rights) of children when those rights can no longer be protected by their natural parents.

The later reform movement (circa 1900–1920) directed much of its energy toward engaging state governments in the provision and supervision of programs for children. States developed mechanisms to ensure that local care of homeless and dependent children was humane and consistent with child-care standards of that day. States also developed legislation that gave legal recognition to differences between children and adults. Illinois created the first juvenile court in 1899, and half the states had laws regulating child labor by 1900. Beginning with Illinois in 1911, states initiated financial aid programs to support dependent children in their own homes.

The suffrage movement gave further thrust to public policy for children. As women organized to obtain the right to vote, they also advocated strongly for the rights of children. The first White House conference ever called by a president was one concerning children convened by Theodore Roosevelt in 1909, and the delegation of hundreds of national leaders who attended the meeting generated enough concern to create the Children's Bureau in the U.S. Department of Labor in 1912. In 1921 women won a long-fought struggle to convince Congress to approve a health program for new mothers and their newborns.[1] This, the Sheppard-Towner Act, was a prototype of future social welfare programs. The Maternal and Child Health program (discussed p. 239 and also in Chapter 6) became its lasting legacy.

By 1935, when the Social Security Act was legislated, the architecture for modern child welfare programs had been partly established. Because state-supervised and state-administered programs of financial aid were already in place, the child welfare policy of the Social Security Act layered federal funds over existing state-level foundations. The child welfare programs created by the Social Security Act thus were new only to the extent that they established a uniform framework for administration, to which a specified number of existing state programs were required to conform. These programs comprised a mixture of services for dependent children—foster care and health services, for example—and income support for children in the form of "pensions" for mothers, which became Aid to Dependent Children under the Social Security Act.

NORMATIVE ISSUES

Three normative issues have shaped child welfare policy and programs today and perpetuate crosscurrents of debate in child welfare policy analysis: (1) parental responsibility versus children's rights, (2) protection of children versus liberation, and (3) need-based versus universal children's services. Although these normative concerns are similar to many of those related to income maintenance policy, with respect to children they take on a unique significance.

Parental Responsibility versus Children's Rights

The conflicting issues of parental responsibility and children's rights arise from two different conceptions of childhood. Prior to the nineteenth century, children were perceived as miniature adults and were expected to become part of the adult world as soon as they were physically able. "Childhood" was restricted to the helpless and dependent phases of infancy and the very early years. Childhood ceased when children were able to carry out adult tasks. This did not mean, however, that children achieved true independence and autonomy at an early age. A unique feature of family history throughout much of the world is the amount of legal authority fathers have traditionally possessed over the lives of family members. Decisions about children have been an important part of this system of family authority. This dual conception of child and family has shaped child welfare policy that distinguishes sharply between children who are in families where fathers are present, and children who are not.

Law and custom have shaped theories of parental responsibility for children. If a child damages property, parents are held liable. Parents are responsible for their children's school attendance, and they are expected to ensure that their children satisfy other social obligations. In exchange for compliance with such basic social expectations, parents are left free to deal with their children as they see fit in almost every area of physical and social development. The welfare of the child is the responsibility of the parent. From nutrition to dating, from health care to school achievement, from clothing and dress to decisions about the family car, parents are responsible for their children.

In the nineteenth century, with the spread of the romantic movement and its ideas, a changed concept of separate identity in childhood initiated new views about children. Children were now seen as good, innocent, and subject to corruption and danger from an otherwise evil society. Thus childhood problems and problem children could be corrected, and children were held in high esteem as the salvation of future generations. According to one theorist, it was this reformed view of children that led to "child-saving" activities such as those undertaken in New York by the Reverend Brace, which were designed to rescue children from the evils of society.[2] The obligations of society to protect and nurture children, together with the reformed view of childhood as a period of innocence, led to the idea that children not only had rights, but rights peculiar to the status of childhood. Paramount among them, social reformers argued, were the right to an education, the right to life and good health, the right to play, and the right to make their own choices.

Whether rights exist for anyone, and what limitations are placed on them if they do, is an important philosophical question that has intricate overtones in child welfare policy. The emerging idea of children's rights collided sharply with earlier views of parental responsibility. If children had rights independent of their status in the family, how were these rights to be protected and asserted? If children's rights were to prevail, some greater force had to exist outside the authority of the family, and this force was government. Because the "best interests of the child" were placed before the authority of the child's parents, efforts to promote and protect children's rights on this basis raised, and still raise, serious questions of conflict between personal individuality and the privacy of the family.

Protection of Children versus Their Liberation

The newly perceived status of children prompted considerable activity during the early-twentieth-century reform movement. Not only were public policies designed to embrace children's rights, but a vast array of public and private programs were developed that served to protect and promote their interests. Juvenile courts were established to deal with violations of the law in nonadversarial, nonpunitive ways, and in an environment designed to correct delinquent behavior and help young people develop into productive members of society. When children were found guilty of crimes for which adults would be punished, rehabilitation and treatment were substituted for fines and incarceration. After the Mary Ellen case, states moved quickly to adopt laws to protect children, giving power to state agencies to remove children from their homes if they were abused, neglected, or financially deprived. Families were expected to care for their children in acceptable ways, and if that care could not be provided, public agencies would provide it. Special treatment units for children, with recreational activities, were created in general and psychiatric hospitals.

Such efforts to protect children, to enhance the virtues of childhood, and to reform children's alien and antisocial behaviors into socially acceptable ones, began to conflict with the very rights that child advocates had sought to identify and protect. As new protective programs were introduced, the new definition of childhood came under attack: if children did indeed have rights, would it not make better sense to liberate them to enjoy their rights, rather than enforce their rights on them? From this distinction developed two views of childhood that continue to influence child welfare policy today.

> The *institutional* concept [of childhood] is a legal or quasi-legal one in which in modern society childhood is usually determined by age. . . . The *normative* concept is connected with certain [childhood] capacities, the acquisition of certain elements of knowledge and experience, expertness and possession of certain ethical interests, or reasonable expectations about a person's likely behavior at certain stages of development.[3]

The products of "institutional" and "normative" definitions of childhood have left a legacy of policies and programs with diffuse, often conflicting, goals. For example, public policy now supports early childhood development programs, programs for culturally disadvantaged children, programs for adolescents, preadolescents, postadolescents, and so on. These normative child welfare policies all hinge on somehow defining children's functional capacities to use available resources without limiting their access to those resources by specific age boundaries. In contrast, the products of institutional definitions of childhood, such as mandatory public education, child labor laws, and certain legal privileges (voting, driving, public drinking) are defined by specific age, without regard to functional ability. In effect, normatively produced policies support activities that liberate children from traditional roles, whereas institutional, age-limited programs focus on protection, promote constraints, and communicate traditional paternalistic messages. As programs developed from normative views of childhood have become interlayered with age-specific programs, the purposes of child welfare policies and programs as a whole have become very confused, and all types of programs have lost most of their clarity and focus.

For example, confusion may abound over which programs are best suited for a teenage parent, who can be viewed normatively as an adult but still be defined institutionally as a child. Or suppose a retarded couple in their twenties wish to marry and raise a family; institutionally they are adults, but normatively they may still be children. What policies should apply to them? Allied to these exceptional examples is the almost universal complaint: "If I'm old enough to fight and die for my country, I ought to be old enough to drink." In one case we protect the children; in the other case the children must fend for themselves.

Need-Based versus Universal Services

Need-based and universal services pervade both issues of parental responsibility versus children's rights and protection versus liberation. The recognition that childhood is a special condition would certainly argue for special services for all children, placing special demands on all parents and families to satisfy those special circumstances. Children are expensive, particularly when they are not allowed to support themselves financially until age 16 (or longer in many cases). Some nations, including Great Britain and Canada, provide generous financial allowances for children. The United States provides a standard income tax deduction for each family dependent. Such policies, essentially a variety of income-maintenance programs, give some public support to the idea that all children have special needs.

Various forms of child allowances, however, become a very controversial topic when administered to children who live in high-income families. A reasonable question may be: "Can parents fulfill their responsibility to their children when they do not earn enough money to maintain their children at acceptable social standards?" In the eighteenth and nineteenth centuries, children could indeed be removed from their families for financial reasons, but modern child welfare policy does not support such practices. Nevertheless, the adequacy of parental care for children in low-income families is frequently questioned even today. These children do not benefit from community resources as much as children from families with adequate income. They are at higher risk of accidents, delinquent behavior, poor school performance, and teenage pregnancies, and children with nutritionally inadequate diets do not learn well in school.

In that sense it would be fair to say that poor children require more intense and more specialized services, many designed to protect them or intervene in their lives, in sharp contrast with normative views about freedom and liberation. For example, studies of child abuse and neglect continue to find a close associ-

FIGURE 8.1 | PERCENTAGE OF POOR PERSONS, BY AGE

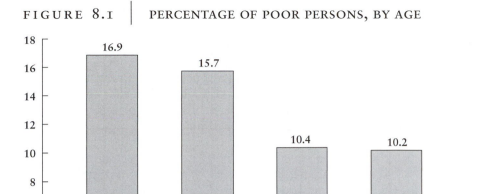

ation between parents' low income and poor child care, and between family stress (as expressed particularly by separation and divorce) and child abuse and neglect.[4] Social programs of family intervention and child protection, which have a universal legal responsibility, usually have a heavy caseload of low-income clients. The success of a program like Head Start, which attempts to mitigate the impact of poverty on learning, is undermined when low-income families are unable to stabilize the home learning environment for their children.

It is abundantly clear that low-income children constitute a special group of children. Among the various age groups, children under the age of five constitute the greatest concentration of persons in poverty. (See Figure 8.1.)

As it presently exists, child welfare policy includes activities to satisfy both sides of this issue. Some programs, such as public education, are clearly universal, whereas others, such as Head Start, are need-based. Yet in most instances the issues are not so clearly separated. For example, policymakers remain undecided as to whether birth control information and supplies should be available without charge to all teenagers who request it. Such information and material is provided without charge to children from low-income families, but critics have objected that these services (whether universally offered or not) bypass parental authority. Other services, such as preventive health service, generally are available to all children, on a cost basis. However, because many low-income families cannot afford routine medical care, many poor children go without some basic health services. For example, a child may not receive standard immunizations against serious childhood diseases until about to enter school. (By state laws, vaccinations are prerequisite for enrollment.)

Universal versus selective child welfare policies raise an additional consideration of how child resources are provided. Child welfare services are usually provided through an adult, usually a parent. Consequently, normative concerns about parental responsibility versus children's rights and about protection versus liberation are also complicated by questions of how benefits should be provided, as outright monetary support or as in-kind benefits? If parents effectively control the use of income-maintenance resources, particularly for low-income children, will those resources be used for products most necessary for the child's well-being? In-kind products do ensure better targeting of resources, and a decision about the first two normative issues may determine the normative orientation for this one. If, for example, one decides to act in the best interest of the child, might not in-kind benefits achieve this objective better than income maintenance?

If the child is considered in the context of the family, the principle of family privacy would seem to dictate that the family knows best how to use income resources to answer the child's needs. This assumption falters, however, when faced with children who are under public charge—who have no families or cannot live with their families. In those circumstances in-kind benefits may seem the safest and fairest alternatives, even though they may override the opportunity for the children, or the adults who attend them, to make their own choices. Hence, in practice, income maintenance and autonomy have become the prime policy choices for children who are within families, whereas in-kind services are preferred for children who are outside the protective influence of the family. This division seems to apply regardless of whether the family does in fact serve the interests of the child, or whether the child has been removed from the family's protection due to his or her own activities or to some other factor.

One of the most significant demographic changes in the United States since the Social Security Act became the foundation for child welfare policy has been the change in the structure of the American family. Traditionally the American family was characterized by two parents of opposite sex and one or more children. No such definition can be applied to the American family of the 2000s. The trend away from the traditional family stereotype has been led by the unexpected increase in single-parent, female-headed families, and the persistent poverty among children is one consequence of these changing demographics. (See Figure 8.2.) All other reasons aside, a child in a single-parent family is highly likely to be poor due to limited income from one parent. And if this parent is a female, the family income is likely to be even more limited. (See Table 8.1.)

Child welfare income-maintenance issues have become more complicated as more children live in single-parent, female-headed households with little or no support from the absent parent. Although public income-maintenance programs exist for these children, critics have long questioned the propriety of supporting children when parents are unable or unwilling to contribute financially to their care. The issue of parental responsibility is thus joined forcibly with policy choices concerning income maintenance and in-kind products. The TANF program has undermined historical unconditional support for depen-

FIGURE 8.2 | SINGLE-PARENT FEMALE-HEADED FAMILIES WITH CHILDREN (IN THOUSANDS)

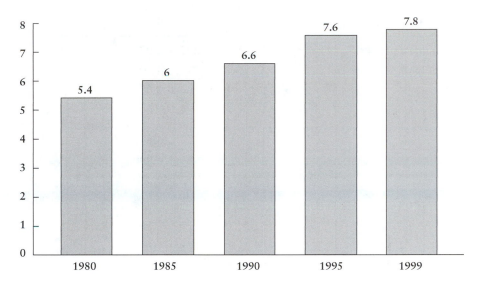

dent children by linking financial aid to children with parental responsibility by forcing work on mothers and taking parents to court when they do not financially support their children. As appropriate as work and child-support obligations are in their own right, mixing them with income-maintenance activities has resulted in complex and confusing policies that force child welfare policy into parental responsibility issues, and away from inherent concerns for children. In other words, adequate family income is important, and parental responsibility is also highly valued, but neither assures the welfare of the child.

Most normative debates over child welfare policy can usually be understood in terms of children's rights versus parents' responsibility, public protection of children versus public liberation of children (issues that affect definitions of childhood), and universal versus special public services for children. Child welfare policy in its present state has not clearly distinguished these normative questions, and consequently it sustains and creates policy products that often have arisen from conflicting normative bases. A profile of American children may give some objective vantage point for reviewing these normative issues and policies against the current state of child welfare across the nation.

A PROFILE OF AMERICAN CHILDREN

The basic normative issues reviewed above ultimately revolve around the conditions in which children actually live, and public expectations about them. The

TABLE 8.1 | PROFILE OF CHILDREN IN THE UNITED STATES (1999, 1998)

Population Group*	Number	Percentage
Total population (1999)	272,691,000	
Children (under age 18)	72,274,000	27
Male	36,140,000	50
Female	36,107,000	50
White (1998)	56,124,000	81
African American	11,414,000	16
Other	2,049,000	3
Total	72,274,000	(100)
Children under age 5 of all children	18,942,000	26
Children under 18 living in families	71,371,000	
Living with both parents	48,071,000	68
(White—74%)		
(African American—36%)		
(Other—64%)		
Living with mother only	17,308,000	24
(White —18%)		
(African American—51%)		
(Other—27%)		
Living with father or relative	6,270,000	8
Total		(100)
Children living below poverty (1999)	12,845,000	
(18% of all children)		
In white families	7,935,000	62
In African American families	4,073,000	36

following profile of American children suggests some areas of special concern for child welfare policy. Table 8.1 presents a composite view of children that highlights their social and economic status. Children under age 18 constitute about 27% of the total population. A child welfare policy that served all children would cover a lot of people—over 72 million. Thus, at the outset, compre-

Population Group*	Number	Percentage
In other families	237,000	2
Total		(100)
Children under age 18 by presence of parents		
White mothers		
Married, spouse present		74
Divorced or widowed		9
Married, spouse absent		4
Never married		5
White fathers only		5
Neither		3
Total		(100)
African American mothers		
Married, spouse present		36
Divorced or widowed		10
Married, spouse absent		9
Never married		32
African American fathers only		4
Neither		9
Total		(100)
Other mothers		
Married, spouse present		64
Divorced or widowed		7
Married, spouse absent		8
Never married		12
Other father only		4
Neither		5
Total		(100)

Source: *Statistical Abstract of the United States*, 2001, tables 13, 19, 64, 65, 68, 69, and 755.

*According to this census report, Hispanic population can be of any race and thus is included in white, African American, and other data.

hensive child welfare policies are likely to be very expensive, and indeed most are. In FY 1999, federal funds for educational activities for children in public primary and secondary schools totaled almost 4.4% of the entire federal budget; but even this large sum amounted only to 10% of all federal expenditures on children's education. Total educational expenditures for elementary and secondary education in 1999 amounted to more than $400 billion, and many experts believe education is still underfunded in the United States.[5]

Children in Poverty

Because of the potentially high costs of any policy that serves all children, most child welfare policy is directed toward special groups of children, most usually children who seem particularly in economic and/or social need. Table 8.1 suggests that children in single-parent, female-headed families are likely to be poor and likely to be African American, two special overlapping classes of children for whom child welfare policy can have very significant effects. Research on children over the years suggests that children in single-parent, female-headed families are more likely to do poorly in school and display more antisocial behavior (including tendencies toward delinquency and difficulty in social adjustments),[6] problems all complicated by poverty. Overall, poor performance by children may be due as much to their poverty as to their family situation.

The fact that children are two and a half times as likely to be poor if they live in single-parent, female-headed families is a special concern. About 24% of all children live in such families, and almost all of them have living fathers, who by law are required to provide financial support for them. Uncollected child support is one of the most pervasive child welfare problems today. In the only study of parental failure to pay child support that has examined fathers' financial capacity to pay, researchers found that $26.6 billion in child support was owed and could be paid by absent fathers in 1984. Only $6.1 billion was actually paid, leaving $20.5 billion uncollected.[7] By 1999, if uncollected child support were distributed equally, it would have provided every child $1,647 per year. The average amount of child support received by a single-parent family in 1999 was $2,995, according to the U.S. Bureau of the Census, and this amount provided only about 19% of the family's income. (See Chapter 5.)

The Racial Factor

Table 8.1 also highlights a striking difference in family structures for African American and white children. Fifty-one percent of all African American children are living with a single parent, 49% in female-headed households, and 32% live with women who have never been married. The poverty rate among these children is twice as high as that for children in similar white families; about one out of three African American children in single-parent, female-headed homes are living in poverty; only 19% of white children in such families are poor.

For these and other reasons over the years, scholars and analysts have debated how the differences between African American and white family structures may affect the rearing of children. Writing in the 1940s, Gunnar Myrdal identified this difference as a continuing product of the American system of slavery, which had deliberately destroyed family bonds and established the black matriarchal family.[8] Two decades later, in 1965, a critique of the African American family by Patrick Moynihan, written while he was an assistant director of the Office of Planning and Policy of the U.S. Department of Labor, stirred considerable controversy. Moynihan identified high rates of out-of-wedlock births, dissolved marriages, and the relatively high proportion of female-headed families among African Americans as a cause for alarm and argued that the African American family was no longer able to rear children properly.[9] Many African American social scientists had expressed concern about African American family structure before Moynihan issued his report. Most notable was the social psychologist Kenneth Clark, an influential scholar whose work helped shape civil rights laws and policy of the 1960s.[10]

More recently, Andrew Billingsley and anthropologist Carol Stack have presented research that confirms important differences between white and African American family structures.[11] This does not mean, however, that African American families are somehow inadequate or are unable to raise their children properly. Research has also shown that African American women may rely more customarily on the extended family for surrogate parenting resources, an option that may not be as commonly available among white families. In other ways, African American family structures serve important functions for African Americans that are not necessary for the white family, and that should not be minimized: "Negroes have created . . . a range of institutions to structure the tasks of living a victimized life and to minimize the pain it inevitably produces. Predominant among these institutions are those of the nuclear family, the social network—the extended kinship system . . . by which they instruct, explain and accept themselves."[12]

On the negative side, however valuable they are to African American families, these important structural differences continue to isolate African Americans and their children from the mainstream of American life, which has provided the energy for upward mobility for other American minorities. The difficulty and appropriateness of developing public policy designed deliberately to modify forms of family life raises huge issues of ethics and public expense. Because so many public child-welfare policies do indeed have an influence on various forms of family life, it might seem tempting to suggest new policies that would modify present forms of African American family life as one means of addressing the degrading experience of poverty that more than half of all African American children undergo. From the perspective of policy analysis, however, family policy and child welfare policy are two separate issues, and they must be addressed independently. Focus on the family as the subject for policy analysis raises a host of normative issues that differ profoundly from those surrounding child welfare policy. For that reason, analysis in this chapter concentrates on the problems of children. Thus it is important to digress briefly here to consider conclusions drawn from research about family patterns generally and specifically about the African American family. The alternative patterns so evident in African American family structure have not deprived children of basic maternal care, but serious doubts about that care must be raised when adequate funds to support this and other analogous forms of maternal care are not available, and when women are poorly prepared for the maternal roles that today's complex urban society forces on them.

The Changing Character of American Families

The changing character of the American family, so dramatically portrayed by our gradual recognition of special African American family structures, has had a significant impact on child welfare in many other ways. More women are working than ever before. They presently compose half the civilian labor force, which means, among other things, that many more mothers are working. In fact, maternal employment is now greater than at any time since World War II. Table 8.2 provides some information about maternal employment and women's participation in the workforce that has direct bearing on child welfare.

Married women compose almost half of the female labor force. Of all the married women with school-age children, 65% work. Many studies have explored why women work and the impact of their changing roles on families and on the care of children. In general, women work because they need money and are seeking meaningful lives. Work itself does not diminish women's maternal interests and abilities. However, lack of supportive resources for working mothers makes mothering more difficult. Perhaps because women traditionally have been expected to stay home and provide nurturing and care for children and spouses, few public resources have been developed that substitute for traditional maternal activities during mothers' working hours.

But not all mothers have a choice about whether to stay home and provide child care. Poor mothers, in particular, are expected to work, and from time to time poor mothers who receive welfare support will be required to work as the 1996 welfare reform amendments are implemented. But conflicting messages are expressed when enforced work policy fails to anticipate the kinds of resources necessary to support employment for mothers who wish to work and for those who are forced to do so by other policies. Working mothers destabilize child welfare policies in today's social and vocational context. Day care for children becomes a critical issue, particularly for poor mothers who cannot afford to purchase such services. By 1998, the Congressional Budget Office states, there were 2.8 million children under age six living in poverty in female-headed households.[13] At present, publicly funded day care can serve only about 10% of these children. Welfare mothers who work are permitted to deduct child-care expenses from gross earnings, which provides in most cases only a partial subsidy for that expense. And although welfare will guarantee day care to mothers who are required to work, finding adequate day care may be difficult, regardless of one's ability to pay for it. From the standpoint of child welfare, maternal employment without an adequate infrastructure of reliable and trustworthy day-care services and an infrastructure of other family support services for mothers and children is a questionable policy option.

TABLE 8.2 | WOMEN IN THE LABOR FORCE

Category	Number in Labor Force	Percentage of Category	Percentage of Total Labor Force
Total women in the labor force (57.9% of all women)	58,407,000	100.0	100.0
Single women	14,624,000	66.4	25.0
Married women	31,978,000	59.4	54.8
Widowed and divorced	11,805,000	47.1	20.2
Married women with children to 6 years	7,300,000	59.6	
Married women with children 6–17 years	9,700,000	79.4	
Single women with children to 6 years	1,100,000	47.4	
Single women with children 6–17 years	700,000	70.2	
Widowed, divorced, or separated			
with children to 6 years	1,200,000	60.0	
with children 6–17 years	3,000,000	78.3	

Source: *Statistical Abstract of the United States*, 1994, tables 625 and 626.

Special Issues of Health and Social Welfare

The health status of children was discussed to some extent in Chapter 6. Poor mothers are more likely to bear low-birth-weight (premature) babies, who in turn are at risk of frequent and serious childhood health problems. This is a critical issue not only of early childhood welfare, but also of the welfare of older children who themselves bear children. Teenage pregnancy and motherhood is a serious problem for both mother and child. The birthrate had dropped from 1 birth for every 1,000 women age 10–14 in 1950, to 0.8 in 1965, but it rose to 1.3 in 1975 and stabilized at 1.1 in the 1990s. An unusually high percentage of these births were children with low birth weights, born to mothers without financial and social resources to care for them adequately.

A number of other health problems of older children have not been addressed adequately by child welfare policies generally, or by public health programs specifically. Drug use, auto accidents, and suicides are persistent problems that ignore boundaries of class, race, or economic status. Emotional health, both immediately and in the long term, may be greatly affected by success or failure in school and its influence on employment. African American children and poor children are more likely to drop out of school before they complete high school. The nationwide dropout rate among white teenagers is currently about 7%, for African American teenagers, about 15%; these rates tend to be higher in impoverished areas.

This profile of American children suggests that traditional issues of rights and responsibilities, protection or liberation, or universal or specialized services are amplified by the present status of children. In particular, changes in family roles and structures have severely strained child welfare policies that originally emerged to deal with children in traditional contexts. Single-parent, female-headed families are seriously limited financially in caring for their children. Families with working mothers may have increased difficulty finding adequate child care and other supportive services. African American children, in particular, are at great risk of poverty and resulting inadequate care. These facts raise concern about how well children really are being protected from a variety of social risks, how well parents are capable of meeting traditional child-care expectations, and how well current social services and income-maintenance programs provide protection for all children, but especially the poor ones.

POLICY BACKGROUND

As indicated above, child welfare policy has a rich history of efforts to protect and promote the welfare of all children. Of particular significance for this policy analysis is the contemporary policy background directed at disadvantaged American children. One analyst has put the picture in somewhat reductive terms: "It may develop that private families really are not equipped to meet most children's needs. . . . Unless and until that case is made more persuasively than it has been, however, a children's policy will be successful enough if it concentrates on ways to compensate demonstrably unlucky children whose bodies or minds are sick, or whose families are unstable or in poverty."[14]

Table 8.3 gives an overview of current child welfare policy for the disadvantaged and comparable expenditures for each program. The number of children served and the amount of federal money spent on them suggests that, except for Social Security benefits to the retired and disabled, children's policies constitute in aggregate the nation's most expensive federal welfare program.

THE SOCIAL SECURITY ACT
AND CHILD WELFARE POLICY

Most child welfare policy is part of the Social Security Act. Eight program titles in the act have some bearing on the welfare of children (see Figure 8.3 and Table 8.4). One of these, Title IV, composes the fundamental federal child welfare policy for disadvantaged children.

TABLE 8.3 | FEDERAL EXPENDITURES ON PROGRAMS THAT PRIMARILY AFFECT CHILDREN

Program	Number of Beneficiaries (est.)*	Expenditures (in Billions)
Total civilian population	272,691,000	
Total children	71,371,000	
Social Security children	3,759,000	$17.0
TANF recipients	8,770,000	21.5
Food stamps	21,000,000	22.4
School lunch and breakfast	21,400,000	6.5
Medicaid	41,360,000	177.4
Public housing	4,296,000	20.1
Head Start children	822,000	5.4
Total		$270.3

Source: *Statistical Abstract of the United States*, 2001, table 606.

*In 1990 the Congressional Budget Office estimated that approximately 3.5 benefits are provided to each recipient.

TABLE 8.4 | CHILDREN'S FOCUS UNDER THE SOCIAL SECURITY ACT

Title	Function	Children's Focus	1996 Welfare Reforms
Social Security (Title II)	Social insurance	In covered families	Unchanged
Unemployment Insurance (Title III)	Social insurance	In covered families	Unchanged
Aid to Families with Dependent Children (AFDC):			
• Assistance Payments (Title IV-A)	Income maintenance	Cash for dependent children in own homes	Changed to block grant under TANF
• Child Welfare Services (Title IV-B)	Social services	Dependent children in foster or adoptive homes	Block grant
• Demonstration and Training (Title IV-C)	Social services	Work programs and demonstrations	Block grant

(*continued*)

TABLE 8.4 | CHILDREN'S FOCUS UNDER THE SOCIAL
SECURITY ACT (CONTINUED)

Title	Function	Children's Focus	1996 Welfare Reforms
• Child Support Enforcement (CSE) (Title IV-D)	Social services	Child support collection for poor and nonpoor	Unchanged
• Permanency Planning (Title IV-E)	Social services	Home finding and placement	Block grant
• TANF (Title IV-G	Income maintenance	Cash for dependent children	Created this subtitle
• Jobs Program (Title IV-F)	Services	Put parents to work	Changed to block grant under TANF
Maternal and Child Health (MCH) (Title V)	Health services	Health care children and others	Unchanged
Supplemental Security Income (SSI) (Title XVI)	Income maintenance	For severely disabled children	Unchanged
Medicaid (Title XIX)	Health income	Health care for poor children	Unchanged
Social Services Block Grant (SSBG) (formerly Title XX)	Social services	Various services	Unchanged
State Child Health Insurance (Title XXI)	Health care	All low-income children	Unchanged

Source: U.S. Department of Health and Human Services, *The Green Book* (Washington, D.C.: Government Printing Office, 2001) (www.hhs.gov).

Social Security Benefits (Title II)

Title II of the Social Security Act, which provides benefits to the retired and disabled—what most people mean when they say "social security"—also benefits many children, a fact that has gone relatively unnoticed in current Social Security debates. Children to age 18 are covered under Social Security if their parents are or were covered. This eligibility may be the result of a covered parent's retirement, death, or disability. Because Social Security has become so universal, children are protected by its "safety net" feature. Social Security was intended to perform this function for children, with the expectation that the need-based program, AFDC (now TANF, see Title IV below), would eventually become unnecessary. AFDC was, in fact, designed as a temporary program; Social Security was expected to carry the burden of income maintenance for children. AFDC's origin as a temporary measure is important to recall for later discussion.

Unemployment Insurance (Title III)

Unemployment insurance, discussed in detail in Chapter 5, provides income maintenance to children when they are part of a family in which the wage earner becomes unemployed through no fault of his or her own. There is no clear figure for how many children are covered under this program, but by counting the number of families who receive the service, one can estimate that a great many children must benefit. Single-parent, female-headed families are covered if the woman is employed in covered employment. The way the program is set up, however, makes it difficult for many low-income, single-parent, female heads of families to qualify for unemployment insurance, for many of them are employed in jobs that are not covered by unemployment insurance laws. On the other hand, because unemployment insurance is not means-tested, its universal applicability provides important income protection to many children.

Assistance to Needy Families (Title IV)

As Figure 8.3 shows, Title IV has had a prominent position in child welfare policy, since it authorizes both income maintenance and social services on behalf of disadvantaged children and their adult caretakers—usually their mothers, but also foster and adoptive parents and institutions. Title IV contains subtitles all specifically directed at poor children. (In some cases other children are eligible.) The legislative development of Title IV is worth noting because it exemplifies many practical confusions of the normative questions discussed at the beginning of this chapter. Also, as noted above (and in Chapter 5), the program was originally designed as a temporary program, because it was assumed that as the Social Security program expanded its coverage, public aid for dependent children would not be necessary. In this context states were given great discretionary authority over setting payment standards and criteria for eligibility. This was in keeping with the fact that all states had public programs to support dependent children before 1935; the new federal program was essentially intended to provide additional funding to brace these earlier efforts.

Title IV began with two parts. Part A was the financial assistance program; Part B was for child welfare services, mostly supporting dependents in other than their own homes. Later Part C was added to provide funds for demonstration and training activities. The financial assistance program (Part A), originally called Aid to Dependent Children (ADC), made matching federal funds available to states, provided that state programs met uniform federal administrative standards. Fourteen original standards—modified frequently over subsequent

FIGURE 8.3 | PROGRAMS UNDER THE SOCIAL SECURITY ACT WITH IMPORTANT CONSEQUENCES FOR CHILDREN

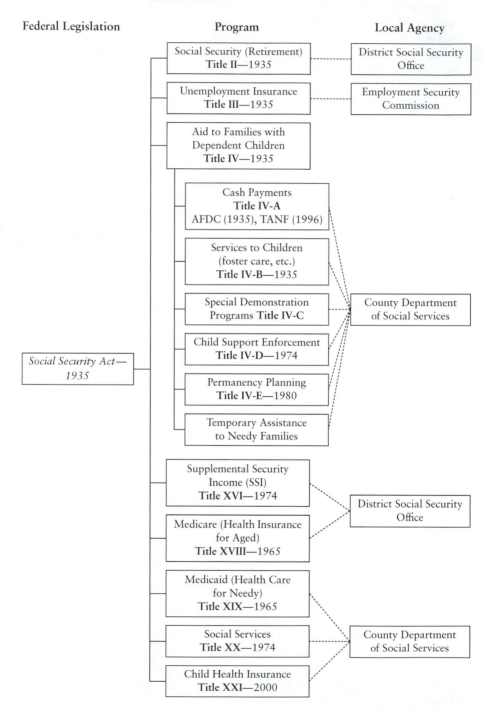

Federal Legislation · Program · Local Agency

Social Security (Retirement) Title II—1935 — District Social Security Office

Unemployment Insurance Title III—1935 — Employment Security Commission

Aid to Families with Dependent Children Title IV—1935

Cash Payments Title IV-A AFDC (1935), TANF (1996)

Services to Children (foster care, etc.) Title IV-B—1935

Special Demonstration Programs Title IV-C

Child Support Enforcement Title IV-D—1974

Permanency Planning Title IV-E—1980

Temporary Assistance to Needy Families

County Department of Social Services

Social Security Act—1935

Supplemental Security Income (SSI) Title XVI—1974

Medicare (Health Insurance for Aged) Title XVIII—1965

District Social Security Office

Medicaid (Health Care for Needy) Title XIX—1965

Social Services Title XX—1974

Child Health Insurance Title XXI—2000

County Department of Social Services

years—established a federal context that protected individual rights from possible infringements during the process of providing assistance. Nevertheless, noneconomic standards for determining eligibility often crept into the administration of the program. For example, in 1956 Louisiana established a condition of eligibility that denied ADC to mothers who had a second out-of-wedlock birth. The federal government threatened to withdraw funds from Louisiana's program, which appeared blatantly prejudiced racially, but Louisiana contested the case in court. A compromise was reached before a court decision was made, but the case clearly illustrated states' ability to set ADC policy that could circumvent guarantees established by federal statute. Child welfare policymaking continues to be a joint responsibility of the federal government and the states.

In 1959, after six years of increased attention to matters of the family, Title IV as a whole was renamed Aid to Families with Dependent Children (AFDC), signifying a movement away from its original, more exclusive emphasis on the child. The late 1950s brought a spate of studies that linked family welfare to child welfare. The most important one, conducted by the American Public Welfare Association in 1956, established the importance of families to healthy child development and documented a strong association between families who received social service counseling and shorter stays on welfare.[15] These and similar findings of the period led to the development of a new policy for children that included federal funding for social services designed, in the words of the 1962 amendments to the Social Security Act, "to maintain and strengthen family life for children."[16]

Bringing a focus on the family into child welfare policy through the AFDC program seemed a logical extension of child welfare policy: Protect the family, and you protect children; strong families provide strong children. Thus there developed perceptions that policy did, could, and should manipulate the family to achieve wide-ranging public objectives including improved child health and welfare. At the programmatic level, the changes introduced into Title IV during the 1950s and 1960s were designed to deal, directly, with family issues. Provisions were made to provide financial support for unemployed parents (usually fathers), to keep the family together through casework counseling, and to establish programs of work training and placement to help families become economically self-sufficient. The change in name reflected a substantial shift in the direction of child welfare policy.

Despite this strong interest in "family impact statements" and family policy studies, the Orwellian overtones of such efforts did not go unnoticed by public critics.[17] Nor, for all the additional assistance children and their parents received through these special services programs, did AFDC caseloads decrease as hoped. Not only did the number of AFDC recipients increase during the 1960s, but more and more AFDC families were becoming financially dependent because a parent was absent from the home, due to out-of-wedlock births, desertion, or informal separation. Welfare critics blamed AFDC for causing "family breakup" and argued for stronger policy to keep families together. Amid all this clamor, the welfare of children, the original purpose of Title IV, seemed to have become lost, so much so that the seventh decennial White House conference on children, proposed for 1979, was modified to become a conference on the family. But even then, preliminary discussion could not establish a definition of the family, and under a wave of discontent the conference was canceled—nor has a White House conference on children been held since.

There is little doubt that the family is an important institution in the United States, but there is still little professional or public consensus on just exactly what a family is. The disagreements early on in planning the 1979 White House conference on the family opened a Pandora's box of normative issues. The planners initially defined a family as a husband who probably worked and a wife who usually stayed at home and took care of (approximately) two children, despite the fact that less than 10% of American families then fit that stereotype. But women in particular objected to having single-parent, female-headed families categorized as "broken" families. Many separated and divorced women argued that they had much more "intact" families than they had while they were married. Religious organizations, however, could not accept single-parent families as "full-fledged" families, any more than they could accept the idea that homosexual couples (even those with dependent children) should be included in the cornucopia of wholesome American families.

It is impossible to make good policy for an abstraction. The concerns of women's advocacy groups over new family policies did help redirect attention of Title IV back to children's financial concerns. The increase in absent and nonsupporting fathers became viewed less as a problem of "family breakdown" and more as an issue of financial support for children that might lift them out of poverty or keep them off welfare in the first place.

Temporary Assistance for Needy Families (TANF)   As reported in Chapter 5, Temporary Assistance for Needy Families (TANF) was created in 1996 by combining the old Aid to Families with Dependent Children program with the Job Opportunity and Basic Skills program (Title IV-F, 1988), and Emergency Assistance into a block grant to states.

Title IV-B   An original title of the Social Security Act, Title IV-B was created to provide assistance to children who could not live in their own homes. These funds are used to support foster care, adoptive placements and services, and care of children in nonhome environments such as group homes and institutions. They are also used for diagnosis, counseling, and treatment for children who are experiencing difficulty in their own homes or the homes of others, even though they may otherwise be ineligible to be served under this program. Over the years, Title IV-B programs have become the launching pad for a number of related programs that attempt to help children stay in their own homes. Federal legislation under Title IV-B was strengthened in 1984 to provide the funds to identify and address abuse and neglect among dependent children and to provide assistance to abused and neglected children, and in 1993 Family Preservation services were funded under this part.

These changes in Title IV-B have led to the development of a much larger network of services to children. Title IV-E, which was added in 1980, became a companion program, and it too has spawned a large number of specific service programs designed to stabilize families so that they become suitable for children. With the advent of TANF a shortage of substitute homes has developed, according to the Urban Institute. Additionally, the ever-expanding service programs now appropriate for funding under Titles IV-B and IV-E have begun to overwhelm the child welfare system. For example, the Urban Institute reports that under the Family Preservation and Family Support Act of 1993 (Title IV-B, subpart 2) a system of waivers has allowed states to use IV-B funding for a wide variety of activities, including development of mediation programs and joint training for child welfare agency and court personnel.[18]

Title IV-E: Permanency Planning   Title IV-E was created in 1980 as an extension of the IV-B program in an effort to reduce out-of-home placements for children and to try to ensure that every child had a permanent home. Because out-of-home care is expensive and has always been considered a temporary alternative to care at home, concern was voiced in Congress during 1976–79 that not enough effort was being put forward to establish a permanent home environment for many of the children served with Title IV-B funds. In particular, many children with special medical and psychological problems were maintained in "temporary" environments for long periods and frequently shifted from one such setting to another. African American children especially were often kept in these uncertain settings, in many cases for the whole of their childhood. Title IV-E was created to motivate states to review the status of children supported by IV-B resources, and to develop permanent plans for all of them, emphasizing adoptive alternatives or return to their own rehabilitated homes. The program requires the recruitment of adoptive homes and also assistance to families who may, with some adjustment, be able to accept their children back into the original home.

Title IV-E has probably already achieved the maximum benefit of its original policy objective. States quickly developed classification systems for reviewing the status of AFDC children in foster placements and made dramatic strides to provide permanent homes for children. Out-of-home child-care populations decreased in 1981, stabilized in 1982, but then began to rise again. Since 1990 there has been a steady increase in both the number of children in foster care and adoptive care under the IV-E program. Foster care cases increased from 168,000 in 1990 to 233,000 in 1993, a 29% increase in four years. IV-E adoption assistance cases increased from 44,000 in 1990 to 81,000 in 1993, a 46% increase. Thus while the Title IV-E program has succeeded in getting children into permanent homes, it has not reduced the number of children in foster care. At present there are about 390,000 children in foster care, and 20,000 awaiting adoption in both the Title IV-B and Title IV-E programs.[19]

If the Title IV-E program has not significantly reduced the substitute-care population, it has provided an unusually good understanding of the problems of this group of children. More than 75% of children in substitute care have been there for two or more years; 60% have special physical, mental, or emotional problems; 39% are African American; and 69% are more than six years old. The discovery that so many children need substitute care because of abuse and neglect provided firm evidence of the seriousness of child abuse and neglect in the general population. Changes in IV-B and IV-E legislation have integrated these two provisions under what is now called "Family Preservation."[20] In other words, the focus of the policy underlying both subtitles IV-B and IV-E is to help children obtain and live in permanent and stable homes. For children whose substitute care is terminated successfully in a permanent home, the IV-E program is invaluable, but the program has not efficiently reduced the use of or need for substitute care.

Child Support Enforcement Program (CSE)   In 1974 a fourth part was added to Title IV—Part D, known as Child Support Enforcement. In 1984 this program was enlarged and broadened to give it more authority over collecting financial support owed to children from absent parents. CSE represents a departure from original child welfare policy under Title IV, in two ways. First, the federal government provides help to the states in their effort to collect child support. All states have statutes that make parents' failure to support their child a crime, and all states have procedures enforcing these statutes. CSE policy requires, as a condition of receiving welfare, that the applicant (usually a mother) sign over to the state his or her right, and the right of the dependent child or children, to support from the absent parent. The state then collects the support from the absent parent and uses the collected funds to lower the state's share of welfare costs. If the family is eventually able to leave the welfare program, the support payments revert to the family. But as long as the family is on welfare, the state keeps the collections. This is an important shift in policy: the state "owns" the right to child-support payments for welfare families; the money owed belongs to the state and the federal government.

Second, through CSE the federal government provides funds to help parents and children who are not on welfare collect any child support that might be due to them. This also departs from traditional Title IV policy, which was applicable only to poor children. Consequently this new policy creates considerable confusion in program administration. States do not benefit directly from child-support collections on behalf of nonwelfare families because those collections go directly to the families. Hence states have been slow to spend their own resources to help collect money that goes to someone else. States may levy a fee on these services, but fees are apt to discourage those who need the service from using it. The fact that the greatest amount of uncollected child support (about $24 billion in 1992) is owed by parents whose children are not on welfare has presented a serious obstruction to implementing CSE successfully. States are reluctant to help collect child support for these children because it costs states more than they are repaid for their services. Thus a potentially important child welfare policy that would help all children has become seriously compromised in its administration by a normative conflict over whether different standards should apply when all children or only needy children are served by it.

Title IV-C: Research, Demonstration, and Training   Title IV-C, originally instituted to provide funds to states to educate child welfare workers, now provides funds for research, demonstration, and training. When work programs were first required in the 1960s, they were also put under this subtitle. Later, the earlier work programs administered under Title IV-C were reorganized by Title IV-F, the JOBS program created by the 1988 welfare reform amendments. The 1996 welfare reform lumps the IV-F program into the overall welfare block grant. Work programs have had many individual successes but limited universal application. For parents who have a foundation of education and skill and strong work motivation, work programs have been helpful stepping stones for getting back into the workforce. But for those who have little employment potential, the program has no meaning.

The experiences with work-related research and demonstration programs under Title IV-C have provided a considerable amount of information that should be useful in planning how present TANF recipients might be helped to become economically self-sufficient. For example, we have learned that more than 60% of all adult welfare recipients either have never worked or have not worked in the five years prior to receiving welfare. The creation of a single new job may require as much as $5,000 to $10,000 in capital investment, another $2,000 to supervise that job for a year, and about $5,000 to train a person to do the job. At this rate a newly created job may take five to ten years to pay for itself.[21] Welfare reform does not provide funding for these purposes, and consequently work programs have poor potential for assisting welfare parents and their children. One recent study of work demonstration programs has found that only 7 to 10% of welfare beneficiaries who participate in such programs do find steady jobs.[22]

Maternal and Child Health

Maternal and Child Health (MCH, formerly Title V of the Social Security Act) was also discussed in Chapter 6. Originally part of the Social Security Act, federal funds for this program are now distributed to the states through a block grant. Although children with special medical problems, such as crippling conditions, are identified in the block grant as a specific service population, the states otherwise use MCH funds in widely divergent ways. Because all states provide a complex mixture of types and amounts of health-care services for mothers and children, funds from MCH frequently are used to supplement programs that states are already providing. In most cases services that are supplemented with MCH funds are provided at local (usually county) departments of health. Such programs include pre- and postnatal care and child health follow-up services for preschool children.

As mentioned in Chapter 6, MCH and other public health programs that serve children have thus far given comparatively little attention to problems of older children, such as alcohol and drug abuse, auto accidents, suicide, and teenage pregnancies (although many teenage mothers do receive help as mothers of children themselves). Although MCH funds could be used for services that deal with a variety of teenage problems, the lack of specificity in the use of these funds perpetuates financial support for existing service programs rather than encouraging ventures in new directions.[23]

Medicaid (Title XIX)

Like MCH, Medicaid has been discussed in detail in Chapter 6. Table 8.3 shows the importance of Medicaid for needy children. One little noted section of the Supplemental Security Income (SSI) program, discussed in Chapter 5, allows income maintenance from SSI to support children with medically handicapping conditions. Because SSI payments are larger than TANF payments, and because many medically handicapped children require social services but may not meet TANF eligibility requirements, the SSI program is important for this very small group of children.

Social Services (Title XX)

Social services for children are provided under the Social Services Block Grant, Title XX of the Social Security Act. SSBG provides states with funds for a wide variety of services that may be initiated at their own discretion. Although under SSBG there are no services that states are required to provide for children, well over half of services that states do provide with SSBG funds are directly or indirectly for children. Since SSBG services do not have to be means-tested (restricted for use only by the poor), many SSBG programs provided for children complement and extend other services offered under Title IV. For example, adoption, foster care, residential care and treatment, and protective services are provided by most states in harmony with services supported with funds from SSBG, with the net effect of developing an infrastructure of services for all children that is not possible under any single Title IV program alone. At the same time, states have used SSBG to develop services not likely to be funded through other sources. Day care, for example, is the most commonly provided such service, because SSBG funding permits widespread support for day-care programs and subsidies—though not nearly enough to meet the growing demand for more day care. States are also allowed to transfer a portion of their TANF block grant to their SSBG.

Both social services and Maternal and Child Health programs are funded with block grants. The block grant method of financing social programs is itself an important policy issue with a number of normative questions of its own. These issues were discussed thoroughly in Chapter 3, but child welfare policy provides a good practical illustration. Among other issues, the block grant virtually eliminates any federal authority over decisions about what kinds of services states may provide, or under what circumstances. Block grants allow states to shift funds around as the need arises. This increased flexibility has been accompanied by decreasing federal financial support for these programs. Several studies have demonstrated that, in turn, state service patterns have changed as a result of block grant funding. For example, the policy infrastructure of service, which had had some commonality from state to state, has been eroded, and decisions about what services should be provided have shifted from professional groups to political forums.[24] Moreover, although states generally have made up for federal funding decreases, they have modified their programs, shifted programs to other federal funding sources, restricted eligibility for services, and eliminated some programs completely, both to save money and to make the services more consistent with their political realities.[25]

A wide array of policies and programs are available for a wide range of children's needs. These programs engage many of the normative issues inherent in child welfare policy. For the most part these policies are directed toward poor children, which is consistent with the general policy orientation of Title IV of the Social Security Act. Additionally, child welfare policy has become increasingly intertwined with normative views of the American family, making it very difficult to develop child welfare policy independent from efforts that seek to modify the American family to stereotyped, idealized forms. The extent to which child welfare policy is viewed in traditional or contemporary contexts may determine its effectiveness in coping with child welfare problems.

State Child Health Insurance (Title XXI)

The addition of State Child Health Insurance (Title XXI) to the Social Security Act in 2000 is discussed in some detail in Chapter 6. States have been slow to adopt this program and either integrate it into their Medicaid program or establish it as a separate program. One difficulty has been the level of co-payments and deductibles that states have established, which has discouraged many poor families from applying and using the program. (See Chapter 6.)

The 1996 Welfare Reform

The impact of the 1996 federal welfare reform was discussed at length in Chapter 5. As significant as the creation of TANF has become, it has not altered the basic structure of child welfare policy as administered under the Social Security Act. TANF has altered the way federal funds to needy children are distributed by giving states authority over setting conditions of welfare eligibility, thus removing the concept of legal entitlement to welfare support. However, TANF did not alter the legal entitlement to other services to children, as shown in Table 8.4. Reauthorization of TANF means simply continuing the TANF program, rather than any abrupt change in child welfare policy.

POLICY ANALYSIS

The long-standing and traditional national experience with child welfare policy, the relative clarity of the normative issues, and the lack of marginal utility for many of the policy alternatives already in place suggests that analysis of child welfare policy would best be assisted by the behavioral or "rational" model. Despite some disagreements, the amount and depth of consensus on normative issues of child welfare indicate that child welfare policy first considers the best ways to protect children through maximizing parental responsibility, buttressing this protection with programs of income support and social services that can be made available to all children when needed. The major question in policy analysis here is not so much what kinds of policies and programs are needed, but how to modify the existing ones, within the normative environment discussed above, to deal more satisfactorily with circumstances in which children presently live. Under the behavioral model we might thus see the analysis in terms of three major alternatives, each with measurable subsets.

1. Protection of children
    a. Protection of income
    b. Protection of health
2. Parental responsibility
    a. In two-parent traditional families
    b. In alternative family forms
3. Income maintenance and service mix
    a. For poor children only
    b. For all children

These alternatives can be analyzed by examining their subsets and setting the costs of policy alternatives against their benefits to illustrate which choices would most likely realize the best benefits for children generally. The analysis is based on an understanding of existing programs, as described earlier in this chapter. Because the behavioral model may identify several "best" alternatives, more than one recommendation may be suggested for child welfare policy.

The alternatives are described in the following sections.

Protection of Children

Income Protection   There were approximately 80.2 million children in the United States in 1999 (2000 census), and approximately 13 million of them were living in poverty. Income-maintenance programs discussed in Chapter 5 and in-kind programs such as housing, as well as income from work, significantly reduces the amount of funds needed to keep children above the poverty line. As suggested in Chapter 5, the combination of existing cash and in-kind benefits may, in the aggregate, be sufficient to raise all children above poverty, depending on how these resources are distributed. Table 8.3 confirms this position by suggesting that $270.3 billion is already being spent on children, most of this spending focused on low-income children.

Health Protection   Protecting the health of children is more difficult to calculate in terms of costs and benefits. The analysis of health policy presented in Chapter 6 mentions the high benefit and low cost of pre- and postnatal care programs for children. Expenditures for the Medicaid and the Child Health Insurance program again seem adequate to meet the needs of low-income children if distributed wisely.

Parental Responsibility

Parental responsibility for children would require analysis of traditional families—mother, father, and children living together as a primary social and economic unit—and nontraditional families (all other kinds of families). The costs of promoting and protecting the traditional family structure would have to be weighed against the benefits—social development of children, happiness of children, and so forth. The preceding discussion, however, has suggested that although the traditional form still dominates the national ideal, nontraditional families also provide viable structures for realizing parental responsibility to children. The single-parent, female-headed family and the matriarchal extended family are two family structures that depart significantly from traditional ideas of family structure, but there is no evidence that parenting responsibility is better or worse in these families. These two dominant nontraditional family forms are both characterized by absent fathers; in the case of the single-parent, female-headed family, the father is most likely known. In the matriarchal extended family, the father is most likely unknown.[26]

There are currently about 9.5 million single-parent families. Thirty-two percent of all children under age 18 live in a single-parent family. In contrast, 64% of all African American children under age 18 live in a single-parent family, and 31% of those children live with an unmarried mother. This evidence supports the idea that the form of African American families differs significantly from that of other American families. Thus most efforts to reestablish traditional families in the United States would have to take place in the African American community, would be extremely difficult to accomplish by public policy, and probably represents a poor policy alternative.

There is no good way to measure either the costs or the benefits of reestablishing traditional families in the United States, if indeed such a social objective is desirable or possible. From time to time social critics have suggested that some policies may encourage the development of nontraditional families. During the 1950s, for example, AFDC was blamed for breaking up families because fathers had to be absent before the family could become eligible for benefits. Some states consequently amended their AFDC programs to permit eligibility for benefits without the absence of a parent; but the number of absent-parent families has not diminished perceptibly as a result. The Guaranteed Annual Income studies completed in the 1970s provided evidence that middle-income families that received income maintenance tended to separate more frequently than families that did not receive such support.[27]

Such findings may simply illustrate what is already known: the family, however it is defined, is an economic as well as a social unit. Hence economic changes result in change in family form, just as social changes do. In other words, the form of families can be manipulated by financial incentives. Whether policy should try to change the form of the family remains an unresolved normative issue.

Although it is virtually impossible to establish the costs and benefits of maintaining the traditional family as an American ideal—except for purely economic benefits—it is possible, and appropriate, to discuss parents' financial responsibility under this rubric. This can be measured. Statistics mentioned earlier in this chapter (and also in Chapter 5) amply demonstrate the immense difference that efficient retrieval of uncollected child-support payments from absent parents could make in child welfare, perhaps to the point of virtually eliminating childhood poverty. The costs of obtaining this child support may in some cases exceed the financial benefits of collecting it, particularly for financially marginal families. At least one study has found, for instance, that low-income, absent African American fathers did not appear to have sufficient earnings to make collection efforts fiscally beneficial to their children. The same study also demonstrated, however, that low-income African American fathers took considerable parental responsibility for their children, even if that did not take the form of paying much child support.[28]

Although this analysis suggests that by maximizing parental financial responsibility in the aggregate, money could be made available to provide much more support to children, the distribution of such funds, however, might not result in a benefit to children who are most in need of financial protection. African American families are most in need of financial support, but white, upper-income fathers owe by far the greatest proportion of the unpaid child support. Pressing African American fathers to become more financially responsible would not necessarily generate sufficient funds to aid poor African American children, at least in overall terms.

To the extent that more child support can be collected through the assistance of programs like CSE (Title IV-D), all children will benefit. Encouraging parental financial responsibility in the process may be desirable in its own right. However, as the situation now stands, it may not be cost-effective to pursue CSE collection efforts. Low-income families do not have enough money to make the program work for poor children. States find the costs of collecting support payments for other families so great that they are discouraged from pursuing the program, and even new policy initiatives such as wage garnishment requirements have failed to generate additional collections.

Income Maintenance and In-Kind Services for Children

Income maintenance and in-kind services for children might be the very best policy to pursue at this time. The preceding discussion has suggested that the income gap for children in poverty might be eliminated, and that expanded health services could be offered. This, along with slight modifications in other services for children, could realize significant improvements in child welfare. CSE in particular could be modified to increase its efficiency among nonwelfare households that need the service. Less emphasis could be given to collecting child support from low-income absent parents. Additional services might be provided through SSBG, especially expanded child care and better vocational training for the working poor. Because one full-time job at the minimum wage currently pays only 60% of the poverty index for a family of four, raising the

TABLE 8.5 | SUMMARY OF CHILD WELFARE POLICY ANALYSIS, USING THE BEHAVIORAL MODEL

Alternative	Benefit	Cost
1. Protection of children		
a. Protection of income[a]	High	Low
b. Protection of health[a]	High	Low
2. Parental responsibility		
a. Two-parent families	Low	High
b. Alternative family forms	Medium-high	High
3. Income maintenance and services		
a. For poor children	High	Low
b. For all children[a]	High	Very high

[a] Best alternatives.

minimum wage could have an important influence on reducing poverty, without additional outlays in public funding.

From the normative perspective, some decision about what kinds of services should be given to which children is a problem that is difficult to resolve. From a financial perspective, the cost of such a policy would be extremely high, making the policy less desirable than one that focused primarily on poor children.

A summary of the conclusions from this brief analysis appears in Table 8.5. Protection of children's income and health and income maintenance for poor children seem the best alternatives. Parental responsibility in alternative family forms is also an intriguing possibility, but normative controversies about alternative family forms would probably inhibit effective implementation of such a policy.

CONCLUSION

Child welfare policy covers a wide spectrum of public efforts on behalf of children. Child welfare policy is also the best-developed sector of public welfare policy. Consequently, child welfare is difficult to analyze, and recommendations for policy choices are often laden with implications for other policy sectors. This analysis has attempted to focus child welfare considerations around two normative issues—protection for children and parental responsibility—and to restrict the scope of analysis to matters of health and economic welfare for poor children. (The full scope of child welfare policy often necessitates an examination of other policy sectors; policy on childhood education is an obvious example.) Within these limitations, and on the basis of data mentioned previously, analysis yields a series of "best" alternatives that can be recommended.

First, there is an income gap for families in poverty, but it is a manageable one. The AFDC program has been modified by TANF, and total income maintenance and supportive services for children are now hard to estimate. Modifications brought about by the TANF block grant may make the use of these funds more effective, and this modified distribution mechanism could well be used to distribute additional funds without significantly greater costs. Current proposals to make other welfare programs the exclusive responsibility of states would be appropriate, so long as provisions were made to ensure that adequate funding existed.

Second, children would be served better at less cost by preventive health-care services. Funds spent on pre- and postnatal care for mothers and infants already contribute to reducing short- and long-term medical costs, as well as improving the welfare of all participating children significantly.

Third, parental financial responsibility has become a more important issue as nontraditional families have become more common in American society. Collection of unpaid child support, an important element for parental responsibility, clearly has great potential for substantially decreasing childhood poverty. However, unless there is greater public acceptance of nontraditional families, collection and distribution of such resources will probably be used to achieve social conformity and will have little impact on the children who need financial resources.

QUESTIONS FOR DISCUSSION

1. Why does child welfare policy hold such an important place in the development of all social welfare policy?
2. The development of child welfare policy today is confounded by different views about childhood. How do these different views play out in the child welfare programs that are presently in force?
3. Many child welfare policy debates argue that policy should be directed to the development of healthy two-parent families as the foundation for all subsequent child welfare policy. How are these debates different from the debates that shaped present-day child welfare policy? If policies could be developed that put strong families at the foundation of all subsequent child welfare policies, do you think this would contribute significantly to the overall welfare of children?
4. To what extent do you think child welfare policy should focus on children who are having problems, instead of trying to provide policy that would apply to all children? Defend your answer.

OLDER ADULTS

INTRODUCTION

If policies for children have a long and rich tradition in the United States, dating to the nineteenth century, policies for older people have been perhaps the most lasting legacy of the Great Depression's New Deal. During the 2000–2002 recession, unemployment offices were jammed with people filing claims; but during the Great Depression there was no unemployment insurance. There was no Social Security and no Medicare. And the 2000–2002 recession did not send crowds of older adults into shantytowns and the streets in search of shelter and sustenance. For the most part, older adults were spared the worst suffering of the 2000–2002 recession, even as they were the greatest victims of the 1929–34 depression. In 2000 there was an economic safety net that did not exist in 1929–34, and that safety net held.

That this remarkable development in public policy for older people could take root in less than seventy-five years is due almost entirely to growing political pressure from older adults. Unlike children, older adults vote, and they vote in greater percentages than any other age group. The increase in the number of older people and the emergence of new, politically oriented groups of older people provided the energy for the creation of Social Security and Aid for the Aged (1935), Medicare (1965), and the Older Americans Act (1965). Once slighted by public policy, today older people, both independent and dependent financially, are treated to a cornucopia of benefits through public policy.

On the one hand, then, public policies have developed significantly for older people. But, on the other hand, severe and lasting problems for Amer-

ica's older people persist. The multiple issues faced by older adults are best reflected in the following story.

Haddie Wilson had been living alone for two years after her husband died.
At age 82 she was able to take care of herself in her own home since her children stopped by each day and generally helped her with shopping and other
things she could not always do for herself. She still smoked a pack and a half of
cigarettes a day, stayed up for the late news, and thought any form of exercise
was a mortal sin. Her 78-year-old sister usually came to Haddie's every after-
noon, stayed overnight, and returned to her own apartment at about ten o'clock
the next morning. Sarah said the arrangement kept Haddie from getting scared
at night, but, in truth, Sarah was often frightened at night when she was alone
in *her* apartment, so the arrangement seemed to have great value for both sisters.

Early one morning, Haddie had a heart attack and was rushed to the emergency room. Open-heart surgery was deferred in place of angioplasty, a procedure Haddie had undergone three years earlier. Her recovery was perilous, then
slow, and when it looked as though she would survive she was moved to the local nursing home. Although she suffered a small stroke, and her memory began
to fail more rapidly, gradually her health improved. As she improved, she was
moved to intermediate care, and, day by day, her health continued to improve
so that within three months after her heart attack she had pretty much recov-
ered most of her physical abilities. Her mental condition, however, remained
weak and at times borderline.

With two sons, living and with local, grown-up families, and with two
daughters, also with adult families, and with the attention of Sarah who had
become more or less a live-in sister, it seemed like Haddie could leave the nursing home and return home, provided that adequate in-home care and support
could be found. Money was not a problem. Haddie had a comfortable estate
left by her husband. Finding help was not a problem. A number of persons answered ads for a live-in homemaker at a reasonable monthly salary. Additional
in-home nursing care was also available as needed.

The problem was that the children did not want the responsibility of ar-
ranging and supervising the plan to move Haddie out of the nursing home
and into her own home. Sarah was willing to continue to spend nights with
Haddie, but she felt she was too frail herself to be responsible for her sister.
However, homemakers were available to stay overnight with both of them. The
youngest daughter was willing to arrange, and even supervise, the in-home
living plan, but the other siblings expressed their reluctance to become too involved, fearing that their commitments to an in-home plan would increase as
time went on. And the longer Haddie stayed in the nursing home, the less dissatisfied she became with it. The screaming, putrid odors, bland food, and constant intrusions that bothered her so much at first became commonplace in her
life as she began to settle into the nursing home routine.

The nursing home was one of the best in the city, yet it was a depressing
place. Sometimes wheelchairs so clogged the hallways that it was impossible to
walk through them. Other days the smells were so overpowering one almost
gasped for breath. Yet more than half of those who spent their lives in this nurs-

ing home were like Haddie. They had been sick. Their health had returned to
the extent that they no longer needed the kind of care offered in a nursing home,
but there was no plan for them to go anywhere else, and they had adjusted to
nursing home life.

Although this is not a true story, similar situations are repeated day by day
across the whole United States. This story does help to identify the most important problems facing older adults today.

NORMATIVE ISSUES

Three normative issues dominate policy debates about older adults: (1) adequacy of postemployment (retirement) income, (2) independence for self-
maintenance and care, and (3) overall quality of life.

Postretirement Income

Adequacy of resources may be the most significant normative policy question
that concerns the welfare of older adults, especially because it influences definitions of adequate income in retirement. Except for those who have amassed
large fortunes, most older people live on much less income than they were accustomed to during the years immediately preceding their retirement. In theory,
reduced retirement income is justified on the grounds that everyday costs of living are less after retirement. The house is probably paid for, and the state may
grant a tax exemption for it. Children are grown. Cars are paid for.

But the economics of retirement must take into account the overall standard
of preretirement living. People who have enjoyed a high or modest standard of
living before retirement might reasonably expect to continue a similar level
of existence during retirement; hence questions of income adequacy interlock
with normative concerns about equity and quality of life. For example, suppose
that during the working years a family manages to live comfortably in a very
nice house and maybe even manages to purchase a summer cottage at the lake,
with a boat and near a golf course. In fact, the family anticipates retirement as
a time when they will be able to enjoy more fully what they have obtained. This
family can look forward to retirement income from personal savings, Social Security, and reduced taxes. From one standpoint of equity, it might be asked why
this family should benefit from public funds and live very well, when a retired
family in the city slums has barely enough food to eat. It might also be asked,
however, why a lifetime of inequity should be adjusted only after retirement.
Does not the comfortable family deserve what it has earned? Or, should the
public largesse be shared with this comfortable family when it is needed more
by the poor family?

The source of retirement income, therefore, is an issue closely related to
questions of adequacy of income. Retirement income usually is a mixture of
funds from three major sources: Social Security, earnings, and income from savings, in the form of annuity programs or interest (see Table 9.1). Although no

TABLE 9.1 | PERCENTAGE OF INCOME FROM VARIOUS SOURCES FOR OLDER ADULT (AGE 65 AND OLDER) FAMILIES

Percentage Income From	All Families	1st Quintile $0–$8,792 Income / Year (Poorest)	5th Quintile $22,255–$37,962 Income / Year (Richest)
Earnings	20.7%	0.7%	31.1%
Social Security	37.6	82.1	18.3
Other government pensions	8.9	1.2	10.1
Private pensions	9.8	2.0	10.3
SSI/Public assistance	0.7	9.8	0.0
Assets and interests	19.9	2.4	27.9
Other	2.4	1.8	2.3
Total	100	100	100

Source: U.S. Social Security Administration, *Income Statistics, Older Adults* (Washington, D.C., 2000), table VII.5, p. 123.

exact formulas for estimating retirement income have ever been established, President Roosevelt seemed to suggest one when he commemorated the Social Security Act in 1945: "It seems necessary to adopt three principles for old age security: old age pensions for those unable to build up their own pensions . . . compulsory annuities which will in time establish a self-supporting system for those now young and for future generations . . . and voluntary contributory annuities by which individual initiative can increase the amounts received in old age."

He also warned that Social Security "does not offer anyone either individually or collectively an easy life—nor was it intended to do so."[1] Social Security was originally meant to be a major source of retirement income, but not the *only* source.

Nearly 98% of all retired people in the United States receive Social Security. But, as discussed in Chapter 5, Social Security payments may be quite modest, often less than enough to keep recipients above the poverty line. In many instances Social Security amounts to less than half of a person's retirement income, yet the other sources that contribute to that income may not be sufficient to bring the total up to the poverty line, or to any other agreed-on definition of adequate resources. Table 9.1 summarizes the sources of income for older adult families—poor and nonpoor. From this table it can be seen that the income from Social Security is the most important income source for older people, but it is not the only source. Social Security provides 82.1% of income for the poor, but only 18.3% of income for the nonpoor. For the nonpoor, other pensions,

FIGURE 9.1 | INCOME DISTRIBUTION: ANNUAL INCOME, OLDER ADULT FAMILIES

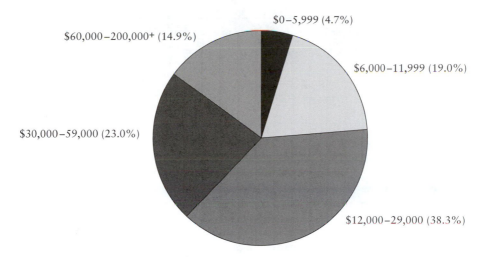

usually private pensions, make up 20.4% of their income. Earnings also constitute 31.1% of the incomes of those over 65 who are not poor.

Figure 9.1 shows the distribution of couple families age 65 and older by income categories. While over 60% of these families have incomes over $12,000, in fact about 15% of these families have incomes over $60,000. There are approximately 295,000 elders with incomes less than $1,000 per year, but 222,000 older adults with incomes over $200,000 per year. This general income distribution remains consistent for all elderly age groups, including families with a householder age of 75 and older.

Independence for Self-Maintenance and Care

Independent living is an important normative issue in policy for older adults. It stems from deeply held, traditional American values of freedom and independence, as well as the contemporary emphasis on self-sufficiency that permeates the whole of public domestic policy.

Drastic changes in the structure of the American way of life have taken place in the middle decades of the twentieth century. Not only are there increasing numbers of single-parent, female-headed families, as outlined in Chapter 8, but the extended family wherein younger households accommodate their elders, a prominent social structure well into the present century, has almost disappeared since World War II. Some explain this change by saying that the extended family ceased to be an efficient economic unit, whereas the smaller, one-generation family unit that is most common today functions more efficiently in the modern American economy.[2] Others have argued that children sought to be free of the

TABLE 9.2 │ COHORT OF OLDER ADULTS

Age at time of critical events

Age in Years, 2000	World War I (1914–17)	Great Depression (1929–35)	World War II (1942–45)	"Baby Boom" (1946–50)
90 (b. 1910)	9–12	24–35 Young families	37–45 Possibly in war	41–50 Steady period
80 (b. 1920)	1–2	14–25 Older children in Depression-era families	27–35 Probably in war	31–40 Families
70 (b. 1930)		4–15 Young children in Depression-era families	17–25 Probably in war	21–230 Starting families
60 (b. 1940)			7–15 Living with Depression-era parents	11–20
50 (b. 1950)				1–10 "Baby boom" generation

burden of their older adult relatives; still others hold that older adults wanted to be free of their children. From whatever perspective, generationally independent households are highly prized today in the United States. Few modern households contain more than one adult generation.[3]

To the extent that *cohorts* of people (age-linked groups such as the "sixties generation") share similar experiences and carry these experiences with them throughout their lives, there may be a cohort effect that currently supports independent living as a normative policy issue. Table 9.2 demonstrates how this phenomenon may have led current generations of older people to value highly independent lives. Everyone who is 75 years old today, or older, experienced the Great Depression in some way. The depression was such a profound economic crisis that it had some influence on all who lived through it. Those who are now 70 years old would have been just born during the early 1930s, the most severe part of the depression. They may remember their parents struggling to make ends meet, and they may recall their own personal sacrifices as their families began a slow economic recovery.

Those who are now 85 years old, however, had different experiences, with perhaps more chilling and more devastating effects. During the height of the depression these people were young adults, possibly married, perhaps even with a family of one or two small children. Already on tight personal budgets, with great responsibilities, they faced the depression under severe personal stress due to total loss or serious reduction of income. They had babies to feed and clothe, without any public resources. For assistance they may have stood in line for free food. The specter of hunger, sickness, and perhaps even the death of loved ones is not fantasy for this cohort. Having had some personal financial security before the depression and suddenly having it disappear through no fault of their own left a profound psychological impression on many of them. They experienced a loss of self-sufficiency in a most personal way. On this basis it is easy to understand the fierce sense of personal independence that is virtually the hallmark value of this cohort of older people today.

Those who are 65 to 70 years old today and just facing the prospect of retirement were small children during the depression. They had few personal experiences of the economic crisis that were bad enough to have a lasting effect on their lives. They heard stories from their parents, perhaps, but they are a cohort with a different orientation. Instead they probably recall—vividly—World War II. That event made a strong impression on them and is likely to influence how they view the problems and challenges of older age.

Another factor that increasingly affects policy founded on normative concerns for self-sufficiency is that older people are living longer than ever before. As discussed in Chapter 6, the tremendous improvements in medical science over the course of this century not only keep more people alive longer, but also keep older people in better health. At the turn of the century an average person could expect to live to age 47. Today the average life expectancy is 74 years.

Increased longevity means that older people have many years for independent activities after the usual retirement age of 65. In 2000 the average 65-year-old American could expect to live another 20.3 years. Many older adults today begin second careers or undertake activities that engage them in a broad range of social and vocational pursuits. Often these activities have considerable economic and social value for their communities as a whole.

Living independently, however, requires more than sufficient financial resources. Social supports are also necessary, particularly if health begins to deteriorate. In-home services such as chores services, shopping assistance, and companionship have become increasingly essential to helping an aging population stay in its own homes and communities, where it wants to be. When such support services are available and accessible, the cost of living independently remains far less than the cost of living in dependent care facilities.

Quality of Life

With increased longevity has come increased concern for the quality of life for older people. Personal well-being and personal satisfaction contribute greatly to how well older people live within the resources available to them. Key elements are a sense of safety and security, the opportunity for personal choice, and a sense of contentment. Quality of life can only be defined very subjectively by each individual, but several important social conditions contribute to circumstances that improve the quality of life for older people.

Where people live determines the context of the quality of life. Although as many as 65% of all older people live in homes that they own, free of debt, nearly 20% live in housing that is not appropriate to their present needs. Many lack the financial resources to purchase or rent more appropriate housing. About 70% live in urban areas, 35% specifically in central city areas. The urban elderly are more likely to live in older neighborhoods; even if the housing in which they live is adequate and appropriate to their needs, their surroundings may have become undesirable and unsafe. It is not uncommon for older people to remain virtual prisoners in their city homes and apartments, not because of physical limitations, but because it is not safe to venture out on the streets. Even when the threat of crime is minimized, urban environments can challenge older people in many ways. Congested sidewalks, which may be cracked and crumbling; wide, busy streets without monitored crosswalks; and difficult access to public transportation all contribute to stressful living conditions. Lack of access to public facilities may be more troublesome for these older people than for their counterparts in rural areas, who have never had such resources to rely on in the first place.

In 1997 older adults owned 25% of all occupied housing units, but 13% of those owner-occupied units had one or more housing deficiencies. Fourteen percent of all elderly housing, both owner and renter occupied, suffers from some sort of housing deficiency. (See Table 9.3.) Housing contributes to or detracts from quality of life in another way. Housing is more than shelter. It constitutes a base for emotional security, a feeling of being at home and close to one's own. It accords a sense of independence and mastery. Unfortunately, maintenance, high utility costs, and rapidly escalating taxes force many older people to relocate to housing that is presumed to meet their economic needs but often fails to meet their emotional and aesthetic needs. Even when older people move from less to more appropriate and desirable housing, they may suffer a sense of dislocation and emotional trauma and loss. Thus there are no clear-cut choices for improving the quality of housing for older people. In some cases the familiarity and security of a longtime home may more than offset the dangers of an undesirable physical environment. In others, the comfort, convenience, and safety of new quarters may soon overcome the sadness of leaving an old home behind.

Finally, the use of postemployment time has become one of the most complex issues in quality of life for older people. In most cases older people suddenly find inordinate amounts of extra time in their daily lives when they retire from full-time employment. Not only is more time available, but it is available during periods of the day that previously were occupied by other activities. All too often preretirement dreams of unfettered leisure are quickly transformed into a postretirement reality of boredom, aimlessness, depression, and subsequent frustration and personal deterioration. Many older people are unprepared for these increased amounts of personal time, and many come to realize that re-

TABLE 9.3 | CONDITION OF ELDERLY HOUSING (NUMBERS IN THOUSANDS)

Total of Elderly Housing	Total	Owner Occupied	Renter Occupied
Total of elderly housing	20,906,000	16,493,000	4,413,000
With internal deficiencies	2, 915,000	2,063,000	852,000
Percentage internal deficiencies	14%	13%	19%
Type of internal deficiencies:	*100%*	*100%*	*100%*
Rats	4%	4%	4%
Holes in floor	5%	5%	5%
Open cracks and holes	22%	20%	24%
Paint or plaster problem	12%	12%	14%
Inadequate electrical service	18%	19%	18%
Water leakage/damage	39%	40%	36%

Source: *Statistical Abstract of the United States*, 2000, table 1220.

tirement is not a long vacation, as they may have anticipated during their working years.

In short, work is still an important factor in quality of life for most older people. Older people want and need work opportunities to enhance the quality of their lives. Work for wages has been discouraged by public and private employment policies, yet many older people would prefer to continue working at their jobs—and many do. Many others seek second careers by going back to school and by exploiting hobbies and productive activities, transforming them into vocational pursuits. And for many older people, especially craftsmen, writers, artists, and various professionals, some of the best, most creative, and most useful work comes in later years, when some of life's pressures are reduced.

Planning ahead can enhance the quality of use of retirement time and help identify personal and interpersonal problems that might arise after retirement. For example, one spouse may look forward to retirement as a time for increased recreation; the other may view the additional time as an opportunity to pursue a new career. Without prior discussion and planning, these different expectations may cause serious conflicts during the early retirement years. Quality of life for older people would be improved considerably if the public and private sectors offered routine counseling for employees about the use of time after retirement. Such counseling would, on the average, cost less than the traditional "gold watch" and retirement luncheon, but it would be much more valuable to the person who retires.

Normative issues in aging policy focus on adequacy of income in retirement and its sources, on self-sufficient, independent living, and on quality of life. To a great extent the policies that have developed for older people since the 1930s have dealt with these concerns, and new policy efforts for older people must continue to do so.

POLICY CONTEXT

The contemporary context of policy for older people is found mostly in the Social Security Act, the Older Americans Act, special provisions in the Health Services Act, and the Housing Act. Other policies are scattered through state and local programs. Health services and housing policies for older adults have been discussed in earlier chapters of this book, as have relevant sections of the Social Security Act. Title II, Social Security (retirement), and Title XVI, Supplemental Security Income (SSI), were analyzed in Chapter 5. Title XVIII, Medicare, was featured in Chapter 6. The policy context on aging created by these programs is briefly described below, as it reflects normative concerns differently from policy oriented solely toward income maintenance or solely toward health or housing. A full discussion of the Older Americans Act, not previously mentioned, completes the review.

Policy for Older People under the Social Security Act

The original Social Security Act contained two financial support programs for older people: Social Security (then called Old Age and Survivors Insurance, OASI), an insurance program; and Aid for the Aged, a welfare program. Social Security benefits were to be based on contributions to the Social Security System. Aid for the Aged benefits were to be based on financial need. The federal government administered Social Security, but Aid for the Aged was administered cooperatively by the federal government and the states. Because of intense political pressure from older people during the formative years of Social Security, these two programs were developed as the first titles of the Social Security Act. Aid for the Aged was Title I, Social Security was Title II. Thus at the outset two categories of financial assistance were available to older people: one for the poor, the other for those who were not. Social Security was provided not only to retirees but also to spouses, children, and survivors of retirees. Partly from political motivations, and partly from practical considerations, amounts of financial payment under Aid for the Aged were established by the states. Although the federal government would have preferred to set national standards for Aid for the Aged, as it had with Social Security, Congress opposed efforts that appeared to override state authority. Instead Congress agreed to let states control the payments as long as they were of amounts sufficient to meet a "standard of health and decency," though it did not stipulate what constituted those standards.

These ideological differences extended to program financing. Social Security was financed by a tax on employers and employees, with revenues reserved exclusively for the Social Security program. The constitutionality of this tax was upheld in 1937. Aid for the Aged was financed by a categorical grant-in-aid similar in pattern to the one devised for the Aid for Dependent Children (ADC) program. States were free to choose whether they wanted to have the program, as well as the level of support they wanted to provide. Thus separate financial issues affected each program. Although states were more or less forced to participate in Aid for the Aged, they still had options about their level of participation.

Medical coverage for older people was added to the Social Security Act in 1965 as Medicare. A separate payroll tax was established to support Medicare, and a separate trust fund was established to secure employer and employee contributions. The name of the program absorbed OASI to become Old Age and Survivors Disability and Hospital Insurance (OASDHI). In 1972 Congress modified the original Aid to the Aged program by combining it with aid for the blind and disabled into a consolidated program called Supplemental Security Income (SSI), incorporated under Title XVI of the Social Security Act.

Social Security (Title II)   Social Security under Title II of the Social Security Act is available to older people under a variety of circumstances. Currently there are more than 35 different criteria by which people may become eligible. In 1999 there were 44.6 million beneficiaries receiving Social Security benefits. Retired workers constituted only 62% of all Social Security beneficiaries. (Table 5.7, based on slightly earlier figures, shows a general breakdown. Social Security benefits to others, especially children of covered retirees and disabled, are discussed in Chapters 5 and 8.)

Supplemental Security Income (SSI) (Title XVI)   Supplementary Security Income (SSI) was created by Congress in 1972 by combining Aid for the Aged (Title I) with Aid for the Disabled and Aid for the Blind. Thus, in principle, SSI operates for older people in the same way that Aid for the Aged did. It was presumed that, generally, fewer and fewer older people would need public assistance of this kind because they would be increasingly covered by Social Security, and indeed the number of older people receiving SSI is comparatively small. In 1998 only 6.5% of all persons over the age of 65 were receiving SSI, but 54% of all poor elderly received SSI payments.

About 65% of all SSI recipients also receive a Social Security benefit. SSI is a means-tested program, and Social Security benefits are counted as part of income when determining an applicant's eligibility. Any resulting SSI benefit is reduced by the amount of Social Security the beneficiary receives (with a $20 "pass-through" exclusion). As discussed at some length in Chapter 5 (see especially Table 5.13), this policy poses a problem in that it essentially devalues Social Security. A person who has worked to earn Social Security will receive little more in combined Social Security and SSI than will a person who receives SSI only.

The Older Americans Act

Unlike the Social Security Act, the Older Americans Act is not a policy instrument designed to transfer funds or resources to older people. Instead it provides legislative authority for combining and organizing a variety of public resources for older people. Legislated in 1965, the Older Americans Act was part of the Great Society programs, which provided income support, housing, food, jobs, self-help, and medical care to poor people with the full support and assistance of the federal government. In particular, the Older Americans Act was designed to provide governmental authority for coordinating these apparently abundant resources in order to make them more effective for older people. That the federal government should provide resources for such coordinating activities represented considerable ideological development beyond the philosophy that supported the Social Security Act. The Older Americans Act stated that federal funds would be used to excite, stimulate, and encourage the development and refinement of efforts to get greater shares of the social welfare "pie" for older people.

The Older Americans Act has a number of provisions, but Title III has the greatest importance as policy. It contains four subparts: (1) Area-wide Agencies on Aging (AAAs), (2) social services, (3) senior centers, and (4) nutrition services.

Area-wide Agencies on Aging (AAAs)   The Area-wide Agencies on Aging (AAA) is the crucial policy structure under Title III. Each state is required to establish distinct planning and service areas in which the details of Title III mandates will be carried out. These planning and service areas may be geographically or politically defined regions, general-purpose local government centers, or other subsections of state and local administrative structures. As illustrated in Chapter 3, the AAA may be a public or a private nonprofit organization. Thus, even though each state must designate AAAs, each AAA is different.

The AAA's main purpose is to develop for its service area an "area plan" that is submitted to the state. These area plans generally tell how the services available to older people in each area will be prepared and presented. In practice, the work of the area-wide planner is to make some judgments about which agencies and organizations within the area will receive funds for providing the services that are covered under the act. The planner must take into account the extent to which resources and services, *overall,* will be improved for older people by choosing one local organization as opposed to another, as the recipient of funds provided through Title III.

Social Services   Specific social services are provided through the Older Americans Act, even though their exact form may vary from place to place. Some of these services are available to meet specific objectives; others meet general objectives. Services to meet specific objectives—health education, training, "welfare," information, recreation, homemaker-aides, counseling, referral, and transportation—are funded discretely. Although the names of these services are very clear, the elements that constitute the actual services may vary greatly from place to place. Usually area-wide planners decide which sets of activities qualify as services according to the act. For example, are inoculations against influenza and discussions about body care both health services? If they are, which service is more likely to achieve the objective of a health service? The degree of interpretation of services varies so widely that ultimately no one exact pattern of social services is provided under the Older Americans Act.

Services designed to meet general objectives include those that encourage older people to use other services, those that help them attain adequate housing, crime prevention programs, victim assistance programs, and similar programs, including, to round out a list of 14 such general programs, "any other service . . . necessary for the welfare of older individuals." As a result of this latitude in the scope of the policy, each community and each social service agency competes vigorously for funds available from the Older Americans Act. In many cases, however, the funding decisions are based on political expediency. There are no established standards that could guide decision making.

Senior Centers   Senior centers are developed as "focal points" and operate as informal community resources where older people can come for planned services or just drop in for fellowship. The National Council for Senior Centers has established elaborate criteria for development of such centers, and these are frequently used as standards for evaluation and funding. The programs offered at senior centers vary from community to community. In most cases the resources and services of the centers are available to all older people without charge.

Nutrition Services   Ideally, nutrition services are the center of activity at the senior center. Nutrition services essentially consist of three distinct activities rolled into one: (1) a hot meal (usually lunch) served in a group environment, (2) nutrition education, aimed at instructing older people about good eating habits, and (3) a program designed to help older people learn about other resources in the community that would contribute to a satisfactory life. The meal is available without charge, although participants are encouraged to make a contribution to defray some of the expenses. The meal must meet nutritional standards established by the National Academy of Sciences. Although some of these meals may be delivered to older people who are unable to leave their homes, most of the meals must be provided in a friendly and inviting group environment.

Despite its fairly clear policy guidelines, the purpose of this program has often been misunderstood. Because it is available without charge, it is *not* a means-tested program, yet it is an in-kind program. The purpose of the program is to use the meal as an inducement to get older people out of their homes and into some healthy social interactions with others, as well as to link them to useful information that affects their well-being. Therefore nutrition services are available to anyone age 60 and older, and to their spouses, even if the spouses are not yet 60 years old.

Other Services and Programs

The programs that have been discussed constitute some of the major efforts to assist older people in their retirement years. These programs cover a wide array of resources available in one form or another across the United States. But because both the needs and interests of older people are so varied, programs other than those discussed may also be available in different localities, and under different circumstances. For example, many localities offer abuse and protective services for older people, in-home care services to help elders remain at home, and chore services to help with minor household maintenance. These and other specialized services would likely be provided with funding from the Social Services Block Grant (Title XX of the Social Security Act).

More and more elderly are concerned with the issue of prolonging their lives with artificial life-support systems, beyond a time where life as we usually think of it no longer exists. Recently states are beginning to face legal challenges to acts such as "assisted suicide," "living wills," and other documents that give authority to guardians to discontinue life-support systems. While popular among many elderly, and legal in most states, these measures designed to prevent routine efforts to prolong life at all costs contribute greatly to the enhancement of independence and self-determination among today's elderly.

In spite of the expanded use of home care, in lieu of nursing home care and of various forms of respite care that are now available, sometimes supported by Medicaid and Medicare, sometimes not, the problems faced by persons like Haddie continue. In the face of expanded policies and programs for older people, there remains a reservoir of problems in the later years of life that cannot be solved by public policies, but, instead, must be dealt with by individual, private decisions.

Summary and Overview

The programs offered to older people under the Social Security Act and the Older Americans Act provide a rich array of income-support services, medical assistance, and social services to needy and non-needy older people. Consequently, policy for older adults has sometimes been criticized as contributing to a mass distribution of resources to older people at the expense of children.[4] Whether or not such a competitive situation exists, public priority for older people has caught up to other policy sectors in comprehensiveness in a relatively short period of time.

POLICY ANALYSIS

Taking into account the normative issues involved and the varied centers of policymaking that serve older people, policy directed at the welfare of older adults might best be analyzed using the criteria-based model. Of particular relevance are normative issues pertaining to adequacy of income, independence, and quality of life. Table 9.4 offers a policy analysis geared to those issues.

TABLE 9.4 | ANALYSIS OF POLICY FOR OLDER ADULTS, USING THE CRITERIA-BASED MODEL

Alternatives

Normative Orientations	Income-Maintenance Programs		Older Americans Act				Health Services		Other
	Social Security	SSI	AAAs	Social Services	Senior Centers	Nutrition Program	Medicare	Medicaid	Existing Housing Programs
Universal criteria									
Equity									
Horizontal	Med	Lo	Med	Med	Med	Hi	—	Hi	Hi
Vertical	Hi	Lo	—	Lo	Med	Lo	—	—	—
Efficiency (low-cost/high value)	Hi	Lo	—	Lo	Med	Lo	Lo	Lo	Lo
Nonstigmatizing	Hi	Lo	—	Hi	Med	Hi	Hi	Lo	Lo
Preference satisfaction	Hi	Lo	—	Hi	Med	Med	Hi	Med	Lo
Policy-specific criteria									
Income adequacy	Hi	Lo	—	—	—	—	—	—	Med
Independence for self-maintenance	Med	Med	Hi	Hi	Hi	Hi	Hi	Med	Med
Quality of life	Med	Lo	Hi	Hi	Hi	Hi	Hi	Lo	Lo
	Hi = 5 Med = 3 Lo = 0	Hi = 0 Med = 1 Lo = 7	Hi = 2 Med = 1 Lo = 0	Hi = 4 Med = 1 Lo = 2	Hi = 2 Med = 5 Lo = 2	Hi = 4 Med = 1 Lo = 2	Hi = 4 Med = 0 Lo = 1	Hi = 1 Med = 2 Lo = 3	Hi = 1 Med = 2 Lo = 4

As one might expect, Social Security does the best job of meeting the universal criteria outlined in the table, whereas programs under the Older Americans Act are best at meeting the program-specific criteria. All the means-tested programs—SSI, Medicaid, and existing housing programs—satisfy very few criteria, because policy for poor older adults must consider, in a comprehensive way, the needs of all older adults to some extent. From this analysis it appears that if Social Security could be improved to provide greater income adequacy, and if some of the services of the Older Americans Act could be expanded, policy for older adults could be improved considerably.

Attention to the normative issues of existing policy alternatives, particularly those that would enhance the policy-specific criteria, is especially crucial in view of the rapidly expanding older adult population—called by some the "graying of America." In other words, the increasing proportion of older people in American society means that policy for older people has a special obligation to consider income adequacy, independence for self-maintenance, and quality of life. Without attention to these normative concerns, policy for older adults will become as inflexible as policy for children has become under current income-maintenance programs.

Adequacy of Income

Perhaps the most significant fact of most older adults' income is that it was fixed upon their retirement and remains fixed through the retirement period. Therefore, older people are usually not as well off financially as the adult population as a whole, and without deliberate policy efforts adequacy of income will deteriorate. Economic disparities among older people are striking. There are approximately 65,000 men and women in the United States who are worth more than $1 million, and of these, 50%—28% men, 22% women—are more than 50 years old. Yet in 1998 the average family income in older adult families was only $22,771 per year. Forty-one percent of this annual income came from Social Security retirement payments.

Net worth is another way to look at income adequacy for older people. In 1988, for example, the average net worth of an elderly married couple householder was $124,400, but $78,500 of this was in housing, leaving only about $45,800 net worth in liquid assets. By today's standards, if Social Security retirement was discontinued, the average elderly household would exhaust liquid assets in about 6 years and would probably have to sell its home, or get a loan to live on during the additional 11 years of its life expectancy. This scenario does not take into account increased living expenses that might be brought about by illness. The limited net worth of most elderly families may be an important issue to consider in the continuing debate over whether the Social Security program should be privatized. Invested assets would contribute significantly to the net worth of the elderly, although if they completely replaced Social Security as sources of income the assets would have to be protected for retirement use.

Perhaps aided by the robust economy, poverty rates for older people decreased to 9.7%, a steady decrease from 12.9% in poverty in 1992. For the ten years prior to 1992, poverty rates for elders remained constant. This is a little lower than the rate for the nation's population as a whole (11.2%) and lower than the rate for children (16.9%). (The corresponding rate for white elderly was 8.3% and for African American elderly 22.7%.)[5] And, as mentioned earlier in this chapter, a great many more older people live on incomes just above the poverty level, with another cluster in the higher income brackets. This pattern bespeaks an inequity in the distribution of income among the nation's older population, despite the presence of Social Security as a major source of income maintenance for retirees over the past half-century.

Serious economic inequities can be observed for many kinds of people in the United States—the young, minorities, the poor, and women—but the inequities that older adults confront are striking. Most older people are retired and are not part of the labor force. Their income must come from prior savings, income from stocks and bonds or similar investments, rents, support from children or other relatives, or government income-transfer programs. By comparison, as much as 93% of all income for individuals and families under age 55 comes from earned wages and salaries in the workforce. For those over age 65, earned income has decreased to the point that it composes only about 30% of total family income. Depending on the health and previous employment pattern of the older person, earned income may be at best an unstable and unreliable source of income. More than 95% of all older adults have worked at some time, or have, or had, spouses who have worked in the past. This degree of attachment to the workforce conveys something of the magnitude of the loss that results from the cessation of earned income—which must be made up by other resources.

The single greatest source of wealth among older people is their homes. This wealth does provide some income protection in old age, but it lacks liquidity, and from a personal standpoint it is not a reliable form of income support in old age. For people whose savings are mostly personal real estate, Social Security is a much better investment. A worker who entered the Social Security system in 1937 and who contributed $20,741 toward his (not her) retirement and would have $186,000 (average) in benefits in 1986, amounting to about 6% of total earnings of more than $3 million.[6] The same $20,741 invested in a home would have yielded assets upon retirement valued at approximately $65,000. In this view, "contributing" to Social Security is more valuable than building retirement assets in housing.

Cash programs such as Social Security and SSI are also essential because they provide maximum autonomy to older people. With cash, the older person can satisfy personal preferences in meeting particular needs, wants, and desires. The use of cash is compatible with the economic system to which most older people have become accustomed. In-kind programs, on the other hand, may seem an alien resource. Since Social Security is the mainstay of retirement income, it must be adequately funded to preserve adequacy of income. That a large number of Social Security beneficiaries must accept SSI because their Social Security benefit is so low also attests to the importance of assuring adequate income through Social Security. Table 9.4 suggests that enhancing Social Security would provide the best opportunity to realize a number of the most important policy goals for older adults.

Independent Living

Presently it is estimated that 32.15 million older people are covered by Medicare, representing about 85% of the older population and about 92% of older, eligible Social Security recipients. However, only 21% of those covered will receive reimbursed services. The amount of medical treatment costs paid by Medicare and Medicaid is astonishing. Approximately 51% of all Medicare expenditures are for hospital-based care. Reimbursements for physicians' services amounted to 24.7% of the rest of Medicare costs. Only 21% of those covered under Medicare received reimbursable services. By contrast, costs for home health care are about 10% of the costs of in-hospital care, yet most medical services cover expenses other than in-home care. Even with these levels of expenditure, only 77.4% of total physician costs and 55% of total outpatient hospital costs were reimbursed through Medicare. The balance was paid by the individual, either through private insurance coverage or out of pocket.[7] By these standards the cost of medical care for older people is truly alarming.

Most of the Medicare payments to older people are used to reimburse hospitals, nursing homes, intermediate-care homes, and group homes, for prolonged care of older people in those facilities. Recent studies by the federal General Accounting Office substantiate, however, that in many circumstances home-based care could substitute for these various forms of institutionalized care. Not only would the costs be more reasonable, but the care itself would be more personalized and, in most cases, more desirable from the patient's point of view inasmuch as home offers a base of emotional security and a vantage point for maximizing independence. Yet the rules for Medicare reimbursement do not permit routine payments for in-home services, since most of these services are not identified as "medical" in the strictest sense of "treatment." They belong more to the category of "care" during convalescence or terminal illness—a distinction discussed at some length in Chapter 6. Thus older adult policy would be enhanced by modifications in Medicare that would permit greater use of in-home services and encourage independence and personal autonomy.

Quality of Life

Table 9.4 does not rate housing alternatives for older people very high in terms of important normative issues. Because housing policy in general offers so little opportunity for improving the housing stock for disadvantaged groups, improving housing for older people through existing housing programs does not seem to be a viable alternative. However, improved housing is important if older adults are to maintain decent quality of life and reasonable independence. This issue will grow in importance as the population of older adults continues to swell in succeeding decades. Rather than seek housing improvement for older people through existing housing programs, policymakers might investigate the possibility of making housing services available to older people through modifications in Title III of the Older Americans Act. If this housing emphasis could be shifted to Title III services, in combination with changes in Medicare policy that would permit reimbursement for in-home care on a broader basis, quality of life for older people could be improved substantially.

CONCLUSION

Unlike policy for children, policy for older adults has a more focused context. Three specific normative issues—adequacy of income, independent living, and quality of life—have the greatest salience in policy directed at older people. Fortunately, a strong base of public policy exists for older people that is already capable of addressing these normative issues. Among the major recommendations from analysis of existing programs for older adults are (1) ensuring that Social Security is financed and administered sufficiently to provide the foundation for an adequate income for all older people, (2) redirecting Medicare reimbursements for older people so as to cover a greater number and variety of in-home care services, and (3) developing housing policy efforts directed specifically at bringing the home situation of older people in line with other support for in-home care and independent living in general. The second of these recommendations is consistent with a recommendation in Chapter 6 that proposes a general shift in public medical expenditures away from treatment and cure and toward prevention and care. The third recommendation might be accomplished by diversifying social services under Title III of the Older Americans Act to accommodate home improvement and similar home-based services. Improving the physical living environment of older people means improving their quality of life as well.

Public policy for children must ensure an opportunity for full growth and development. Public policy for older people must act to protect and enhance what these citizens have already obtained. In this view, policy for children does not compete with policy for older people, but rather both sets of public policy, together, offer opportunity to construct a safety net for two vulnerable populations. Both, too, are based on a respect for the dignity of individuals regardless of limitations imposed by age.

QUESTIONS FOR DISCUSSION

1. Why are economic problems of older adults so important in the development of older adult policy?
2. Evaluate the effectiveness of the Social Security program for older people.
3. One of the most striking features of American demographics is the "graying of America." Over time the size of the older adult population will continue

to grow relative to other population groups. Aside from the various policies now in place to assist older adults to live independently in environments that enhance and protect the quality of their lives, what other alternatives might be promoted as forms of policy that would help achieve these goals? Considering the constraints on policy development, how reasonable would it be to achieve such policies?

ASSESSING WELFARE POLICY AND ITS POLICY PRODUCTS

POLICY OVERVIEW

Part I presented policy analysis as an applied social science discipline. The analyst may be in any one of the many private or public units where policy is shaped, refined, made, and partially, at least, implemented. The policy analyst may be the policymaker, but most likely the policy analyst will be asked to provide systematic information to policymakers. The policy analysis is most useful when the information it provides helps policymakers as they reach for a decision. The lament that "they had all the information in front of them and made the wrong decision anyway" is much more an indictment of the policy analyst than of the policymaker, because such statements bring into question whether the information was provided in a useful way. Policy is made in a unique political environment in the United States. There is no clear center of policy decision. Rather, policy is made and remade in a constant stream of decision making. The various policymaking models presented in Chapter 4 attest to the wide variety of policymaking activities, each with its own process, each with its unique information needs.

Despite such complexity in policymaking, it is possible to identify focal points of policy activity—executives, legislators, administrators, judges, private organizations—all regulated by the actors and interaction among policymaking centers, giving some definition and clarity to a policy process at a particular point in time. Thus, policies become settled. Programs flow from the policies. Professional people make the programs come alive by connecting people with the programs that assist them. Therefore, a policy analysis necessary at one policy focal point is likely to be different from that necessary at another policy center. But while no single approach to policy analysis is likely to satisfy these divergent requirements, a range of models is available to guide the analyst in organizing, examining, and presenting information useful to the policy decision process. Most of the necessary information for policy analysis already exists in some form. Sometimes new information has to be created. But whether new or old, the information has to be communicated, unencumbered and clear.

Part II identified the five most significant sectors of social welfare policy. More than 50 of the most widely used social programs are produced from policies created within these five policy sectors. A brief policy analysis was undertaken of each policy sector, not only to demonstrate a method of policy analysis that could be applied to each, but perhaps more significantly, to acquaint the human service practitioner with important programs and their characteristics. Because policy locates the public interest, reflects the time in which we live, or charts a course for action by allocating resources, normative views about the times in which we live and the problems we face shape both the ways we understand our problems and how we go about developing programs that attempt to solve them. Particularly in a diverse nation, it is not at all unusual for people to see the same things differently. For some the issue of children's policy may be seen as a responsibility of the state to protect children from harm. Others may see the critical issue in children's policy as an erosion of parental responsibility. Policy analysis must provide information that will illuminate how one set of choices will enhance resolution of one set of normative positions or another.

Because policy is a reflection of our current social world, changing times bring restructuring of the policy contexts in which problems are viewed and addressed. Policy contexts have been shaped and reshaped over many years. For example, income-maintenance policies have developed a rich repertory of policy and programs. Because some policy sectors have long policy histories, policies and programs that are products of these contexts often contain divergent, sometimes conflicting elements, since the way a problem was seen and resolved in one historical context may not fit in another context. Thus a good bit of policy analysis, particularly at the administrative level, or level of policy transitions, is directed toward how these widespread policy mandates can be harmonized and redirected to fit with the ways issues are presently understood.

THE UNRESOLVED POLICY AGENDA

Even though these sectors are fairly comprehensive of current welfare policy, an emphasis on five policy sectors leaves many public welfare policy issues unattended. For example, current concerns about violence against women may be a law enforcement issue, but it may also be a concern for health policy and policy for older adults. Treatment of gays and lesbians may be a civil rights issue, and also an issue for family policy. Unresolved racial issues are often approached as civil rights issues, although they may find better resolution as child welfare issues. Thus many policy problems raised by contemporary social issues have not been sufficiently addressed specifically as social welfare policy issues. For example, abortion is a highly volatile policy issue. In *Roe v. Wade*, the U.S. Supreme Court ruled that state laws could not interfere with a woman's choice to have an abortion. But striking down the illegality of abortion laws has not resolved the policy debates over abortion. In 1978, the Hyde Amendment to federal spending bills, another form of public policy that forbade federal funding of abortions, did not resolve the controversy either. In fact, more than half the states continued to provide publicly funded abortions using state funds after the Hyde Amendment. In 1987, the Department of Health and Human Services (DHHS) proposed requirements that would have terminated all federal funding to any program providing abortions, even if the abortions were a separate program activity funded by entirely separate funds. Under these policies a hospital could lose all its federal funds if it provided abortions. At present, courts have made policies that say these administrative policies are not legal. When some balance seemed to be achieved with respect to abortion policy in the United States, the issues resurfaced in the 1996 welfare reform debate; same problem, but in a different policy context. Thus a consistent reshaping of normative orientations to problems (e.g., government should not pay to support children born out of wedlock, but we do not want women to have abortions to stay eligible for welfare) forces policymakers to revisit problems that, although seemingly resolved in one policy context, present continuing unresolved issues in a different policy context.

Abortion policy is also a good example of a normative concern that does not have its own clear policy context. Some abortion policy exists as set by the courts and some by legislation, but abortion policy is also played out in newly established policy areas, as in welfare reform, health policy, or stem cell research, for examples. A clear policy environment about abortion does not exist because the normative questions surrounding abortions have not been sufficiently understood and clarified. For the time being, abortion policy is addressed as a health issue, even though "right to life" groups argue that abortion is a moral issue, and "freedom of choice" groups argue that abortion is a constitutionally guaranteed right. Since only a health policy context exists, the normative orientations of the various abortion adversaries must find a more appropriate policy context for their policy debates. Until then, public policy over abortion will remain unresolved, and tension and conflict over abortion is likely to continue.

WELFARE POLICY IN CONTEXT

There are a number of reasons why policies may not be developed, or why existing policies seem to discriminate against some groups in some ways. First, there are other unresolved policy problems like abortion that do not have sufficient independent policy contexts to permit discrete policy analysis. Since the implementation of *Brown v. Board of Education* (1954), the Civil Rights Act and its subsequent amendments, and the Voting Rights Act, racial and sexual discrimination have become less pronounced, although they still exist. While a policy context exists in which issues of discrimination can be addressed in general, the actual practices of discrimination have shifted. Discriminatory treatment of minorities, mostly African Americans in the urban Northeast and rural Southeast, Latinos in the West and Southwest, and Native Americans in the Southwest and Northern Plains, continues to plague American public policy efforts. Minority concerns seek special attention in well-established policy sectors such as child welfare, health, and housing, but these traditional policy sectors are ill equipped to deal with problems of discrimination. In other words, there is not always congruence between a problem and the policy context in which the problem is experienced and a solution is sought.

Sexual discrimination against women had tended to concentrate within the context of the workplace and is most evident in the fact that women in the aggregate earn about 60% of what men earn for similar work. But despite the existence of a policy context, little policy has been developed to address sexual discrimination in a more general way because the normative issues of sexual discrimination have been addressed as work issues. Traditional views of the family and the role of women generally continue to conflict sharply with current social realities. Such a lack of fit between a problem and a policy development context allow some like George Gilder, for example, to argue that women do not want social or economic parity with men: "Government may not be discriminating against women and private companies may not either. Let us at least consider the possibility that many women, desperately rejecting the values of male careerists, are discriminating against the job 'rat race' and in favor of their families." [1]

Consider this example. For years child welfare policy prohibited foster-care payments to relatives of dependent or neglected children under Title IV of the Social Security Act. There were sound child welfare reasons for this policy that need not be discussed here. Recently, however, many African Americans questioned this policy as a form of racial discrimination since it did not take into account the multigenerational, matriarchal nature of the African American family where relative care of children is much more common a practice than in white families. The policy was eventually changed, but for years the policy context of child welfare lacked the capacity to deal with this issue that became identified as one of racial discrimination. The policy contexts for addressing racial discrimination were voting, education, and housing. These latter policy sectors do not overlap very well with the policy sector that deals with child welfare.

GETTING ON THE POLICY AGENDA

The above discussion of unresolved policy problems leads to considering how public issues do get on a policy agenda. Although policy issues and concerns must have some policy context before they enter the stream of policymaking, the processes by which public issues become subjects for policy analysis remain vague. Sometimes public debates become so polarized that conflict develops. Conflict, usually over the allocation of resources, propels such issues onto a public agenda. Policies are then demanded to guide the use of resources. Analysis is undertaken, and a policy process is under way.

Sometimes issues are propelled onto a public agenda by social science findings. For example, after World War II there was a general concern about poverty, and as discussed in Chapter 5, the social science findings of the American Public Welfare Association not only helped to rediscover poverty, but also prompted policy analysis about how the Aid to Dependent Children program could be improved to combat poverty more effectively. In a similar way the findings of Michael Harrington in *The Other America,* and subsequent research by Richard Cloward and Lloyd Ohlin, reintroduced poverty as a public issue. This led to poverty being placed on a policy agenda and to the creation of the Economic Opportunity Act and its many programs by President Johnson and the U.S. Congress.

Sometimes governments initiate public policy agendas independent of conflict or social science discoveries. Often government-initiated policy agendas are products of social and physical planning. Local governments, for example, are engaged in planning land use, transportation, housing, and the need for various public utilities—clean water, waste disposal, communication, schools, and health services, for example. When a particular issue suggests the need for policy, government may initiate a policy process. A local government may initiate a school bond issue, or it may decide to create an urban transportation system. The 1996 welfare reforms were largely initiated by Congress after prolonged frustration over growing welfare needs in the face of increased welfare spending and an environment of fiscal austerity. Issues may get on the policy agenda when there is a major crisis, as when federal funds were quickly provided to shore up economic markets after the September 11, 2001, terrorist attacks. Sometimes items get on a policy agenda for strictly political reasons, as when a legislator puts a "pet project" before a legislature.

Despite these suggestions about how issues become part of a policy agenda, why some items become policy subjects and others do not is not always clear. Robert Eyestone identifies an "Issue Transition Process" in which he describes how an issue becomes transformed to a policy subject:

1. A problem is
2. perceived by groups, and
3. others join groups with related but differing objectives until
4. the problem becomes a social issue.
5. The issue finds some place on some public agenda, due to
6. activities of "issue entrepreneurs" (advocacy groups), and
7. the issue becomes part of a formal policy process.
8. A policy decision of some kind is made, encouraging
9. groups to pursue similar or related issues or
10. wait until the "next round."[2]

Of course, Eyestone also notes that not all issues have to follow the transition pattern he outlines, suggesting that such global formulations do not always explain systematically how specific public policy issues emerge or how the policy process really operates. The materials in Part I of this text, however, suggest various frameworks for abstracting the reasons why some issues *do not* move onto a policy agenda and into policymaking processes. The following constitute conditions that prevent issues from becoming policy concerns:

1. Normative issues may be lacking in clarity so that no firm views can be generated about the problem or concern.
2. There is no policy context in which the issue can be addressed. The issue just does not seem to fit.
3. There is insufficient public concern, or if there is public concern, it is not strong enough to command the resources necessary to develop policy about the issue.
4. The problem area has not become recognized as a public one. In other words, the problem is seen as a private rather than a public concern.
5. The problem has been addressed by an element of policy process that is not appropriate to develop policy on that particular problem. For example, the federal government may be engaged to assist in developing more effective elementary education, when, in reality, states and local communities have policy authority over this issue. Or the DHHS may try to resolve abortion issues through administrative policy, when the matter is really one for the U.S. Supreme Court.

As discussed in detail in earlier chapters, whenever one or more of these conditions exist it is unlikely that an issue will be transformed into a policy question. Unfortunately, it does not follow that if all these conditions are met, the issue will emerge on a policy agenda.

POLICY REFLECTS MAJORITY VIEWS

One defining characteristic of all public policy, and particularly social welfare policy, focuses policy outcomes on issues comfortable to the majority. In other words, policy is made for the general situation, not for the specific case. Racial, sexual, and gender prejudice and other forms of social bias, for example, have been some of the most vexing problems confronting welfare policy. The long-standing discriminatory treatment of African Americans, the more recent concerns over the unequal treatment of women, particularly in the workplace, and presently the concerns expressed by gay and lesbian persons over legal nuances in marriage and family law, all call forth charges that present policy, welfare policy included, discriminates against minorities on the basis of race, gender, ethnicity, and choice of lifestyle. Human service workers are most concerned about uneven treatment of individuals with respect to the social programs they offer their clients. There workers often seek policy changes that might mitigate perceived discrimination in providing these services. This kind of policy discrimination, however, may be due less to the effects of particular policies than to changes in the nature of American society that render policy made to address one problem inappropriate for addressing a problem in a changed social context—a form of unintended policy consequences. Policy created for the majority is likely to have an adverse effect on the minority. In other words, social welfare policies may discriminate in treatment of clients, but correcting the discrimination may not be possible within the particular welfare policy context. For example, one might argue that Social Security discriminates against women and African Americans in the way benefits are distributed. But such discrimination cannot be corrected by changing Social Security policy; it must be addressed by employment and wage policy.

Since there are multiple centers of policymaking in the American system—the "branches" of government, the various governmental units at the federal, state, and local levels—policies made in one or another of these units, perhaps consistent with majority views represented by that unit, become prejudicial when passed to groups operating in other spheres of public life. Discriminatory treatment of African Americans following the Civil War was supported by stringent racial policies in the southern states, but it was completely dysfunctional policy for African Americans who sought to live their lives in the broader sphere of American life. Indeed it was the intervention of the federal government that moved civil rights for African Americans to where they are today. Thus the complexity of the policymaking process, a product of noncentralized policy decision centers, functions to bring issues of policy discrimination into a policymaking arena.

MAJOR ISSUES SEEKING POLICY RESOLUTION

There are many and various public issues seeking policy resolution depending on which organized group, outspoken individuals, or policy centers are focused on them. The authoritative and nonpartisan Congressional Quarterly Research Service identified five general public issues with accompanying subissues that were vying for policy attention in the year 2002: education, health care, welfare and social services, criminal justice, and civil rights.

Educational issues raise debates over the use of school vouchers, "zero tolerance" school behavior, and safety concerns. Criminal justice issues raise debates over the death penalty, rising prison populations, and the use of private prisons. Death penalty debates often focus on civil rights issues, pointing to what appears to be discriminatory treatment of African Americans receiving the death penalty. Gay and lesbian issues will continue to be on the civil rights agenda. These issues touch on property rights, health care, and family and children's policy.

Health care and welfare and social services are discussed in preceding chapters of this text. Managed care, according to the Congressional Quarterly Research Service, is often discussed as discriminatory treatment of individuals who seek needed health services that are denied by the managed care company. Embryo stem cell research, identified as a health issue, raises debate among religious groups. The executive order on stem cell research issued by President George W. Bush will only delay future debate on this question. Many of the welfare and social service issues identified by the Congressional Quarterly Research Service touch on concerns discussed in Chapter 5. Privatizing Social Security heads the top of the list, along with future directions for welfare reform. Thus there are many, many social welfare issues that will continue to seek policy decisions in the next few years. Some will fall into traditional social welfare policy arenas, while others will require the development of new policy sectors of decision making if successful policy solutions to them are to be found.

THE INTELLECTUAL FOUNDATION
FOR SOCIAL WELFARE POLICY DEVELOPMENT

Much of the discussion of welfare policy and its programs appears equivocal. When a welfare policymaking process is presented, it is accompanied by cautions that not all processes operate the same way in the complex American system. Policy analysis procedures are modified by warnings that the exact procedures depend on the expectations of the policymakers. When public programs are discussed, practitioners are warned to expect deviations in their implementation. The many welfare policies do not address many of the public social issues churning throughout American society today. These constant cautions are designed to remind human service professionals that much of the energy behind the development of welfare policy and programs is generated by a distinctly American political and economic tradition. This tradition emerges from the tension created by the interplay of American capitalism and democratic political principles. The American economic system is based on the idea of a free-market economy in which the accumulation of capital is left in the hands of private individuals. The American political system is based on a system of representative democracy in which individuals exchange a measure of individual freedom for protection and pursuit of common, nation-enhancing goals. The tension between these two pursuits creates the need for welfare programs, on the one hand, but does not guarantee the access to the resources necessary to provide them. As Chapter 1 illustrates, public policy is the way questions are resolved by the allocation of political and economic power between individual pursuits and public goals.

As welfare policy has become a more familiar element in American society, functional distinctions between public and private spheres of welfare-type activity have become less clear. Consequently, as discussed in Chapter 3, functional distinctions in the scope of public policy have been replaced by a more dynamic interaction between public and private interests. Recently, serious debate over the question of the scope of public policy has spawned widespread political assaults on the entire social welfare policy enterprise that has been crafted since the Great Depression. President Clinton's goal, to change the character of welfare, as represented by the 1996 welfare reform, recreates welfare as a work program in contrast with an earlier tradition of efforts to support those in financial need without insisting that they work for their welfare. These recent reevaluations of the scope and justification of public welfare policy have raised serious doubt in the minds of many about the wisdom and appropriateness of pursuing nation-enhancing social welfare goals at the expense of reduced personal liberties. To do as one sees fit with one's own private wealth and property has been a constant theme of neoconservative critics of expanded social welfare policy. This neoconservative trend was supported by the unprecedented economic prosperity of the 1990s. The 1996 welfare reforms are part of this reevaluation. Curiously enough, this neoconservative pattern persisted throughout President Clinton's welfare reform efforts.

Neoconservative Economics and Welfare Policy

Charles Murray in *Losing Ground* and George Gilder in *Wealth and Poverty* present widely read critiques of American social policy today. Both Murray and Gilder argue that the products of social policy—contemporary social programs—do not provide a substantial social benefit and that there is little justification for government to provide them. The substance of the Murray and Gilder arguments derives from the neoconservative view that the federal government has no authority to provide social welfare benefits, and that this form of public policy represents an unwarranted intrusion on the rights of people to do what they please with their possessions.[3]

Another neoconservative critic, Richard Epstein, former dean of the University of Chicago Law School, presents a more substantial critique of social welfare policy than Murray and Gilder. Basing his argument on an "original intent" interpretation of the U.S. Constitution and subsequent constitutional law, Epstein says that social programs constitute an unjustified "taking" by the federal government and that therefore Social Security, medical insurance, workers' compensation, and welfare payments should be abandoned.[4] "The fundamental problem in a system of welfare is that it conflicts with a theory of private rights that lies behind any system of representative government. There is quite simply no private cause of action for want of a benevolence that remotely resembles those causes allowable under the domain actions of tort, contract and restitution."[5]

Epstein's arguments are unequivocal. Unlike Murray and Gilder, Epstein develops both a social and a legal theory to support his contentions. Epstein argues that the "just compensation" clause of the U.S. Constitution in Article V of the Bill of Rights should be the controlling constitutional element for examining the legitimacy of a welfare function. A welfare function represents a "taking," without satisfying a definition of public use and without just compensation, Epstein argues; welfare is an unconstitutional taking of property, with no support in legal doctrine or social theory.

Neoconservative economists object to social welfare programs, particularly those discussed in Chapter 5, because they do not meet economic conditions that usually justify the public use of private property. It is at this point that economic neoconservative welfare critics discuss specific social programs as if they are similar in public purpose and rest on similar economic foundations. The discussion in Part II of this book, however, demonstrates the wide economic diversity among social programs offered by the federal government and those offered cooperatively with states and local governments. Differences abound among insurance programs, worker protection programs, social services programs, and cash assistance programs. The unwillingness of neoconservative economists to distinguish among these programs leads them to criticize all social welfare programs as if they served the same economic and political purpose and as if they were, therefore, founded on the same economic and political principles. For example, Chapters 3 and 5 discuss how welfare cash payments are cooperative policies funded through the states. The federal government makes grants for many social purposes. It seems specious to isolate welfare cash payments for special criticisms when highway and airport construction, education, law enforcement, environmental protection, and a variety of other domestic programs are funded similarly with federal grants.

If neoconservative economists mean to criticize only those welfare cash programs administered directly by the federal government, this criticism should be limited and directed to Social Security, Unemployment Insurance, and Supplemental Security Income. But neither Social Security nor unemployment insurance are "welfare takings." They are insurance programs in which beneficiaries pay into the program and receive benefits from the program. The economic justification for these programs reflects the same macroeconomic necessity as other federal government policies that provide a range of federally guaranteed subsidies, such as the U.S. Postal Service, Conrail, Fannie Mae, farm and oil price supports, and the 2002 airline bailout. These macroeconomic necessities stem from the public need to protect economically fragile industry. Social Security protects economically fragile people.

In fact, Social Security and unemployment insurance meet one of the best economic tests used to distinguish between public and private activities—market externalities, sometimes called "spillover" effects. As the policy analysis in Part II identifies, external but often hidden costs are part of the real costs of a product that for many reasons are not reflected in the price of the product. For example, scarce resources may be used to produce a product without acknowledging their replacement costs, as in the case of oil depletion, or costly by-products of production may not be included in production costs, as in the case of environmental pollution. In the same vein, the true value of any product must also include a true measure of the costs of labor. True labor costs include the cost of maintaining an adequate labor supply during times when prices of products force the firm to save by laying off personnel. The unemployment tax levied against the employer, therefore, ought to be reflected in the overall price of the product, and it is, through the unemployment tax levied on employers. In this view the unemployment tax is a legitimate cost of producing a particular product. It does not represent a taking of private property.

The Neoliberal Critique

Liberals have been quick to defend contemporary social welfare policy from neoconservative attacks. Stung by the Reagan administration's successful social welfare retrenchments, a number of well-known liberal policy analysts sought to neutralize growing dissatisfaction with social welfare policy by restating timeworn liberal dogma. Robert Morris, for example, asks for a return to "traditional" values of justice and mutual obligation:

> Welfare becomes a proxy term for values, a lightning rod for differing views about the obligations we owe each other, the virtues of selfishness, the limits of obligation, and political behaviors that will either unify or further divide a multiethnic population. Though limited in its singularity, social welfare provides a means of addressing certain questions related to human values and their expression in our society.[6]

With a similar plea, Alvin Schorr chides the neoconservative policy objectives and urges a return to decency and just treatment. "Next to the discovery of sex and the invention of money, the Reagan administration will rank high in history as a force in the promotion of selfishness."[7] Schorr concludes his liberal defense of social welfare by writing: "If we will express decency through policy as well as in personal relationships, if we will understand that in the modern world one affects us as deeply as the other, and if we will call on the skill and sophistication that are widely available, we may yet build a society that is just and fraternal."[8]

The difficulty with the neoliberal position lies in the high value given to individualism in liberal thought. While liberals and conservatives both agree that social policy should pursue just and decent social goals, neither liberals nor conservatives are likely to agree on what constitutes either justice or a decent society. Jeffrey Galper put the liberal dilemma in perspective many years ago when he wrote:

> Twentieth century liberalism has developed in a collectivist fashion. Individual well-being is pursued through state intervention, the welfare state being the limiting case. Despite the collectivist superstructure, however, modern liberalism retains its individualistic bias. Our welfare state, consequently, does not generally establish specific policy goals for the society as a whole. Rather, public policy establishes a framework for individual effort.[9]

Theodore Lowi offered the most salient critique of liberalism some years ago, pointing out that the individualism of traditional liberalism had become infested with special interests (interest groups) and no longer offered consensus about social goals, such as justice or a decent society. "Modern [liberal] policymakers have fallen into believing that public policy involves merely the identification of problems toward which government ought to be aimed. It pretends . . . that the unsentimental business of coercion need not be involved and that the unsentimental decisions about how to employ coercion need not really to be made at all."[10]

Social Welfare and American Political Institutions

American political institutions were established within the intellectual tradition of the seventeenth century—reason, enlightenment, individual dignity, and human rights. Perhaps more than any other, it was the political philosophy of John Locke (1632–1704) that inspired the form of America's political institutions as we know them today. In particular, the foundations of the modern constitutional state were drawn from Locke's expression of individualism, which was later called popular sovereignty, and his theories of the social contract.

Personal property provided the most tangible expression of Locke's theories of individuality. Personal property was a novel idea in Locke's times. Locke's belief in individual property rights was an important part of his political philosophy. But the great theoretical problem for Locke continues to this day: How is it possible to have personal rights and to have an ordered society at the same time? If all citizens do as they please, how are the rights of some protected against the abuses of others? As far as public policy is concerned, the question is raised sharply by the neoconservative social welfare policy critics. How can my private property be taken and given to others in the form of welfare benefits with no compensation to me?

Locke understood the development of the state, or the commonwealth, as necessary to protect private property through a contractual process in which individuals exchange exclusive rights to property that existed in the state of nature for rights determined by government. Locke understood that civil societies had obligations to its citizens. He did not think civil societies could agree to make all kinds of rules, particularly rules that offended personal rights. Locke, however, wrote that all rights were limited by social obligation, and in particular, the right to own and use private property was limited by the social obligation of charity. Locke stated the conditions of charity on the use of private property quite clearly when he wrote:

> But we know God hath not left one Man so to the Mercy of another, that he may starve him if he please. . . . [H]e has given his needy Brother a Right to the Surplusage of his Goods; so that it cannot be justly denied him, when his pressing Wants call for it. . . . As *Justice* gives every Man a title to the products of his honest Industry, and the fair Acquisition of his Ancestors descended to him; so *Charity* gives every Man Title to so much out of another's Plenty as will keep him from extreme want, where he has no means to subsist otherwise; and a Man can no more justly make use of another's necessity to force him to become his Vassal, by the withholding that Relief . . . than he that has more strength can seize upon a weaker . . . and . . . offer him Death or Slavery.[11]

Locke's idea of charity derives from an "inclusive" right to property and the claim that property was held in common by all. "Charity gives every Man Title to so much of another's Plenty." James Tully, a Locke scholar, says this about Locke's limitation of private property: "If a case or need arise then *ipso facto,* one man's individual right is overridden by another's claim and the goods become his property."[12] Locke's idea of charity would prevent society from using want or need to force someone to work, and stands in sobering opposition to the neoconservative ideology articulated by Gilder, Murray, and others. Labor, for Locke, was the way one laid claim to property, not the foundation for a vassal–master relationship. The 1996 forced-work welfare reform, and other efforts to deny welfare to those unwilling to work find no support in liberalism reflected by Locke's theories. Locke states clearly that a claim right exists to the property of others: "A man may labor for himself or he may work for another but only if an alternative is available. If it is not, he cannot labor for himself and he cannot be forced to work for another; he is simply given the necessary relief." [13] Locke's theories were the original "contract for America." It might do well to review his ideas upon entering the twenty-first century and contemplate further welfare reforms.

Welfare's Erosion of Moral Advocacy

So what went wrong? Why do neoconservative ideologies seem a more compelling foundation for welfare development than the classic liberal ideology laid down by John Locke, an ideology that remains so central to how Americans have crafted their government? The major unresolved policy issues reviewed briefly in this chapter hold the key to this answer. They reflect a common theme: an inability to cast these issues in a morally relevant policy environment. To the extent that these issues are converted into political issues, with competing political factions seeking favorable policies, the issues will continue to be raised again and again. It is wrong to deprive inner-city and minority youth a good education; it is wrong to deny forms of medical treatment to save money or to deny medical care to some altogether; it is wrong to withhold adequate retirement benefits to elders, regardless of their work histories; it is wrong to allow children in the United States to grow up in poverty when sufficient wealth exists to prevent it; the death penalty is wrong. The genius of American government that insists on a separation between religion and government, between "church and state," has also separated welfare policy development from its earlier moral foundations. [14] It appears that our present approach to welfare has failed because it has lost its connection with important moral values. No one, no profession, no group is advocating for morally relevant welfare values.

Welfare policy and programs today are empty of most of their moral authority. Without moral authority, welfare has become empty of meaning necessary to give the help most welfare families need. While the poor need money, much more is required of welfare. The pathetic public payments made to those who need them barely serve to keep them alive. Instead, welfare's financial support enslaves the poor in the misery of poor housing, inadequate schools, dirty streets, crime-ridden neighborhoods, and hostile police. Welfare is dehumanizing because it fails to enrich or improve the character of those who need it.

The loss of welfare's moral authority is twofold. On the one hand, a deep moral decay has set into the way Americans understand and use their wealth. America's parsimonious use of its unprecedented wealth on behalf of those less fortunate points to a deep moral cavity in the American community. When compared with America's wealth, America's welfare activities are a disgrace. On the other hand, welfare has lost its moral authority in its use. Originally welfare was a means to help people achieve a better life. Today it is a means in itself.

As it developed, the social work profession championed morally relevant welfare policy. Social workers in the early 1900s sought to establish a welfare system that would improve the lives of the poor, fully recognizing the judgmental character of their efforts. But as social work became more professionalized in later years, it undertook the development and operation of welfare programs consistent with the framework of its professional interests, values, and areas of expertness. In so doing social work moved away from the morally relevant values that energized its work to begin with.

> The origins of social work as a profession was founded on concern for the welfare of others. This concern focused on the character of the poor, sick, uneducated, and addicted, and on the character of the community in which these people and the rest of us live. Mary Richmond focused on the character issues of individuals who were in need; Jane Addams focused on the character of the community. Both laid the ground work for modern Social Work as a profession that raised up issues of character.[15]

Over the years social work's continued involvement in welfare policy development moved away from its originally morally relevant values, and instead promoted a growth in federal programs without a clear sense of moral purpose. Presumably the American community was expecting social welfare to continue its efforts to restore character. Instead it got social welfare policy that was sterile of expectations for welfare recipients and welfare administrators. The community was expecting social welfare to eradicate problems and restore character. "Self-determination" was substituted as the guiding principle of this post–World War II welfare policy, replacing the earlier principles of obligation and responsibility.

The social work emphasis on the value of "self-determination," as significant as this value seems to be, lacks moral authority. It does not guide either individuals or communities in the proper way either should behave. Self-determination does not guide the needy as to how they should behave toward the community, nor does it guide the members of the community as to how they should behave toward the needy. Self-determination as an ethic is the cornerstone of the "me first" generation. Self-determination has had a corrosive effect on the fundamental American value of personal responsibility that couples with freedom in the expression of traditional Lockean American liberalism. "On the one hand, self-determination expresses a value in social work that has about it something of an absolute: Thou shalt not impose personal preferences upon clients. On the other it makes clear a . . . belief . . . that goals, standard solutions, and morals are, in fact, personal things, belonging not to humanity as a whole, but to the [person] as an individual."[16] The value of self-determination in social work replaced earlier values that stressed character development and behaving responsibly. "Self-determination in Social Work removed the individual from the social consequences of the individual's behavior, shifting the burden of social responsibility to the community. Thus the reciprocity of individual and social responsibility became broken, and the bond between welfare and the community was lost."[17]

Christopher Lasch captures a similar sentiment when he writes:

> Public policies based on a therapeutic model of the state have failed miserably over and over again. . . . Far from promoting self-respect, they have created a nation of dependents. They have given rise to the cult of the victim in which entitlements are

based on the display of accumulated injuries inflicted by an uncaring society. The professionalization of compassion has not made us a kinder, gentler nation. Instead it institutionalizes inequality under the pretense that everyone is "special" in his own way. Since the pretense is transparent, the attempt to make people feel good about themselves only makes them cynical instead. "Caring" is no substitute for candor.[18]

The net result is that charity in the Lockean sense has become politicized. Welfare reform is not a reformulation of how we think and act about the problems of the needy; instead, it has become a political process of how we change welfare products and how they might be provided. In spite of its major moralistic themes, the 1996 welfare reform that created Temporary Assistance to Needy Families (TANF) actually represents a shift away from morally based welfare policy. Using work to limit welfare benefits has a long-standing history in the development of welfare policy, less to keep people from using welfare benefits than from a belief that, in the United States, people improve their lives by active involvement in work. Most people prefer to work because they realize the opportunity for character building that work provides, not because they are dissatisfied with their welfare payments.

> The 1996 welfare reform reflected a mean-spirited effort to achieve a narrow political agenda at the expense of the very neediest people. Nowhere in the debate, or in the remarks of President Clinton, were the moral virtues of work extolled. Nor were there efforts to help those who were needy experience the uplifting virtues of having a job and paying one's own way. Peter Edelman rightly complained that welfare reform was one of President Clinton's meanest acts.[19]

The morally relevant value of work speaks to work's character-building capacity and its serving as an integrating force in the community. Promoting the values of work in these terms would lead to a welfare policy that would help individuals achieve more meaningful lives through work.

There is good reason why the current welfare reform efforts stumble over morally relevant values. It is almost impossible for government to instruct persons in how to lead a moral life. Government must operate in morally responsible ways, but government is not the moral authority. Personal morality is not the business of government, and efforts to make it so have eroded the authority of government itself. Government oversteps its authority in the United States when it prescribes moral behavior. For example, a criminal law against giving birth out of wedlock even if out-of-wedlock births were morally wrong would in itself be morally wrong. Welfare is just as morally reprehensible if it is anything more than a "hand out." Moral authority rests with the church, the family, other members of a community, and with professional associations who commit to serve the poor. A government worker may not be allowed to advise a young woman or a young man on sexual morality, but a good friend, a parent, or member of the clergy can. Unless various professions like social work can raise up morally relevant values, welfare policy will continue to stumble in its twenty-first-century abyss of interest-group politics.

The faith-based initiatives announced by President Bush that propose to allow religious organizations to use public monies for welfare work should have strong appeal for social welfare reform. The skepticism with which mainline faith-based organizations have approached the president's initiatives, however, may be more a sign of how far religious organizations have moved away from their historic social missions than an indictment of the initiative itself. For years the work of the Salvation Army has been held at arm's length from traditional social welfare activity, even as such efforts to connect social welfare with moral relevance seems to be growing. As one clergy street worker recently remarked about prohibitions on the use of public funds by faith-based organizations: "After running four twelve-week [previously unsuccessful] training sessions . . . we realized it just wasn't working without Bible study, and so we gave the [federal] money back." [20] This and similar activities are worth examining for the contribution they may make to infusing welfare with the moral authority it needs to do what Americans expect it to do. The importance of moral direction, in general, and as it might apply to welfare is clearly identified by Christopher Lasch:

> Every culture has to narrow the range of choices in some way, however arbitrary such limitations may seem. To be sure, it also has to see to it that its controls do not reach too far into people's private lives. But if it allows every impulse a public expression—if it boldly declares that "it is forbidden to forbid," in the revolutionary slogan of 1968—then it not only invites anarchy but also abolishes the sacred distances on which the category of truth finally depends. When every expression is equally permissible, nothing is true. [21]

Certainly it is easier for the wealthy person to pay taxes, or make a sizable donation to the United Way, than to use this wealth and influence to improve the character of the community. In the same way, it is easier for the teenager to stumble from one day to the next, blaming the community for his or her wretched condition. Welfare has always been about morally relevant values. Welfare has been about doing the right thing, not only by welfare recipients but by members of the community. Welfare has been about right and wrong behavior. Thus a true welfare reform begins by putting responsibility before rights, as it has been traditionally in liberal thought, and linking the value of work with a traditional aesthetic use of wealth. Separating rights from responsibility and work from the use of wealth have taken welfare beyond its ability to build both individual and community character—a major purpose for welfare as suggested by Wilensky and Lebeaux (see Chapter 1). For without a welfare approach resting solidly on these values, it becomes "a form of piracy for the rich and cynical hoax played on the poor." [22]

A meaningful welfare reform calls for the role of government welfare programs to change significantly. Government must provide adequate welfare resources just as it provides the resources for law enforcement. But government is severely limited in carrying out welfare activities because government cannot be the moral authority. Moral authority rests with the Church, the professions, and, in the context of traditional liberalism, with each individual. Thus, the kinds of welfare activities that need to be undertaken are as diverse as the centers of moral authority. Moral authority in the United States is so uncentralized and individualistic that a morally based welfare program may look quite chaotic, as different morally relevant interpretations are attached to and direct similar and different welfare activities. Even though this picture would reflect the nature of American society itself, it would drive the existing welfare bureaucracy out of business, perhaps a true welfare reform.[23]

While government is not the moral authority, it must act in a morally responsible way. Whether it is the federal government, the states, or local governments, government in the American tradition has the obligation to ensure that its laws are consistent with the moral rules. In this respect government has the obligation to set the rules of the game. "Governments are instituted among men," the Declaration of Independence reads, "deriving their just powers from the consent of the governed . . . laying [their] foundations on such principles . . . most likely to effect their Safety and Happiness." Thus, for example, it would be just as improper for government to determine that welfare funds may not be used to support children born out of wedlock, or to forbid out-of-wedlock births, or to require marriage as it would be improper for government to refuse to use private property for highway construction, parks, and other form of public use. Government has the obligation and responsibility to set limits on personal behavior in order to create a society that assures "Safety and Happiness," but those limits must not violate fundamental moral principles. Balance between these two compelling forces is the constantly changing dynamic in American welfare policy. It is in this dynamic environment that professions such as social work have the opportunity to lift up welfare's morally relevant foundations.

From the perspective of welfare policy, therefore, without a strong advocacy for morally relevant policy, such as that originally provided by the profession of social work, little will be accomplished to truly end welfare as we know it. This, then, may be the challenge for social work, or for other professional groups that purport to serve the poor, for the twenty-first century.[24]

THE CONTRIBUTIONS OF POLICY ANALYSIS

Perhaps the most significant contribution that policy analysis can make to the development of better welfare policies may lie not in its scientific analysis of information, but in the development of the information itself. Welfare policy has become so politicized, as its moral center has eroded, that information generated by most policy analysis comes with a bias, or a "spin" favorable to a particular normative view, without articulating the wide range of values each welfare policy issue raises. Policy is about values, and policy analysis will find it impossible to deal with welfare values in the policy development process unless policy analysis first acknowledges the influence values exert on the policy process, and makes them an explicit part of the policy analysis process.[25]

Government, and therefore welfare, is about values; policy is about values. Present debates over values are necessary to clarify what relevance we want welfare to hold in twenty-first-century America. Taking this perspective, policy debates that deal with contestable issues are positive steps not only in the reformulation of welfare values, but also in the reformulation of American values. Only by examining the moral relevance of welfare can the neoconservative criticism of social welfare policy development or the helplessness of neoliberal efforts to reestablish an authority for further policy development be successfully addressed. Policy analysis can bring clarity to the issues being faced by American society in the first decade of the twenty-first century. As stated in Chapter 1, public policy (1) clarifies normative positions, (2) offers alternatives that can be adopted through the political process, (3) attracts public attention to issues that may have been obscured by their uncertain normative contexts, and (4) offers an environment for settling disputes of conflicting claims for scarce resources.

Policy analysis requires information that can be shared. A democratic political system needs information if it is to address problems. Good policy analysis provides good information, usable information, which enhances the process of policymaking, even when political processes do not operate flawlessly. By its nature, policy analysis becomes involved in ideological struggles, not theoretically or philosophically, but by providing information to policymakers as to which choices might best achieve sought-after political objectives. These political choices must be just, and while policy analysis cannot define justice, it can provide information that helps separate just from unjust alternatives. For example, policy analysis can show that enforced work programs have neither reduced welfare caseloads nor put welfare recipients to work. Consequently, enforced work programs must serve other purposes. Policymakers then can evaluate whether these other purposes are just or not.

Policy analysis provides an essential product in the American system. Despite the complexity of the policymaking process, and in spite of its lack of specificity, policy analysis takes confusing information about highly emotionally charged subjects, sorts out important considerations from unimportant ones, and then provides information that will enhance the quality of policy decisions. Without policy analysis it would be difficult to determine the relative value of the ever-increasing numbers of conflicting choices. Without policy analysis it would be difficult to categorize the many normative orientations to many policy options. And without policy analysis, the American political system would fall far short of meeting its commitments to its citizens.

The continued development of social welfare policy as it is known today finds strong intellectual support from those economic, political, and legal actions that were so critical to the founding of the contemporary American state. Through careful policy analysis, progressive social policies can be realized that are consistent with the American economic and political systems, and the moral values our country was founded on.

QUESTIONS FOR DISCUSSION

1. What are the major focal points for policymaking?
2. Why are there so many issues that continue to exist without policy to address them today?

3. What are some of the reasons that neoliberals seek welfare solutions from the federal government rather than support individualized welfare solutions? Is this present-day liberal position the same as or different from the traditional liberal views prevalent at the founding of America?

4. How does the traditional view of private property, as espoused by John Locke, influence the development of welfare policy in America today?

5. There is substantive and continuing debate over whether welfare policy should be developed on the basis of some set of moral standards, or whether it should be developed in respect to the needs of individuals and the society at large. Even in the current welfare reforms, debate rages over whether welfare should encourage the development of families as the best place for providing care for children, and for years public debate has continued over the morality of abortion policy. Discuss the issue of morally relevant vs. need-based public policy with respect to what you have learned in this course.

ONLINE INFORMATION SOURCES

Information for Policy Analysis and Program Outcomes

In recent years more and more official statistical information has been placed online and can be easily accessed from the computer laboratory or home computer that has access to the Internet. Many of the statistics provided in this book were obtained from these on-line sources. The policy analyst, too, can get up-to-date information without waiting for published materials to appear.

Some of the most useful on-line information services are the following:

http://www.acf.dhhs.gov/
U.S. Department of Health and Human Services, Administration for Children and Families

http://www.census.gov/
U.S. Census Bureau

http://www.aspe.hhs.gov/2000gb/index.htm
Source of the "Green Book," a collection of descriptions of and historical data about programs under the authority of U.S. Department of Health and Human Resources

http://aspe.hhs.gov/
U.S. Department of Health and Human Services, Assistant Secretary for Policy and Evaluation

http://www.census.gov/prod/www/statistical-abstract-us.html
Source for *Statistical Abstract of the United States*

http://www.hcfa.gov/
U.S. Department of Health and Human Services, Health Care Financing Administration

http://www.acf.dhhs.gov/programs/opre/
U.S. Department of Health and Human Services, Administration for Children and Families, with links to Children's Bureau

http://www.access.gpo.gov/nara/index.htm
U.S. Department of National Archives and Records Administration—*Federal Register* and other related administrative documents

http://www.federalreserve.gov/
U.S. Department of the Treasury, Office of Federal Reserve

INVENTORY OF COMMUNITY SOCIAL WELFARE PROGRAMS

A Professional Responsibility

A responsible professional social worker must know which basic programs are available to help those in need. A summary of 40 of the most useful social programs is posted on the publisher's social welfare policy resource center Web site at http://socialwork.wadsworth.com/socialwelfarepolicy/. Use this site as a supplement to the text to find information on programs administered under the Social Security Act, housing programs, programs for older people, and other significant programs.

On the Web site you will find materials identifying:

- the program's common name
- its legal name
- its statutory (what statute created it), legal, and administrative authority
- a brief description of who is eligible for the program
- the benefits that program participants are likely to receive
- program providers at the local level
- information on how the program is funded

The material is provided for several reasons. The details of what the program is likely to provide are spelled out in the *Code of Federal Regulations* (Administrative Authority or CFR). Thus, CFR Title 20, chapter 3, part 404 spells out rules for the Disability Program, and, by turning to this section of the federal regulations, the practitioner can become more informed about the details of this specific program. The *Code of Federal Regulations* is updated and issued in a new edition every year, available in any university or well-equipped public library. By consulting the appropriate part of the *Code of Federal Regulations*, practitioners are able to keep up with the rules for specific programs and make sure that the services provided to clients are appropriate, and thus this appendix provides a resource tool for practicing social welfare practitioners.

For policy practitioners, the materials in on the Web site at http://social work.wadsworth.com/socialwelfarepolicy/ provide opportunity for further policy research. With the information on the statutory authority and the legal authority for the program, the policy analyst can explore the law as it created the particular program in question and thereby determine how future policy changes might be made. For example, the statutory authority for the Disability Insurance program is the Social Security Act, Title II (as discussed in chapters 5 and 6.) This is the law that Congress passed and subsequently amended to set up the program. The up-to-date legal authority, the law as it has been amended (codified), can be found in the *United States Code* (USC). Thus Title 42, chapter 7, subchapter 2 of the *United States Code* contains all the latest statutory changes that have been made to the Disability Insurance program since its inception. The *United States Code* provides the legal base for the operation of the program today.

Like the *Federal Code of Regulations*, the *United States Code* is also updated each year and can be found in most libraries. Policy analysts are usually aware that the way a program is administered must be consistent with the statute that created it and the present laws under which it operates. Thus, policy analysis in an administrative agency must constantly refer to the statute and legal authority to determine whether the policy alternatives under consideration are possible.

Finally, it is important for the practitioner to have some knowledge of what agency in the local community has the responsibility for linking the program with the client. It is important to make sure that the client gets to the right place to get all the benefits the program can supply.

NOTES

Chapter 1: Understanding Social Welfare as a Part of Public Policy

1. "House Passes Welfare Bill; Senate Likely to Alter It," *Congressional Quarterly Weekly Report*, 25 March 1995, 872.

2. Vee Burke, "Cash and Non-Cash Benefits for Persons with Limited Income: Eligibility Rules, Recipient and Expenditure Data, FY 1990–92" (Washington, D.C.: Congressional Research Service), September 1993.

3. Jack A. Meyer, "Health Care Policy: Historical Backgrounds and Recent Developments," in *Incentives vs. Controls in Health Policy,* ed. Jack Meyer (Washington, D.C.: American Enterprise Institute, 1985), 1–9.

4. Harold Wilensky and Charles Lebeaux, *Industrial Society and Social Welfare* (New York: Free Press, 1965), 138–47.

5. Messages of the President, Articles of the United States, vol. 24 (1964).

6. Frederic N. Cleaveland, *Congress and Urban Problems* (Washington, D.C.: Brookings Institution, 1973), 279–310.

7. Messages of the President, Articles of the United States, vol. 24 (1964).

8. C. Wright Mills, *The Power Elite* (New York: Oxford, 1956), 187.

9. Amitai Etzioni, *Modern Organizations* (Englewood Cliffs, N.J.: Prentice-Hall, 1963), 16.

10. Ibid., 67.

11. Ibid., 71.

12. Edward Banfield and Martin Myerson, *Politics, Planning, and the Public Interest* (Glencoe, Ill.: Free Press, 1955), 287.

13. Mel Scott, *American City Planning since 1890* (Berkeley: University of California Press, 1969), 88.

14. Ibid., 75. *Recent Economic Trends and Recent Social Trends* were documents produced by the Hoover administration's Research Committee on Social Trends.

15. 45 *CFR* 1331. All policy students should become familiar with the *Code of Federal Regulations*, the repository of all policy of the administrative agencies of the federal government.

16. *Executive Order of the President 12291*, 17 February 1981 (Washington, D.C.: Government Printing Office, 1983).

17. Howard Ball, "Presidential Control of the Federal Bureaucracy," in *Federal Administrative Agencies*, ed. Howard Ball (Englewood Cliffs, N.J.: Prentice-Hall, 1984), 224.

18. Theodore Becker, *Comparative Judicial Politics* (Chicago: Rand McNally, 1970), 137.

Chapter 2: Social Welfare Policymaking

1. Andrew Dobelstein, *Politics, Economics, and Public Welfare* (Englewood Cliffs, N.J.: Prentice-Hall, 1985), 57

2. See John Palmer and Isabel Sawhill, eds., *The Reagan Record* (Cambridge, Mass.: Ballinger, 1984), ch. 6 and 7.

3. K. J. Meir and C. G. Nigro, "Representative Bureaucracy and Policy Preferences," *Public Administration Review* 36 (1976): 458–469.

4. Roger H. Davidson, "Representation and Congressional Committees," *Annals of the American Academy of Political and Social Sciences* 12 (January 1974): 49.

5. See, for example, Hanna Pitkin, *The Concept of Representation* (Berkeley: University of California Press, 1967), 144–167.

6. John R. Wright, *Interest Groups and Congress* (Boston: Allyn & Bacon, 1996).

7. James Madison, *The Federalist Papers* (No. 48).

8. Woodrow Wilson, "Public Administration," *Political Science Quarterly* 2 (June 1887): 128.

9. Herbert Simon, "Comments on the Theory of Organization," *American Political Science Review* 54, no. 2 (1954): 157.

10. Paul Appleby, *Big Democracy* (New York: Knopf, 1949), 39–47, 128–134.

11. Dwight Waldo, *Public Administration in a Time of Turbulence* (Scranton, Pa.: Chandler, 1971), 108–115.

12. Robert Dahl and Charles Lindblom, *Politics, Economics, and Welfare* (Englewood Cliffs, N.J.: Prentice-Hall, 1953), 88–104.

13. Wallace Sayre, ed., *The Federal Government Service* (Englewood Cliffs, N.J.: Prentice-Hall, 1965), 6.

14. Andrew Dobelstein, The 1996 Federal Welfare Reform in North Carolina: The Politics of Bureaucratic Behavior (Lewiston, N.Y.: Edwin Mellen Press, 2001).

15. B. Guy Peters, *The Politics of Bureaucracy* (New York: Longman, 1984).

16. T. H. Marshall, "Citizenship and Social Class," in *Social Development* (New York: Doubleday, 1965), 89–126.

17. Wright, Interest Groups and Congress, 169.

18. Randall Ripley and Grace Franklin, *Congress, the Bureaucracy, and Public Policy*, 3d ed. (Homewood, Ill.: Dorsey Press, 1984), 42–46.

19. Peters, Politics of Bureaucracy, 31–32.

20. Charles Barrilleaux, "Statehouse Bureaucracy: Institutional Consistency in a Changing Environment," in *American State and Local Politics*, ed. Ronald Weber and Paul Brace (New York: Chatham House, 1999), 113.

21. Dobelstein, *Welfare Reform*, 45.

22. Glendon Schubert, *Judicial Policy-Making* (Chicago: Scott, Foresman, 1965), 11, 85.

23. *Gilliard v. Craig*, 272 US Fed. (1972).

24. *Helvering v. Davis*, US 633 at 640.

25. "Individual Rights and Emerging Social Welfare Issues," *Yale Law Journal* 74 (1965): 90.

26. 329 US 309.66 (1963).

27. 349 US 618 (1969).

28. 400 US 309–310 (1971).

29. U.S. Congress, House of Representatives, Committee on Ways and Means, *Overview of Entitlement Programs (The Green Book)* (Washington, D.C.: Government Printing Office, 1993), 781, 798, 803.

30. John W. Kingdon, *Agendas, Alternatives, and Public Policies,* 2d ed. (New York: HarperCollins, 1995).

31. Nikolaos Zahariadis, "Ambiguity, Time and Multiple Streams," in *Theories of the Policy Process,* ed. Paul A. Sabatier (Boulder, Colo.: Westview Press, 1999), 76.

Chapter 3: Policymaking at the Subnational Level

1. See Dobelstein, Politics, Economics, and Public Welfare, 64–72.

2. See Andrew Dobelstein, *Moral Authority, Ideology, and the Future of American Social Welfare* (Boulder, Colo.: Westview Press, 1999), ch. 3.

3. City of Clinton v. The Cedar Rapids and Missouri River Railroad, 24 Iowa 455 (1868).

4. *Akins v. Kansas,* 191 US 207, 220 (1903).

5. See, for example, Martin Grodzins, "The Federal System," in *Goals for Americans* (Englewood Cliffs, N.J.: Prentice-Hall, 1960), 265–82.

6. Deil Wright, *Understanding Intergovernmental Relations,* 2d ed. (Monterey, Calif.: Brooks/Cole, 1982), 69.

7. Ibid., 307–309.

8. U.S. General Accounting Office, *Block Grants: Overview of Experiences to Date* (Washington, D.C.: Government Printing Office, 1985), 14–17.

9. Andrew Dobelstein, "The Bifurcation of Social Work and Social Services," *Urban and Social Change Review* 18, no. 1 (1985): 13.

10. Charles Brecher and Colin Chellman, "Fiscal Federalism: Placing the Clinton Years in Context" (paper presented at the American Political Science Association, San Francisco, Calif., August 2001).

11. David Easton, *The Political System* (New York: Knopf, 1964), 129ff.

12. Randall Ripley, Grace Franklin, William Holmes, and William Moreland, *Structure, Environment, and Policy Actions: Exploring a Model of Policy-Making* (Beverly Hills, Calif.: Sage, 1973), esp. 13–17.

13. Ripley and Franklin, Congress, the Bureaucracy, and Public Policy, 3d ed., 10.

14. Ibid., 11–12.

Chapter 4: Framework for Policy Analysis and Development

1. Robert Mayer and Ernest Greenwood, *The Design of Social Policy Research* (Englewood Cliffs, N.J.: Prentice-Hall, 1980), 20.

2. John Hallowell, *Main Currents in Modern Political Thought* (New York: Holt, Rinehart & Winston, 1950), 292.

3. Ibid., 307.

4. See Dobelstein, The 1996 Federal Welfare Reform in North Carolina.

5. Andrew Dobelstein, "The Bifurcation of Social Work and Social Services," *Urban and Social Change Review* 18, no. 1 (1985): 12–17.

6. Sheldon Danzier, "Statement," in U.S. Congress, Joint Economic Committee, *New Federalism: Its Impact to Date* (Washington, D.C.: Government Printing Office, 1983), 444–466.

7. C. Arden Miller, "Infant Mortality in the United States," *Scientific American* 253, no. 1 (July 1985): 31.

8. John Palmer and Isabel Sawhill, *The Reagan Record* (Cambridge, Mass.: Ballinger, 1984), 345.

9. Stuart Nagel and Marion Neef, *Policy Analysis in Social Science Research* (Beverly Hills, Calif.: Sage, 1979), 11.

10. Paul A. Sabatier, ed., *Theories of the Policy Process* (Boulder, Colo.: Westview Press, 1999), 4.

11. Herbert Simon, "A Behavioral Model of Rational Choice," in *The Making of Decisions*, ed. William Gore and J. W. Dyson (Glencoe, Ill.: Free Press, 1964), 119.

12. Ibid., 122.

13. Ibid., 119 (emphasis added).

14. Charles Lindblom, "The Science of Muddling Through," *Public Administration Review* 19 (1959) (reprinted in Gore and Dyson, *Making of Decisions*).

15. Charles Lindblom and David Cohen, *Usable Knowledge* (New Haven, Conn.: Yale University Press, 1975), 10.

16. Ibid., 160.

17. Ibid., 155.

18. Ibid., 166.

19. Ibid., 162.

20. *Toward a Social Report* (Washington, D.C.: Department of Health, Education, and Welfare, 1969), 57–112.

21. *Indicators of Welfare Dependence, Annual Report to Congress* (Washington, D.C.: U.S. Department of Health and Human Services, nd).

22. Duncan MacRae, *Policy Indicators: Links Between Social Science and Public Debate* (Chapel Hill: University of North Carolina Press, 1985), 127–128.

23. David Greenberg and Philip Robins, "The Changing Role of Social Experiments in Policy Analysis," in *Evaluation Studies Review Annual*, vol. 10, ed. Robert Aiken and Paul Keher (Beverly Hills, Calif.: Sage, 1985), 23.

24. Aiken and Keher, introduction to *Evaluation Studies*, 12.

25. Harold Linstone and Murray Turoff, eds., *The Delphi Method: Techniques and Applications* (Reading, Mass.: Addison-Wesley, 1975), ch. 6.

26. An excellent beginning text is Robert Weinbach and Richard Grinnell Jr., *Statistics for Social Workers* (New York: Longman, 1987).

Chapter 5: Income Maintenance

1. For purposes of consistency and comparison, all data referenced in the text in this and subsequent chapters are drawn from U.S. Bureau of Census, *Statistical Abstract of the United States* 1994 and 2000, unless otherwise noted. This makes it possible to compare data from one chapter to the next. Although more current data sets may exist

in specific cases, the U.S. Census provides one of the most reliable and universal data bases. See the appendix for a discussion of obtaining up-to-date Web-based data.

2. Ibid., 18.

3. *Indicators of Welfare Dependence, Annual Report to Congress* (Washington, D.C.: U.S. Department of Health and Human Services, n.d.), part 2, p. 5.

4. Programs available to persons who do work or have worked are (1) Social Security, (2) Unemployment Compensation, (3) Railroad Employees Retirement Insurance, (4) Veterans' Disability Pension, (5) Medical Hospital and Medical Insurance, and (6) federally assisted home loans. Programs for those who do not work are (1) Supplemental Security Income, (2) AFDC, (3) general assistance, (4) veterans' pensions, and (5) Job Training Partnership Act.

5. Harold Watts and Albert Reece, eds., *Final Report of the New Jersey Graduated Work Incentive Experiment*, vol. 1 (Madison: University of Wisconsin Press, 1974), 78–235.

6. See also Leonard Goodwin, *Causes and Cures of Welfare* (Lexington, Mass.: Lexington Books, 1983), 87.

7. Kathryn Porter, Robert Greenstein, and John Bickerman, *Smaller Slices of the Pie* (Washington, D.C.: Center on Budget and Policy Priorities, 1985), 1.

8. U.S. Department of Commerce, Bureau of the Census, "Estimates of Poverty," 22–23, and Burke, "Cash and Non-Cash Benefits," 21.

9. Testimony of Chairman Alan Greenspan Before the Committee on the Budget, U.S. Senate, *Outlook for the Federal Budget and Implications for Fiscal Policy*, January 25, 2001

10. See *Social Security and the Changing Roles of Women* (Washington, D.C.: Department of Health and Human Services, 1979). U.S. Congress, Committee on Ways and Means, *Overview of Entitlement Programs (The Green Book)* (Washington, D.C.: Government Printing Office, 1993), 488.

11. U.S. Department of Health and Human Services, *Overview of Entitlement Programs (The Green Book)* (Washington, D.C., 2000).

12. Ibid., 528.

13. Ibid., 535.

14. Gregory Acs and Pamela Loprest, "Initial Synthesis Report of the Findings from ASPE's 'Leavers' Grants" (Washington, D.C.: Urban Institute, January, 2001).

15. National Conference of State Legislators, "State Study Initiative," Lexington, Kentucky, 1999.

16. Andrew W. Dobelstein, "Leaving Work First: A Survey of Persons Who Left the Welfare Roles in Chatham County" (Chapel Hill, N.C.: The Conference on Poverty, 1999), 14.

17. *Green Book*, 2000.

18. Data on the Child Support Enforcement Program were taken from Ron Haskins, Brad Schwartz, John Akin, and Andrew Dobelstein, "How Much Child Support Can Absent Fathers Pay?" *Policy Studies Journal* 6, no. 6 (December 1985): 201–223.

Chapter 6: Health

1. David Mechanic, *Medical Sociology: A Selective View* (New York: Free Press, 1968), 16.

2. U.S. Congress, Committee on Ways and Means, *The Hospital Cost Containment Act of 1977* (Washington, D.C.: Government Printing Office, 1977), 3.

3. Michael D. Reagan, *The Accidental System: Health Care Policy in America* (Boulder, Colo.: Westview Press, 1999).

4. "Health Care Debate Takes Off," *Congressional Quarterly Almanac* (Washington, D.C.: Congressional Quarterly, 1993), 335–347.

5. Odin Anderson, *Blue Cross Since 1929: Accountability and the Public Trust* (Cambridge, Mass.: Ballinger, 1975). See ch. 3 in particular.

6. Andrew Dobelstein, "Impact of Behavioral Sciences in Medical Practice," in *The Environment Affecting Health Science Behaviors,* ed. Robert Cheshire (Cleveland, Ohio: Case Western Reserve Press, 1978), 115–166.

7. C. Arden Miller, "The Cost Effectiveness of Pre-natal Care" (unpublished, University of North Carolina, Department of Maternal and Child Health, 1989).

8. Jack Meyer, *Incentives Versus Controls in Health Policy* (Washington, D.C.: American Enterprise Institute, 1985), 3–4.

9. Congressional Budget Office, *Containing Medical Care Costs through Market Forces* (Washington, D.C.: Government Printing Office, 1982).

10. Karen Davis and Cathy Schoen, *Health and the War on Poverty: A Ten-Year Appraisal* (Washington, D.C.: Brookings Institution, 1978), ch. 2.

Chapter 7: Housing

1. See Department of Housing and Urban Development, *Environmental Review Guide, for Community Development Block Grant Programs* (Washington, D.C.: Department of Housing and Community Development, 1986).

2. See Anthony Downs, *Federal Housing Subsidies: How Are They Working?* (Washington. D.C.: Brookings Institution, 1973), 30–33.

3. Office of the President, Report of the Commission on the Causes of Racial Disorder (Washington, D.C., 1968).

4. U.S. Congress, Senate, Subcommittee on Housing and Urban Affairs, *Hearings* (Washington, D.C.: Government Printing Office, 1970).

5. Alvin Schorr, *Slums and Social Insecurity* (London: Nelson, 1964).

6. See George Von Furstenberg, "The Distribution of Federally Assisted Rental Housing Services by Regions and States," in *Housing, 1971–72: An AMS Anthology,* ed. George Sternlieb and Virginia Paulus (New York: AMS Press, 1973), 9–45.

Chapter 8: Child Welfare

1. Joseph Chepaitis, "Federal Social Welfare Progressivism in the 1920s," *Social Service Review* 45, no. 2 (June 1971): 213–228.

2. R. Takamishi, "Childhood as a Social Issue: Historical Roots of Contemporary Child Advocacy Movements," *Journal of Social Issues* 35 (1978): 8–28.

3. Olin A. Wringe, *Children's Rights: A Philosophical Study* (Boston: Routledge & Kegan Paul, 1981), 88 (emphasis added).

4. Norman A. Polansky, Mary Ann Chalmers, Elizabeth Werthan Buttenwieser, and David P. Williams, *Damaged Parents* (Chicago: University of Chicago Press, 1981), ch. 1.

5. U.S. Bureau of the Census, *County Statistics* (Washington, D.C.: Bureau of the Census, 1994), tables 142, 143.

6. Ron Haskins, Andrew Dobelstein, John Akin, and Brad Schwartz, "Estimates of National Child Support Collections," Grant No. 18-P-00259-4-10 (Washington, D.C.: Office of Child Support Enforcement, 1985). No similar studies have been done since.

7. Ron Haskins, Brad Schwartz, John Akin, and Andrew Dobelstein, "How Much Child Support Can Absent Fathers Pay?" *Policy Studies Journal* 14, no. 2 (December 1985): 201–222.

8. Gunnar Myrdal, *An American Dilemma* (New York: Harper & Row, 1962).

9. Office of Policy Planning and Research, *The Negro Family: The Case for National Action* (Washington, D.C.: Department of Labor, 1965).

10. Kenneth Clark, *The Negro American* (Boston: Houghton Mifflin, 1966).

11. See Andrew Billingsley and Jeanne Giovannoni, *Children of the Storm* (New York: Harper & Row, 1975).

12. Lee Rainwater, ed., *Black Experience* (New York: Transaction Books, 1970), 6.

13. See Gilbert Steiner, *The Abortion Dispute and the American System* (Washington, D.C.: Brookings Institution, 1983).

14. Gilbert Steiner, *The Children's Cause* (Washington, D.C.: Brookings Institution, 1976), 255.

15. Gordon Blackwell, *Future Citizens All* (Chicago, Ill.: American Public Welfare Association, 1952).

16. PL 87-543 (Public Welfare Amendments of 1962), Title I, part A, sec. 101.

17. Gilbert Steiner, *The State of Welfare* (Washington, D.C.: Brookings Institution, 1971).

18. Karin Malm, Roseana Bess, Jacob Leos-Urbel, and Robert Geen, *Running to Keep in Place: The Continuing Evolution of Our Nation's Child Welfare System* (Washington, D.C.: Urban Institute, 2001).

19. Council of Economic Advisors, *Economic Report to the President* (Washington, D.C.: Government Printing Office, 1987).

20. Manpower Demonstration Research Corporation, *Summary and Findings of the National Supported Work Demonstration* (Cambridge, Mass.: Ballinger, 1980).

21. U.S. Congress, House of Representatives, Committee on Ways and Means, *Overview of Entitlement Programs (The Green Book)* (Washington, D.C.: Government Printing Office, 1993), 889–891.

22. *Compilation of Titles IV-B, IV-E, and Related Sections of the Social Security Act* (Washington, D.C.: U.S. Department of Health and Human Services, 2000). See particularly subpart 2, "Providing Safe and Stable Families."

23. Frank Bolton Jr., *The Pregnant Adolescent* (Beverly Hills, Calif.: Sage, 1980), ch. 7.

24. Andrew Dobelstein, "The Bifurcation of Social Work and Social Services," *Urban and Social Change Review* 18, no. 1 (1985): 9–13.

25. Comptroller General of the United States, Report to Congress: States Use Several Strategies to Cope with Funding Reductions under the Social Services Block Grant (Washington, D.C.: GAO, August 1984).

26. Carol Stack, *All Our Kin: Strategies for Survival in a Black Community* (New York: Harper & Row, 1974), ch. 3 and 4.

27. Harold Watts and Albert Reece, eds., *Final Report of the New Jersey Graduated Work Incentive Experiment,* vol. 1 (Madison: University of Wisconsin Press, 1974).

28. Haskins et al., "How Much Child Support," 27.

Chapter 9: Older Adults

1. Quoted in Andrew Dobelstein, *Politics, Economics, and Public Welfare,* 2d ed. (Englewood Cliffs, N.J.: Prentice Hall, 1985), 81.

2. See, for example, Rosabeth M. Kanter, *Work and Family in the United States* (New York: Sage, 1977), 18ff.

3. Andrew Dobelstein and Ann Johnson, *Services to Older Adults* (Englewood Cliffs, N.J.: Prentice Hall, 1980).

4. For example, Robert Finch, who was at the time secretary of health, education, and welfare, complained that "federal benefits and services of all kinds in 1970 will average about $1,750 per aged person and only $190 per young person" (*Parade Magazine*, November 27, 1970).

5. U.S. Congress, House of Representatives, Committee on Ways and Means, *Overview of Entitlement Programs (The Green Book)* (Washington, D.C.: Government Printing Office, 1993), 889–891, 1559–60.

6. U.S. Congress, Committee on Ways and Means, *Background Material and Data on Programs within the Jurisdiction of the Committee on Ways and Means* (Washington, D.C.: Government Printing Office, 1986), 60 and 68. Unfortunately no current similar study has been conducted.

7. *Statistical Abstracts* (2000), table 715.

Chapter 10: Assessing Welfare Policy and Its Policy Products

1. George Gilder, "Women in the Work Force," *Atlantic Monthly*, September 1984, 24.

2. Robert Eyestone, *From Social Issues to Public Policy* (New York: Wiley, 1978), 104.

3. Charles Murray, *Losing Ground: American Social Policy, 1950–1980* (New York: Basic Books, 1984).

4. Richard Epstein, *Takings: Private Property and the Power of Eminent Domain* (Cambridge, Mass.: Harvard University Press, 1985).

5. Ibid., 318.

6. Robert Morris, *Rethinking Social Welfare* (New York: Longman, 1986), 5.

7. Alvin Schorr, *Common Decency: Domestic Policies after Reagan* (New York: Yale University Press, 1986), 5.

8. Ibid., 216.

9. Jeffrey Galper, "Social Work, Public Welfare and the Limits of Liberal Reform," *Public Welfare*, spring 1973, 34.

10. Theodore Lowi, *The End of Liberalism* (New York: Norton, 1979), 85.

11. John Locke, *Two Treatises of Government* (London: Black Swan, 1698), I, IV, 42. (Locke's original title was "Two Treatises of Government: In the Former, the False Principles and Foundation of Sir Robert Filmer, and his Followers, are Detected and Overthrown.") Emphasis in original, unless specifically stated otherwise.

12. James Tally, *A Discourse on Property: John Locke and His Adversaries* (Cambridge: Cambridge University Press, 1982), 61, 63.

13. Quoted in Dobelstein, Moral Authority, Ideology, and the Future of American Social Welfare. See ch. 2 and 3.

14. Ibid., 138.

15. Ibid., 246.

16. Alan Keith-Lucas, "The Political Theory Implicit in Social Casework Theory," *American Political Science Review* 47, no. 4 (1953): 1091.

17. Dobelstein, *Moral Authority*, 249.

18. Christopher Lasch, *The Revolt of the Elites and the Betrayal of Democracy* (New York: Norton, 1955), 210.

19. Dobelstein, *Moral Authority*, 250. See also Peter Edelman, "The Worst Thing Bill Clinton Has Done," *Atlantic Monthly*, December–January 1997, 43–58.

20. Quoted by Joe Klein, "In God They Trust," *New Yorker,* June 16, 1997, 48.

21. Lasch, *Revolt of the Elites,* 222–223.

22. Kenneth Boulding, "The Boundaries of Social Policy," *Social Work,* January 1967, 7.

23. See Clarence Y. H. Lo and Michael Schwartz, *Social Policy and the Conservative Agenda* (Malden, Mass.: Blackwell, 1998), particularly part 2.

24. See Robert Morris, "Social Work's Century of Evolution as a Profession: Choices Made, Opportunities Lost from the Individual and Society to the Individual," in *Social Work at the Millennium,* ed. June Gary Hopps and Robert Morris (New York: Free Press, 2000), 42–70. "As to the shrunken aims to lead in social change, social work will more likely perform best by bearing witness to the needs it discovers through its daily work, while leaving to others the crafting of the changes to be tried out. To do more would require a major change in social work education . . . far beyond any demonstrated ability to do so" (70).

25. See S. Wojciech Sokowski, "Beneath the Veil of Market Rationality: Cognitive Lumping and Splitting in Narratives of Economic Development," in *Ideology and the Social Sciences,* ed. Graham Kinloch and Raj Mohan (Westport, Conn.: Greenwood Press, 2000).

INDEX